Insiders' Guide® Series

Insiders' Guide®
to Yellowstone
and Grand Teton

Third Edition

By Brian Hurlbut
and
Seabring Davis

Guilford, Connecticut
An imprint of The Globe Pequot Press

Insiders' Guide is a registered trademark of The Globe Pequot Press.

Front cover photo: Index Stock Imagery
Back cover photos: Libby Kingsbury

Library of Congress Cataloging-in-Publication Data is available.
ISBN 1-57380-153-4

Manufactured in the United States of America
Third Edition/First Printing

Contents

Directory of Maps

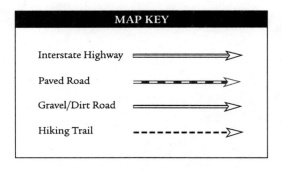

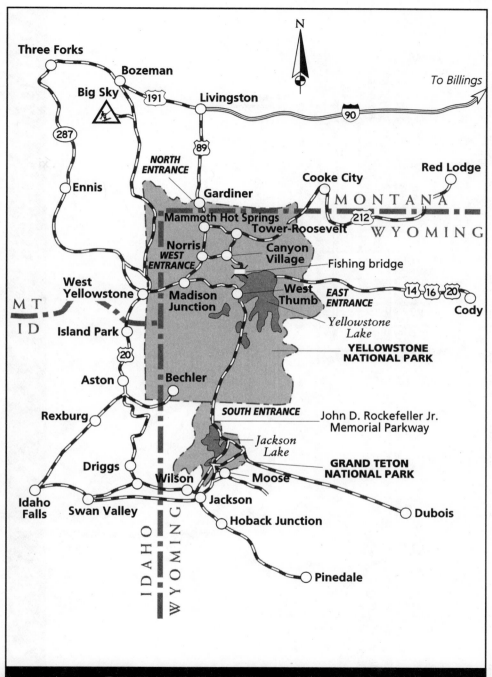

GREATER YELLOWSTONE AREA

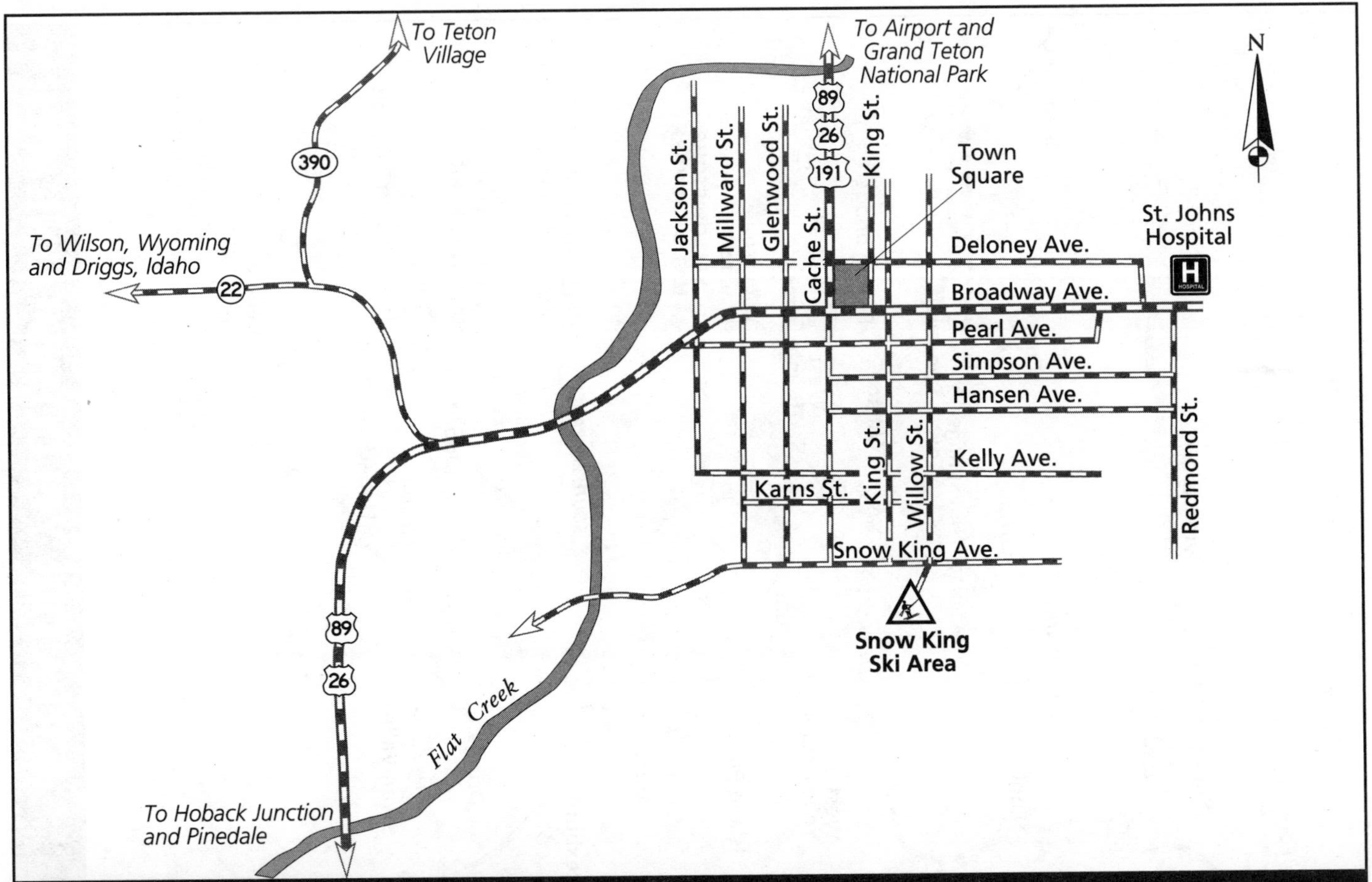

JACKSON, WYOMING

St. Johns Hospital

Town Square

Deloney Ave.
Broadway Ave.
Pearl Ave.
Simpson Ave.
Hansen Ave.
Kelly Ave.
Snow King Ave.

Redmond St.

Willow St.
King St.
King St.

Snow King Ski Area

Karns St.
Cache St.
Glenwood St.
Millward St.
Jackson St.

To Airport and Grand Teton National Park

89 26 191

To Teton Village

Flat Creek

390

22

89 26

To Wilson, Wyoming and Driggs, Idaho

To Hoback Junction and Pinedale

N

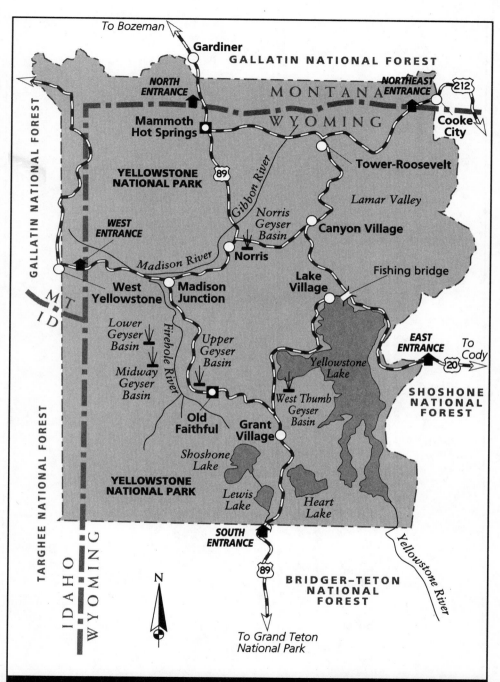

YELLOWSTONE NATIONAL PARK

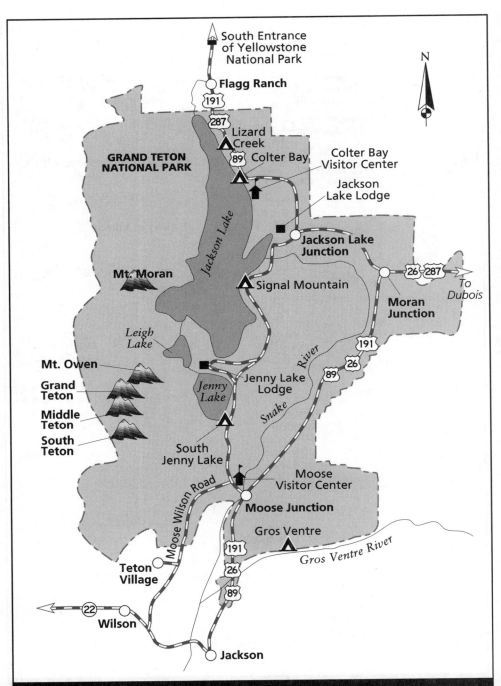

GRAND TETON NATIONAL PARK

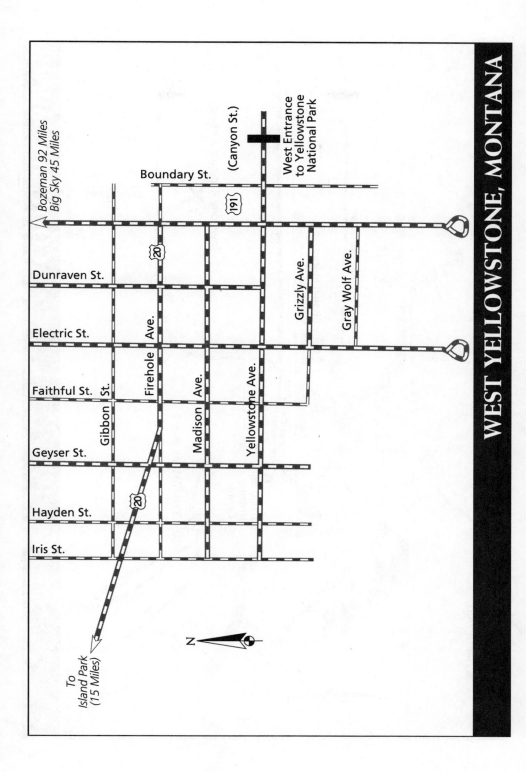

WEST YELLOWSTONE, MONTANA

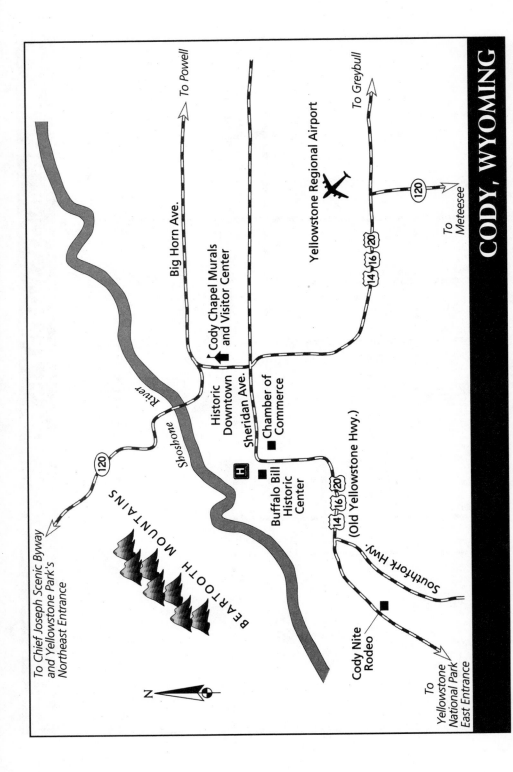

CODY, WYOMING

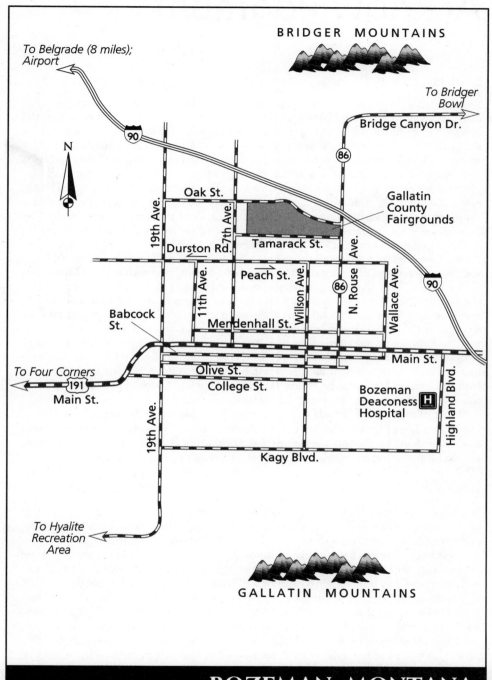

BRIDGER MOUNTAINS

To Belgrade (8 miles);
Airport

To Bridger
Bowl

Bridge Canyon Dr.

N

90

86

Oak St.

19th Ave.

7th Ave.

Gallatin
County
Fairgrounds

Durston Rd.

Tamarack St.

N. Rouse Ave.

90

11th Ave.

Peach St.

Willson Ave.

86

Wallace Ave.

Babcock
St.

Mendenhall St.

To Four Corners

191

Main St.

Olive St.

College St.

Main St.

Bozeman
Deaconess
Hospital

H
HOSPITAL

Highland Blvd.

19th Ave.

Kagy Blvd.

To Hyalite
Recreation
Area

GALLATIN MOUNTAINS

BOZEMAN, MONTANA

Acknowledgments

Seabring Davis

Writing this book has re-opened my eyes to the things I see every day. I realized that I so often focus on the physical beauty of this place that I had forgotten to notice all the quirks that made me fall in love with this area more than a decade ago—the small town things, like the fact that businesses in Cooke City, Montana, don't actually have street addresses. Or that most people I know don't drive anywhere without their dog in the car and that when I go to the bank or to the local coffee shop in Livingston they always supply complimentary dog biscuits for my own mutts. Or that most of us don't even bat an eye at the prospect of driving 100 miles round-trip for dinner and a movie. Or that a shopkeeper can still hang a handwritten sign on his door that reads "gone fishing." Or that folks out here still stop to help a person on the side of the road. These idiosyncrasies are what make Yellowstone Country so endearing and unique.

So, I would like to thank all the people who indirectly made this book possible—the waitress at Martin's Cafe, the guy who drives around Livingston with his Jack Russell terrier on his shoulder, the garbage men who smile and wave as they do their job every week, the person passing on the street who says hello to strangers, the old timers who sit in every bar and diner and cafe in every little town of Greater Yellowstone, and also my neighbors. These are the people who give this region character and depth.

This book also would never have been complete without the help of Claudia Wade at the Cody Chamber of Commerce, Pattie Kinderlin at the Livingston Chamber of Commerce, Yellowstone National Park superintendent Mike Finley, Marsha Karle with Yellowstone National Park Public Affairs, David Knight at Red Lodge's Pollard Hotel, Travel Montana, and the many other local businesses who endured "just one more question."

Most of all I would like offer my complete gratitude to my husband, Colin Kurth Davis, Jain Davis, Carter Walker, and my mother, Renee Becht, for their support and encouragement. Thank you also to my co-author, Brian Hurlbut, and my editor Erika Serviss for including me in this project. Above all, thank you to my daughter, Isabel.

Brian Hurlbut

Writing a book is a difficult, trying task, one that can not be possible without the help of many individuals and organizations. This Insider's Guide has been a tremendous experience for me, one that I certainly will never forget. I owe my gratitude to many.

First and foremost, I would like to thank my editor Erika Serviss for giving me the opportunity to be an Insider, and for her patience and guidance through the difficult circumstances of this project. My co-author and friend Seabring Davis was a tremendous help, taking the time out of her busy day for brainstorming sessions—usually involving large amounts of coffee. I need to thank my partner Lindsie Feldner for being supportive, helpful, and encouraging, and for not getting too down on me as I was holed up in my office for six months. All of my friends at the Farmhouse were so supportive of this project, as well as of my move from Bozeman to Big Sky—which came in the middle of writing this book. I can't list everybody, but you know who you are! The various chambers of commerce used in this book were extremely helpful, as were the organizations responsible for gathering the wonderful photos you see throughout the book. An extra special thanks goes out to Donnie Sexton at Travel Montana and Dax Schieffer at Big Sky Resort. My parents, of course, were extremely supportive of this opportunity and were a big help in many ways. I would also like to thank my sister, Diane, whose various excursions in the outdoors continue to motivate me to get out there and write—and to try and keep up with her.

Lastly, I would like to add that I am extremely grateful to be able to live in such a beautiful place. Montana is like no place on earth, full of friendly people and incredible scenery—a place I'm proud to call home. Writing this book served as a reminder of just how lucky I am.

Yellowstone National Park offers some of the most dramatic scenery in the world. PHOTO: NATIONAL PARK SERVICE

Area Overview

The Yellowstone and Grand Teton region is one of contrasts. From the geothermal pools and rugged peaks of Yellowstone National Park, to the warm, dry summers and cold, snowy winters, contrast is everywhere. It is what makes this region so interesting to visitors and residents alike, and is one thing constant in this ever-changing environment. While here, you'll drive on flat, straight roads and winding, mountain passes. You'll have mountain ranges on your left and farmland on your right. It can be hot during the day and cold at night, and you might have the best meal ever at an out-of-the-way café in a town you never thought you'd be in. This is contrast, and people here live by it, right down to how they feel about their environment and land.

Exploration is another theme of our region. From Lewis and Clark's epic journey in the beginning of the nineteenth century and the first expedition to Yellowstone in 1866 to the millions of tourists that flock here each year, exploration is at the heart of Yellowstone Country. But you don't just have to stay on the beaten path. Some of the area's greatest charms are hidden—from small towns to lesser-known trails to scenic backroads, all of which will leave a lasting impression on anyone who visits. And don't forget the friendly people, all of whom want to help you in your own quest for exploration.

The Gallatin Gateway Inn's railroad station was an elegant stopover for early travelers. PHOTO: GALLATIN GATEWAY INN

Native American performers compete in dance contests at the annual powwow in Cody, Wyoming.
PHOTO: BUFFALO BILL HISTORICAL CENTER

The Lay of the Land

For our purposes, the Yellowstone Region is defined as the area surrounding Yellowstone and Grand Teton National Parks. This is a large area, yes, but you'll soon find out that all of it is worth exploring—even if it means coming back again and again.

From north to south, the region extends close to 200 miles; from east to west is nearly 150. But the great thing about such a large area is that there is always something, or somewhere, to explore.

From its inception as the country's first national park in 1872, the 2.2 million acres of Yellowstone have been one of the world's most popular destinations. With 10,000 thermal features, abundant wildlife, miles of hiking trails, and hundreds of lakes, streams, and waterfalls, Yellowstone is a nature lover's paradise that sees more than 4 million visitors a year.

Grand Teton National Park, created in 1929 and expanded in 1950 to include the Jackson Hole portion, offers more than 300,000 acres of some of the most dramatic scenery in the world. With peaks rising above the valley floor to nearly 14,000 feet, the Teton Range's famous silhouette will never leave your memory, and neither will the lakes, trails, and scenic byways.

Because of these two parks, tourism is at the center of what we call "gateway towns," places which you can use as your base camp for exploring the region. All of these towns offer everything a visitor needs to stay for a day, a week, a year, or more for the person wishing to relocate. We will cover the following Montana gateway towns: Bozeman/Big Sky, Livingston/Gardiner, West Yellowstone, and Red Lodge/Cooke City. In Wyoming, we cover Cody and Jackson Hole, and we include Idaho's Driggs and Island Park. As we want to keep you informed of all of the little gems around the Gateway towns, we give information on smaller towns like Ennis, which we included in the West Yellowstone chapter. We have decided to leave out larger cities like Billings, Montana, and Idaho Falls, Idaho, other than including them as options for starting and ending your visit.

These gateway towns swell in the summer with busloads of visitors, and in the winter skiers and snowmobilers flock here eager to see the park as few have. These same towns are quiet in the off-season, giving locals a chance to rest a little and the occasional visitor a different atmosphere altogether.

But again, contrast is here. While tourism may be the driving force behind these towns, each offers a different look into what makes the Yellowstone Region so special. Annual events, arts and music, outdoor adventures, great dining, history—these towns have it all, whether they are on the map or not. Music festivals, museums, and art shows abound, including Bozeman's Sweet Pea Festival of the Arts, Jackson Hole's Grand Teton Music Festival and Cody's Buffalo Bill Historical Center. Even the smallest of towns will have plenty going on, offering a glimpse into what living here is really like. For us, it is a place where folks still talk about community, where the landscape dominates the soul, and where hard times are made easier by the surrounding beauty. Simply put, people choose to live here for all the same reasons people want to visit.

Things to Remember

1. This can be a busy place—Millions of people flock to the area in the summer, so plan accordingly. Book your accommodations (including campsites) early, and always have another option. If big crowds aren't your thing, do some research and pick out a smaller town to stay in and different trails to hike. You may even want to visit the area in one of the "shoulder" seasons, in the spring or fall. During this time, most of the crowds have dispersed and room rates are significantly lower. However, check for closures—roads and services—if you choose this option.

2. Be careful!—Whether driving on a winding road or hiking on a backcountry trail, be alert to possible dangers. On roads, watch out for wildlife and heed large trucks and recreational vehicles, and constantly adjust your driving to the conditions. On trails, remember that wildlife is just that—wild, and do not approach anything you may encounter. Check with rangers in the parks and forests to find out what to expect on a trail, and know what to do in case of an encounter. Precaution is the key here, and the more you know, the better and safer you'll feel.

3. Tread lightly—Much of this region is pristine and removed from human intrusion, and we want to keep it this way. Be aware of rules and heed them. For example, leaving the marked boardwalks around Yellowstone's geothermal features is a no-no, and doing so can be dangerous. Stay on marked trails, don't switchback, and

> ### Insiders' Tip
> When you get here, pick up a few road maps of Montana, Wyoming, and Idaho. These maps will have roads that a larger travel atlas may leave out, and many are worth driving on. They will also have information on campgrounds, historic sites, and other points of interest.

use a "leave no trace" ethic. Remember that everyone has the same privilege to enjoy the area.

4. Respect—From wildlife to locals, make sure to be considerate of your surroundings. When watching wildlife, don't get so close that you disturb the natural actions, and refrain from making loud noises. Even the most streetwise wildlife—like the roaming elk in Mammoth and Gardiner—can be extremely dangerous. Be courteous to the locals. They are here to make sure your visit is enjoyable, but keep in mind that they have to deal with volumes of people just like you. Do your best to let them know they're appreciated.

5. Have fun—If you keep all of this information in mind, your visit will be an enjoyable one. It's a chance for many to do things they may have never thought of—swim in a mountain lake, glimpse a grizzly bear, and stand in snow in August—and remember it for the rest of their life. Take lots of pictures and read about the area's history; visit local museums and out-of-the-way attractions. But most of all, keep a smile on your face as you enjoy our area. We'll be smiling back.

Yellowstone Country is home to the largest elk population in North America. PHOTO: JACKSON HOLE CHAMBER OF COMMERCE

Getting Here, Getting Around

By Air
By Train
By Bus/Shuttle
Snowcoaches

The Greater Yellowstone region encompasses three states, and the variety of ways to get here is equally impressive. The changes over the past century have made getting to this once remote area easier on the itinerary—and wallet. Once you're here, though, you'll need to remember just how big the area is and plan accordingly. Our roads are often windier and hillier than most, making for scenic but sometimes slow driving. And, believe it or not, traffic can exist in even the most remote places. Visit either Yellowstone or Grand Teton National Park in the summer and you will often see vehicles backed up for miles. Small towns may not offer all of the services you require, and long stretches can go by without services at all. All of this may make your trip take a little longer, but no one here will mind. This is the West, and life creeps along just a little bit slower than most other places.

Weather is the other factor to consider when traveling in this region. Whatever your mode of transportation, it can be affected by quickly changing conditions. Even in the summer, high altitudes and cool weather can mean snow. Take this into consideration and always give yourself some extra time.

With all this in mind, the Greater Yellowstone offers all modes of transportation, from airplanes to snowcoaches, and many choices of where to begin and end your trip. Modern methods of travel have made getting here and getting around easier. All of the airports described here are within a few hours—or miles—of Yellowstone Country, and there are plenty of scenic byways that allow you to see much of the region in a single trip. Whatever method you choose, just remember that getting to your destination is half the fun.

By Air

Seven airports regularly serve the Greater Yellowstone region: They are located in Salt Lake City, Utah; Bozeman, West Yellowstone, and Billings, Montana; Jackson and Cody, Wyoming; and Idaho Falls, Idaho. There are no distinct advantages for any one of these, although Jackson Hole is the most centrally located. However, a higher price may make up for this smaller airport. Either way, you will most likely rent a car to drive around the region, and all are worthy options for starting and ending your trip. If you prefer, the proximity of these airports allow for a nice change of pace—to fly into one and out of another. There are also other regional airports in Butte, Helena, and Missoula, Montana and Pocatello, Idaho.

Salt Lake International Airport
776 N. Terminal Dr., Salt Lake City, UT
(801) 575-2400

This airport should be history by 2002, as Salt Lake City is preparing for the major influx of visitors expected during the 2002 Winter Olympics by building a brand new airport just northwest of the current one. The airport, which is the largest in the Yellowstone Region and handles more than 20 million passengers per year, serves 10 major airlines: American, United, Northwest, Delta, SkyWest,

Continental, Frontier, Southwest, America West, and TWA.

Rental cars from Alamo, Avis, Budget, Dollar, Hertz, and National are available at the airport, and calling the number above can connect you with all of these.

There are several shuttle options to choose from if you are not renting a car. The Salt Lake airport, (801) 575-2400, offers numerous shuttles into eastern Idaho towns. The Salt Lake Airport Shuttle Hop (SLASH), (800) 359-6826, has up to three shuttles a day going to Pocatello, Idaho Falls, and Rexburg, Idaho, and offers summer shuttles to Jackson Hole, Wyoming. Rates to Rexburg are under $40. Recently, the company updated their fleet by adding brand-new vans. Jackson Hole Express offers two shuttles a day from the Salt Lake airport to Jackson Hole for under $50 one way.

If you're renting a car at the airport and driving to Jackson Hole, the quickest way is I-15 north out of Salt Lake City to Idaho Falls, then U.S. Highway 26 right into Jackson. In good weather this should take about five hours. In the summer, exiting I-15 at Brigham City to U.S. Highway 89 north will take you on a longer, more scenic route. Take U.S. 89 north to Montpelier, then take U.S. Highway 30, also known as the Bear Lake-Caribou Scenic Byway, to Soda Springs, Idaho, then take Idaho Highway 34 (The Pioneer Historic Byway) to Freedom, Wyoming, then north to Alpine and on to Jackson via U.S. Highway 26. This route is not recommended in winter, but in the summer it is well worth the extra time. The gorgeous road takes you through the northern tip of the Wasatch National Forest, past Bear Lake and Mead Peak (10,541 feet) and along the Salt River to Palisades Reservoir. Make sure to call the Wyoming, (307) 772-0824, and Idaho, (888) IDA-ROAD, road reports for up-to-date information on conditions and closures.

Logan International Airport
1901 Terminal Circle, Billings, MT 59101
(406) 657-8495

Located about 130 miles from the Northeast entrance to Yellowstone National Park, Billings is Montana's largest city with just under 100,000 area residents. Flying into Logan is kind of a hair-raising experience, as it is perched above the city on the Rimrocks, a shelf-like rock band that drops off precipitously in several spots. Montana's largest airport services more than 300,000 passengers a year on Horizon, Delta, Northwest, and United airlines, as well as offering regional service from Big Sky and SkyWest. Flights here connect to Denver, Minneapolis, Seattle, and Salt Lake City, and you can fly within Montana as well. Car rentals from Avis, (406) 252-8007, Budget, (406) 259-4168, Hertz, (406) 248-9151, and National, (406) 252-8700, are available at the airport. You can also call City Cab at (406) 252-8700 or Yellow Cab at (406) 245-3033.

There are a few options to get to Yellowstone National Park from Billings. To get to the northeast entrance of the park at Cooke City, head west out of Billings on I-90 and turn south on U.S. Highway 212. This will take you through Red Lodge and over the beautiful Beartooth Pass, topping out at around 11,000 feet, before descending toward Cooke City and the park. Allow about four hours if you choose this route. You can also continue west on I-90 to Livingston, Montana, about 120 miles from

Insiders' Tip

If you're flying in from another country or the other end of the U.S., try the Salt Lake City International Airport. Flights and car rentals may be significantly cheaper, and Yellowstone country is only a few hours away by car.

Yellowstone's bear population thrives within park boundaries. PHOTO: NATIONAL PARK SERVICE

Billings. At Livingston, head south on U.S. Highway 89 toward Gardiner and the north entrance to the park. This route shortens the driving time considerably, and in the winter is the only option since Beartooth Pass is closed from mid-October through the end of May. Call the Montana road report at (800) 226-7623 even during the summer, as inclement weather can close roads.

Gallatin Field Airport
850 Gallatin Field Rd., Belgrade, MT 59714
(406) 388-8321

Gallatin Field is Bozeman's airport, even though it is located eight miles west of the city in the small town of Belgrade. The beautiful airport, elegantly remodeled in 1996, is a great representation of the Montana post and beam architectural style and has a friendly feel. It's small size makes getting in and getting out easy, and Delta, Northwest, United, Horizon, and SkyWest all serve Gallatin Field. Rental cars are available in the terminal from Avis, (406) 388-6414, Hertz, (406) 388-

6939, Budget, (406) 388-4091, and National, (406) 388-6694. Karst Stage (406) 388-2293 and 4 X 4 Stage (406) 388-6404 offer ground transportation from the airport, and you can get a taxi by calling (406) 388-9999.

To get to Bozeman from the airport, make a left out of the airport onto the Frontage Road. Stay on this road for about 7 miles and it will take you right into the city. The easiest way to get to Yellowstone from the airport is to make a right out of the airport exit, then turn left

Insiders' Tip
Don't wait until your gas tank is near empty to fill up. Smaller towns have limited services and are often spaced far apart.

onto Jackrabbit Lane. This road will turn into U.S. Highway 191 and take you right to West Yellowstone and the west entrance of the park. There are well-marked signs at the airport's exit that will point you right toward the park or Bozeman.

Jackson Hole International Airport
Jackson, WY 83001
(307) 733-7682

This small airport with a spectacular backdrop is located northeast of the town, within the boundaries of Grand Teton National Park. It is serviced by American, United/United Express, Delta, and SkyWest airlines. Daily buses run to and from the Jackson airport via Idaho Falls and Salt Lake City. Schedules change with each season, but you can check times and dates by calling (800) 652-9510. Alltrans, (800) 443-6133, also has daily shuttles to Jackson, Grand Targhee, and the south entrance to Yellowstone. Rental cars from Alamo, (307) 733-0671, Avis, (307) 733-3422, Budget, (307) 733-2206, and Hertz, (307) 733-2272, are available at the airport. Thrifty, (307) 739-9300, and Aspen Rent-A-Car, (877) 222-7736, are located in downtown Jackson but offer free airport pickups. When you exit the airport, heading north will lead you to Moose Junction, at which point you can choose your route through the park. Heading south on U.S. Highway 191 out of the airport will take you right into the center of Jackson.

Yellowstone Regional Airport
3001 Duggleby Dr., Cody, WY 82421
(307) 587-5096
www.flyyra.com

Cody's airport is located just a few minutes from downtown, approximately 52 miles from the east entrance to Yellowstone. It is serviced year round by Delta, SkyWest, and United/United Express. Rental cars from Hertz, Avis, and Thrifty are available in the terminal. The east entrance to Yellowstone National Park is reached by taking U.S. Highway 20 west from Cody.

Idaho Falls Municipal Airport/Fanning Field
2140 Skyline Dr., Idaho Falls, ID
(208) 529-1221

This airport serves SkyWest, Horizon (Alaska Airlines partner), and Northwest Airlines. Flights go through Salt Lake City and Boise before touching down in Idaho Falls. You can rent cars by calling Avis at (208) 522-4245, Budget at (208) 522-8800, Hertz at (208) 529-3101 or National at (208) 522-5276. Jackson Hole Express, (800) 652-9510, can take you from the airport to Jackson Hole for under $30.

West Yellowstone Airport
1515 Gallatin Rd., West Yellowstone, MT
(406) 646-7351 (800) 453-9417

SkyWest provides daily scheduled air service here from June through September 30, and you'll find rental cars available from Budget, (406) 646-7882, and Avis, (406) 646-7635. Although only open during the summer, this high-elevation airport (6,642 feet) gets good business from its three daily SkyWest flights and private pilots.

Insiders' Tip

If you're renting a car in the winter, you may want to consider a four-wheel drive vehicle. Winter roads around the region can get nasty in a hurry, and many of the region's out-of-the-way places require travel on primitive roads. Most car rental agencies offer a variety of four-wheel-drive vehicles. Just ask when making your reservations.

By Train

You won't find any direct service to the gateway towns, but Amtrak does offer service to Salt Lake City, Utah, Laramie, Wyoming, and Idaho Falls and Pocatello, Idaho. Depending on the route, connecting services may be provided by train, motorcoach, van, or taxi. Call Amtrak at (800) USA-RAIL for further information.

By Bus/Shuttle

Greyhound Lines
(800) 229-9424
www.greyhound.com

The closest Greyhound bus stops are in Wyoming at Powell and Cody, near the east entrance of Yellowstone. In Montana, Greyhound serves Billings, West Yellowstone, Livingston, and Bozeman, and in Idaho at Island Park, Idaho Falls, Pocatello, and Ashton. Call the number above for a complete list of fare and terminal information.

4 x 4 Stage
1765 Alaska Rd. S., Belgrade, MT 59714
(406) 388-6404, (800) 517-8243

Bozeman-based 4 x 4 Stage offers personalized transportation to and from the Bozeman airport, including West Yellowstone, Big Sky, and Yellowstone National Park. Reservations are advised.

Karst Stage
511 N. Wallace Ave., Bozeman, MT 59771
(406) 388-2293, (800) 287-4759

This charter motorcoach company offers year-round service to West Yellowstone, Big Sky, and Mammoth Hot Springs from the Bozeman airport and the surrounding area. In the winter, Karst runs an early morning shuttle between West Yellowstone and Big Sky. Karst has two locations, one in downtown Bozeman (above) and one in the airport.

Buffalo Bus Touring Co.
429 Yellowstone St., West Yellowstone, MT 59758
(406) 646-9564, (800) 426-7669
www.yellowstonevacations.com

Buffalo bus has daily, narrated sightseeing tours of Yellowstone Park and offers free pick up at motels and campgrounds around West Yellowstone.

Alltrans, Inc.
P.O. Box 96, Jackson, WY 83001
(307) 733-3135 (800)-443-6133

Alltrans offers airport shuttles, taxis, and charters, as well as single- and multi-day tours of the Grand Teton area. Alltrans meets every flight at the airport and also offers shuttle service to the Grand Targhee ski area.

Southern Teton Area Rapid Transit
P.O. Box 1687, Jackson, WY 83001
(307) 733-4521
www.startbus.com

The START bus is a public bus service offering year-round transportation around Jackson and to and from Teton Village, where the ski area is located. Fares are $1 for in-town service and $2 for the trip to Teton Village, with children under 8 riding free with an accompanying adult. In the winter and summer, the bus runs seven days a week, five days a week during the off-season (usually October through November). The bus has ski racks in the winter and bike racks in the summer. You can also find discount booklets available at most motels. Times and schedules may vary, so call the number above for information.

Insiders' Tip

Don't rely on your cell phone. Although service is getting better, the mountainous terrain may often block signals and antenna towers can be few and far between.

Close-up

The Beartooth Highway

Few roads in the country rival the majestic beauty of the Beartooth Highway, which runs from Red Lodge to Cooke City, Montana. The highway opened in 1936, and it remains an engineering feat. Topping out at a dizzying 10,946 feet, the highway winds its way through high alpine country with stunning views in every direction.

To reach the highway, drive south of the small community of Red Lodge on U.S. Highway 212 or east from the northeast entrance to Yellowstone Park. Red Lodge's downtown shops, restaurants, and attractions aren't this western town's only draw. It is also home to Red Lodge Mountain ski resort, one of the state's major ski areas, and numerous bed and breakfasts and other lodging options (see Red Lodge chapter in this book).

From Red Lodge, nestled in the Beartooth Mountains at around 5,500 feet, the highway begins to climb with a series of sharp switchbacks. There are numerous turnouts that provide panoramic views and spots for larger vehicles to pull over and let others pass. Driving on this road is slow going, but for good reason. The hair-raising road drops off steeply in several spots.

For campers, Ratine and Sheridan campgrounds just south of Red Lodge offer numerous sites along Rock Creek, one of the major drainages originating from the large cirque to the south. Here, you'll see the charred remains of the 2000 Willie Fire, named for country singer Willie Nelson, who happened to be performing in Red Lodge the day the fire broke out.

As the highway continues to rise, you'll cross over into Wyoming and eventually come back into Montana. At the first border, stop your vehicle where you can to get a great view of the alpine sage fields and the Bear's Tooth, a jutting rock that looks just like its name. Granite Peak, Montana's highest at 12,799 feet, is also in the distance, and dozens of lakes and snowfields dot the horizon.

You'll also pass by the site of the Red Lodge International Ski Race Camp and the Beartooth Freeride Camp, a permanent snowfield used for summer training. The top of the pass is also popular for backcountry skiing and snowboarding, as many diehards flock to the Rock Creek and Gardiner Headwalls when the highway is open. Most likely there will be patches of snow at the top any time of year, making for great photo opportunities.

After the top of the pass, you'll see far into the mountains of Wyoming and Yellowstone National Park. The Top of the World store offers lodging, gas, food, and other services, and numerous opportunities for hiking exist. The Beartooth Loop National Recreation Trail, Beartooth Butte, and Beartooth Falls are all worth exploring. Campgrounds on this side of the pass include Island Lake, Crazy Creek, and Fox Creek. The highway descends to follow the Clark's Fork of the Yellowstone River, past the burned areas of the devastating 1988 fires, through the old mining town of Cooke City, and terminates at the northeast entrance of Yellowstone National Park. Of course, you can also drive the road in the opposite direction described here.

The weather can change instantly, and snow can close the road even in the summer. Typically the road is open Memorial Day through the middle of October. Call the Montana road report at (800) 226-7623 or the Wyoming report at (307) 772-0824.

The scenic Beartooth Highway climbs to 11,000 feet. PHOTO: DONNIE SEXTON/TRAVEL MONTANA

Snowcoaches serve as winter transportation in Yellowstone and Grand Teton National Park. PHOTO: JACKSON HOLE CHAMBER OF COMMERCE

Snowcoaches

Yellowstone Alpen Guides
555 Yellowstone St., West Yellowstone, MT 59758
(406) 646-9591 (800) 858-3502
www.yellowstoneguides.com

Yellowstone Alpen Guides offers guided tours daily from West Yellowstone to Old Faithful or the Grand Canyon of the Yellowstone on 10-passenger, heated, traditional snowcoaches. The tours make many stops along the way, including opportunities for seeing geysers, paint pots, and wildlife. The adventurous can bring along cross-country skis and take a few side trips. Biscuit Basin is an option on the Old Faithful tour which allows members of your group to ski the easy 2½ miles along the Firehole River through the Upper Geyser Basin right to Old Faithful while the rest of your group continues by snowcoach.

Yellowstone National Park Lodges
P.O. Box 165, Yellowstone National Park, WY 82190
(307) 344-7311
www.travelyellowstone.com

This company offers daily snowcoach and snowvan tours to Old Faithful from Mammoth, West Yellowstone, and the South entrance, as well as trips from Mammoth and Old Faithful to Canyon. Prices run about $90 round-trip.

History

A land of contradictions, a spectacular pageant, a world incomprehensible . . . a wonderful gift to men from a benign God—all this and more.

—Olin Wheeler, 1914

Yellowstone National Park has been dubbed "America's best idea," "the great American experiment" and "Wonderland." Because it is all of these things it continues to fascinate and unite and sustain millions of people today, as it has for centuries. Those of us who live in and love the Greater Yellowstone Area—that vast stretch of land ringed by blurry borders within Idaho, Montana, and Wyoming—are continually pulled by the paradox of Yellowstone Park as a place to be preserved and protected, yet promoted.

Long before the idea of a national park existed, the Yellowstone region was revered by Native Americans. This land was essential for hunting and gathering, and considered splendid enough to inspire spiritual practices. They considered Yellowstone a sacred gift.

Likewise, when early explorers and later white settlers came to the area, Yellowstone left them awed. Its beauty and abundance was too incredible to be consumed by industry or development; we knew this even before understanding its magnitude. This undeniable truth eventually led to the creation of Yellowstone National Park in 1872 and subsequently brought hordes of other people who wanted to experience the wilderness, too.

In that way, Yellowstone National Park shaped its corner of the West, becoming a hub for tall tales of the frontier, for industry, and population. At a time when America was still creating itself, the eerie geysers, impossibly tall mountains, and sheer vastness of this region gave our country identity—the opportunity to say, "There is no place like this anywhere on the planet." And this is true. In Yellowstone, we found the undiscovered and embraced its wildness as a place to live and cultivate new communities, new traditions, and new ideals. From Yellowstone our country gained its most long-standing legends: the explorer, the cowboy, and the rugged individualist.

Almost 200 years later, people continue to come here to gawk, study, commune with nature, and capitalize on the awesome treasures Yellowstone holds. Our methods may be different in modern times, but in a way the sentiment is much the same as early inhabitants who revered and utilized the riches of this land. At the heart of Yellowstone's influence is its power to inspire a sense of place.

Today's Greater Yellowstone Area encompasses roughly 18 million acres of land. With Yellowstone and Grand Teton National Parks at its core, the area includes seven national forests and three national wildlife refuges, plus thousands of acres of private lands. Because this region is so huge, diverse, and complex, in this chapter we'll highlight how Yellowstone's history relates to this region and its individual communities.

Early Residents

Today 25 different Native American tribes incorporate Yellowstone into their tribal history or customs. With this, the area surrounding what is now known as Yellowstone National Park could have been called "the land of many tribes." The Native American people of the Sioux, Bannock, Shoshone, Crow, Blackfeet, Kiowa, Nez Perce, Flathead, and Assiniboine nations valued the land of "Yellow Stone" or "Smoke from the Ground" for its abundant hunting grounds inhabited by bison, big horn sheep, and elk, among other animals. The area's hot springs were used for spiritual rituals, and several tribal deities resided in the mountains of Yellowstone country—the Absarokas, the Gallatins, and the Tetons.

Although many tribes made annual hunting and foraging forays to the region, no single group claimed exclusive territorial rights to the area. Several tribal territories did overlap with Yellowstone's boundaries, such as the Crow to the east in present day Cody, Wyoming, and the Blackfeet to the west near Three Forks, Montana. But because of the harsh winters and rugged terrain, this mountainous region was considered uninhabitable.

Historically, the Sheepeaters (a band of the Shoshone) were the only known year-round residents here. Archeologists speculate that the Sheepeaters may have migrated from the Great Basin to the intermountain area of Montana and Wyoming as early as 1,200 A.D. Reports from the earliest EuroAmerican explorers indicate that the Sheepeaters made their living hunting big horn sheep and were well known for the high quality bows they made from their horns. Additionally, the historic shelters called wickiups found throughout Yellowstone were undoubtedly made by the Sheepeaters.

Although early American explorers claim to have discovered the "unknown wilderness," it was more accurately Native American homes, gardens, and hunting territory. Even the name "Yellowstone" is derived from Native Americans. The Minnetaree Indian expression *Mi tsi a-da-zi* translated to Rock Yellow or Stone Yellow and is thought to refer to the yellowish sandstone bluffs that border the Yellowstone River near present-day Billings, Montana.

The rugged Grand Teton Range makes Greater Yellowstone one of the country's most popular destinations. PHOTO: GRAND TETON LODGE COMPANY

Opening the Western Frontier

Both the French and the Spanish had interests in the land now considered Greater Yellowstone. Early EuroAmerican explorers reported a land of abundant wildlife and vast natural resources. Although most of the area was unexplored, there was no doubt the land was valuable.

In the end, it was President Thomas Jefferson who claimed this region as American soil when he signed the Louisiana Purchase in 1803. The United States bought the rights to 828,000 square miles of uncharted land west of the Mississippi River from France for $15 million. Jefferson had big plans to develop a trade route from St. Louis, Missouri to the Pacific and to further American power through land ownership. Critics of Jefferson saw the Purchase as a waste. But the visionary president knew that the acquisition would change the course of American history, further cultivating the image of democracy with the fact that there was enough land for every man.

By 1805 Jefferson had enlisted Merriweather Lewis and William Clark to lead the Corps of Discovery into this newly acquired territory. The expedition's primary goal was to locate a waterway that could be used as a northwest passage to transport goods across the continent. (At the time the only way to ship commodities was by way of Cape Horn.) Lewis and Clark were also sent to make contact with Native American people and to survey this vast, new property. Their travels crossed much of what would later become the states of Idaho and Montana.

Historically, the Lewis and Clark expedition left an indelible mark upon the development of the West, but technically it was considered unsuccessful because they were unable to locate a viable trade route. What Lewis and Clark did do is plant the seed of opportunity on the western frontier. They reported a wealth of furs and timber stores for potential development.

Ironically, however, the Corps of Discovery's efforts skirted around today's Yellowstone, bringing them within 50 miles of Mammoth Hot Springs. It was actually John Colter, an original member of the Lewis and Clark expedition, who discovered the awesome geysers and hot springs of the region in 1807. Colter had joined a hunting party with the intent of establishing a fur trading relationship with Native Americans. He spent three years hunting and trapping. His travels took him on an epic 500-mile trip from the Bighorn River, along the Shoshone River near present day Cody, Wyoming, into

Close-up

Greater Yellowstone Area Timeline

1803—Thomas Jefferson signs The Louisiana Purchase. The United States pays France $15 million for the rights to 828,000 square miles of uncharted land west of the Mississippi River.

1805 to 1806—The Lewis and Clark Expedition passes west and east through Greater Yellowstone, missing the Mammoth Hot Springs by 50 miles.

1807—John Colter explores the area that will eventually become Yellowstone National Park.

1869—Cook-Folsom-Peterson Expedition of 1869 travels through Yellowstone seeing geysers and hot pools. The three men return to Montana Territory with tales that many doubted.

1870—Gen. Henry Washburn and Nathaniel Langford (who later became the first park superintendent) are among the members of the official exploration party. Old Faithful is discovered and named.

1871—The Hayden Expedition, including photographer William Jackson and artist Thomas Moran, chronicle the area. Moran's paintings and Jackson's photos help convince Congress to preserve the area.

March 1, 1872—President Ulysses S. Grant signs the National Park Act, which creates Yellowstone National Park. It is the first national park in the world.

1877—The Nez Perce Indians, led by Chief Joseph, pass through Yellowstone during a retreat after a series of summer battles in which they lost 300 people. The retreat is later hailed as a masterful tactical display.

1882—Gen. Philip Sheridan tours Yellowstone Park. Appalled by rampant poaching of wildlife in the park, he plants the first seeds for the Greater Yellowstone idea by promoting park expansion to encompass wildlife migratory and wintering grounds.

1883—Yellowstone National Park Superintendent Philetus W. Norris persuades Congress to allocate funds to build access roads into Yellowstone. This effort establishes the road system that is known today as the Grand Loop Road.

1883—The first grand hotel, the National Hotel at Mammoth Hot Springs, is built by the Yellowstone Park Improvement Company.

1885—The Army Corps of Engineers completes Yellowstone National Park's Golden Gate Bridge.

1886—The U.S. Army takes over Yellowstone National Park's administration.

1888—Excelsior Geyser, which erupted up to 300 feet in height, resumes major eruptions.

1891—Congress passes the Forest Reserve Act, and President Benjamin Harrison creates the Yellowstone National Park Timberland Reserve, precursor to today's national forests and a key component of Greater Yellowstone.

1892—The Northern Pacific Railroad completes tracks within three miles of Yellowstone's northern entrance, making visits to the park more accessible to wealthy tourists.

1894—The Lacey Act is passed to "protect the birds and animals in Yellowstone National Park, and to punish crimes in said park." The act leads to the end of hunting, with heavy penalties for poaching game in Yellowstone.

1895—Army begins predator control by poisoning coyotes.

1900—Approximately 9,000 people visit the park this year.

1901 to mid-1950s—The world's largest trout hatchery operates on the shores of Yellowstone Lake.

1902—Park officials count only 22 bison.

1903—President Theodore Roosevelt dedicates the Roosevelt Arch on August 24.

1904—Old Faithful Inn, the world's largest log hostelry, opens.

1905—President Theodore Roosevelt creates the U.S. Forest Service and appoints Gifford Pinchot as its first director.

1915—The first automobile is allowed to enter Yellowstone.

1916—President Woodrow Wilson signs Act of Congress on August 25, creating the National Park Service as a bureau of the Department of the Interior. Shortly thereafter, civilian superintendents are appointed, replacing the park's military overseers.

1927 to 1943—John D. Rockefeller, hoping to create Grand Teton National Park, buys thousands of acres of private land in Jackson Hole.

1929—Congress creates Grand Teton National Park, which includes only the Teton Mountains.

1941—Park officials end bear feeding shows at Canyon. The shows, during which the bears were fed garbage, began as a way to entertain visitors during the days when the Army controlled the park.

1943—President Franklin Roosevelt creates the 221,000-acre Jackson Hole National Monument.

1946—Bison are fed their last hay at the Buffalo Ranch in nearby Lamar Valley. The herd numbers over 1,000 animals.

1950—Jackson Hole National Monument is incorporated into Grand Teton Park.

1958—Canyon Hotel closes.

1959—An earthquake causes considerable damage, including a rock slide at Golden Gate Bridge. The quake's epicenter is at Hebgen Lake, Montana.

1965—The number of park visitors exceeds 2 million.

1973—Yellowstone National Park managers institute catch-and-release fishing.

1985—Excelsior Geyser erupts for the first time in 95 years and hurls large pieces of rock into the Firehole River for 47 hours.

1988—Summer fires sweep through two-thirds of the park, the largest burn in Yellowstone history.

1995—The National Park Service re-introduces the gray wolf into Yellowstone National Park.

1996—Yellowstone's bison herd numbers reach 3,500 animals.

1997—Yellowstone turns 125 years old, with an average of 30,000 to 40,000 visitors each day of the summer.

(Continued)

1999—Congress orders a partial ban on snowmobiling in Yellowstone Park because of its impact on wildlife.

2000—The National Park Service and other federal agencies create a management plan for population size and disease to maintain the Yellowstone bison herd.

Insiders' Tip

Yellowstone National Park is twice the size of the state of Delaware.

Jackson Hole. From there he traversed Teton Pass and came into Idaho's Teton Basin until he apparently headed onto the Yellowstone Plateau through Cooke City and back into the Bighorn Basin. Finally in 1810, Colter returned to St. Louis, Missouri, with his stories of great steaming valleys, geysers that shot hundreds of feet out of the earth, and more beaver than any man could trap.

Despite the fact that Colter's tales of a steaming, bubbling, boiling land were met with disbelief, people listened intently to the confirmation of abundant trading and trapping opportunities. A new economic boom began in America: the mountain man era of fur trading. If St. Louis, Missouri, was the gateway to the West, then Yellowstone was its heartland.

From the 1820s through the 1930s demands for fashionable beaver skin hats fostered the fur trading industry. Most notably, the Rocky Mountain Fur Company and the Hudson Bay Trading Company dominated in Idaho, Wyoming, and Montana. Highly competitive Canadian, American, and English fur trading companies vied for beaver pelts, which were worth as much as $6 apiece. Some trappers even vowed to trap areas into "deserts" before allowing anyone to infringe on their territory.

This rugged new breed of opportunists etched out their own culture in the wilderness. They endured hardships of the climate, fought unfriendly Indians, and endured most of the year in solitude until rendezvous. Rather than establishing formal trading posts, mountain men gathered annually at designated sites such as Red Lodge, Montana, or Jackson Hole, where they would sell their furs and trade for supplies. Rendezvous was also a social event, where they drank, caroused, gambled, swapped stories, and feasted.

With the influence of mountain men, the door of this untouched frontier was open. Legendary names like Jedediah Smith, Jim Bridger, Don MacKenzie, Nathaniel Wyeth, David Jackson, William Sublette, and Major William Ashley still dot the landscape of the northern Rockies in the form of towns, mountain ranges, and other usages. These men paved the way for many of the routes that would later be used in the settlement of the Western frontier. About the time the beaver were disappearing in the 1840s, mountain men traded their traps in for positions as guides to the steady stream of pilgrims traveling to California in search of gold and rich farming land. Famous overland passages such as the Oregon Trail brought a flood of more than 500,000 settlers in what became the greatest overland migration this country has ever known.

Miners and Settlers

From the coast of California to the high hills of Idaho the cries of "Gold! Gold! Gold!" resounded. Throngs of fortune-seekers journeyed through the Yellowstone region first to California and Oregon in 1848 and gradually into the interiors of Montana, Wyoming and Idaho. Here and there prospectors hit pay dirt outside the present-day park. In 1863 gold was found—lots of it—to the north in Virginia City, Montana. The rush continued in this region until 1870, when a group of miners staked their claims on a gold strike in Cooke City, Montana.

Recklessly, miners chipped at the frontier, settling in camps which later became official towns. Gold strikes became scarce as supplies were depleted, and people found other ways to eke out a living. Many settlers realized the futility of gold mining and made their living instead by supplying goods to miners. A few others raised cattle, while still others opened hotels, saloons, and stores.

It was providence that protected the heart of Yellowstone country from gold discoveries. Protected by high, unpassable mountain ranges, it remained relatively unexplored and uninhabited until the late 1860s. But accounts of the area's other treasures trickled back to Washington, DC.

Exploring Yellowstone

It is a testimonial to Yellowstone's spectacular wonders that three "discovery" expeditions were required before the American public would believe such a place existed. Even journalists refused to print stories of ghostly geysers and steaming valleys for fear of being dubbed liars. In the end, exploring parties of 1869, 1870, and 1871 each played an integral role in revealing Yellowstone to the world.

Persistent rumors of unfathomable curiosities led three prospectors from Diamond City in Montana Territory (near present day Helena) into the wilds of Yellowstone. In September of 1869 these men, known as the Folsom-Cook-Peterson Expedition, left to explore the area near the headwaters of the Yellowstone River. They spent 36 days exploring and mapping the region and were astounded by what they saw. When they stumbled upon the Grand Canyon of the Yellowstone, Charles Cook wrote, "It seemed to me that it was five minutes before anyone spoke." Upon their return, they wrote a magazine article about their experiences and suggested the area be reserved for its natural wonders.

> **Insiders' Tip**
>
> For more details on the park's history, read *The Yellowstone Story*, by Aubrey L. Haines.

By the next year, excitement over Yellowstone was feverish. The Washburn-Langford-Doane Expedition left Bozeman in August of 1870 to further investigate the region. This group spent a month exploring the present park, naming many of its features, including Old Faithful Geyser. Following the expedition's return, Nathaniel P. Langford (an employee of the Northern Pacific Railroad, which would play a prominent role in advertising the future park) traveled to the East coast to promote their "discovery." Dr. Ferdinand Hayden, then head of what would become the U.S. Geological Survey, was in one of the Washington, DC, audiences. Intrigued by Langford's story, Hayden petitioned Congress for a $40,000 grant to outfit a government party to explore Yellowstone country.

The Hayden Expedition spent many months in Yellowstone during the summer of 1871 and confirmed much of what Washburn's party had found. The group of about 30 men included artist Thomas Moran and photographer William H. Jackson. Their visual images were the proof needed to confirm Yellowstone's existence. It was their work that tipped the scales in favor of the world's first national park in the eyes of Congress.

Creating a New Ideal

If there were any pure intentions in the creation of Yellowstone National Park, they stem from the sheer awe felt by explorers when they first experienced the geothermal features of the area. Amidst the smell of sulfur, the eerie spouting, steaming earth seemed other-worldly and sparked wonder in the men who first laid their eyes upon it. And although no one person can be credited for creating Yellowstone, it was Ferdinand Hayden who first approached Congress with the idea of setting aside this chunk of land following his 1871 expedition.

At the time there was substantial debate within Washington about what to do with the land they considered "worthless" because its climate was too harsh to be utilized for farming or ranching. They considered exploiting it for timber and mining but did not yet have a way to access the expanse of property or to affordably transport their goods. The suggestion of a national park seemed preposterous and wasteful in this era where conservation wasn't practiced yet.

The first hurdle Hayden had to clear was making people believe in the astounding "wonders and curiosities" that made the proposed 2 million acres of land worthy of preservation. Since photographer William Jackson and painter Thomas Moran had accompanied the expedition, their works were presented to Congress. Historians attribute the artful representations of Moran's paintings as a key factor that clinched the national park deal.

The next obstacle was funding for this proposed park. For this, Hayden had help. Following the creation of Yellowstone, the railroad barons of the Northern Pacific hoped to lay tracks into Yellowstone country bringing curious tourists to see the sights of this wild place. The collective thinking of park supporters at the time was that Yellowstone would support itself through fees paid by concessionaires who would build hotels and by tourists who would pay entrance fees. With the agreement that this Yellowstone National Park would not require federal funding, Congress passed the bill.

On March 1, 1872 President Ulysses S. Grant signed the National Park Act and created a new ideal for American wilderness.

Making Tracks

While the depths of America's wild lands were being explored, railroad companies were frenetically racing to lay tracks across it. The Union Pacific Railroad was first, completing its transcontinental railroad in 1869. Not to be outdone, investors in the Northern Pacific Railroad turned their interests toward discoveries in Yellowstone, hoping to be the first to access it.

The railroad's influence reaches back to the actual exploration of Yellowstone country, beginning with Nathaniel Langford's connection to the Northern Pacific Railroad when he accompanied the Washburn Expedition. In fact, it was partially the lobbying of railroad supporters such as Minnesota governor William Marshall (Langford's brother-in-law) and Judge William Darrah Kelley who helped push the National Park Act through Congress in 1872. It was no coincidence that only the year before the federal government had issued a series of railroad land grants on which to continue the newly established transcontinental rail system to encourage western settlement. What railroad barons saw in Yellowstone was a hugely profitable tourist destination. The idea was for the Northern Pacific (other smaller lines had similar interests as well) to haul in visitors along tracks leading right to attractions such as Old Faithful and the Grand Canyon of the Yellowstone.

Although advances toward developing Yellowstone as a "summer resort" came to a standstill for a decade due to Northern Pacific's financial difficulties, by 1882 the idea of building a railroad to service attractions inside Yellowstone's boundaries was refueled. The best evidence of this was the construction of a branch line from Livingston, Montana, to Cinnabar, just three miles from the National Park's Gardiner entrance. This multi-million dollar investment was done with the intention of continuing the tracks through the actual park. But it would be a long time before the railroad would even come close to attaining its goal.

Over the next decade, railroad monopolists and Yellowstone supporters within Congress debated over the railroad's intent to develop Yellowstone National Park. The first stone of opposition to railroad development within the boundaries of Yellowstone Park was thrown by General P. H. Sheridan in 1882. After a summer of vacationing in Yellowstone, Sheridan succeeded in convincing the secretary of the interior to forbid the building of any railroad within the park. This began the Yellowstone war, as historian Aubrey Haines called it in his book, *The Yellowstone Story*.

Despite clever and aggressive efforts by railroad lobbyists who approached the Yellowstone railway project from every angle, including the attempt to access mining claims along Yellowstone's northern border, near Cooke City, they were consistently defeated in Congress. One of Yellowstone National Park's biggest supporters was Senator George Vest, who said, "allowing any railroad to enter Yellowstone would end in the destruction of the Park."

While the Northern Pacific lost to park supporters, it was still integral in the promotion and success of Yellowstone National Park. The park branch line eventually extended to Yellowstone's northern entrance in 1903 and was marked by President Teddy Roosevelt's dedication of the Roosevelt Arch for the "benefit and enjoyment of the people."

For the next three decades railroad interests tapped into every aspect of Yellowstone, from its management practices, stage transportation, and lodging to national advertising campaigns. The Burlington Northern, Northern Pacific, Oregon Short Line, and later the Chicago Milwaukee and St. Paul railroads all invested money in regional depots. Both the Sacajawea Inn in Three Forks, Montana, and the Gallatin Gateway Inn outside of Bozeman, Montana, are testaments to the railroad marketing of Yellowstone. Trains made it possible for hundreds of wealthy travelers to experience "Wonderland" in style. After traveling thousands of miles, passengers disembarked and would often stay over night in a railroad luxury hotel before being carted off by stage for the "Grand Tour" of Yellowstone's wonders. Explorations of the park thrived until automobile travel finally replaced trains after World War II.

As it turned out, railroad spur lines originally built to access coal-mining areas later became the major entrances to Yellowstone National Park. Without the railroads there would be no Cody, Wyoming, or Livingston, Red Lodge, West Yellowstone, or Bozeman, Montana. Public access to the park and to the western frontier eventually solidified the railroad's success.

The Grand Tour

While debates over access to Yellowstone raged in Washington, the park was left to its wildness. Without real roadways or formal tour guides, it was mainly accessible by horseback or on foot. In fact, the park's first superintendent, Nathaniel Langford, refused to issue leases to a number of entrepreneurs who proposed building hotels, because there were no roads to access them. (Historians claim he denied other concessionaire ventures because he was in cahoots with the Northern Pacific Railroad.)

By the turn of the century, railroad travel opened the gates of Yellowstone National Park to throngs of wealthy tourists. They traveled long distances from the East and West Coasts first to the Northern Pacific Railroad's outpost in Cinnabar, Montana. Those early tourists purchased a five- or six-day travel package from the railroad and were shuttled along the Grand Loop Road.

From Cinnabar visitors embarked on a rough and dusty stagecoach ride to Gardiner's east entrance into the park and on to Mammoth Hot Springs. The National Hotel at Mammoth was the first to offer luxurious accommodations in the park. It served as home base for the "grand tour of Wonderland."

After a night's stay at Mammoth and a tour of the terraces, folks were herded into 11-person coaches, assigned a driver, and sent on their way. Stagecoach drivers were barraged with questions from the tourists, and though most did right by their guests, others spun yarns about the wonders of the park just for fun. But these guides brought tourists to the edge of the Grand Canyon and to the foot of the major geyser basins throughout Yellowstone for six glorious days before returning to Mammoth and then the train terminal at Cinnabar.

Until 1891, when the modern Fountain Hotel was built in the Upper Geyser Basin, travelers were subjected to the simplest of rustic accommodations. The lavish grand hotels built at Lake Yellowstone and Canyon replaced a rustic Firehole Hotel where the rooms held two beds and had canvas walls. Even that was an improvement over other accommodations in which guests slept shoulder to shoulder on plank floors in hotels with broken windows.

Because these early tourists were accustomed to luxury, concessionaires knew the rustic accommodations wouldn't be accepted for long. With the opening of the Fountain Hotel—with its steam heat, electric lights, and hot baths—a new precedent was set for lodging within Yellowstone. All of the new hotels were equipped with formal dining areas and grand rooms for lounging, reading, and socializing. The majestic Old Faithful Inn opened in 1904 as the pinnacle of Yellowstone's hotels with its massive Douglas fir and native stone construction.

The Grand Tour of Wonderland continued this way for thirty years. As a result, the park remained largely an elitist vacation spot, because train travel was so expensive. But all that changed in 1915 when automobiles were first permitted to tour Wonderland independently.

Traffic

In a sense, by making Yellowstone accessible to just about everyone in America, the automobile restored the democratic intentions upon which the park was founded. When the gates opened in 1915, more than 50,000 mostly middle-class Americans flooded Yellowstone National Park. Honking their horns, vehicles lined up 100-deep at the entrance gates. After that, visitation numbers climbed steadily for the next 15 years.

Old Faithful Inn. PHOTO: THE WAGNER PERSPECTIVE

Unlike the upper-class railroad tourist who had packed trunks full of fine clothing to dress for dinner and dancing, these working people loaded up a gaggle of relatives into the Ford and headed for the park. Following a route from St. Paul to Bozeman mapped out by the Minnesota Automobile Association, the slow-moving cars inched along with wash basins, tents, pots, pans and chairs, bedding, and a couple of spare tires strapped on top. They followed a string of platter-sized orange signs marking the rough rural roads that would later become today's Interstate 90 and 94.

Inside the park, Model Ts blocked attractions and the sighting of a bear, bison, or buffalo from the road was enough to jam up traffic as well. Objections were raised (mostly from the park concessionaires who were losing money) about the affects of automobile traffic within the park. Some said it would lead to the ruin the whole place. It took only a year for the noisy automobiles to oust outdated stagecoaches and horse-drawn carriages, and the three former transportation companies were outraged.

With the automobile came change and reorganization. In 1916 Stephen T. Mather, director of the newly formed National Park Service, streamlined concession operations when he designated the Yellowstone Park Transportation Company as sole provider of transportation; Frank M. Haynes, who owned several hotels and other businesses was told to sell them and become the photographic concessionaire; and the Yellowstone Park Hotel Company merged with Wylie Permanent Camps to be the only hotelier in the park. Each was asked to contribute four percent of its gross profits to the National Park Service for the leases. The changes were not easily accepted, but in the long run concessionaires provided better service for the public.

Order in the Wilderness

Since Yellowstone was theoretically set aside for the benefit of the public good, it seemed natural that it would be governed by civilians. The Secretary of the Interior appointed civilian superintendents from 1872 until 1886. This new creation of the government came with no instructions or manual to maintain its pristine state, and early managers struggled to maintain order.

Because of his Washington connections, Nathaniel Langford became the park's first superintendent and held the post from 1872 to 1877. An absentee manager in this unpaid position, he made only three visits to Yellowstone and filed one report during his tenure. Otherwise, the park was unguarded, unregulated, and unmaintained. Yet it had been discovered, so it was at the mercy of squatters and vandals. Hunters brazenly poached elk by the thousands; would-be concessionaires camped at major attractions; tourists stuffed rocks, logs, and clothing into geysers and then poured soap into them to get them to blow; they skinny-dipped in hot springs and hauled home whole petrified trees as souvenirs.

Yellowstone's second superintendent, Philetus W. Norris, saw a monument that was underfunded and neglected. For his part, Norris reasoned with Congress, saying Yellowstone would forever falter if there were no roads leading to its attractions. He received enough money to map out the early portion of the Grand Loop Road. He served until 1882, when he was ousted for supporting a railroad through the park.

By 1886 Yellowstone National Park had been branded with scandals. News of visitors victimized by stagecoach robberies, rampant poaching, shameless bootlegging, and destruction of geothermal formations reached Washington. Congress was so fed up that it refused to allocate funds for that year. This action in turn stirred vengefulness from park employees, who trashed public facilities and even started numerous forest fires.

Yellowstone had gone amok. There were grumblings within Congress that the national park idea was a failure and even talk of abolishing Yellowstone. The Department of the Interior pulled its trump card: it called in the U.S. Cavalry.

When Captain Moses Harris rode into Mammoth Hot Springs with his Troop M on August 20, 1886, he immediately relieved Superintendent Wear from his duties and restored order to Yellowstone. This began a 30-year era of military administration in Yellowstone. Although the enlisted men endured great public criticism, their presence restored the park's integrity and saved it from ruin.

By World War I, the military was needed for other, more pressing national situations. That and the fact that the national parks system had grown to 30 national parks and monuments throughout the country called for the creation of an agency to manage these special places. On August 25, 1916, Congress created the National Park Service, and two years later the Cavalry left Yellowstone.

The Yellowstone Park left to the National Park Service was now a full-fledged business. Unlike the soldiers, whose job it was to prosecute poachers, bootleggers, and robbers, the rangers were there to manage people. They greeted cars at entrance gates, investigated accidents, patrolled popular areas on foot, horseback, and on motorcycles, maintained public buildings, managed wildlife problems, administered first aid, and conducted interpretive talks about Yellowstone. From 1919 to 1929 visitation numbers jumped from about 62,000 to 260,000 people, and the fleet of 71 park rangers struggled to maintain order.

Into the 1930s and World War II, Yellowstone seriously suffered from the impacts of the Great Depression and wartime America. Visitor numbers were so low that concessionaires literally boarded up their facilities and left. Our national park fell into severe disrepair and so was later not prepared when tourists returned to Yellowstone in droves. By 1948 more than 1 million people visited Yellowstone, tipping it into a new era of tourism.

Since its creation the National Park Service has persevered in its impossible task of balancing preservation of Yellowstone with the needs and desires of visitors. Then as now, park service administrators work under the demands of tight federal budgets, changing politics, and ever-increasing visitation.

From Great Idea to Greater Yellowstone

Even as Yellowstone became more of the "pleasuring ground" it was set aside to be, concern for the health of the park heightened. While tourists reveled in the natural curiosities of Yellowstone, they did little to preserve it. Camp sites and attractions were littered with trash, observation areas were built to watch park rangers feed garbage to bears and debris was tossed into mud pots or geysers. Gradually Yellowstone began to show signs of duress, and the National Park Service experimented with how to maintain the park's natural integrity.

Ironically, because of Yellowstone's aesthetic and recreational appeal, gateway communities to the park have created an isolated wilderness troubled by problems of wildlife overpopulation (grizzly bears, wolves, elk, and bison), overgrazing (elk and bison) and predator conflicts with human pursuits (wolves versus cattle and sheep ranching). These conflicts have historically escalated and at times created a climate of resentment and polarization among recreationists, environmentalists, scientists, ranchers, developers, and politicians. Yet the lives affected most by these issues are Yellowstone's plants and animals. Because they know no boundaries and don't abide by state or federal laws, they are caught in the middle of human battles about public access, mining, ranching, noxious weeds, non-native species infiltration, disease, and forest fires—to name a few.

As one of the last intact ecosystems, Yellowstone is an experiment not only of federal policy, but of nature. During its tenure the National Park Service has tested both boundaries, often learning from mistakes. Park service employees have stocked Yellowstone waters with exotic non-native fish; fed bears for visitor entertainment; nearly brought the extinction of bison and later bred them; implemented the "let-burn" forest fire policy to the extreme that two-thirds of Yellowstone was charred in the fires of 1988; and exterminated the grey wolf and then in 1995 reintroduced it.

As early as 1882 Yellowstone was a place of conflict and controversy. Following a tour through Yellowstone with President Chester Alan Arthur, General Phil Sheridan suggested the national park's boundaries should be doubled to protect wildlife. Even then it was evident that Yellowstone National Park's boundary lines were drawn when

Insiders' Tip

Greater Yellowstone encompasses the intersection of three wild Western states: Idaho, the most populous with more than 1 million people; Montana, with around 900,000; and Wyoming, the ninth-largest in the nation geographically, with only 481,000 residents.

Close-up

From Tribe to Tribe

Bozeman, Montana's, history is a short one. The town's beginnings only reach back a little more than a century. The Gallatin Valley's history, where Bozeman sits, however, is ancient. Historian Phyllis Smith wrote in her book *Bozeman and the Gallatin Valley: A History*:

"The first migration through the Gallatin Valley may have occurred more than 30,000 years ago after small groups of hunters from Asia tentatively crossed a 56-mile-long land bridge to this hemisphere, now underwater as the Bering Strait. As these early travelers tracked mastodon, caribou, mammoth, and giant bison with wide-spreading horns, they may have watched small horses and camels traveling in the opposite direction to Asia. They passed along grassy corridors through towering glaciers and filtered slowly down the eastern face of the Rockies along what is sometimes called the Old North Trail. They seldom went into the mountains to hunt because the remaining glaciers blocked their passage. They avoided the high plains as well because they felt vulnerable without forest cover."

This purported migration was a slow population process for North America. Hunting and gathering tribes moved methodically and at a pace that would accommodate a large group of women and children. Approximately 12,000 years ago, paleontologists believe that other small bands of hunters ventured to this continent after hearing legends about the plentiful game and abundance of clean water.

"We don't know who the people were that lived here thousands of years ago and even who they turned into isn't known," said Walter Fleming, professor for Native American Studies at Montana State University in Bozeman.

About 5,000 years ago the Gallatin Valley's weather patterns gradually changed. It became a barren high desert in a drought that lasted approximately 2,000 years. A people from the southwest, accustomed to such conditions, ventured into the region, wrote Smith. They trapped small animals and foraged for plants to survive that long dry period.

Fleming claimed that it is difficult to know the cultural habits or lifestyle of these early people because any artifacts of their existence have long since decayed.

The most significant remains of a native people in this area date back 4,000 years ago along the Madison River. The valley's climate had shifted again, presumably bringing it to a state much like today's. Traces of an early village remain in the form of about 100 circles of boulders lining the river and marking temporary lodges. Pieces of primitive tools and weapons were found in this area as well as points, chips, and fragments of knives made mostly of basalt and occasionally obsidian or jasper. According to Smith, other early camps exist in the valley, the most notable in Kelly Canyon.

Additionally, the famous Madison Buffalo Jump is estimated to have been used by those same people who laid camp along the Madison River. This 30-foot cliff is located just seven miles south of Logan.

"For possibly 4,000 years or more, these early Gallatin Valley people utilized the steep cliffs generally associated with the high plains country to force grazing bison to run to their death over the drop," according to Fleming.

More recently, dating back to the 1500s, the cliffs were used by the Flathead, Crow, Blackfeet, and possibly other High Plains Indian tribes.

"This valley was an important crossroads for tribes heading into the plains to hunt buffalo," Fleming explained. "You really can't say this was one single tribe's territory because all tribes crossed through and fought in this area. Tribal lore refers to it as a common hunting ground, which implies some kind of mutual agreement that no single tribe could exert its control over it."

On the fringe of several tribal territories, such as the Crow and the Blackfeet, Fleming said, the Gallatin Valley became disputed territory in the 1850s with the advent of white settlement and railroad surveys. The first Fort Laramie Treaty was passed in 1851, promising the land to the Blackfeet, but new treaty signers reneged in 1855 and changed the Gallatin Valley to open territory. According to Smith, the three forks and the Gallatin Valley were named "common Indian hunting grounds for 99 years."

This new treaty ultimately allowed wagon trains following overland routes such as the Bozeman Trail to cross directly through essential tribal hunting territory, despite Indian protests saying the traffic would alter their way of life entirely. This route, which crested at 5,500-foot Bozeman Pass, later became known as "The Bloody Bozeman," because of conflicts with Indian warriors. Ultimately, the trail was abandoned for alternative routes that were less dangerous.

A new migration began in the 1860s and on through the turn of the century as trappers, traders, explorers, and prospectors opened up the Western frontier. These new people brought customs and cultures that were different than those of early Gallatin Valley inhabitants. As the railroads solidified this region's change, existing tribes were pushed to different boundaries of the West. By the 1870s almost all Native Americans were placed on reservations. Wheat fields replaced rolling grassland and hunting grounds, cattle eventually replaced bison, and houses replaced teepees. The Gallatin Valley, like so many other parts of the West, became the single territory of white settlers.

Bison. PHOTO: NATIONAL PARK SERVICE

there was little knowledge of ecosystems or animal migration patterns. That lack of knowledge has resulted in an on-going debate over park management and the ecological value of land bordering the park.

The Greater Yellowstone concept took root in 1917 when a 1,200-square-mile addition to the south of Yellowstone National Park was proposed. Congress nearly passed the bill, which would have included land from the Absaroka Range ridge to the Buffalo Fork of the Snake River, then west, just south of Jackson and Leigh and Jenny Lakes, including some National Forest Service land. But when the ranching community caught wind of it, they protested the move and urged the Wyoming Legislature to oppose the bill. The debate continued for a decade and tangled U.S. courts with political twists and turns regarding grazing leases and paranoia over too much federal land control.

Finally, someone tried a new approach. Senator Gerald Nye proposed a bill not for the expansion of Yellowstone Park, but for the creation of a whole new park: Grand Teton National Park. Echoing sentiments expressed by General Sheridan almost 40 years earlier, Nye outlined the new park boundaries around the dramatically beautiful Teton Mountains, which were too steep and high for livestock. Congress passed it with flying colors on February 26, 1929.

Encouraged by this, John D. Rockefeller Jr. also wanted to keep the whole area outside of Jackson Hole protected from commercial development. He formed the Snake River Land Company and purchased 35,000 acres of land (worth $2 million) from area residents. He offered to donate the property to Grand Teton National Park, but was thwarted by congressional and local opposition. Again, the issue of national park expansion went to the courts.

A man accustomed to getting his way, Rockefeller wouldn't have it. In 1943 he told President Franklin Roosevelt that he would happily sell the land on the open market. Roosevelt was moved to action. He set aside the 221,000-acre Jackson Hole Monument by presidential decree.

Roosevelt's decision set fire to a new war that was battled out in congressional and legislative sessions for nearly another decade. Congress passed a bill abolishing the decree, but Roosevelt vetoed it. Then the state of Wyoming sued the Grand Teton National Park superintendent—and lost. Finally Congress cut funding for the monument's maintenance. At last, in 1950 a compromise was reached. It included allowances for lifetime grazing leases, permanent family homes, and monetary compensation for displaced land owners. But that same year the Jackson Hole Monument and Grand Teton National Park lands were combined.

Consequently, the founding of Grand Teton National Park stands as a historic victory for American wildlands. In addition, the creation of the National Forest Service in 1905 and the Wilderness Act of 1964 are hallmarks in our country's conservation history, which began with the Yellowstone story. When so much of the world is being urbanized, we can turn to the legacy of lands preserved for beauty and splendor.

Beyond Borders

Side by side with economic growth, Yellowstone Park has fostered its own environmental movement. Rumblings of the controversial Greater Yellowstone Ecosystem concept cropped up in the 1970s. A biological study proved that the Yellowstone grizzly bear range extended over more than 5 million acres (only 2 million were contained within the park). The term implies that Yellowstone's health can only truly be sustained if it is managed like an ecosystem extending beyond its formal borders to maintain the long-term viability of its natural processes. The idea was heavily promoted by the Greater Yellowstone Coalition, a prominent conservation group based in Bozeman, Montana. The mention of Greater Yellowstone Ecosystem was once considered fightin' words. With time, however, the concept of an interconnected ecosystem seemed logical and has attained a certain level of common acceptance. That acceptance, however, has been hard won and brought Yellowstone to the brink of disaster more than once.

In 1990, for example, the Church Universal and Triumphant, a religious group headquartered near Gardiner, wanted to tap a geothermal feature on their land but bordering the park. Concerned because thermal areas in the U.S. and other countries have been ruined by outside intrusion of connected systems, authorities studied the problem. They determined that tapping geothermal features outside the park could damage the geothermal features inside it. They denied the religious group access and almost 10 years later the same parcel of land was purchased by the federal government to prevent the situation from occurring again.

Additionally, in 1990 a proposed open-pit gold mine near Cooke City threatened to leak mining tailings into the Clark's Fork of the Yellowstone River and Soda Butte Creek and potentially further infringe wildlife habitat. The Noranda, Inc. mining company estimated a $600 million return in precious metal from the proposed site and promised high-paying jobs. Cooke City residents were divided and debate over the issue raged until 1996. After flying over the New World Mining District bordering Yellowstone, President Bill Clinton cut a deal with the mining company. He traded $65 million worth of federal land for Noranda's mining rights.

These examples are neither the first or last controversies spurred by Yellowstone National Park. As residents of the Greater Yellowstone, we struggle with the dilemma of how best to preserve our park. The realities of population, pollution, tourism, and industry repeatedly bring us to a threshold where we must ask ourselves, "How will we continue to reap the benefits of Yellowstone while preserving its wild amenities?" Some say the answer is to limit entry into Yellowstone National Park, others say it should be privatized to better fund its preservation, still others say it's fine the way it is. Like the paradigm that exists inside park boundaries, we grapple with issues of loving this place to death.

Gateways

Since its inception Yellowstone was intended to be the economic hub of our region and in this sense, it is a success. If Yellowstone had never been designated an attraction as the world's first national park, there would have been no long term motivation for railroads to extend tracks out here, no reason to transport goods, and no reason to advertise the wonders of the area to the masses. Nineteenth century buzz phrases like "Manifest Destiny" and "Westward expansion" have been replaced with today's "diversified economy," but no matter what you call it, these are the bricks that built the gateway towns of the West. And Yellowstone National Park is the cornerstone of our greater community.

Indeed, it was economics that brought Yellowstone to our collective attention, although many of us don't like to think of it this way. Undeniably, without Yellowstone National Park it is difficult to say whether the communities along its borders would even exist today. The boom and bust economies of mining and logging fostered Cody, Wyoming, Cooke City, Montana, and Island Park, Idaho, to name a few, but it is the natural beauty of Yellowstone and its surrounding area that fosters long-term economic health. The forests, rivers, and wildlands encompassed by the national park ideal employ thousands of people in the region. Yellowstone intrinsically connects us as a benefactor and a commodity.

The towns that make up the Greater Yellowstone area are divided by individual cultures, whether through ventures in agriculture, triumph in natural resource industries, endeavors in recreation, or forays into art. Yet there is a pervasive knowledge that no one industry can solely sustain a viable economy in this part of the West. Yellowstone's millions of visitors contribute to the financial fuel keeping these gateway towns alive, while the park's preservation guarantees a certain quality of life in our towns. You'll see that the entire region, consciously or not, is wholly bound and marvelously intertwined in the same story of beauty and natural wonders that have drawn people here for centuries.

Yellowstone's Past Is Our Future

Surely our people do not understand even yet the rich heritage that is theirs. There can be nothing in the world more beautiful than the Yosemite, the groves of giant sequoias and redwoods, the Canyon of the Colorado, the Canyon of the Yellowstone, the three Tetons; and our people should see to it that they are preserved for their children forever, with their majestic beauty all unmarred.

—Theodore Roosevelt

Out of the national park experiment, the Greater Yellowstone Area emerged. Within our collective tri-state community we are both divided and connected by Yellowstone's wonders, yet the truth of Greater Yellowstone continues to grow. Finally (though pessimists say it's too late) we are realizing that this area is interconnected—towns and wilderness; waterways and valleys; grazing lands and conservation properties; animals and people; past and present. What we will do with this knowledge remains to be seen, but cooperative efforts between unlikely partners, such as mining companies and conservationists or developers and environmentalists, continue to emerge. Our communities are revamping city plans to include open space, wildlife migration corridors, and view sheds. With the help of private conservation groups such as the Jackson Hole Land Alliance or the Montana Land Alliance, we are preserving more valuable acreage for aesthetic and environmental qualities than ever before.

The West continues to be the fastest growing region in the U.S. Some towns have seen their populations jump 50 percent in the last decade, and with that growth comes new issues. But most of us are here for the love of the land and lifestyle. Because of the Park and the natural beauty that surrounds us, we concern ourselves with what we will have to pass on to the coming generations. In Yellowstone there is a reverence for the actual spirit upon which our country was founded—the frontier of possibility that says anything can happen, if you believe in it.

Wildflowers and clean mountain streams crisscross Yellowstone Country. PHOTO: SEABRING DAVIS

Our Natural World

The Landscape
Flora and Fauna
Wildlife Watching Tips

We are blessed here in Yellowstone Country with some of the most unspoiled, unparalleled, and beautiful land in the world. Many landscapes and features look the same to us as they did when the first settlers moved through the area in the early 1800s. Much of the same wildlife still roams the area, many of the same forests still stand, and many of the same trails crisscross the region.

Most people who call this area home are in touch with their surroundings. It isn't the same as living in the concrete jungle, where you occasionally have to look up to see blue sky. Here, the vast landscape constantly encompasses you and it is omnipresent—a factor in every aspect of our life: recreation, economy, and politics.

The mountains are sure nice to look at and are reason enough to live here for most of us. But what's out there to someone who hasn't been here before? More than just trees, animals, and rocks, that's for sure.

The Landscape

A constant theme in this book and our daily lives is contrast, and the landscape is no different. If need be, Yellowstone Country can be broken down into two divisions: mountains and valleys. You'll notice as you drive around that roads will travel across valleys, up mountains, and down again. Take, for example, the drive from Ennis to Livingston, Montana: In less than 80 miles, you begin in the Madison Valley, where the Madison River cuts through the Tobacco Root and Madison Ranges, from there you'll cross the latter and drop into the Gallatin Valley. Continuing east, up over Bozeman Pass and down into Livingston takes you through the upper end of the Gallatin Range. Once you're in Livingston, the Paradise Valley stretches between the Gallatin and Absaroka Mountains, and the cycle continues. You can be on flat land or up near the clouds, all in a matter of miles. Isn't it beautiful?

Of course, there's water, too. Lots of it. Miles of blue-ribbon trout streams and loads of pristine alpine lakes ensure the region's popularity among outdoor lovers. The area's rivers—which include the Snake, Madison, Yellowstone, and more—and the mountains and valleys they run through are the result of a complex geologic history.

Most of the region's geologic features were formed by movement of the earth. Thirty

> ## Insiders' Tip
> The large stands of Aspen trees you'll see around the region are havens for wildlife. Look for woodpeckers, owls, and ruffed grouse hovering around branches of the white-barked trees, and keep an eye out for elk and deer foraging on plants and bark on the ground.

Insiders' Tip

If you do any hiking up to some of our backcountry alpine lakes, keep an eye out for mountain goats on the rocky cliffs above you. They can be hard to spot—the goats often blend into their back-grounds—but a nice set of binoculars can make it easier for you. They are curious creatures and will seem unwary of your presence, mak-ing for great wildlife view-ing in the mountains.

to eighty million years ago, the area's mountains were created along a fault when two of the Earth's plates collided, sending rock in all directions. The exception is the Tetons, which stretched sky-ward only two to three million years ago from massive earthquakes. The Tetons' granite peaks were exposed when the ground cracked, lifting the west side up and dropping the east side down nearly 24,000 feet. After millions of years of erosion, what's left are some of the oldest rocks on earth. In fact, a thin layer of rock on top of Grand Teton National Park's Mount Moran—12,605 feet above sea level—was once part of a layer that now lies buried nearly five miles below the valley floor.

As the earth's giant masses of molten rock continued to thrust upward, the peaks you see today stretched up through the surface to create this dramatic landscape. Some of these peaks were buried under miles of thick ice during an era of cold climates and massive snowfall. Eventually, these snow accumulations turned into glaciers, massive rivers of ice that gouged and carved out the present-day valleys. The result of all of this activity is broad river basins flanked by mountains—just the type of scenery our region is known for.

Incidentally, glaciers still permeate some of our region's mountains. Although not the behemoth size of the past, they are evidence of ice ages that this area went through—the most recent occured only about 13,000 years ago. Although most mountain ranges have them, glaciers are most easily found in the Tetons, the Wind Rivers, and the Beartooths. These fluctuate with the temperature and the annual snowfall. As the earth is warming, these glaciers recede little by little each year.

Yellowstone National Park was created by a series of volcanic eruptions, the biggest of which occurred about 600,000 years ago. Big is an understatement here, as the blast is estimated to be as much as 10,000 times greater than the Mount St. Helens explosion of 1980. The Yellowstone explosion spewed gases and hot ash across the continent, with some fragments landing more than 1,000 miles away. What's left is a giant caldera—the cylindrical cone of the volcano—that continues to erupt through the surface in the form of geysers, bubbling cauldrons, hot springs, and fumaroles. And yes, Yellowstone was also covered by ice at one time. In fact, geologists theorize as much of 90 percent of the park was buried under 3,000 feet of ice between 20,000 and 25,000 years ago.

Yellowstone is renowned for its geysers, even though they only count for about three percent of geothermal activity. A geyser is an underground hot spring that ejects steam and water on a regular basis. Below the geyser is a narrow rock chimney fed by a constant supply of superheated water. The water wants to boil into steam but doesn't have room, so it has no place to go but up. Since steam has a much greater volume than water, the increasing pressure causes the water and steam to erupt out of the earth and into the air. The most famous geyser in the park is Old Faithful, named for its reliable eruption about every 81 minutes.

Dog sledding is a peaceful way to see the wildreness around Yellowstone in the winter. PHOTO: SEABRING DAVIS

Mud pots, also called mud volcanoes or paint pots, make up some of the more interesting features in the park. These bubbling cauldrons are formed far below the earth when rising steam dissolves the surrounding rock into a watery, clay-like substance. The clay bubbles and spits when it reaches the surface, with bigger bubbles meaning more steam is being forced through. On the surface, the edges of these formations are colored by minerals. Yellow is formed by sulfur deposits, while oranges, reds, browns, and blacks come from iron sulfides and oxides. The resulting colorful mix is what gives mud pots their alternate name—paint pots.

A fumerole is like a geyser running low on water. What little amount of water there is converts to steam immediately after hitting the boiling point, sending the rising steam up through a small vent in the ground. Listen closely and you'll hear the steam hissing as it comes up to the surface.

You'll also see a variety of hot springs and pools around the park. Mammoth has the most dramatic—the water deposits calcium carbonate (limestone) as it trickles down marble-like terraces, creating beautiful, colored sculptures in the earth. Small hot pools can be found all over the park, usually in brilliant shades of blue or green. It looks like these would be great for soaking, but be careful. Most of them are scalding hot and the ground around them is extremely fragile. Stay on the park's boardwalks that pass nearby these geothermal features.

Flora and Fauna

Coupled with the dramatic mountain landscape is a plant and animal community that comprises one of the largest protected natural areas in the United States. The Greater Yellowstone Ecosystem stretches across our entire region and is home to an awesome variety of species, from miniature wildflowers and animals to old-growth conifers and large ungulates–elk, deer, and moose.

The national parks are where you'll see the most wildlife. Bison, elk, deer, coyotes, and bald eagles will cross your path the most, and keen observers will have no trouble spotting moose, trumpeter swans, pronghorns, and others. The following information will give you hints on where you are most likely to see certain wildlife.

Forget-me-nots are only one of Yellowstone's many wildflowers. PHOTO: SEABRING DAVIS

Most of the lower elevations around our region are almost desertlike and composed of sagebrush, grasses, shrubs, and wildflowers. Areas like the Teton valley floor—made up of coarse, rocky soil with very few large trees—support squirrels, badgers, pronghorns, sage grouse, hawks, and eagles. Around June, a variety of wildflowers burst with the bright colors of summer.

You'll notice while driving around our region that there is a lot of water—rivers, creeks, and lakes. These areas support water-dependent wildlife such as moose, beaver, muskrat, swans, ducks, ospreys, and eagles, and offer excellent viewing opportunities. The Lamar Valley in Yellowstone National Park is a great example. Here, you're likely to see bison, eagles, osprey, elk, and an occasional wolf all within a matter of miles.

Lodgepole pine trees—found on the lower elevations of hillsides and on the valley floor—harbor bears, elk, deer, coyotes, porcupines, owls, woodpeckers, and golden eagles. Just about any hiking trail in our region will take you through this type of forest, a veritable jungle of interesting plants and active animals. Consequently, this is bear country. Stay alert when hiking and camping and obey all rules of food storage and waste disposal. Signs at trailheads will inform you of precautions and rules to follow.

At higher elevations, subalpine fir, spruce, and other conifers take over the territory, with the trees getting smaller and more sparse the higher you climb. Moose, mule deer, and the elusive mountain lion live here year round, while bears and elk can occasionally wander up. You'll see lots of birds here, including nuthatches, chickadees, golden eagles, grouse, and flycatchers.

Above treeline, the elevation of which varies depending on where you are, the land seems inhospitable to living things. But look closely and you'll find a vast community of hardy plants and animals that call this country home. In the summer you can find patches of colorful wildflowers like phlox, glacier lilies, and forget-me-nots, as well as marmots, golden eagles, bighorn sheep, and mountain goats. Grizzlies can also wander high in the spring, digging for a good meal of glacier lily bulbs.

Insiders' Tip

If you're staying in or around Big Sky, you should be able to see lots of wildlife. As you turn off of U.S. Highway 191 and head toward the ski resort, scan the rocky mountainside on the right side of the highway for bighorn sheep. You'll enter a large meadow just a little further up the road where you can often spot elk, moose, and eagles. On the east side of U.S. 191, just past Big Sky, elk roam the meadows surrounding the Gallatin River nearly every morning in the winter, along with an occasional moose. If you don't have any luck with these spots, keep your eye open while going up the chairlifts at Big Sky Resort. Bald eagles have been spotted soaring above the slopes.

Wildlife Watching Tips

Looking for wildlife is one of the best things about a visit to Yellowstone Country, but there are rules to follow. Remember that they were here first and you're usually on their turf.

Before your visit, do some research on the area's wildlife. Find out about their habitat and what time of the day they are out and about. This will give you a good idea of where to go when you're here, so you'll have your camera ready for that award-winning shot.

Try not to startle animals. Generally most won't even notice you're nearby and will continue going about their business, until you get too close. Carrying a set of binoculars and a bigger lens for your camera is a good idea. Never approach wildlife, and never feed any animal.

Insiders' Tip

Yellowstone Country's petrified forests are reminders of the region's geologic past, and were created when mud and ash from volcanic eruptions buried entire forests. Yellowstone National Park has 40 square miles of petrified forest, while another large but remote stand can be found in the Gallatin National Forest.

Close-up

Sure Things

You say there's no such thing as a sure thing? Well, in Yellowstone Country that's not entirely true with regards to wildlife viewing. Patient observers can almost always find their favorite animal, and the list below will help guide you to areas where the chances are greater.

Everybody wants to see elk. Royal and majestic, these large ungulates frequent our region and never fail to impress. Just inside the north entrance to Yellowstone National Park at Mammoth, elk wander around and mingle with visitors. In the fall, big bulls can be seen lying in the lush grass between the roads. Also, the National Elk Refuge just north of Jackson Hole is home to as many as 10,000 elk during the winter. See the Attractions chapter for details on the refuge.

You should have no trouble seeing bison in Yellowstone. A full day of driving around the park's main roads should net you more than one sighting, and you may even have to stop your car to let them pass. If you're driving south from Bozeman on U.S. Highway 191, a drive back on the Spanish Creek Road will let you gaze upon media mogul Ted Turner's private herd. Look for the sign to Spanish Creek on the highway about five miles after you enter Gallatin Canyon.

Your best chance to see a wolf may be in the winter, when packs will travel Yellowstone National Park's Lamar Valley in search of a good meal (usually a fallen elk). Huge herds of elk invade the valley floor looking for food, and wolves, in turn, hunt the elk. Bring a good set of binoculars and scan the elk herds and the valley floor, particularly in the morning.

Coyotes are smaller than wolves but just as interesting to watch. If you're driving around Yellowstone or Grand Teton, coyotes can often be spotted walking swiftly along the roadside, hurrying to their next meal. You can also find them wandering around river basins and open meadows.

If you're staying in or around Big Sky, you should be able to glimpse some bighorn sheep. As you turn off U.S. Highway 191 and head toward the ski resort, scan the rocky mountainside on the right side of the highway. Occasionally the sheep will cross the road and stop traffic, allowing you a rare close-up view of this amazing animal.

Driving along the Snake River in Grand Teton National Park from the Jackson Lake Dam south to Moose allows for opportunities to see bald eagles, ospreys, and great blue herons.

Most people associate pelicans with tropical climates, but the American white pelican thrives around Yellowstone Lake in Yellowstone National Park and at the Snake River's Oxbow Bend in Grand Teton. Look for bald eagles here, too.

The best times of day to see wildlife are in the early morning or late evening—feeding time for most animals. As you drive around, look for the signs with the brown and white binoculars logo and the words "Wildlife Viewing Area," which signal roadside turnouts with viewing opportunities.

Insiders' Tip

The Red Rock Lakes National Wildlife Refuge in southwest Montana is one of North America's important resting sites for the trumpeter swan—the largest of all North American waterfowl. In the remote Centennial Valley, more than 500 nesting swans in the Yellowstone area are joined in the winter by as many as 1,000 migrating birds from Canada and Alaska. Established in 1935, when there were only 100 trumpeters in the country, the refuge's lakes, marshes, and creeks are also home to more than 20 other species of waterfowl. You'll find the refuge on County Route 509, about 40 miles west of West Yellowstone, Montana.

Yellowstone National Park

Entering the Park
Accommodations
Restaurants
Shopping

The creation of Yellowstone National Park was an expansive act uniting unprecedented philanthropic and political intentions. But it almost didn't happen.

At the time, there was lackluster support from the federal government for the proposal to designate 2.2 million acres of land as the world's first national park despite reports from three exploratory expeditions in 1869, 1870, and 1871 stating that no other region was so rich in beauty and natural wonders. Congress argued over the "worthlessness" of the Yellowstone area. Devoid of substantial timber, minerals, and other resources, the property was deemed "useless." With most of the land located above 7,000 feet, it was considered too barren for agriculture or settlement and therefore not economically viable. On top of all this, some skeptics doubted the reports of the area's geysers and inexhaustible wildlife.

That all changed, however, when the members of Congress saw Yellowstone's beauty for themselves through the work of artist Thomas Moran and photographer William Henry Jackson, who documented the scenery for the Hayden Expedition in 1871. Moran's watercolors depicting the dramatic yellow, orange, and red walls in the Grand Canyon of the Yellowstone and other sketches of the area dispersed any doubts about the region's majesty. A mere seven months later Congress passed the legislation that made Yellowstone National Park a reality. When President Ulysses S. Grant signed the park bill on March 1, 1872, it was a precedent-setting moment in history for our nation and the world.

Today it doesn't take as much convincing for people to believe that Yellowstone is a wondrous place. Each year, over 3 million visitors travel here from all over the world. While it is still fairly remote, the area makes its geysers, hot springs, waterfalls, and wildlife accessible to everyone. The number of visitors Yellowstone draws proves that it is a priceless resource not for its economic value, but for its intrinsic natural beauty.

Unlike the early travelers who came to Yellowstone, today we have many options in which to explore our park. With over 1,200 miles of trails and 300 miles of public roads, you can experience Yellowstone on or off the road. You are only limited by what you want to see and how much time you want to spend here. One thing is for sure, you can't see it in just one trip. So whether you tour the park hopping from campground to campground, in the comfort of the historic hotels, or via the backcountry, enjoy every moment and plan on coming back again. Above all, no matter how you experience Yellowstone, respect this national treasure by obeying park rules and regulations for your safety and the preservation of Yellowstone for our future generations.

Insiders' Tip

Yellowstone Park Lodges offer special discounts for on-line reservations, especially during "shoulder seasons"—autumn or spring. Click on "special offers" at www.travelyellowstone.com.

Entering the Park

Entrances to Yellowstone National Park are generally open to automobile traffic from mid-April or May through the first of November. The road from Gardiner to Cooke City is open year round to auto traffic. But from about November 1 until the end of May, the road dead-ends in Cooke City. Depending on the weather, the Beartooth Highway closes in mid-October and the Chief Joseph Highway to Cody closes approximately the first of November. In mid-December, when the park re-opens for winter recreation, snowmobilers and snowcoaches line up at the West Entrance to travel approximately 150 miles of groomed roads.

Yellowstone National Park entrance fees

- ◆ $20 per vehicle
- ◆ $15 per individual motorcycle or snowmobile
- ◆ $10 per individual (hiker, bicyclist, skier, or snowcoach passenger)
- ◆ Free admittance for children 16 and under. All passes provide entrance to both Yellowstone and Grand Teton National Parks for seven days. You can purchase an annual pass, also good for both parks, for $40. Golden Eagle Passports cost $65 and offer additional benefits to the seniors who purchase them, including discounted camping fees.

Once inside the park, expect to travel park roads slowly, since most are winding two-lane highways. The routes mostly circle around the center of the park past major attractions through villages equipped with an array of tourist amenities. Park roads are easy to navigate since they are well-marked and generally named after the attractions which they lead to and from, such as the Mammoth-Tower Junction Road, Mammoth-Norris Road, or the Madison-Old Faithful Road. The main roads are dubbed the Grand Loop, Lower Loop, and Upper Loop. Most tour operators offer trips on all three routes.

West Entrance
West Yellowstone, MT

More than one-third of the park's visitors travel through the West Yellowstone gate annually, making it the No. 1 entrance. This is probably because of its accessibility by three main routes: U.S. Highway 20, U.S. Highway 191, and U.S. Highway 287. Expect to wait in line first thing in the morning at this entrance during peak season in summer or winter. The town of West Yellowstone, adjacent to the park, is packed with motels, campgrounds, restaurants, and attractions of its own.

South Entrance
Via Grand Teton National Park

Being greeted by the Teton Mountains jutting up seemingly out of nowhere makes this the most scenic route to enter Yellowstone. The second-most used entrance, it is accessed by the north-south highway traveling through Grand Teton National Park.

North Entrance
Gardiner, MT

The historic, 50-foot Roosevelt Arch still marks the original entrance to Yellowstone. It is the park's only gate that is open to automobile traffic year-round, but the road dead ends in Cooke City, 57 miles to the east. The third-most popular gate in the park, it is grounded by the small western town of Gardiner. With the Yellowstone River cutting through town, Gardiner is a scenic stopover before starting into the park. The road begins to wind quickly after this gate and offers great views of the Absarokee Mountains to the south.

East Entrance
U.S. Hwy. 20

This entrance is not as easy to access as some of the more popular gates, but given the surrounding scenery it makes for a wonderful beginning to a trip through Yellowstone. The stretch of highway between Cody, Wyoming and the East gate was dubbed "the most scenic 50 miles in America," by President Theodore Roosevelt. Bordering the park boundary is historic Pahaska Teepee, once Buffalo Bill Cody's hunting lodge, which offers all-in-one lodging, gas station, convenience store, and guest ranch. Winter months are popular with cross-country skiers since the entrance is open to automobiles only during the summer.

Northeast Entrance
Silver Gate/Cooke City

During the summer months, visitors entering at this gate will have just been to the "Top Of The World"—the highest point of the preceding Beartooth Highway. But in the winter this entrance becomes a cul de sac for skiers and snowmobilers, since this is as far as the National Park Service is able to plow the road. The tiny hamlet of Silver Gate, located about one mile from the Northeast gate, shuts down during this time, but nearby Cooke City bulges with hearty visitors. The 300 residents of Cooke City endure nine months of winter and offer simple, year-round attractions for tourists (see our Cooke City chapter for more details).

Visitor Centers

The cornerstone of information, Yellowstone National Park's visitor centers anchor curious travelers who want to experience everything the park has to offer. Many of them are treasure troves of park legend and lore, and all of them offer current details on hiking trails, interpretive programs, and park road closures. Most have nearby amenities such as shopping, refueling, and dining that are generally open from the last week in May to the first week of September. (We've noted those that stay open longer.)

An extensive bookstore, specializing in Yellowstone-specific publications, is located at each center. Run by the non-profit Yellowstone Association, proceeds from your book purchases help support educational, historical, and scientific projects. Operating since 1933, the Yellowstone Association has contributed more than $5 million to the park.

Albright Visitor Center
Mammoth Hot Springs
(307) 344-2263

Located within the historic Bachelor's Quarters at Mammoth Hot Springs, the Albright Center is an integral part of today's park headquarters. Not only do the center's cheery rangers answer all your questions, they can also direct you to the Center's extensive research library and rare book room. The rangers offer regular naturalist tours starting on the facility's front steps and direct you toward informative movies about Yellowstone's history, which are shown every half-hour.

Once the location of Fort Yellowstone, Mammoth's historic stone buildings now house the offices of the National Park Service employees. Besides the administrative buildings, Mammoth has a hotel, cabins, campground, a bar, and two restaurants operated by AmFac, the park's main concessionaire. Hamilton Stores, the oldest established concessionaire in Yellowstone, operates a store here. Other Mammoth amenities include a gas station, post office, and ice machine.

Canyon Visitor Center
Canyon Village
(307) 242-2550

This is arguably the busiest visitor center in the park, since it is the first information hub visitors encounter after driving through the West entrance. Tucked into a horseshoe-shaped complex, this is a full service stop for fuel, food, camping gear, and shopping. You can find anything you may have forgotten at the two Hamilton Stores (one a new nature store), post office, and gas station. You'll also find a restaurant, cafeteria, fast-food places, a hotel, cabins, and a campground. Laundry facilities and shower are attached to the campground office. What's most attractive about this center, however, is the extensive bison exhibit—it's worth wading through the crowds to view it.

Fishing Bridge Visitor Center
North Shore of Yellowstone Lake
(307) 242-2450

The view alone is worth a stop at this visitor center, which is located on the north end of Yellowstone Lake. Housed in a historic building designed by renowned Yellowstone architect Robert Reamer in 1929, this center showcases exhibits on Yellowstone's birds, wildlife, and lake geology. Services here are not as extensive as other centers since it's located in grizzly country. But you will find a Hamilton Store, RV park, a gas station, lunch counter, and shower and laundry facilities.

Grant Village Visitor Center
Grant Village
(307) 242-2650

This center's extensive exhibit about the 1988 Yellowstone fires will make your tour through some of the charred forests in the park more interesting. The film, which plays throughout the day, details what to look for as the forest regenerates and explains this natural process that occurs every 250 to 400 years. Located on the west shore of Yellowstone Lake, Grant Village facilities include one Hamilton General Store, a post office, showers, laundry facility, and an ice machine. You'll also find motel-style lodging and a large campground by the lake. You must register and purchase a permit at the center's backcountry office if you plan to camp in this part of the park.

Norris Geyser Basin Museum
Norris Geyser Basin
(307) 344-2812

Don't confuse the stone building on the hill above the Norris Geyser Basin with a visitor center. The building you're looking for is the small log structure across the way. Inside, you'll find an interesting collection of information on geothermal features in the park. We recommend stopping here before venturing into the basin.

Old Faithful Visitor Center
Old Faithful Geyser
(307) 344-2750

Located near the famous geyser, this center bustles with anxious visitors curious to know when Old Faithful will erupt next. The center features exhibits that explain and predict geyser eruptions in the area. In this way, the friendly and knowledgeable staff work to dispel the myth that Old Faithful erupts every hour on the hour; the truth is that although this thermal feature is the park's most consistent geyser, eruptions take place every 80 to 90 minutes. An informative film, shown throughout the day, details the anomaly of geothermal features. Old Faithful is a busy place with two hotels, a lodge, more than 100 cabins, two gas stations, a post office, and shower facilities. Other attractions include several restaurants, a couple of gift shops, and two Hamilton Stores. The center is open from the end of May until the first of November.

Lake Yellowstone Hotel. PHOTO: NATIONAL PARK SERVICE

Accommodations

Hotels, Motels, and Cabins

Price Code

Keep in mind that some rates are based on availability. The average nightly rates for two adults are based upon that establishment's lowest price during the most expensive season (primarily summer).

$ . . . . $25 to $49

$$ . . . . $50 to $75

$$$ . . . . $76 to 100

$$$$ . . . . $101 and more

Staying in Yellowstone National Park is half the fun of visiting the area. Several of the hotels date back to the park's early forays into tourism and their architecture and location tell much about that era. These hotels are not just places to sleep, they are pieces of history to experience and relive. Imagine being among the first visitors to stay at the Lake Yellowstone Hotel or the Old Faithful Inn at the turn of the last century.

Of course not all the rooms in Yellowstone are quaint slices of history. With 2,500 rooms, including 1,232 cabins, the park offers a diverse array of accommodations from luxurious suites to rustic cabins. What you should know about Yellowstone's lodging is that the hotels were never intended to be the main attraction, so in some cases the accommodations are downright simple. When you read that Roosevelt Lodge's cabins are "rustic," indeed, they are. Heated only by a wood stove and with communal bathrooms, some would consider the tiny, barrack-style log buildings akin to roughing it in a campground. But that's all part of the experience. Remember that Yellowstone is a place of natural wonders, so none of the hotel rooms have televisions, and only a few have private phones. Some folks might consider this a drawback, but look at it instead as a way to get back to basics—read a book, sit by the fire, enjoy this time to talk with your family and friends, get outside. Some of the rooms in motel-style facilities are simply places to lay your head for the night, and the truth is that after a full day of sight-seeing in this wondrous country, that's probably all you will need. Remember that although the area is still somewhat remote, it isn't undiscovered. To ensure that your vacation is hassle-free, make lodging reservations as soon as possible. Millions of people visit the area each year and sometimes it will feel very hectic, particularly if you are scrambling to find a place to sleep—be it campsite, luxury suite, or motel room. Most facilities are open only during summer months, except the Old Faithful Snow Lodge and Mammoth Hot Springs Hotel, which also accept reservations from mid-December through early March. The park offers early-bird specials for spring bookings and also for autumn; these are considered the "shoulder" seasons when the number of visitors thins out. All park accommodations are operated by AmFac Parks and Resorts. They accept all major credit cards. For reservations at all park hotels and cabins call AmFac Reservations at (307) 344-7311 or book on-line at www.travelyellowstone.com.

Canyon Lodge and Cabins
Canyon Village, Yellowstone National Park
(307) 344-7311
$$

Constructed in the 1950s and '60s, the Canyon Lodge offers some standard hotel-type rooms along with cabins that sleep from two to five people. All the cabins have private bathrooms. The main lodge has an activities desk in the lobby, along with restrooms, a lounge, gift shop, and several dining options. Separate from the main lodge, two other buildings, Cascade Lodge and Dunraven Lodge, offer more updated accommodations decorated with lodgepole pine furniture and western influences. Built in 1993, the 30 hotel-style rooms in Cascade each have two double beds. The 3-story, 44 room Dunraven was built in 1999 and features rooms with your choice of one or two double beds. There are a few wheelchair-accessible rooms with a double and a single bed in each, as well.

Canyon Village is centrally located in the park, but serves primarily as an ideal place from which to explore the Grand Canyon of the Yellowstone. The bustling village hosts plenty of traffic and people. The community has a visitor information center with a Hamilton Store, a post office, and a photo shop.

Grant Village
Grant Village, Yellowstone National Park
(307) 344-7311
$$$

Named after President Ulysses S. Grant, who signed the legislation to create Yellowstone National Park in 1872, Grant Village is located in the southeastern portion of the park. Built in 1984, it is one of Yellowstone's newer lodging options and offers regular, motel-style accommodations. Six two-story complexes house fifty rooms each, all with two double beds and private bathrooms. You'll find two restaurants, a lounge, a gift shop, and a laundry facility nearby. This village is a pick-up and drop-off point for Yellowstone Park Tour buses and an ideal location to explore Yellowstone Lake and Grand Teton National Park.

Lake Lodge Cabins
Lake Village, Yellowstone National Park
(307) 344-7311
$

The Lake Lodge Cabins are a more affordable alternative to the grandeur of Lake Yellowstone Hotel, but with all the perks of a great lakeside location. Only paces from the convenience of a gift shop, cafeteria, laundry facilities, and the shore, these cozy cabins create a great family atmosphere. The massive log lodge offers a rocking chair view of the lake. It is also an ideal perch for watching an early morning moose or deer tiptoe through the yard. The huge fireplace, the focal point of the lodge's expansive lobby, beckons guests to cozy up with late night cocktails and good books. Each of the 186 Western and Frontier cabins encircling the lodge sleeps two to five people all in one main room with various bed configurations. You are only a stone's throw from The Bridge Bay Marina, headquarters for scenic cruises, guided fishing trips, and boat rentals.

Insiders' Tip

If you are longing for a more extensive educational experience in America's first National Park, the Yellowstone Institute offers 80 field courses throughout the year. The classes last anywhere from one day to one month and cover anything from wildlife photography to wolf watching in the Lamar Valley. Call for a catalog of classes at (307) 344-2294.

Lake Yellowstone Hotel and Cabins
Lake Village, Yellowstone National Park
(307) 344-7311
$$$

The Lake Hotel will captivate your whimsical side when you first see this majestic 1920s building. Huge white columns reach up to the sky on the front porch facing the vastness of Yellowstone Lake. The hotel entrance's high arching ceilings will remind you of a classic period of elegance. Originally, the hotel was but a shoebox building when it was constructed by the Northern Pacific Railroad in 1891. A 1920s remodel by Seattle architect Robert Reamer transformed the place to its present beauty. He drew in details like the blue tile fireplace and the sweeping staircase, but probably the best attribute of this classic hostelry is the sun room looking out at the lake. You could spend most of a morning or late afternoon contemplating life from the comfort of an antique wicker chair in the enclosed sun room. A cool glass of lemonade or sweet ice tea will make it even better.

In the 1980s this grand hotel and its 194 guest rooms underwent a 10-year restoration project that eventually landed it on the National Historic Register. The old rooms are spacious with high ceilings and private bathrooms. The newer rooms, built in 1980s, follow suit. Most have two queen-size beds. There is one presidential suite. The 110 cabins are painted a buttery yellow to match the main hotel and all feature private bathrooms as well.

Mammoth Hot Springs Hotel
Mammoth, Yellowstone National Park
(307) 344-7311
$$

For early visitors who traveled by train to the nation's first national park, Mammoth Hot Springs was where it all began. Built in 1911 and completed in 1937, Mammoth is a testament to the day when only the wealthy could afford to visit Yellowstone. This stately hotel is located just five miles from the north entrance of the park and is accessible throughout the year

Terraces at Mammoth Hot Springs. PHOTO: NATIONAL PARK SERVICE

by car. During summer months a total of 98 rooms and 136 in winter are available within the main hotel and annex behind it. Most rooms have two double beds and there are two suites. In addition to hotel rooms, the complex has 128 cabins, which mostly have two double beds. Some have communal facilities with toilets and showers instead of private baths. To encourage advance bookings, AmFac offers early bird rates for any reservations made before the first of April; a hotel room or cabin without bath goes for just $25 per night. Its location makes Mammoth ideal as a base for daytrips into the nearby Lamar Valley for wildlife viewing and of course to explore the terraces of its namesake, Mammoth Hot Springs. During the winter, Mammoth is the starting point for winter adventures, including snowcoach rides, snowmobiling, and skiing.

Mammoth Hot Springs is the official park headquarters and was once Fort Yellowstone when the U.S. Army was in charge of the park. Today the original stone structures built by the military now house administrative offices for the National Park Service. The hotel is situated across from the Albright Visitor Center. You'll find fine dining at the Mammoth dining room and a pleasant atmosphere in the adjacent lounge. Sunday brunch in the Mammoth Dining Room is one of the best things about staying here; don't miss it. At the other end of the building is a fast food outlet. There is also a Hamilton Store on site. Mammoth is a pick-up and drop-off point for Yellowstone Park Tour buses.

Old Faithful Inn
Old Faithful, Yellowstone National Park
(307) 344-7311
$$

Of all the places in Yellowstone, this hotel has the most character. Walking through the 85-foot high lobby you feel the history of old Yellowstone greet you, whispering its memories from the high knarled pine balconies overlooking the lobby. The huge roughstone fireplace and its newly restored wrought iron tower clock have been the centerpiece of the room since the hotel was built in 1903-1904. Designed by famed Yellowstone architect Robert Reamer, Old Faithful Inn is filled with custom detail, including wrought iron details on door handles, light fixtures, and even the numerals for guest rooms. It took 1,500 men to build this log and stone structure which now stands as a testament to the ingenuity of the Western spirit.

Originally the inn housed 146 guest rooms and was equipped with electricity, water, and steam heat—unprecedented for the era. Today, the remaining 75 rooms are much like they were at the turn of the century. With the great public spaces for lounging and people watching, the actual sleeping quarters are small and dimly lit with a dangling bulb—the only thing missing is the chamber pot. Down the hall you'll find restrooms, showers, and two rooms with elegant clawfoot bathtubs for soaking. But during peak summer months the odds are against a relaxing soak; you're more likely to have other guests banging on the door. In the newer wing, 250 somewhat larger, brighter rooms are equipped with the "luxury" of private bathrooms. Several of the older balcony rooms, which are larger suites overlooking the geyser basin in front of the inn, are so sought-after they're reserved two years in advance. In all, the inn has 327 rooms ranging from two single beds to two double beds.

Situated next to the famous Old Faithful Geyser, you won't spend much time in your room anyway. Take a stroll along one of the paths winding through the geyser basin just a few hundred yards from the inn. Or settle into one of the chairs on the outside balcony of the hotel and take in all the beauty. However you pass the time, a stay in the world's largest log structure is one you won't soon forget. Ask some of the employees here to tell you a couple ghost stories, if you dare. In addition to the formal dining room, the Old Faithful Inn houses a fast-food outlet, an ice cream counter, espresso cart, a lounge, and gift

Insiders' Tip

The Horace Albright visitor center at Mammoth Hot Springs contains an extensive library with volumes of material relating to Yellowstone, including a rare book room which has most rare or hard to find books published about the park.

shop. You'll also find a gas station and general store nearby. The park's tour buses pick up passengers here, as well.

Old Faithful Lodge Cabins
Old Faithful, Yellowstone National Park
(307) 344-7311
$

Built to accommodate the overflow of guests wanting to stay near the famous Old Faithful Geyser, these cabins and sleek stone lodge were built in the 1950s. The lodge itself houses a gift shop, two snack shops, a cafeteria, and an espresso cart. The 132 cabins are classically practical, barrack-style structures. The rooms range from those with two singles to two double beds. Forty-seven rooms have private bathrooms, while everyone else uses the communal bathrooms scattered throughout the complex.

Old Faithful Snow Lodge
Old Faithful, Yellowstone National Park
(307) 344-7311
$$$$

Built in 1998, this huge timber frame structure is a much needed new addition to Yellowstone's lodging options. Architecturally the Snow Lodge is the modern counterpart to its neighbor, the Old Faithful Inn. It is an impressive heavy timber structure with wrought iron accents, custom designed furniture, and light fixtures. High vaulted ceilings, a massive native rock fireplace, picture windows, and deep cushioned chairs in the lobby invite you to hunker down by the fire on a cold winter night. All rooms have built-in armoires, some have window seats, each has two double beds, and there isn't a room with a bad view in the whole hotel. An additional 34 cabins feature two double beds and bathrooms. A family restaurant and a gift shop are on the premises. The Snow Lodge is open both summer and winter.

Roosevelt Lodge Cabins
Yellowstone National Park
(307) 344-7311
$

This historic lodge and cabins are located near President Theodore Roosevelt's favorite camping spot. Built in 1908, the lodge and barracks-style cabins are tucked beneath the trees. Roughrider and Economy units have wood-burning stoves, but no private bathrooms. Communal bathing facilities are scattered throughout the cabin area. The Frontier cabins come with the luxuries of private bath and propane heat. But in actuality, all the cabins qualify as "rustic." From the ambling front porch of the lodge you almost feel as if you've been transported back to the old West, sitting in a rocking chair as the evening air grows cooler. Inside is a large lodgepole pine family-style dining room. Staying here truly feels like a step back in time. Stagecoach and horseback rides are available and can take you to the corral, where a wholesome real western cookout is offered nightly. Roosevelt Lodge activities fill up quickly; it's best to book well in advance.

Campgrounds and RV Parks

Campground Rates

$	Less than $9
$$	$10 to $16
$$$	$17 to $23
$$$$	$24 and more

Yellowstone National Park has 11 campgrounds and one RV park with a total of 2,145 campsites. Seven sites are operated on a first-come, first-served basis and require no reservations. The other five—Madison, Canyon Village, Grant Village, Bridge Bay, and the Fishing Bridge RV Park—contain more than 1,700 spaces that may be reserved in advance by calling AmFac, the main park concessionaire.

You'll find at least minimal amenities such as tables, fire grills, drinking water, and flush or pit toilets at every campground. The reservation campgrounds generally have more amenities, including firewood for sale, showers, and laundries. They are often conveniently located near general stores, post offices, restaurants, and gas stations. You can learn more about any of the Yellowstone National Park campgrounds by calling at (307) 344-7311 or visiting the website at www.travelyellowstone.com. For backcountry camping you must obtain a permit from a visitor center or ranger station. Advance reservations for overnight camping in the backcountry cost $15. Permits are free without reservations. For more information call (307) 344-2160.

Old Faithful Lodge. PHOTO: NATIONAL PARK SERVICE

Bridge Bay Campground
West Thumb-Fishing Bridge Rd.
Yellowstone National Park
$$

Don't be shocked if you wake up with an uninvited bison tromping through your camp here. Despite Bridge Bay being the largest of Yellowstone's campgrounds, the bison still roam the area and share their territory with thousands of people each summer. The main feature here is Yellowstone Lake and the adjacent marina (see our Attractions chapter). At the marina you can launch your boat, enjoy a scenic cruise, or take a guided fishing trip on the lake. With 429 sites, this campground sprawls along the lake shore. Open from late May through September, Bridge Bay is a reservations campground. You'll find firewood sold here, flush toilets, an RV dump station, and boat access. Everything else you might need can be found just three miles to the south at Lake Village.

Canyon Village Campground
Canyon Village, Yellowstone National Park
$$

Canyon Village is the most centrally located of all Yellowstone's campgrounds. It offers such easy driving access to nearly all of the park's major attractions—from Yellowstone Lake to Mammoth Hot Springs to Old Faithful—you may want to call this home for the duration of your trip. From here you can drive in different directions each day and get a whirlwind view of Yellowstone. Canyon is open from early June to early September and reservations are required. This full-service campground's 271 spaces are within walking distance from the actual Canyon Village. There you can stock up on gifts, groceries, and any outdoor gear you might have forgotten. Take a break from camp cooking and choose from the number of dining options, including a huge lunch counter, fast-food counter, cafeteria, and a full-service dining room.

Fishing Bridge RV Park
East Entrance Rd., Yellowstone National Park
$$$$

There isn't exactly a sign here that says "no tents allowed," but the fact is that only hard-sided RVs are welcome to camp at this area near Fishing Bridge and Yellowstone Lake. These 341 sites, open from mid-May through early October, feature a general store, laundry, pay showers, electricity, water, sewer hook-ups, and a dump station. The maximum RV length is 40 feet. The Fishing Bridge RV Park's central location makes it ideal for exploring the lower portion of the park, but it is also a place where you must be cautious storing food because it's smack in the middle of bear country. It is also close to the Pelican Valley Trailhead, which leads to incredible hiking. Call ahead for reservations.

Grant Village Campground
Grant Village, Yellowstone National Park
$$

Grant Village is a good staging spot for daytrips into geyser and lake countries. The 425 campsites ramble along the shore of Yellowstone Lake and are an easy bike ride away from the geyser basin at the West Thumb. You'll find a laundry, showers, a Hamilton Store, gas station, and post office at Grant Village. This is a reservations campground open from late June through September.

> ## Insiders' Tip
> Every year the staff at the Old Faithful Inn celebrates Christmas on August 25—complete with elaborately decorated trees, mistletoe, and holiday carolers. The tradition was spurred by a freak snow storm which stranded a group of visitors at the inn during the early 1900s. Reveling in their "misfortune," the group decided to have a "Christmas party."

Indian Creek Campground
Norris-Mammoth Rd., Yellowstone National Park
$$

Obsidian Cliff, the Mammoth Terraces, and the Boiling River are just a few of the attractions you can access easily from this small campground. Wake up early and jump in the car to drive a couple miles down to the Boiling River trailhead and stroll about a mile to a natural hot spring that melts the icy Gardiner River to create the perfect temperature for a relaxing soak. Indian Creek doesn't take reservations and since it is only eight miles south of Mammoth Hot Springs and National Park Service headquarters, the spaces fill up quickly. Situated in an open meadow where bison and elk graze nearby, its namesake Indian Creek flows through the campground. Within walking distance is Sheepeater Cliff, the former home of the Sheepeater band of Shoshone Indians, Yellowstone's only resident tribe. Indian Creek is open from early June until mid-September. Firewood is sold here.

Lewis Lake Campground
South Entrance Rd., Yellowstone National Park
$$

Situated above Lewis Lake—renowned for its trout fishing—this campground is open from mid-June to early November on a first-come, first-served basis. It is a fine halfway point to explore Yellowstone's Lake country and Grand Teton National Park. These 85 campsites are hard to come by during peak season, so mark your claim early in the day. A boat launch in the campground offers access to Lewis Lake.

Madison Campground
West Entrance Rd., Yellowstone National Park
$$

This campground is often called Madison Junction, because it is near the confluence of the Madison, Gibbon, and Firehole Rivers. Located just 14 miles from the West Yellowstone entrance and 16 miles north of Old Faithful, Madison Campground is a prime location for exploring Geyser country. You can see a good portion of the area at a leisurely pace in three or four days. And if fishing is your love, you can't beat the proximity to such beautiful, highly fishable rivers. Within biking or hiking distance, you'll find the turnoff for the one-way, two-mile Firehole Canyon Drive, where you'll see several cascades and waterfalls up close.

Although there are 280 campsites, this campground still manages to feel peaceful and enclosed by the forest. Every night at the amphitheater, a naturalist presents programs on such topics as the bison, mountains, geology, or hiking in the park. More in-depth material is also available at the adjacent log and stone building, a former ranger station that now serves as a small Information Station where you will find educational books for sale. Madison Campground, a reservation campground operated by Amfac, offers a sanitary dump station and flush toilets and sells firewood. Madison is open from early May to late October.

Mammoth Campground
Mammoth Hot Springs, Yellowstone
National Park
$$

Located at the base of a winding road, this is one of the most popular campgrounds in Yellowstone. Its 85 campsites are full from Memorial Day to Labor Day. At the top of the hill is Mammoth Hot Springs and the National Park Service headquarters. It's an easy walk, though somewhat perilous because the path is dusty and easy to slip on. But wear some walking shoes and leave the car behind to explore the Mammoth complex, including the Albright Visitor Center, where you'll find exhibits on the controversial Yellowstone wolves, historic photos, and an interesting film on the history of the park. From there you'll want to walk up to the Mammoth Terraces and follow the boardwalk through stacks of sculpturesque mineral deposits (see our Attractions chapter). Mammoth is the only year-round campground in the park. During the summer months it's ideal for a one or two night stay. Camping sites are available on a first-come, first-served basis.

Norris Campground
Mammoth-Norris Rd., Yellowstone
National Park
$$

With only 112 campsites, Norris Campground is one of the park's smaller campgrounds. That's a good thing, because the location is nice enough that you just might want to linger here a bit longer. The campground sits at the edge of a wildflower-covered meadow where elk like to graze in the summer months. Within walking or biking distance is the Norris Geyser Basin, as well as several hiking trails. To the north of the campground you'll find open meadows and Whiterock Spring. Then to the east follow Solfatara Creek through a large burned area. From there it's an uphill climb to Ice Lake. For a short walk and a little company, head to the Museum of the National Park Ranger, at the edge of the meadow. Former Park Service employees rotate through this old ranger station and educate visitors with their historical anecdotes that paint a colorful picture of the past. Each evening a naturalist gives presentations at the Norris Campfire Circle near the "C" Loop.

Norris is within easy driving distance of the Grand Canyon of the Yellowstone and the geyser basin below Madison. To the north, Mammoth Hot Springs is only 21 miles away, with many attractions along the way. Give yourself a few days to see the diverse sights in the area.

Norris is open from mid-May to late September. Amenities include flush toilets and firewood for sale. Reservations are not accepted.

Pebble Creek Campground
Northeast Entrance Rd., Yellowstone National Park
$$

To get away from the crowds, seek out this small, shady campground just 10 miles southwest of the Northeast Entrance at Silver Gate. With Pebble Creek running through the campground, there isn't a bad choice among these 36 campsites. This is a nice spot to regroup and relax before hitting the road again to tour the rest of the park. With access to Pebble Creek Trail, this is a nice location for a good day hike. Pebble Creek Campground is open from mid-June through September and is a non-reservation campground.

Slough Creek Campground
Northeast Entrance Rd., Yellowstone National Park
$$

Slough Creek could easily be called the "Wildlife Watcher's Campground," with its proximity to the Lamar Valley. Tucked in a lush drainage just a mile from the main road, the rolling hills and open meadows surrounding this campground easily qualify it as Yellowstone's most beautiful. Eight miles northeast of the Tower-Roosevelt Junction, this is a quiet area known for its lack of crowds and unbelievable fishing (see our Fishing and Watersports chapter). Located on the northern edge of the Lamar Valley, you are likely to see moose in the spring; coyote, trumpeter swans, and birds of prey in the summer; and elk and bison in autumn. Some of Yellowstone's wolves are also frequently sighted in this area; ask park rangers if they know of any perches you can seek out to catch a glimpse of these elusive creatures on your own. Also only a half-mile from camp is the Slough Creek trailhead, which leads to the park's northern boundary.

Slough Creek's 29 campsites are situated in prime grizzly habitat, so take extra precautions in storing food and garbage. Bring everything you need for cooking and cleaning up, as there are no frills at this first-come, first-served campground. Slough Creek is open from late May to early November.

Tower Fall Campground
Tower-Roosevelt-Canyon Rd., Yellowstone National Park
$$

This conveniently located campground is popular because of its access to amenities, hiking, and organized activities at Roosevelt Lodge. Staying here is more like summer camp than roughing it. Though they are hidden in the trees, these 32 campsites are located directly across from a Hamilton Store and only three miles from the Tower-Roosevelt Junction. Hiking trails abound here. The most popular leads to 132-foot Tower Fall, a breathtaking waterfall that tumbles between columns of rocks. Another begins at the campground entrance and travels three miles up Tower Creek. There are several other trails near the Tower-Roosevelt Junction. One of them, the Yellowstone Picnic Area Trail, follows the Grand Canyon of the Yellowstone for about two miles. Open only during the summer months, campsites fill up fast on a first-come, first-served basis.

Morning Glory Pool. PHOTO: NATIONAL PARK SERVICE

Close-up

Pedaling Yellowstone National Park

The sight of a bison grazing across an open meadow and being able to smell the air it smells, the heat of day, and the sounds it hears are just some of the reasons many people would say that pedaling Yellowstone Park is the best way to experience its beauty.

You may be able to cover more ground by driving Yellowstone in the comfort of an air conditioned car, but there's also a lot you can miss. On a bicycle, however, every mile you rack up is earned and unforgettable. Over 300 miles of road are available to cyclists within Yellowstone. From short day rides on old gravel service roads and bike trails made for fat tires or week-long tours from one entrance to another, autumn is the best time to hop on two wheels in the park. Though July and August are typically the most popular months to bike in the park, September and October are even better because the days are clear and cool. Summer tourist traffic slows, making it easier to access trails without crowds and creating a safer atmosphere for road biking, as well. Snowy roads and mountain passes prevent bicycling from November through most of April.

Bicycling through Yellowstone is a rewarding experience, but planning in advance is essential. This type of trip is not for beginners or the faint of heart. Distances between developed areas are long and some of the most notable climbs range in elevation from 5,300 to 8,860 feet. Some favorite climbs require extra time, energy, and food, such as Craig Pass (8,261), Sylvan Pass (8,530), and Dunraven Pass (8,859). If you're attempting a long ride crossing mountain passes, things to consider are camping reservations, packing extra food and water, bringing clothes that can be layered for any type of weather, and carrying supplies for bicycle repairs.

Though experiencing the wonders of Yellowstone on a bike is like nothing else, there are rules, according to the National Park Service. Bicyclists on public roads are required to obey the same traffic regulations that apply to motorized vehicles.

Bikes are not allowed on any park trails or in backcountry areas, and service roads are closed to bikes unless specified. All riders must have a white light on the front and a red light or reflector on the rear of their bikes during times of low visibility. And riding abreast on a public road is prohibited.

Beyond that, safety and common sense also factor in to the quintessential bike trip in the park. Road conditions predate today's bicycling popularity, to say the least, so Yellowstone's roads are narrow, rough, and typically don't have a shoulder. Always ride single file. Be aware of heavy traffic and wide recreational vehicles near places like Old Faithful, Mammoth, and other major points of interest throughout the park. Remember that traffic swells highest from mid-morning to late afternoon.

Despite obvious hazards that exist everywhere for cyclists, Yellowstone by bike is a way to see the park at your own pace. Smell the air, feel the sun on your face, work a little harder to see the view at the top. It's a worthwhile experience that will stick with you forever.

Bicycling Routes

Mammoth area

1. The abandoned railroad bed paralleling the Yellowstone River between Gardiner and the park boundary at Reese Creek. 5 miles.
2. Golden Gate service road between Golden Gate and Joffee Lake. Approximately 1.5 miles.

3. Mammoth service road beginning at the top of the hill on the Old Gardiner Road above Mammoth running northwest to the telephone microwave station. 1.5 miles.

4. Swan Lake gravel pit road, six miles south of Mammoth. Approximately 1 mile.

5. Superintendant's campground road, adjacent to the entrance to the Indian Creek Campground. 0.4 mile.

West entrance

6. Riverside trail from entrance area to Barns Road. 1.4 miles.

Old Faithful area

7. Lone Star Geyser Road from the Grand Loop Road to the Lone Star Geyser parking lot. 2 miles.

8. The paved trail beginning in front of the Lower Hamilton Store at Old Faithful to Morning Glory Pool. 2 miles.

9. Fountain Freight Road located six miles north of Old Faithful.

10. Daisy Geyser cut-off to Biscuit Basin. Abandoned service road. 1.4 miles.

11. Natural Bridge Road near Bridge Bay. 1 mile.

12. The old roadbed near the lake shore between Lake Hotel and where the roadbed joins the main road south of Lake Junction. 1 mile.

Tower-Lamar areas

13. Mount Washburn Service Road, from the Chittenden Road parking area to the summit of Mt. Washburn. 3 miles.

14. Old Chittenden service road, between Grand Loop Road and Tower Falls campground. 2 miles.

15. Rose Creek Service Road behind the Lamar Ranger Station. 1 mile.

Mountain biking trails abound in Yellowstone Country. PHOTO: BOZEMAN CHAMBER OF COMMERCE

Restaurants

Restaurant Rates

For two people, excluding beverages, tip, and tax.

$ . . . . $10 to $19
$$ . . . . $20 to $27
$$$ . . . . $28 to $35
$$$$ . . . . $36 and more

Lake Hotel
Lake Village, Yellowstone National Park
(307) 344-7311
$$$

With the sound of a piano hanging in the air each evening, chandeliers and candles casting warm light across this elegant dining room, there is one word that captures the scene: romantic. In the 1920s, guests were required to dress for dinner—coat tails for men and silk dresses for women. Supper was served at six o'clock sharp and offered a prix fixe, European-style menu. Today you can choose whatever you fancy from this seasonal menu, although the blackened prime rib is the restaurant's hallmark. And although formal dress is not a requirement, why not make it just a little more special? Whatever you wear, savor the time, come hungry, and order several courses—be lavish. Before your meal, opt for a cocktail and lounge in the sun room. The menu and wine list are extensive. The hotel recommends reservations.

Mammoth Hot Springs Hotel
Mammoth, Yellowstone National Park
(307) 344-7311
$$

The Dining Room at Mammoth Hot Springs is the kind of place where you might enjoy a high tea. It's spacious and grand; at a glance it seems prim, as if you should sit up straight and be careful not to use the wrong fork. But in actuality the atmosphere is very casual, with a menu that reflects its clientele—a cheeseburger for the kids; orange roughy for the light eater; and prime rib for the hungry. Wine or mixed drinks are available to complete your meal.

Mammoth is a popular dining spot because, like the pioneers, many tourists today begin and end their Yellowstone visit here. The winter months, December 20 through early March, bring a lot of locals to the Dining Room. The restaurant is also open from the first week in May through mid-October. Reservations are accepted.

Old Faithful Inn
Old Faithful, Yellowstone National Park
(307) 344-7311
$$$

At the turn of the century, when there wasn't another restaurant for hundreds of miles, Old Faithful Inn offered formal dinner service and dancing. The band played from the Crow's Nest some 50 feet above the lobby.

The scene isn't quite as formal these days, but the knotty pine furniture and decor still take you back to the Old West era. Today's menu is contemporary, offering Rocky Mountain Trout; honey-lemon chicken; and fettuccine with mushrooms, artichoke hearts, and olives. And though it's not necessary to break out your best attire like the early visitors, one thing you can do is take your time dining here as the pioneers did. Old Faithful has a full bar and a reasonably sized wine list. The restaurant, which suggests reservations, is open during summer months, approximately May 1 through mid-October.

Old Faithful Snow Lodge. PHOTO: NATIONAL PARK SERVICE

Old Faithful Snow Lodge
Old Faithful, Yellowstone National Park
(307) 344-7311
$$

The digs are new, but the food is hearty and traditional. Comfort food staples like chicken-fried steak, meat loaf, and fried chicken are some of your options in this relaxed Western setting. Besides your entree, the meal is served family style—so you can't be too polite to ask a fellow guest to pass the big bowl of mashed potatoes down to your end of the table. The grand picture windows, cathedral ceilings, and pine chairs adorned with wildlife carvings make an easy atmosphere. The Old Faithful Snow Lodge opens and closes with the park, serves liquor and wine, but does not accept reservations in the restaurant.

Roosevelt Lodge
Yellowstone National Park
(307) 344-7311
$$

Barbecued ribs are the house specialty, whether you nosh on them at the table of the family-style dining room or outside at the picnic tables after a wagon ride. Either way, the atmosphere is like a dude ranch with huge platters of potatoes, meat, and green beans passed around the table. You can almost imagine yourself among gruff Teddy Roosevelt and his Roughriders, sipping whiskey and smoking pipes on full bellies. Only today, in addition to the massive rib eye steaks and juicy prime rib, you'll also find some lighter salads, pasta dishes, and fish specials on the menu. One thing is certain, a good old American cheeseburger tastes a little better when you're sitting in this turn-of-the-century log dining room. Roosevelt is open only during summer, mid-June through September. Reservations are not accepted.

Shopping

Hamilton Stores
Various locations throughout the park

Hamilton Stores have served park visitors since 1915. In the early days, these general stores catered to the needs of their wealthy visitors and carried hard-to-get beauty products just for the ladies. Today, as Yellowstone's oldest concessionaire, the shops carry camping and fishing equipment, film, groceries, sundries, and souvenirs. In some locations, such as Tower Fall and Lake, you'll find a comparatively limited menu of food, supplies, and gifts. Other areas with greater visitor numbers, like Canyon, sell everything you might need for camping, cooking, traveling, and more. In some of the older locations, like Fishing Bridge and Old Faithful, you can dine at the lunch counter.

Hamilton recently added separate "nature" shops at locations in Mammoth and Canyon. In addition, the stores at Fishing Bridge, Old Faithful, and the Canyon Nature Shop all have on-site, one-hour photo processing. Not to be left behind the times, in 1997 Hamilton Stores, Inc. began offering its Yellowstone On-line Catalog, www.hamiltonstores.com, a useful service if you don't feel like stuffing your bag full of gifts to take home. When you get home you can order anything from Yellowstone souvenirs and apparel, recreation products, jewelry, and Native American handicrafts. It also lists information about road conditions, weather, fishing updates, campgrounds, hotels, and employment.

Yellowstone Association Bookstore
100 Chittenden House, Mammoth
Yellowstone National Park
(307) 344-2293

The thing you should know about this bookstore is that proceeds from any book you purchase here goes to the Yellowstone Association, a non-profit organization that helps Yellowstone National Park with funding, research, and interpretive projects. You'll find an extensive selection of park and nature-related books, many from regional authors. You'll find books on birds, animals, hiking, fishing, geology, history, geysers, and more.

Grand Teton National Park

Entering the Park
In the Park
Visitors Centers
Accommodations
Restaurants
Shopping
Nightlife

Grand Teton National Park celebrated its 50th anniversary in 2000, but its controversial history goes back to before the turn of the twentieth century.

The Teton region first received government protection in 1897, when Congress created the Teton Forest Reserve, made up of land not included in the creation of Yellowstone National Park in 1872. As early as 1917, bills were floating around Congress to create a much larger sanctuary, and three attempts to federalize land around Jackson Hole were defeated by local residents. In 1926, John D. Rockefeller, Jr., toured the park with Yellowstone National Park Superintendent Horace Albright, who thought that the area's beauty would be spoiled if something weren't done quickly. Rockefeller agreed, and his legacy would be left on the park a few years later. In 1929, the central peaks of the Tetons and some lakes at their eastern base officially became Grand Teton National Park, one-third of its present day size.

Still not satisfied with the size of the park, Rockefeller began buying land through the Snake River Land Company—35,000 acres of farm and ranch land between 1927 and the mid-1930s. His goal was to donate the property and expand the park, but congressional and local opposition was tough. Rockefeller finally forced the issue by threatening to sell his holdings on the open market in 1943.

President Franklin D. Roosevelt responded immediately by declaring the 221,000 acres of the Snake River Basin—nearly the entire remaining valley—as the Jackson Hole National Monument. This was a clever move, since this didn't require congressional approval as did the creation of a national park.

The controversy didn't end there, however, as Wyoming residents felt betrayed (most didn't want the park expanded) and sued Grand Teton National Park's superintendent, but lost. Congress passed a bill abolishing the monument, but Roosevelt vetoed it. Finally, in 1950, the Jackson Hole National Monument officially became part of Grand Teton National Park. And in 1972, Congress dedicated a 24,000-acre parcel of land in the northern part of the park in honor of Rockefeller, and named the highway from the south boundary of Grand Teton to West Thumb in Yellowstone after him.

As current Grand Teton National Park Superintendent Jack Neckels wrote in a special anniversary publication, "The struggle for present-day Grand Teton National Park required decades of compromise and defined new horizons in park preservation. Today's park represents conservation through compromise and preserves a more complete ecosystem."

Insiders' Tip

A Grand Teton National Park Ranger is available at the Moose Visitor Center every day but Christmas. To reach the center, call (307) 739-3399.

Lush broad valleys give way to majestic peaks in Grand Teton National Park. PHOTO: JACKSON HOLE CHAMBER OF COMMERCE

Insiders' Tip

Towering more than a mile above the Jackson Hole valley, the Grand Teton rises to 13,770 feet above sea level. Twelve Teton peaks stretch above 12,000 feet, high enough to support a dozen mountain glaciers. In contrast to the abrupt eastern face, the west side of the range slopes gently, highlighting the angle of tilt of the rectangular block of the Earth's crust. The Teton Range is the youngest of the Rocky Mountains, but displays some of North America's oldest rocks.

At the pinnacle of the ecosystem is the mountain range itself, located on a fault line that erupted with massive earthquakes 2 to 3 million years ago. The mountain block uplifted on the west side of the fault and the valley block dropped down to the east. That's why the mountains shoot straight up from the Jackson Hole valley floor while they taper off to the west as the foothills of the Teton Valley. Glaciers finished sculpting the mountains, gouging out deep canyons between the high peaks and forming basins occupied today by lakes like Leigh, Bradley, Jenny, and Taggart. Jackson Lake is what's left of a massive river of ice that covered most of Yellowstone National Park 25,000 years ago, and the Snake River now flows through its glacial moraines toward Jackson Hole.

The range itself is perhaps the most recognizable and photographed in the world, and its silhouette can be picked out from more than a hundred miles away on a clear day. The bent and jagged formation of the Grand Teton—named by French trappers of the Hudson Bay Company, part of "les trois Tetons," meaning "the three beasts"—pokes up to 13,770 feet, and is surrounded by the "cathedral" of peaks—Nez Perce, Middle Teton, Mount Owen, and Teewinot Mountain. Mount Moran, the highest and most recognizable peak on the northern end of the range, tops out at 12,605 feet. It was named by Ferdinand Hayden for Thomas Moran, who traveled with the 1872 Hayden expedition into Yellowstone and Pierre's Hole on the west side of the Teton range.

Besides the mountains, Grand Teton National Park is also known for its wildlife. The center of the ecosystem is the adjacent National Elk Refuge, a 23,754-acre winter refuge for up to 10,000 elk, but the park is also home to moose, bison, mule deer, pronghorn antelope, beavers, birds, mountain goats, bighorn sheep, coyotes, black bears, and grizzly bears. In addition, wolves released in Yellowstone National Park in 1995 have migrated between the two parks. Remember to report all wolf and bear sightings to a park ranger, and always respect the wildlife you encounter—don't put yourself in any danger and keep a safe distance away. Most importantly, never feed any animals.

Today, more than four million visitors see the majestic beauty of Grand Teton National Park each year, whether by car or motorhome or from the top of a 13,000-foot peak and the shore of a hidden backcountry lake. Visitors from all over the world marvel at the awe-inspiring Tetons, rising 7,000 feet off the valley floor. It's not a huge park, and that's one if its strengths. You can explore nearly every nook in a few days, from the miles of awesome hiking trails to the numerous alpine lakes and abundant wildlife. And for those who prefer driving around, the park's easily navigated roads offer views in every direction. Of course, the going may be slow, as you'll most likely want to stop at every turnout to get that postcard-perfect photograph, and by the end of your trip, you're sure to have plenty of those.

Entering the Park

Grand Teton only has three entrance stations. If you're coming from Yellowstone you'll travel the John D. Rockefeller, Jr., Memorial Parkway south through Flagg Ranch, along Jackson Lake, and toward Colter Bay. There's no gate here, as your entrance permit from Yellowstone is also good for Grand Teton.

If you're entering the park on the east side from Dubois, you'll pay your admission fee at the Moran entrance station, a few miles inside the boundaries of the park. The road splits here, and turning right will take you five miles to Jackson Lake Junction and the Jackson Lake Lodge. Heading left will guide you 18 miles along the Snake River toward Moose Junction.

Coming from the south, you won't hit an entrance station until you drive north on Teton Park Road, which can be found by turning left at Moose Junction. Teton Park Road is the park's main thoroughfare, running along Cottonwood Creek and Jenny and Jackson Lakes. You can drive U.S. Highway 26/89/191 from Moose Junction to Moran and out the east entrance without paying an entrance fee.

You'll also find an entrance fee on the less-traveled Moose-Wilson Road (Wyoming Highway 390), which is a summer route from Wilson to Moose Junction. No motorhomes or trailers are allowed on this road once you enter the park boundary, and the road is closed from November 1 to May 1.

Another dirt road, the Grassy Lake Road, starts in Ashton, Idaho, and connects with the Rockefeller Highway at Flagg Ranch. There's no entrance station here, but the road makes for a beautiful drive into the park. It's not recommended for RVs, however, and is closed during the winter.

The entrance fee is $20 per vehicle, good for seven days in Grand Teton and Yellowstone National Parks. Single hikers and bicyclists get in for $10, while motorcycles are $15 each. If you'll be in the area longer than a week or if you're planning to return within a year, consider a Parks Specific Pass. It's $40 and allows entrance to both parks for a full year, or better yet, get a $50 Golden Eagle Pass—good for all national parks.

Insiders' Tip

The map you receive at the park's entrance station shows several picnic areas around the park. A few choices include the Signal Mountain Summit and Overlook, which has tables at a central high point in the Jackson Hole valley, and the Cottonwood Creek Picnic Area, where you can learn about the forest's life cycle by reading interpretive signs. The String Lake Picnic Area, located on a spur road northwest of Jenny Lake, offers beautiful lake vistas and a great view of the Cathedral Group of Teton peaks.

And if you're over 62, a $10 Golden Age Passport allows lifetime entrance to all National Park System areas.

Grand Teton is open during the winter, but not all services are available. The Teton Park Road is closed to motorized vehicles from the Taggart Lake trailhead north to Signal Mountain on November 1. You can drive on U.S. Highway 26/89/191 all the way to Flagg Ranch, but further travel is prohibited. The unpaved portion of the Moose-Wilson Road is also closed, as is the Grassy Lake Road from Asthon to Flagg Ranch. All other main roads are open. Unplowed park roads are open to snowmobiles ($15 entrance fee required) when conditions allow. Refer to the following individual sections on building and service closures.

In the Park

U.S. Highway 89/191 runs through the entire park from north to south, from the town of Jackson up to Yellowstone National Park and out its west entrance. In Grand Teton, the road forks right at Moose Junction and continues along the Snake River to the Moran Junction. Here, U.S. Highway 26/287 goes east out of the park and U.S. Highway 89/191/287 heads west to Jackson Lake Junction, then north toward Yellowstone. It sounds confusing, but looking at the map will set things straight.

Teton Park Road is where you'll find all park visitor centers and most services. Make a left at Moose Junction and follow the signs toward Moose, Jenny Lake, and Jackson Lake. The road skirts Cottonwood Creek and Jenny Lake before winding around Jackson Lake and reconnecting with Highway U.S. 89/191/287 at Jackson Lake Junction.

There are other smaller, less used roads in the park. Refer to park maps for their exact location.

Visitor Centers

Moose Visitor Center
Moose Village
(307) 739-3399

This is one of the main centers of activity in the park, and also where you'll find the park headquarters. The center provides assistance and information, offers audio-visual programs and exhibits, and issues permits for overnight camping and climbing adventures. You can also buy Grand Teton Natural History Association (GTNHA) publications here, and you'll also find a gift shop, restaurant, gas station, post office, cash machine, and a small store that sells basic camping necessities. The center is also the hub of winter activity in the park, where you can get maps of ski trails and information on weather and avalanche and road conditions. From June 5 through September 4, the center is open daily from 8 A.M. to 7 P.M. The rest of the year, it's open from 8 A.M. to 5 P.M. You'll find the Moose Visitor Center one-half mile west of Moose Junction on Teton Park Road.

Colter Bay Visitor Center
Colter Bay Village
(307) 739-3594

This is the main point of activity on the north end of the park. The center offers the same services as the Moose Visitor Center, as well as a marina, campground, RV park, and several lodging options. The center also houses the Colter Bay Indian Arts Museum, which features the spectacular assemblage of Native American artifacts from the David T. Vernon collection. From June to September the museum offers interpretive activities, such as craft demonstrations by tribal members and ranger-led museum tours, to enhance our appreciation of Native American culture. Hours are 8 A.M. to 5 P.M. from May 13 through May 21 and September 5 through October 1; 8 A.M. to 7 P.M. from May 22 through June 4; and 8 A.M. to 8 P.M. from September 5 through October 1. The center is located one-half mile west of Colter Bay Junction of U.S. Highway 89/191/287.

Jenny Lake Visitor Center
Jenny Lake

This small visitor center is located on the Teton Park Road eight miles north of Moose Junction. You'll find basic park information, a small store, geology exhibits, and GTNHA publications for sale. The Visitor Center is close to the South Jenny Lake trailhead and boat dock and the well-known Jenny Lake Lodge. The center is open 8 A.M. to 7 P.M. from June 5 through September 4, and 8 A.M. to 5 P.M. from September 1 through October 1. A ranger is on duty when the center is open.

Flagg Ranch Information Station
Flagg Ranch

While not a full-fledged visitor center, the Flagg Ranch Information Station offers audiovisual programs and backcountry and boating permits, and has a ranger on duty to answer questions. The station is located 15 miles north of Colter Bay on U.S. Highway 89/191/287 and is open daily June 5 through September 4 from 9 A.M. to 6 P.M.

Accommodations

Hotels, Lodges, and Cabins

Hotel, Lodge, and Cabin Rates

Keep in mind that some rates are based on availability. The average nightly rates for two adults at the hotels and motels listed in this section are indicated by a dollar sign ($) ranking in the following chart. Also, the hotels and motels in this chapter accept all or most major credit cards.

$	$50 to $75
$$	$76 to $100
$$$	$101 to $150
$$$$	$151 and more

Jackson Lake Lodge
Jackson Lake
(307) 543-3100, (800) 628-9988
$$$

This magnificent lodge is a full-service hotel located in the heart of Grand Teton National Park on a bluff overlooking Willow Flats with a spectacular view of the Teton skyline and Jackson Lake.

There are 348 guest cottage rooms on either side of the main lodge building and 37 rooms in the lodge itself. Standard cot-

The Jackson Lake Lodge offers unparalleled views of Mt. Moran and the Teton Range. PHOTO: JACKSON HOLE CHAMBER OF COMMERCE

tage rooms have two full beds and a private setting. View cottages have private balconies where you can watch the Teton sunset each evening. View rooms in the main lodge have a huge picture window that frames the mountain range and lake. In keeping with the National Park location, none of the rooms have televisions or radios, and all are comfortably furnished with a Western décor.

The main lodge features 60-foot picture windows with breathtaking views as well as a collection of Indian artifacts and Western art. You'll also find apparel and gift shops and a small newsstand that sells national papers and local reads like the *Jackson Hole Guide* and the *Jackson Hole News*, as well as film, magazines, and snacks.

You can enjoy a beverage and appetizers in the Blue Heron cocktail lounge, which features an amazing outdoor patio. The Pioneer Grill serves counter service of light meals, snacks, and soda fountain

treats, while the Mural Room offers Rocky Mountain walls filled with historic murals.

Other guest facilities include a business center, espresso station, heated outdoor swimming pool, horseback riding, bus tours, float trips, service station, and a medical clinic.

The lodge is open from mid-May through mid-October and a two nights' deposit is required.

Jenny Lake Lodge
Jenny Lake
(307) 733-4647
$$$$

The Jenny Lake Lodge offers a bit of luxury in a charming Old West setting. In the shadow of the Tetons, the Lodge overlooks one of the park's prettiest sights, Jenny Lake. Thirty-seven rustic but elegant cabins surround the main lodge and come complete with handmade log furniture, covered deck, and telephones on request—but no radio or TV. The spacious and recently renovated main lodge has a sitting area with books and games for guests to enjoy.

Breakfast and dinner as well as horseback riding and bicycle usage are included in the room rate. Dinners feature six courses served in the log cabin elegance of the main dining room, which also hosts the locally famous Sunday night buffet dinners. Jackets are appreciated during dinner in the lodge.

The lodge is open from June through early October. A three-night deposit is required.

Colter Bay Village
Colter Bay
(307) 543-3100, (800) 628-9988
$
Colter Bay Village offers a variety of accommodations as well as a full-service marina, two restaurants, laundry facilities, grocery store, gift and apparel shops, corrals, and service stations.

The 166 Colter Bay log cabins are nestled in the woods around Jackson Lake and feature many sizes and configurations that sleep up to six people. The cabins are pretty rustic—some are original settlers' cabins—but most have a complete bath

with shower. No kitchen facilities are available, and the cabins don't have a phone, TV, or radio.

Colter Bay also offers something unique—tent cabins made of canvas and logs. Each has an outdoor grill, wood-burning stove, two double-decker bunks (without bedding) and a picnic table. Restroom facilities with hot running water are included—showers are available for a fee—and sleeping bags, cots, and bedding may be rented at a central utility building.

Signal Mountain Lodge
Inner Park Road
(307) 543-2831
www.signalmountainlodge.com
$$-$$$$
Lakeside suites, log cabins, and motel rooms are offered from early May to early October at the Signal Mountain Lodge, located on the shores of Jackson Lake a few miles south of the Jackson Lake Junction on Teton Park Road. Fireplaces are included in some rooms, and the lodge also features a restaurant, coffee shop, gift shop, and water sports rentals. The Aspens restaurant offers fine dining, while you'll find lighter fare at the Trapper Grill and Deadman's Bar.

Insiders' Tip

There are several regulations that you must follow when boating in the park. Motorized craft use requires a $7 seven-day permit or a $20 annual permit. Nonmotorized craft use requires a $5 seven-day or $10 annual permit. To float the Snake River, you must register your craft with the National Park Service and obtain a $10 annual permit. Motorized craft use is permitted only on Jackson, Jenny, and Phelps Lakes, while nonmotorized craft are allowed on Bearpaw, Bradley, Emma Matilda, Jackson, Jenny, Leigh, Phelps, String, Taggart, and Two Ocean Lakes. Permits can be purchased at the Moose and Colter Bay Visitor Centers.

Guest Ranches and Lodges

Guest Ranch and Lodge Rates

$ . . . . Less than $85

$$ . . . . $86 to $115

$$$ . . . . $116 to $150

$$$$ . . . . $151 and more

Flagg Ranch Resort
John D. Rockefeller, Jr. Memorial Parkway
(307) 543-2861, (800) 443-2311
www.flaggranch.com
$$$

This cowboy-style ranch welcomes visitors year round to its location on the Snake River between Yellowstone and Grand Teton National Parks. While at the ranch, stay in cozy log cabins, comfortably furnished with either two queen beds or one king bed. Each cabin has a private bath, telephone, coffee maker, and patio with rocking chairs.

Book early here for summer, as there is limited lodging between the parks. Summer season lasts from mid-May to early October. During winter, Flagg Ranch is open from mid-December to mid-March, when rates are slightly lower.

Moose Head Ranch
P.O. Box 214, Moose, WY
(307) 733-3141
$$$$

Guests at the Moose Head stay in modern log cabins, nestled among the pine and cottonwood trees of its location on the east fringes of the park. The ranch offers week-long family summer vacations with a wide variety of recreation opportunities. The Snake River flows through the ranch, and Moose Head also has stocked trout ponds. Guests eat family style in the main lodge.

The ranch is open from early June to late August and accommodates up to 40 guests.

Triangle X Ranch
U.S. Hwy. 26/89/191
(307) 733-2183
www.trianglex.com
$$$

For over 60 years, the Turner family has offered real Western dude ranch vacations at the Triangle X Ranch, located just outside Grand Teton National Park. You can enjoy horseback riding, float trips, pack trips, fishing, square dancing, hiking, scenic tours, and more during the day, then relax for a dutch oven cookout dinner and an evening of Western guitar music. Stay here in the winter and enjoy the nearby cross-country and downhill skiing and snowmobiling opportunities.

Guests stay in one-, two-, or three-bedroom log cabins with bathrooms, all attractively furnished with Western décor.

Insiders' Tip

Snow can linger on Teton trails into August, making for slippery spots in some areas. Be extra careful when crossing snowfields. In addition, the weather can turn wintry in a hurry at higher elevations. It's always a good idea to pack extra clothes, food, and water when going out for a day hike—even if it's a short one.

Meals are served family style in the beautiful sun porch dining room of the main lodge.

During the peak summer season, there is a week-long minimum stay requirement, and prices include meals and horseback riding. Winter rates are per person, per night, with a two night minimum stay required. The ranch accommodates up to 70 guests.

Campgrounds and RV Parks

Campground Rates

$ . . . . $12 and less
$$ . . . . $13 to $24
$$$ . . . . $25 and more

Grand Teton National Park has five National Park Service campgrounds within its boundaries, for a total of 905 sites. Jenny Lake Campground is for tents only, while all others accommodate tents, trailers, and RVs. All campgrounds have modern comfort stations but do not have utility hookups (there are others not operated by the park that do), and NPS campgrounds operate on a first-come, first-served basis. Advance reservations are not accepted. The fee is $12 per night, with a 14-day limit at all but Jenny Lake, where the limit is seven days. Doubling up on campsites is not permitted and there are no overflow facilities. Fill-up times are listed below for individual campgrounds.

Free backcountry permits for overnight trips can be obtained at the Moose or Colter Bay Visitor Centers or the Jenny Lake Ranger Station. You can reserve backcountry campsites in advance—January 1 until May 15—by calling the park at (307) 739-3600. The fee is $15 per reservation. Campfires are prohibited except at designated sites depending on fire danger.

Group sites for 10 to 75 people are available at Gros Ventre and Colter Bay campgrounds. Organized youth, religious, or educational groups may use these sites, but advance reservations are required. The nightly use fee is $3 per person, plus a $15 reservation fee. Reservation requests should be made between January 1 and May 15 by writing Campground Reservations, Grand Teton National Park, Moose, WY 83012.

> ## Insiders' Tip
> Each campground in the park has a nightly ranger presentation during the summer, including slide shows and storytelling sessions. Programs are usually offered between 7 P.M. and 9:30 P.M. Check the park's newspaper, *Teewinot*, for information on times, locations, and topics.

Gros Ventre Campground
Gros Ventre-Kelly Rd.
$

This 360-site campground is the largest in the park and is located on the banks of the Gros Ventre River in the southeast corner of the park. It's open from April 29 to October 12, and usually is the last campground to fill up. There's an RV dump station, but no hook-ups. Five group sites are available as well. To get here, take a right at the Gros Ventre Junction upon entering the park from the south, and you'll see the site a few miles ahead on the right.

Jenny Lake Campground
Teton Park Rd.
$

Since this tent-only campground is located in the most popular part of the park, its 49 sites fill up early, usually by 8 A.M. It's open from mid-May to late September. The campground is located next to numerous hiking trails, and a small store is nearby.

Signal Mountain Campground
Teton Park Rd.
$

This scenic campground features 86 sites on the shores of Jackson Lake, with direct views of the Tetons. There's also a dump station for RVs, and nearby you'll find a gas station, marina, and restaurants. Sites usually fill up by 10 A.M., and the campground is open from mid-May to early October.

Lizard Creek Campground
U.S. Hwy. 89/191/287
$

This is the most northern of the NPS campgrounds, located on the edge of Jackson Lake just south of the park boundary. There are 60 sites, and the campground is open from early June to early September. It usually fills up by 2 P.M.

Insiders' Tip

Wayside exhibits at many turnouts along main park roads identify major peaks and explain natural features and wildlife exhibits. Turnouts also insure safe parking for viewing and photographing the mountain scenery.

Colter Bay Campground
Colter Bay Village
$

This 350-site campground is located near the greatest number of park services, including gas, food, stables, self-guiding nature trails, and a marina. There are also laundry and showers, as well as propane and trailer dumping stations. The campground usually fills up by noon, and is located on U.S. Highway 89/191/287 on the shores of Jackson Lake.

Colter Bay RV Park
Colter Bay Village
(307) 543-3100, (800) 628-9988
$$$

This RV park is operated by the Grand Teton Lodge Company and offers 112 trailer spaces, each with sewer, electrical, and water connections and a picnic table. Most sites are pull-thrus and shaded, and showers are available for a fee. Expect to pay $2 more for vehicles more than 38 feet long.

Flagg Ranch RV Park
Flagg Ranch
(307) 543-2861, (800) 443-2311
www.flaggranch.com
$$$

Flagg Ranch has a wooded campground near the Snake River with great views of the surrounding mountains. It features tent and RV sites, with showers, laundry facilities, fire pits, and picnic tables. RV sites are pull-thrus.

Prices are for one or two people, with each additional person paying $2. Reservations are strongly recommended for the summer.

Grand Teton Park RV Resort and Cabins
U.S. Hwy. 26/287
(307) 543-2483, (800) 563-6469
$$$

This is the closest year-round RV park near Grand Teton, located one mile east of the park in Moran. There are 120 RV sites with full services, and 60 tent sites available during the summer. Other amenities include a pool, recreation room, and laundry facility.

Restaurants

Restaurant Rates

Prices include meals for two people, excluding beverages, tip, and tax.

$	$10 to $19
$$	$20 and $27
$$$	$28 to $35
$$$$	$36 and more

The Blue Heron
Jackson Lake Lodge
(307) 543-2811
$

Open mid-May to mid-October, The Blue Heron offers all your favorite latte, espresso, cappuccino, or coffee drinks from 6 A.M. to 10 A.M. The Blue Heron Lounge opens at 11 A.M., serving appetizers and a fine selection of mixed drinks, wine, and beer in a panoramic setting. On nice days you can enjoy the Blue Heron's outdoor patio, and nightly live entertainment is offered during the summer. The lounge is open until midnight.

Chuckwagon Restaurant
Colter Bay Village
$$

The Chuckwagon is a great place to take the family, as it has a special menu just for kids. Steaks and homemade pastas are the specialty here, and dinner includes a bottomless salad bowl. The breakfast buffet is a great way to start your day, and lunch includes an extensive sandwich and salad menu. Breakfast is served from 7:30 A.M. to 10 A.M., lunch hours are 11:30 A.M. to 2 P.M., and dinner is offered from 5:30 P.M. to 9 P.M. The Chuckwagon has a full bar, does not accept reservations, and is open from early June to early September.

Jenny Lake Lodge Dining Room
Jenny Lake Lodge
(307) 543-3300
$$$$

The rustic main lodge at Jenny Lake and its accompanying dining room are park favorites, and are open June through early October. The log structure is the perfect place to enjoy the renowned cuisine for breakfast, lunch, and dinner. Breakfast and the six-course dinner are a fixed price and included in the room rate for lodge guests. Lunch is served a la carte. Besides the innovative dishes and extensive wine list, the dining room is known for its outstanding Sunday buffet dinner, featuring enough food selections to last a week. Reservations are required for dinner and breakfast, and jackets are appreciated on men for dinner.

John Colter Café Court
Colter Bay Village
$

This little café at Colter Bay is a great place to go for a quick meal or a snack. Open 6 A.M. to 10 P.M., the café's breakfast features pastries, breads, and packaged items, while pizza, deli sandwiches, and fresh salads make up the lunch menu. Everything here can be packaged to go for a picnic or lunch on the trail, and beer is available. The café is open from early June to early September.

Leek's Restaurant
North of Colter Bay
(307) 543-2494
$$

Leek's—located on the main park road just north of Colter Bay—offers Italian favorites like specialty pizzas, calzones, pasta, and sandwiches served with a great view of Jackson Lake and the Tetons. An outdoor patio makes for great summer dining, and snacks, desserts, and draft beer are available. Leek's is open 11 A.M. to 10 P.M. from early June to early September.

The Mural Room
Jackson Lake Lodge
(307) 543-2811, ext. 1911
$$$$

Artist Carl Roters's historic murals aren't the only things to look at in the Mural Room. A 100-foot picture window offers dramatic views of the Tetons and serves as a backdrop for diners enjoying Jackson Lake Lodge's finest cuisine. The Mural Room serves breakfast, lunch, and renowned dinners. Hours for breakfast are 7 to 9:30 A.M., lunch hours are noon to 1:30 P.M. and dinner is served from 5:30 to 9 P.M. Reservations are strongly recommended for dinner. The Mural Room is open mid-May to mid-October.

Pioneer Grill
Jackson Lake Lodge
(307) 543-2811
$

The laid-back Pioneer Grill—open from mid May to mid October—serves breakfast, lunch, and dinner in a classic, soda-fountain-style diner. Breakfast includes traditional hot and cold selections, while sandwiches, burgers, and salads are served for lunch. Dinners are served until 10 P.M., but you can get cold sandwiches, beverages, and ice cream until 10:30 P.M. The Pioneer hosts the Pool Grill and BBQ—next to the lodge's heated swimming pool—during July and August.

Sandwiches, pizza, and burgers are served from 11:10 A.M. to 3:30 P.M., with the all-you-can-eat Western BBQ buffet lasting from 6 to 8 P.M. It includes charcoal-broiled steaks, chicken, ribs, and all the fixings. Reservations are required for the BBQ. The Pioneer Grill also offers box lunches to go. Just place your order at the take-out window the evening before your departure.

> ## Insiders' Tip
> While driving north on Teton Park Road, look to the left just before you reach Jackson Lake Lodge. You'll see the spillway of Jackson Lake Dam, which raises the depth of the lake from 389 to 425 feet. Farmers in Idaho paid to have the dam built in 1916, and they still own irrigation rights to the upper 39 feet of Jackson Lake's water.

Shopping

There aren't many places to actually shop in the park—you go to Jackson for that—but stores at Moose, Colter Bay Village, Signal Mountain Lodge, Flagg Ranch, Jackson Lake Lodge, and South Jenny Lake all sell basic camping supplies, groceries, gifts, film, and ice.

Colter Bay has the biggest selection of goods and services during the summer. The General Store, open from 7:30 A.M. to 9:30 P.M., sells everything mentioned above, plus Grand Teton apparel and sporting goods, including a complete line of fishing tackle and backpacking supplies. The Colter Bay Marina Store, open from 7:30 A.M. to 8 P.M. daily during the summer, offers scenic cruises, canoe and boat rentals, fishing equipment and licenses, and guided fishing trips. Film, apparel, postcards, and reference books are also available here.

The Jenny Lake Store, located near the Jenny Lake Ranger Station, offers camping supplies, apparel, postcards, film, gifts, groceries, and ice daily from 8 A.M. to 7 P.M. during the summer. You'll find the same stuff—as well as guided Snake River trips, fishing

Winter in Grand Teton National Park is a snow-capped wonderland. PHOTO: JACKSON HOLE CHAMBER OF COMMERCE

tackle, and licenses—at the Moose Village Store, located across the street from the National Park Headquarters. Hours are 8 A.M. to 6 P.M. daily during the summer.

The Jackson Lake Lodge houses several shops. An apparel shop features casual sportswear and outdoor leisurewear from 8 A.M. to 10 P.M., while the Grand Teton Shop—open 8 A.M. to 10 P.M.—provides a wide assortment of sweatshirts, T-shirts, reference books of the area, and souvenirs. The newsstand sells newspapers, film, magazines, candy, stamps, cigarettes, sundries, and postcards, and offers 24-hour film processing from 7:30 A.M. to 10 P.M. You'll also find a good-sized gift shop, featuring a large collec-

Insiders' Tip

Free, ranger-led naturalist programs and walks take place each day during the summer from the Colter Bay, Moose, and Jenny Lake Visitor Centers and other locations around the park. Check the latest *Teewinot* for schedules and events. From late December to mid-March, ranger-led snowshoe hikes and other winter activities depart daily from the Moose Visitor Center. Reservations are required. Call (307) 739-3399.

tion of Native American crafts and jewelry and local art and photography. The store also sells liquor, beer, and wine and has a small sporting goods section. It's open from 8 A.M. to 10 P.M. daily during the summer.

In the Signal Mountain Lodge, Needles offers gifts, accents, and styles with a Western flavor, while Timbers has cowboy and Western duds and home furnishings.

Nightlife

The park is a quiet place to be when the sun hides behind the Tetons. Other than the occasional howling coyote or bugling elk, you can hear live music nightly during the summer at the Blue Heron Lounge in the Jackson Lake Lodge. Dornan's (307) 733-2415 in Moose has live local and national acts performing year round. To get there, turn left at Moose Junction then make your first right. Dornan's is just down the road next to the Snake River. The real nightlife scene is in Jackson. Refer to the Jackson chapter for more information.

The buckin' bronc in Jackson's town square reflects Wyoming's cowboy past. PHOTO: JACKSON HOLE CHAMBER OF COMMERCE

Jackson

Accommodations
Restaurants
Nightlife
Shopping

Ask anybody around these parts what their favorite town is, and many will answer Jackson Hole. Perhaps more than any other place in Yellowstone Country, Jackson combines all the elements of past and present to create a unique, vibrant destination for visitors to explore during all four seasons.

Jackson Hole, the southern gateway to Grand Teton and Yellowstone National Parks, provides visitors a spectacular introduction to the scenery of the region. It's a bustling place during the summer, when it can seem like everyone you see on the streets is from somewhere else. Literally, busloads of visitors come here from all over the world to enjoy a real Western town with modern clothes on. And this is one of the reasons why it's so popular: You can get a vacation with a Western flair while enjoying the amenities of an upscale destination—renowned restaurants, top-shelf lodging, and exquisite boutiques.

Only about 6,000 people call Jackson home, and 1,500 of them came here within the past ten years. It can be a hard place to live, since real estate costs have skyrocketed and most jobs are in the service sector, but the locals stay here for one reason: the mountains. Jackson truly is a "mountain town" and the birthplace of climbing in North America. Just as early settlers were lured to the valley for the profits of the fur trade, climbers were lured to "the Hole" in the hopes of becoming the first to scale some of the continent's most challenging peaks.

Of course, this led to skiing, and the creation of Jackson Hole Mountain Resort in Teton Village, about ten miles north of Jackson. Containing some of the wildest terrain and some of the deepest powder you'll find anywhere, the resort is a major destination for skiers from all over the world. Young and adventurous ski bums flock here to take any job available just for the chance at catching one of the ski area's epic powder days. Many area businesses also have a "powder clause," meaning that getting work done on a day with more than six inches of new snow will be put on hold—until the mountain gets tracked up.

> ## Insiders' Tip
>
> To see what's happening around town, pick up a copy of *Tempo*, published every Wednesday in the *Jackson Hole Guide*. You'll find information on movies, music, art exhibits, theater, food, and television listings. The *Guide* costs 50 cents.

It's not hard to see why the locals love it here. Looking at the Tetons every day will do something to you, something that can't be described. The majestic skyline of a Teton sunset makes all others seem incomparable. You can literally gaze at the snow-capped peaks for hours and not get bored, but only more amazed as you ponder the way the rocks stretch up more than 7,000 feet from the valley floor. You'll wonder how people can actually scale the Grand Teton—13,770 feet of jagged, twisted rock—and what would possess them do to so. There's no straight answer, really, but climbers say the mountains just beckon them to stand on the top.

The younger population keeps the town from getting too stuffy. Jackson's not all about high-priced galleries and boutiques—there are numerous quaint, out-of-the-way

The famous antler archway of Jackson's beautiful town square. PHOTO: JACKSON HOLE CHAMBER OF COMMERCE

cafés, shops, and bars that are part of the local heritage and show off the town's lesser-known side. Nightlife abounds, with lots of live regional and national acts performing around town, and the après ski scene is one of the most lively around. In short, there's always something fun going on.

It's hard to decide which season is best in Jackson, as each one offers so many different colors—in the scenery and in the town. Summer means blue sky, balmy temperatures, and hiking. In winter, the snow-drenched Tetons seem even more impressive, and the skiing and snowmobiling are world class. Fall is full of warm days, cold nights, and the bright gold leaves of aspen trees, ready to shed as the chill of winter sets in. Spring is a special time where the beauty of the valley comes alive with brilliant wildflowers and bustling wildlife. And events like the Fall Arts Festival, the Stage Stop Sled Dog Race, the spring's Old West Days, and the annual Teton Valley Balloon Festival keep Jackson's vibrant atmosphere kicking all year long.

The best way to describe Jackson is that it has a great vibe. In the summer it can feel a little hurried, but the friendly locals never let the busy atmosphere get them down. After all, many of them work hard to make money for the coming winter, so they can enjoy the benefits of the ski resort without having to work that hard. Walk in any pub or shop and everybody is in a great mood. People on the streets are friendly and say hello as you walk past. Ask questions and you'll get answers. The vibe will certainly do one thing: make you want to come back—maybe even in a different season.

Several outlying towns contribute to the lively atmosphere of the Teton region. Driggs and Victor, Idaho, and Pinedale, Wilson, Alpine, Hoback Junction and Teton Village, Wyoming, all play a role and you'll see them mentioned below.

Accommodations

Hotel and Condominiums

Price Code

Keep in mind that some rates are based on availability. The average nightly rates for two adults at the hotels and motels listed in this section are indicated by a dollar sign ($) ranking in the following chart. Also, the hotels and motels in this chapter accept all or most major credit cards. Rates below are for summer (regular season) rates. Winter rates in downtown Jackson hotels are often significantly cheaper, while Teton Village rates may be more expensive during the ski season and cheaper during the summer.

$ . . . . $50 to $75
$$ . . . . $76 to $100
$$$ . . . . $101 to $150
$$$$ . . . . $151 and more

The Alpine House
285 N. Glenwood St., Jackson
(307) 739-1570
$$$$

The quaint Alpine House—a cozy, country-like inn in the heart of downtown—offers 21 individually decorated guest rooms, each with a private bath and most with fireplaces, TV, and phone. The rooms are light and airy, and include down comforters, plush towels and linens, bathrobes, and European antique furniture. Suites and whirlpool tubs are available. Owners Hans and Nancy Johnstone are both former Olympians—Nancy was on the U.S. biathlon team and Hans was on the Nordic team—who take every measure to make sure your visit to their Scandinavian oasis is an enjoyable one.

Anglers Inn
235 N. Millward St., Jackson
(307) 733-3682, (800) 867-4667
www.anglersinn.net
$$

Handmade lodgepole furniture, locally-made wrought iron lamps, knotty pine accents, and fine art by Jackson Hole artists complete the illusion of staying at a riverside fishing camp, but the Anglers Inn is located within walking distance of all downtown shops, restaurants, and galleries. The 28 rooms feature coffee makers, microwaves, queen size beds, cable TV, and air conditioning.

The Antler Inn
43 W. Pearl St., Jackson
(307) 733-2535, (800) 483-8667
www.antlerinn.com
$$

The Antler Inn is located just a block from the Town Square, which means you can walk to just about everywhere in downtown Jackson from this reasonably priced and full-featured hotel. The two-story building was recently remodeled and offers comfortable rooms with a Western décor, some available with stone fireplaces. A large, indoor hot tub is on the premises, and a complimentary ski shuttle is offered during the winter.

Anvil Motel
215 N. Cache St., Jackson
(307) 733-3668, (800) 234-4507
www.anvilmotel.com
$

The Anvil is the skier's motel, because of its in-room ski racks and on-site waxing room, not to mention its reasonable rates. Built in 1991, the Anvil is located a block from the Town Square and offers refrigerators, microwaves, cable TV, free local phone calls, and an outdoor hot tub. A free continental breakfast is included.

Although Jackson is a busy place during the winter, room rates are significantly cheaper than in the summer. Even with three popular ski resorts nearby, visitor numbers in the winter pale in comparison with summer tourists wanting to get a glimpse of Grand Teton and Yellowstone National Parks.

Buckrail Lodge
110 E. Karns Ave., Jackson
(207) 733-2079
www.buckraillodge.com
$$

The Buckrail is located near the base of Snow King Resort and offers 12 beautifully appointed cedar log rooms with cathedral ceilings and a Western décor. The spacious, park-like grounds feature a large, outdoor hot tub and mature spruce and aspen trees. All rooms include guest-controlled electric heat, two beds, a sitting area, writing desk, and expanded cable television. Furniture is all native western pine. The walls feature original prints from local artists and abundant lighting is provided by custom designed fixtures.

Cowboy Village Log Cabin Resort
120 S. Flat St., Jackson
(307) 733-3121, (800) 962-4988
www.cowboyvillage.com
$$$

Staying at Cowboy Village is a great way to combine convenience with the rustic charm of a log cabin. Located within walking distance of the Town Square, Cowboy Village offers 82 individual log cabins with kitchenettes, full baths, air conditioning, cable TV, phone, queen sized beds, BBQ grills, and covered decks. You'll also find two on-site Jacuzzis and a complimentary continental breakfast in the morning. A free ski shuttle is offered in the winter, and if you will be in the Moran area, try the Cowboy Village at Togwotee, (800) 543-2847. It's 17 miles from the Park's east entrance.

Elk Refuge Inn
1755 N. U.S. Hwy. 89, Jackson
(307) 733-3582, (800) 544-3582
www.elkrefugeinn.com
$$

You can look for elk from your balcony at the Elk Refuge Inn, located across from the National Elk Refuge one mile north of town. The inn has 23 comfortable rooms, 11 of which have full kitchens. All rooms have phones, cable TV, full baths, and a private patio. For summer cookouts there are picnic tables and barbecue grills, and there is a fenced pasture for horses and ample trailer parking for hunters.

Hitching Post Lodge
460 E. Broadway Ave., Jackson
(307) 733-2606, (800) 821-8351
www.hitchingpostlodge.com
$$

Families will love the Hitching Post's covered, outdoor barbecue area, complete with picnic tables, gas and charcoal grills, and a large, outdoor fireplace—perfect for roasting marshmallows. The main lodge was originally built in the early 1900s and has been recently renovated. Choose from either authentic or deluxe cabin-style rooms. Authentic cabins feature a small refrigerator, microwave, private bath, phone, and cable TV. These are one-story buildings with two units each. Deluxe cabins house two units in a two-story building, either one or two bedroom, and include everything the authentic cabins have plus a separate living area, kitchenette, and cookware, glassware, and dishes. Choose from one queen bed, two queens, or a combination of queens and bunks. The Hitching Post is located a few blocks from the Town Square.

Inn on the Creek
295 North Millward St., Jackson
(307) 739-1565, (800) 669-9534
www.innonthecreek.com
$$$$

If it weren't for the small sign in the river-rocked front of this small hotel, you might think it's someone's house, especially because of its location on the more quiet, north side of town. Therefore, the Inn on the Creek is geared more toward couples looking for a romantic getaway than vacationing families. Each room features down comforters, TV and VCR, robes and slippers, queen beds, and breakfast served in your room. Deluxe rooms with Jacuzzis and rock fireplaces are also available, and there is an outdoor Jacuzzi for guests.

Intermountain Lodge
34 Ski Hill Rd., Driggs, ID
(208) 354-8153
$$

The Intermountain Lodge is a great place to stay if you're doing most of your skiing at Grand Targhee, as the lodge is located on the road from Driggs to the ski hill (hence the name of the road). All rooms have kitchenettes, queen beds, phones, and televisions, and there is a large outdoor hot tub to soak in after a day on the hill. The log cabin lodge also offers morning coffee and laundry facilities for guests.

Jackson Hole Resort Lodging
Teton Village, WY
(800) 443-6931
www.jhsnow.com
$$$

If you want to stay on the mountain at the Jackson Hole Mountain Resort, your best bet is to give Jackson Hole Central Reservations a call. Choose from a variety of properties represented by Jackson Hole Resort Lodging, including vacation homes, condominiums, and cabins. Vacation homes range from two to six bedrooms and you can get one with just about any amenity you want, including hot tubs and washer and dryers. Condo-miniums range from reasonably priced one and two bedroom units (Tensleep/Gros Ventre, Sleeping Indian, Nez Perce) to three and four-bedroom luxury (Moose Creek, Snowridge, Timber Ridge, Wind River). The new slope-side Granite Ridge Cabins offer two bedrooms, deck, hot tub, washer/dryer, and single car garage. By calling Jackson Hole Resort Lodging, you can also rent rooms at the Snow King Resort, Grand Targhee Ski and Summer Resort, the Jackson Hole Racquet Club, the Jackson Hole Lodge (downtown), and the Spring Creek Ranch.

Rendezvous Mountain Rentals
P.O. Box 11338, Jackson
(307) 739-9050, (888) 739-2565
www.rmrentals.com
$$$$

Named after the 10,450-foot summit of the Jackson Hole Mountain Resort, Rendezvous has rented budget to deluxe properties around the valley for nearly 30 years. Choose from cabins, vacation homes, and condominiums in Teton Village, Teton Pines, Granite Ridge, and the Aspens at the Jackson Hole Racquet Club.

Insiders' Tip

Brrrr! Jackson can be a cold place in the winter, so bring warm clothes. The average high temperature from November through March is 33 degrees, while the average low for that period is 10 degrees. Luckily, the sun shines often, at least making it feel a bit warmer on those chilly winter days.

Close-up

A Big 'Hole'

Is it Jackson or Jackson Hole? Well, the two are virtually interchangeable, but Jackson is the town and Jackson Hole is the valley. Why "hole?" Early fur traders referred to the high-country valleys of the West as holes, and usually named them after trappers who discovered or frequented them. This one was named after mountain man David Jackson in 1829.

Before that, the valley belonged to the Native Americans. Tribes such as the Crow, Blackfeet, Gros Ventres, and Nez Perce hunted the valley's elk and bison during the warm months of the year.

In the early 1800s, John Colter came to the area and began trading with the tribes at Fort Raymond, at the confluence of the Yellowstone and Bighorn Rivers. He stumbled into the Jackson valley and soon it was a major trapping spot for famous mountain men like Jim Bridger, Jedediah Smith, and Jackson. The boom was short-lived, however, as beaver hats went out of fashion and the fur trade died off by 1850. The valley would remain mostly deserted until government expeditions began mapping the area twenty years later.

The 1872 Hayden Survey was one of the first through the area. William H. Jackson, a member of the expedition team, took the first known photos of the Teton Range, and it didn't take long for the images to appear all over the world. In 1879, painter Thomas Moran put the peaks on canvas and went on to have one of the most beautiful summits in the Tetons named after him. By the mid-1880s, the first permanent settlers began arriving.

Some of the first families were the Wilsons, who founded the town at the bottom of the east side of Teton Pass, and the Driggs, who coined the town on the other side of the pass. Incidentally, that valley—now called Teton Valley or Basin—was originally called Pierre's Hole, named after Iroquois fur trader Pierre Tevanilagen. Other "holes" were Gardner's, Brown's, and Ogden's. Of course, only Jackson still retains its link to the past.

Rusty Parrot Lodge
175 N. Jackson St., Jackson
(307) 733-2000, (800) 458-2004
www.rustyparrot.com
$$$$

This beautiful, three-story log hotel is located just a short walk from downtown, and is one of Jackson's finest in-town hotels. The hotel houses the Body Sage Day Spa, one of the top day spas in the country, and the entire lodge has been featured in a diverse group of national publications, including *Travel & Leisure, Bon Appetit, In Style,* and *Gourmet.* The luxuriously appointed rooms feature handcrafted log furniture, goose-down comforters, terrycloth robes, and an oversized bath. Some rooms also have fireplaces and/or whirlpool baths. Breakfast—included in the price—is nothing short of incredible, with a changing menu that often features world-class dishes like Russian eggs Benedict with smoked trout, spinach, and caviar. Old favorites like French toast are also offered, as well as juices, fresh fruit, and homemade granola and pastries.

Snow King Resort
400 E. Snow King Ave., Jackson
(307) 733-5200, (800) 522-KING
www.snowking.com
$$$

Wyoming's first ski resort has 250 year-round guest rooms, suites, and condominiums for rent six blocks from downtown Jackson. Condominiums include one- to four-bedroom units. Rooms include coffee makers, 27-inch televisions, and queen beds, and guests can also enjoy the swimming pool and an outdoor hot tub. The Atrium restaurant serves breakfast, lunch, and dinner, and the Shady Lady Saloon has occasional live entertainment. Summer visitors can take advantage of Snow King's Alpine Slide—a wild ride, similar to a water slide without the water, where you control your own speed down the mountain through woods and wildflowers. And, of course, winter visitors can enjoy Snow King's 1,571 vertical feet of skiing and the area's only snow tubing park.

Teton Pines Resort
Teton Village Rd., Jackson
(307) 733-1005, (800) 238-2223
www.tetonpines.com
$$$$

This luxury property is located on the road to the Jackson Hole Mountain Resort and boasts amenities such as indoor tennis courts, cross-country skiing trails, health club, and a golf course. Condominium rooms include his and her bathrooms, microwave, wet bar, and more, while individual townhomes are even a step up from that. Each one has three bedrooms with a king size bed, three-and-a-half bathrooms, a full kitchen, washer/dryer, fireplace, two decks, and an attached, one-car garage. Some townhomes also feature a hot tub.

Teton West Best Western
476 N. Main St., Driggs, ID
(208) 354-2363, (800) 528-1234
$$$

Kids under 12 stay free at the Teton West, which offers 40 nicely decorated guest rooms with queen or king size beds, cable TV, and some with Jacuzzi baths. Hotel amenities include an indoor pool and hot tub and a free continental breakfast, and a conference room seats up to 50. It's located right on Idaho Highway 32, Driggs' main thoroughfare.

Insiders' Tip

When you hear people refer to the Teton Village road or the Moose-Wilson road, they're talking about the road north from Idaho Highway 22 near Wilson to Moose, inside the border of Grand Teton National Park. It's the main route to the ski area, but the stretch past Teton Village starting at the park boundary is closed in winter.

The Trapper Inn
235 N. Cache Dr., Jackson
(307) 733-2648, (800) 341-8000
$$

The Trapper is a great bang-for-the-buck hotel, offering nice rooms and a convenient location at a reasonable price. Located one block from the Town Square, the Trapper offers rooms with lodgepole furniture, cable TV, full baths, coffee makers, refrigerators and microwaves, and indoor and outdoor hot tubs.

The Virginian Lodge
750 W. Broadway Ave., Jackson
(307) 733-2792, (800) 262-4999
www.virginianlodge.com
$$

This large, single-story hotel is on the west end of town near the Albertson's shopping center and the turnoff to Teton Village. Nicely sized rooms look out over the Virginian's big courtyard, where an outdoor heated pool is flanked by a year-round, 15-person hot tub. Jacuzzi suites are available, too, if you don't want to walk outside for a soak. The Virginian also houses a restaurant, saloon, liquor store, and a convention center, as well as an RV Park with pull-thrus, cable TV, electric hook-ups, and a dump station.

Wagon Wheel Village
435 N. Cache St., Jackson
(307) 733-2357, (800) 323-9279
www.wagonwheelvillage.com
$$$

The Wagon Wheel offers 97 rooms of log construction, ranging from one bed to three beds in a two-bedroom suite. Some have a fireplace and jetted tub, and rooms with a fireplace, microwave, and mini-fridge are also available. Two outdoor hot tubs, a restaurant, the Log Cabin Saloon, a liquor store, and a laundromat are also on the property. Two daily shuttles to the ski areas are offered, as well as an airport courtesy shuttle.

The Wort Hotel
Broadway and Glenwood, Jackson
(307) 733-2190, (800) THEWORT
www.worthotel.com
$$$$

On the corner of Broadway and Glenwood in downtown Jackson stands the historic Wort, one of the town's landmark and most recognizable hotels. Named one of the "54 Great Inns of America" by *National Geographic Traveler* magazine, the three-story Wort stands out for its elegant, Swiss-chalet look—easy to pick out among Jackson's Western-style buildings. The adjacent Silver Dollar bar features nightly live entertainment and is a popular gathering spot for locals and visitors. The hotel's main restaurant serves excellent continental cuisine with a Western flair.

Guest Ranches and Lodges

Price Code

$	less than $85
$$	$86 to $115
$$$	$116 to $150
$$$$	$151 and more

Alta Lodge Bed and Breakfast
590 Targhee Towne Rd., Alta, WY
(307) 353-2582
www.pdt.net/altalodge
$

Innkeeper Susie Blair has four rooms to offer at the Alta Lodge, located just outside of Driggs, Idaho, and seven minutes from Grand Targhee Resort. The Grande Room features a queen bed and a trundle bed with a private bath. The King Room has a king bed with a private bath, while the Flower and Fish Rooms have queen beds with shared baths. Discounts are given for five- and seven-day stays, and all guests get a delicious, homemade breakfast. Huge, floor-to-ceiling windows offer breathtaking views of the Tetons, and all rooms have great views of the mountains or the beautiful Teton Valley.

Bentwood Bed and Breakfast
4250 Raven Haven Rd., Jackson
(307) 739-1411
www.bentwoodinn.com
$$$$

Bill and Nell Fay offer five rooms in their large log cabin bed and breakfast, nestled in three acres of stately cottonwood and pine trees and only a few casts away from the Snake River. The 5,800 square-foot home was built in 1995, utilizing many logs salvaged from the Yellowstone fires of 1988. Every nook of the Bentwood is impressive, from the slate entry and the three-story living area to the thirty-foot floor-to-ceiling river rock fireplace. A cozy library is stocked with classics and best sellers and a baby grand piano awaits the musical guest. Four of the rooms have Jacuzzi tubs, and each is decorated

As many as 10,000 elk migrate to the National Elk Refuge just north of Jackson. PHOTO: JACKSON HOLE
CHAMBER OF COMMERCE

in its own unique style. All rooms are exquisitely furnished, and Nell's home-made breakfasts and baked goods will roust you out of bed each morning. The Bentwood is located between Teton Village and Jackson, six miles from the ski resort. Rates here are based on double occupancy, with a $50 fee for each additional person, and the Bentwood is a nonsmoking establishment.

Boulder Lake Lodge
P.O. Box 1100, Pinedale, WY
(307) 537-5400, (800) 788-5401
www.boulderlake.com
$$$$

Nestled in the foothills of the Bridger-Teton National Forest and surrounded by the Wind River Mountains is the Boulder Lake Lodge, where families have enjoyed true dude ranch vacations for generations. Part of an original, early 1900s ranch homestead, Boulder Lake features modern guest rooms with a private bath. A main lodge offers opportunity for visiting and relaxation in front of a huge fireplace, and ranch-style meals are served three times a day. Nearby activities include fishing, hiking, horseback riding, and hunting. Guided trips are available.

The Sassy Moose Inn
3859 Miles Rd., Jackson
(307) 733-1277, (800) 356-1277
www.sassymoosejacksonhole.com
$$$

All six rooms in the Sassy Moose have outstanding views of the Tetons, just part of the charm of this bed and breakfast located just minutes from the ski resort. And when you're done skiing, you can relax in the indoor hot tub surrounded by picture windows, or hit the hay under the comfy down comforters. All rooms also have cathedral ceilings, private baths, and bathrobes, and some have fireplaces. Rates at the Sassy Moose peak from June to September, while the low seasons—April and November—find prices nearly cut in half. There's no smoking at the inn, and additional adults are $15 per day. Children under 11 stay free.

Spring Creek Ranch
1800 Spirit Dance Rd., Jackson
(307) 733-8833, (800) 443-6139
www.springcreekranch.com
$$$$

A variety of lodging options—all with dynamite views of the Tetons—are available at this beautiful ranch, located a few

Insiders' Tip

Fall around the Jackson Hole Valley is a quiet and peaceful time, and can be a more relaxing and less expensive time to visit. Most lodging is discounted during the shoulder seasons—the time between the end of one tourist season and the beginning of the next--and you can find well-appointed rooms at a reasonable rate. The streets and trails will also be less crowded, and chances are you'll get to see the first snow of the season dust the high peaks of the Tetons and surrounding mountains. If you do visit in the fall, remember that some park services close in early October. Call Grand Teton National Park, (307) 739-3399, for information.

miles outside of and 1,000 feet above Jackson. Hotel-style rooms offer one king or two queen beds, wood burning fireplace, balcony, coffee maker, mini-fridge, cable TV, and full bath. Studios are one large room with a complete kitchen, sleeping area, fireplace, and sunken living room, with a queen wall bed and queen sofa bed. Sitting suites offer a living room and a bedroom with a connecting bath, while suites with two bedrooms are also available. You can also rent condominiums, which have one, two, or three bedrooms in a variety of configurations. All condos have fireplaces, full kitchens, and balconies. And if you need even more room, Spring Creek has several 4,500 to 6,000 square-foot executive homes for rent. The renowned Granary restaurant and the Rising Sage Café offer lots of dining options for guests, and golf and skiing are just two of the activities just out your door.

The Wildflower Inn
3725 Teton Village Rd., Jackson
(307) 733-4710
www.jacksonholewildflower.com
$$$$

The cozy log cabin confines of The Wildflower Inn have won accolades from magazines like *Sunset, Bon Appetit,* and *Glamour,* and have placed the inn on numerous "Best of" lists. Owners Sherrie and Ken built the Wildflower in 1989, and have five elegant and tastefully decorated rooms for rent, each with handcrafted log beds, down comforters, pedestal sinks, private baths, and beautiful country views. Each room is decorated with its own unique style, and all but one feature a private balcony. The highlight of the inn may be the incredible solarium, complete with a big hot tub and massive hanging plants. Rates range from $160 to $320, depending on the season, and children are welcome.

Campgrounds and RV Parks

Price Code

$ . . . . $10 to $16
$$ . . . . $17 to $23
$$$ . . . . $24 and more

Elk Country Inn and RV Park
480 W. Pearl St., Jackson
(307) 733-2364
$$

This downtown park offers ten RV sites with hook-ups, dump station, restrooms, showers, picnic tables, grills, and drinking water. There are no tent sites here, but the location makes it easy to walk around downtown. The park is open from May 1 to October 1.

Grand Teton Park RV Resort and Cabins
One mile east of Grand Teton Park
(307) 543-2483, (800) 563-6469
$$$$

The closest year-round park is the Grand Teton, which offers 120 RV sites at its location just east of Moran. Full services, including a pool, recreation room, and laundry are offered. Sixty tent sites are offered during the summer.

Lazy J Corral
U.S. Hwy. 89, Hoback
(307) 733-1554
$$$

You'll find this 24-site RV Park 13 miles south of Jackson on the road toward Hoback Junction. The park offers full services, including a recreation room and a pool, but doesn't have any tent sites. The Lazy J is open from May 1 to October 1.

Snake River Park KOA
U.S. Hwy. 89, Jackson
(307) 733-7078, (800) 562-1878
$$$$

This KOA is open from April 12 to October 6 and has 50 RV sites and 30 tent sites. This KOA has no pull-thrus, but you'll find all other services. Snake River Park is south of Jackson on U.S. Highway 89. The nearby Teton Village KOA, five miles west of Jackson on Wyoming Highway 22, offers 150 sites from the beginning of May to October 12. You can reach that KOA by calling (307) 733-5354.

Teton Valley Campground
128 Hwy. 31, Victor, Idaho
(208) 787-2647, (877) 787-3036
$$$–$$$$

Teton Valley has four cabins and 75 RV spaces at its location on the west side of Teton Pass, just south of Driggs and about an hour from Jackson. Pets are allowed here, and the campground has hook-ups, laundry, dump station, showers, pull-through sites, playground, modem hookups, and a swimming pool.

Insiders' Tip

If you're pitching a tent while staying in the area, the earliest campground to open is the Snake River KOA, around April 12. Outlying state and federal campgrounds generally open around June 15, but Colter Bay and Jenny Lake inside the park open a month earlier. Most every campground is closed by the end of October—right before the winter chill.

Restaurants

Price Code

Includes the price of meals for two people, excluding beverages, tip, and tax

$	$10 to $19
$$	$20 to $27
$$$	$28 to $35
$$$$	$36 and more

The Acadian House
180 North Millward St., Jackson
(307) 739-1269
$$

The Acadian dishes up authentic and reasonably priced Cajun cuisine for dinner seven days a week. The menu offers more than 30 selections, from steaks and seafood to catfish, crawfish, and gumbo. Catfish Acadian—blackened with a crawfish étouffée—is the most popular dish. Other recommendations include the Snapper Louisane, the Creole chicken, and the Halibut Orleans, and the Louisiana Alligator appetizer for those wanting something different. All entrees are served with your choice of a house salad or seafood gumbo, vegetable, and starch. Out of all the great items at the Acadian House, the last one you try may be its most famous. The Louisiana Bread Pudding is the only dessert offered, and it only takes one taste to see why. The Acadian House accepts reservations.

The Alpenhof
Teton Village
(307) 733-3462
$$–$$$$

The Alpenhof—at the base of Jackson Hole Mountain Resort—is actually comprised of two great restaurants under one roof. In the main dining room you'll find fantastic regional cuisine, while the bistro, (307) 733-3242, serves lighter gourmet fare. The dining room specializes in game dishes, such as the venison and caribou for two, the Caribou Roulade, venison loin, and medallions of antelope. Vegetarians will love the Mediterranean Timbale, and seafood lovers should try the bouillabaisse. Prices range from $17 to $30 per plate. In the bistro, you'll find smoked duck rolls, grilled portabello mushrooms, salmon pasta, rainbow trout, and grilled honey lime chicken. It's a popular aprés ski spot to grab a drink and an appetizer, and sports a sun deck for those bluebird days. Prices at the bistro top out at around $16, but most items are less. The dining room advises you to make reservations.

The Back Door Deli
410 W. Pearl St., Jackson
(307) 733-3354
$

Need a good sandwich? Well, the Back Door stocks more than 75 domestic and imported meats and cheeses and boasts a whopping 36 choices on the menu. No fast food here, though, as selections include corned beef, pastrami, turkey, prosciutto, salami, and more, served atop cheeses like jarlsberg, gruyere, mortadella, and muenster. If you don't care for the gourmet cheeses, the folks at the Back Door will be happy to whip up any combination you choose, and a full vegetarian menu is offered as well. For the little ones, there's also peanut butter and jelly and kid-sized ham and turkey sandwiches.

The Back Door offers in-town delivery, too. Summer hours are 8 A.M. to 6 P.M. Monday through Friday, and 9 A.M. to 5 P.M. on Saturday. In winter, the hours are 9 A.M. to 7:30 P.M. Monday through Friday, and 10 A.M. to 6 P.M. on Saturday.

Bagel Jax
145 N. Glenwood, Jackson
(307) 733-9148
$

Choose from more than 15 varieties of bagels and seven different cream cheeses at Bagel Jax, where you can also get specialty sandwiches for lunch. Bagel choices include delicious oddities like chocolate chip, apple streusel, and asiago cheese, and you can top them off with cream cheeses like honey maple pecan, tangerine almond, or strawberry. Sandwich selections include turkey avocado, Mediterranean, veggie, and honey cured ham. A baker's dozen of bagels runs under $7, and there isn't a sandwich over $4.

The Blue Lion
160 North Millward St., Jackson
(307) 733-3912
$$$

This quaint little restaurant is one of Jackson's more popular eateries, due to its casual, bistro-like atmosphere, outstanding Continental cuisine, and summer patio dining. The menu offers something for everyone, including exquisite pastas, creative vegetarian, fresh seafood, and hearty beef and game dishes. The signature dish here is the roast rack of New Zealand lamb, but don't hesitate to try the Thai Shrimp Linguine, Rocky Mountain trout filets, or the asparagus and sundried tomato risotto. In fact, it takes an extra long time to decide on what to eat here, as literally every item on the menu is tantalizing. Dinners come with a nicely sized salad and delicious bread, but save room for dessert. Any one of the nightly specials is worth it. In the summer, the patio provides an outside meal away from the hustle and bustle of the town center, as the Blue Lion is located a few blocks north of busy Broadway Avenue, Jack-

Watching the sun rise on the Grand Tetons is one of the benefits of visiting the Jackson area. PHOTO: JACKSON HOLE CHAMBER OF COMMERCE

son's main street. An extensive, affordable wine list and a friendly staff ensure the meal will leave a lasting impression. The Blue Lion has an early bird special—twenty percent of your bill from 6 to 6:30 P.M. with a coupon found each week in the *Jackson Hole Guide*. The Blue Lion serves dinner only and strongly recommends reservations.

Bubba's Bar-B-Que
515 W. Broadway Ave., Jackson
(307) 733-2288
$$

Bubba's is Jackson's place for all things barbecue—chicken, ribs, turkey, and steak. Ribs are slow smoked over a hickory fire and then finished on the char-broiler with Bubba's secret sauce. Dinner plates are served barbecue style, with garlic toast and your choice of two of the following: French fries, cole slaw, potato salad, corn on the cob, and beans. You get the same choices with your lunch, which features numerous reasonably priced specials, as well as a big bowl of beans and franks. If you're not in the mood for barbecue, choose from fish and chips, shrimp, and chili. Bubba's is also open for breakfast, beginning at 7 A.M. seven days a week.

Anthony's Italian Restaurant
62 S. Glenwood St., Jackson
(307) 733-3717
$$

Bring a healthy appetite to Anthony's and plan on leaving stuffed. From traditional noodle and sauce combinations to a variety of meat and seafood selections, Anthony's features nearly 30 choices, and the children's menu makes it a great place to bring the family. If you like it spicy, try the Cajun fettuccine, and vegetable lovers can try the lasagna verde. There's a good selection of antipasto and appetizers and cocktails, beer, and wine. All dinners come with soup, salad, and garlic bread, which means you just may have enough for lunch tomorrow. Anthony's only serves dinner and accepts reservations.

Betty Rock Café
325 W. Pearl St., Jackson
(307) 733-0747
$

The Betty Rock serves great breakfasts, lunches, and dinners Monday through Friday, 7 A.M. to 9 P.M., and on Saturday from 7 A.M. to 4 P.M. Get bagels, coffee, and more in the morning, and salads, sandwiches, pizza, and paninis for lunch and dinner. The café also boasts home-made breads, soups, desserts, fruit smoothies, and a full espresso bar.

The Bunnery
130 N. Cache St., Jackson
(307) 733-5474
$

Breakfast at the Bunnery is a Jackson Hole tradition, and the secret has been let out. In the morning, you'll often see a line extending out the door with people wait-ing to get a taste of fresh-baked breads and pastries, gourmet omelets, and whole grain pancakes and waffles, which is just a sampling of the extensive menu. The wait is worth it, of course, and selections like the Bunnery Benedict, the Glory Bowl, and the Mother Earth will give you plenty of energy for a day on the trail or the slopes. The croissants, sticky buns, and buttermilk coffeecakes make great grab-and-go meals, and fresh juices and espresso are also available. The Bunnery also serves up creative sandwiches, burri-tos, and veggie specialties for lunch, and is open for dinner in the summer.

The Cadillac
55 N. Cache St., Jackson
(307) 733-3279
$$$

From the outside, the Cadillac looks like an unassuming 1950s-era diner, with a lively atmosphere not fit for a typical fine dining experience. And that's just the restaurant's point—you don't have to appear stuffy to serve renowned cuisine. Dining should be a fun experience, and the Cadillac makes sure of it. Selections include Black Angus blue cheese tourne-dos, hazelnut crusted rack of lamb, pan-seared duck, and flame-kissed Atlantic salmon. The menu changes frequently, and the restaurant features an award-winning wine list. The Cadillac suggests reservations.

The Granary
1800 Spirit Dance Rd., Jackson
(307) 733-8833
www.springcreekranch.com
$$$$

It's hard to concentrate on the food at the Granary, located in the Spring Creek Ranch, which sits atop the Gros Ventre Butte and directly in line with one of the best views you'll ever see when sitting at a table. Picture windows frame the Tetons in the distance, while up close you'll be looking at dinner entrees like roast ten-derloin of elk, seared muscovy duck breast, roast rack of Colorado lamb, and garlic sesame encrusted rainbow trout. The Granary also serves lunch, with selec-tions including elk flank fajitas, an ahi tuna sandwich and a portabello mush-room sandwich. The pastry chef also offers a mouthwatering selection of pas-tries and desserts. Reservations are sug-gested for dinner.

The Gun Barrel Steakhouse
862 W. Broadway Ave., Jackson
(307) 733-3287
www.gunbarrel.com
$$$$

The Gun Barrel serves up steak just the way you like it—from traditional cuts like tenderloin, New York, sirloin, and ribeye to game meats such as elk, bison, and caribou. Meats are grilled over mesquite wood imported from Texas, and game cooked over medium rare is discouraged. Roosevelt's Prime Rib—a 10-, 14-, or 20-ounce steak rubbed in lodge seasonings, slow roasted, and served with grated horseradish—is the house specialty. You'll also find baby back ribs, rainbow trout, salmon, and chicken on the menu, as well as a tremendous selection of wine, draft beer, and single malt scotches and bour-bons. And if you have room, the deep-dish apple pie—served warm, of course—is a great way to give yourself a happy ending. Reservations at the Gun Barrel are advised.

Harvest Bakery and Café
130 W. Broadway Ave., Jackson
(307) 733-5418
$

Everything is organic at the Harvest, a natural food lover and vegetarian's delight. Breakfast, lunch, and dinner are served, and there is also a complete retail health store. Choose from selections like chickpea lentil dahl and vegetarian chili for lunch, while early morning eaters can order blue corn pancakes, slow-cooked whole grain cereal, Belgian waffles, and challah French toast. There is also an espresso bar, a smoothie station, and several excellent desserts. Summer hours at the Harvest are 7 A.M. to 8 P.M. daily, and in the winter you'll find the café open daily from 8 A.M. to 6 P.M.

Insiders' Tip

The Teton Public Library has many events for kids, including preschool storytime every Thursday from 10:30 A.M. until 11 A.M. Monthly events like a journal making class and a teen snow sculpture contest are popular for older kids, and the library also hosts art and photography exhibits on a regular basis. The library is located on 125 Virginia Lane, and you can check the schedule by calling (307) 733-2164.

Jedediah's House of Sourdough
135 E. Broadway Ave., Jackson
(307) 733-5671
$$$

Jedediah's serves up great pioneer sourdough cookin' in a historic log cabin decorated with memorabilia and old photographs. You can start your morning in Jackson here, choosing from selections like Teton taters and eggs, sourdough flapjacks, and a variety of omelets. The early riser special, served from 7 A.M. to 9 A.M., is one of the best deals in the valley. You get two eggs, meat, homefries, and all the biscuits and gravy or flapjacks you can eat for under $5. Lunch and dinner menus (summer only) include everything from buffalo burgers to steaks and seafood. No beer or wine here, but the folks at Jedediah's will be happy to provide the glasses and a corkscrew if you bring your own.

The Lame Duck
680 E. Broadway Ave., Jackson
(307) 733-4311
$$

The Lame Duck dishes out above-average Chinese food, from traditional dishes like Kung Pao chicken and pad Thai to original selections such as Thai ginger scallops and red curry prawns. A Jackson favorite for more than 20 years, the Lame Duck also offers a full sushi bar, soups, and appetizers. You can enjoy super mai-tais and hot sake with your meal, as well as a big selection of beer and wine. Dinner is served nightly from 5 P.M., and take-out is available.

Mike's Eats
10 N. Main St., Driggs, ID
(208) 354-2797
$

If you're staying in or passing through Driggs during the summer, a meal at Mike's is a must. The brick-built restaurant is an old-fashioned fifties-style diner, featuring Idaho-raised Buffalo specialties like the Buffalo Dog, the Buffalo Burger, Buffalo Chili, and Buffalo Meatloaf. Many people come in just for the giant stuffed Idaho spuds. Mike's opens for the season on Memorial Day, and serves breakfast, lunch, and dinner. Hours are 7 A.M. to 8 P.M. Monday–Saturday, and 7 A.M. to 2:30 P.M. Sunday. If you're having trouble finding it, just look for the gigantic buffalo on the roof—you can't miss it.

Million Dollar Cowboy Steakhouse
25 N. Cache St., Jackson
(307) 733-4790
www.milliondollarcowboybar.com
$$$

The Million Dollar Cowboy is one of Jackson's most recognizable establishments—a big, flashy sign and lots of Harleys parked out front. Inside, the bar stools are saddles and the atmosphere is Western, right down to the Remington and Russell prints on the walls. The food here is Western, too, with juicy hand-cut steaks, fresh seafood, and wild game. You can get just about any cut of steak you want, and finish off your meal with a homemade dessert. The full bar also features more than two dozen single malt scotches. Dinner reservations are recommended.

Mountain High Pizza Pie
120 W. Broadway Ave., Jackson
(307) 733-3646
$

Mountain High serves up some of Jackson's best pizza, available in traditional, whole wheat, and deep-dish crusts with a variety of fresh toppings. Choose from traditional, tomato-based pizzas or number of specialty pies, including the Santa Fe, Thai pie, sunny chicken pesto, and barbecue chicken. You'll also find huge calzones, subs, salads, and appetizers. Mountain High is open daily until 10 P.M. in the winter, midnight during the summer. Beer, wine, and delivery are available.

Otto Brothers Brew Pub
1295 N. West St., Wilson
(307) 733-9000
www.ottobrothers.com
$

Otto Brothers—the region's oldest brewery and makers of fine beers like Teton Ale and Moose Juice Stout—serves up awesome brick oven pizzas, and hand-tossed calzones. Specialty pizzas include Coal Creek—mozzarella, tomatoes, artichoke hearts, black olives, and feta on a garlic and oil sauce—and the Edelweiss, made with pepperoni, Canadian bacon, sausage, mushroom, and onions. The calzones are huge, and salads and bread sticks are also available. There is also an Otto Brothers on the east side of Teton Pass in Victor, Idaho, just off the side of the highway, (208) 787-9000.

Pearl Street Bagels
Jackson and Wilson
$

Pearl Street has two locations to fix your early morning need for a good bagel. Downtown, head to 145 W. Pearl, (307) 739-1218, and in Wilson you'll find Pearl Street right on Wyoming Highway 22 at the bottom of the pass, (307) 739-1261. Both locations have several varieties of bagels to choose from, as well as sandwiches and coffee to go.

The Range
225 N. Cache St., Jackson
(307) 733-5481
$$$$

Chef Arthur Leech's fare—Continental with a regional flare—has been featured in *Gourmet, Town & Country*, and the *Wine Spectator*, so it's no wonder that this small downtown restaurant is one of Jackson's most popular fine dining establishments. Entrees include goose and foie gras ravioli, filet mignon, elk medallions, duck, trout, and salmon. Game lovers should try the homemade wild game sausages, served with a champagne onion sauce and cognac-hazelnut mashed potatoes. For starters, try the tempera-battered softshell crab or the crispy vegetable spring rolls, and the big salads are meals themselves. The menu changes seasonally at the Range, and there are always nightly fish and game specials. Reservations are appreciated.

Restaurant Terroir
45 S. Glenwood St., Jackson
(307) 739-2500
$$$$

Restaurant Terroir—one of the newer fine dining experiences in Jackson—features French bistro fare with international influences. Head chef Scott Sampson came to Jackson from Las Vegas after cooking at the celebrated Andre's for five years, and his nightly menu features the finest steaks, seafood, and pasta. Seasonal selections you're likely to find are Terroir fish stew, half rack of lamb, Black Angus ribeye, and penne rigate. The wine list is one of the largest in the area, with more than 200 choices stored in a temperature-controlled custom cellar. The cuisine has received accolades from *The New York Times, Food & Wine, USA Today, Wine Spectator*, and many others. Reservations are strongly recommended.

The Silver Dollar Bar and Grille
Broadway and Glenwood, Jackson
(307) 732-3939
$

Located on the first floor of the historic Wort Hotel, the Silver Dollar serves up big sandwiches and tasty appetizers in the bar, and more elaborate fare in the main dining room. The bar is a popular spot to grab a reasonably priced meal, such as a burger, chicken sandwich, or wings or nachos. Dining room entrees include prime rib, trout, elk chops, and chicken pesto primavera. Live entertainment is featured nightly in the bar, making the Silver Dollar a choice après ski destination and a nightlife hotspot.

Snake River Brewing Co.
265 South Millward St., Jackson
(307) 739-2337
$$

If you like a good brew with your meal, there aren't many places better than the Snake River Brewery. Its award winning English-style ales, porters, stouts and European lagers are made on the premises and go perfectly with the variety of pastas, sandwiches, and pizzas served in the restaurant. The pizza, baked in a wood-fired oven, is the most popular and just the right size for one with a hearty appetite, or for two who don't want to stuff themselves. If you don't want to eat a full dinner, the brewery is a great place to hang out, munch on some appetizers, and taste the fine, handcrafted beers. A popular spot with many of the younger locals, the brewery is open daily until midnight.

Snake River Grill
84 E. Broadway Ave., Jackson
(307) 733-0557
$$$$

Make reservations if you want to eat the Snake River Grill, one of Jackson's most popular and well-known restaurants. Located across from the Town Square, the restaurant features a variety of fresh fish, free-range veal and chicken, wood-fired pizza, and wild game. Selections you're apt to find on the menu include Chilean sea bass, grilled ahi tuna, venison chops, braised antelope, fresh Idaho trout, and fettuccine with grilled chicken. The wine list continues to be praised by *Wine Spectator* for its more than 200 selections, and outside dining is available in the summer. The Snake River Grill serves dinner nightly from 6 P.M.

Vista Grande
Teton Village Rd., Jackson
(307) 733-6964
$$

Vista Grande has dished out delicious Mexican dinners for more than 20 years. The fajitas are the house specialty, and you can choose from steak, chicken, or shrimp served on a sizzling platter with onions and green peppers. There are numerous seafood selections, including crab rellenos, fish tacos, crab enchiladas, and the Acapulco seafood platter. You'll find all the traditional items here, too, like burritos, chimichangas, enchiladas, and tacos. If you're not feeling like Mexican, there are steaks, burgers, and sandwiches to choose from. Vista Grande is open at 5 P.M. daily, and asks that you make reservations if your party numbers more than eight. You'll find the restaurant on the Teton Village road on your way to the ski resort.

Nightlife

There's a lot to do after the sun sets in Jackson, and both summer and winter have vibrant nightlife scenes. A night on the town wouldn't be complete without a stop in at the legendary **Million Dollar Cowboy Bar**, (307) 733-4790, directly across from the Town Square. With saddle-shaped bar stools and Thursday night swing dance lessons—and a lot of cowboy hats—the Cowboy Bar is a true Western experience.

    The Mangy Moose, (307) 733-9779, found at the base of the ski resort in Teton Village, is the most popular bar for live music and features local and national acts. The walls and ceilings of the bar are covered in Jackson Hole memorabilia—looking is entertainment in itself—and the Mangy Moose is the ski resort's most celebrated après ski spot. For live music in town, also check out the **Silver Dollar Bar**, (307) 732-3239, in the Wort Hotel, **Sidewinders**, (307) 734-5766, and the **Shady Lady Saloon** at Snow King Resort, (307) 733-5200, which features live music on Wednesdays. **Teton Pines**, (307) 733-1005, and the **Granary Lounge** at Spring Creek Ranch, (307) 733-8833, feature live pianists several nights a week. If you want to drive a little bit, the **Bull Moose Saloon**, (307) 654-7593, in Alpine and **Dornan's** in Moose (307) 733-2415, feature local and national bands on a regular basis. The **Snake River Pub and Brewery**, (307) 739-2337, is a mellow hot spot for the younger crowd.

    The Performing Arts Company of Jackson Hole puts on numerous productions throughout the year in the Pink Garter Mainstage Theater, (307) 733-9787. **The Jackson Hole Playhouse**, (307) 733-6994, does a dinner and theater combination in the tradition of the old Western playhouse, which usually makes for a side-splitting evening of raucous entertainment.

    Sports fans may want to check out the **Jackson Hole Moose**, a Senior A hockey team that plays at the Snow King Center several times per month. Call (307) 733-5200 for information.

Shopping

Shopping is what many people come to Jackson for. For a small town, it has a remarkable number of galleries, boutiques, clothiers, and specialty shops. The list below includes only a few of the more well known shops, but contains only a fraction Jackson's shopping options. It also doesn't include art galleries or clothing stores—you could write a book just on those—concentrating instead on specialty stores you may have trouble finding. Jackson is the kind of place where you really need to just start walking around downtown. There will be several neat shops around every corner you turn, and hardcore shoppers can spend a lot of time looking around.

Broadway Bottle
200 W. Broadway Ave., Jackson
(307) 739-WINE

You can get beer, liquor, and wine at this shop on the corner of Millward and Broadway, two blocks from the Town Square. You'll find a large selection of regional microbrews and fine wines to choose from, as well as an array of spirits and liquors.

Ski Shops

Jackson Hole may just have the most ski shops per capita of anywhere in the world—too many to list in this guide. But to give you an Insiders' peek, here's a few of the best: Skinny Skis (65 W. Delaney, (307) 733-6094) is your cross-country and backcountry touring headquarters, offering top-of-the-line gear and accessories, as well as rentals and demos. Wilson Backcountry Sports (1230 Ida Drive, (307) 733-5228) offers sales and rentals of telemark, randonne, cross-country, and snowshoe equipment, as well as advice and tips on where to go. Hoback Sports (40 S. Millward St., (307) 733-5335) features demo and high performance rentals, snowboards, clothing, and a repair shop, while the Edge (490 W. Broadway Ave., (307) 734-3916) offers beginner to advanced ski sales, ski demos from Atomic, Stockli, and Dynastar, and a Wintersteiger-equipped tuning center. In Teton Village, Wildernest Sports, (307) 733-4297, has one of the largest rental shops in the valley, including kids' and high performance gear, as well as Burton snowboard rentals and an overnight repair service. Teton Village Sports, (307) 733-2181, also has a high performance demo ski center, featuring equipment from Rossignol, Volkl, Salomon, Tecnica, Marker, and more. And it's worth a drive to Driggs to stop in and say hello to the friendly staff at Yöstmark Mountain Equipment (12 E. Little Avenue, (208) 354-2828) where Clair Yöst has been making and selling his legendary Mountain Noodle telemark ski since 1990. You'll find a huge selection of backcountry gear here, as well as snowboards and clothing, and a knowledgeable group of employees full of Insiders' tips on favorite places to go.

Cayuse
255 N. Glenwood St., Jackson
(307) 739-1940
www.cayusewa.com

If you're looking for Old West artifacts, Cayuse is your best bet. The shop specializes in antique Western art and artifacts, early lodge furnishings, and National Park memorabilia, as well as early Jackson and Yellowstone material. Cayuse also features the contemporary buckles of Clint Orms Silversmiths and Engravers.

D.D. Camera Corral
60 S. Cache St., Jackson
(307) 733-3831

This Jackson shop has served locals and visitors for more than 40 years. You'll find all major brands of film and equipment here, as well as two-hour photo finishing and five-minute color enlargements. Also, if you want a recorded memoir of your vacation, the Camera Corral offers camcorder and camera rentals.

Fish Creek Center
WY Hwy. 22, Willson

Coming to Jackson, you'll pass by this little shopping center on the south side of the highway. You'll find Pearl Street Bagels (307) 739-1261, which offers coffee, bagels, and sandwiches, and Willson Backcountry Sports (307) 733-5228, which has everything you need for safe and effective travel in the outdoors. The center is also home to Prime Properties and Fish Creek Construction Services.

Hole in the Wall Snowboard Shop
Teton Village
(307) 739-2689

One of Jackson's original snowboard shops, Hole in the Wall offers sales, demos, tuning, and clothing in its location at the base of the Bridger Gondola at the Jackson Hole Mountain Resort. The shop is open from 8 A.M. to 6 P.M. daily, and carries gear by Lib Tech, Salomon, Burton, K2, Roxy, Bonfire, DaKine, and more. If you want your ride back in a hurry, Hole in the Wall will tune or repair it overnight.

Jackson Hole Chamber of Commerce
990 W. Broadway Ave., Jackson
(307) 733-3316
www.jhchamber.com

Shopping at the Chamber? Well, not exactly. But if you're looking for the highly sought after posters from past and present Old West Days and Fall Arts Festivals, this is the place. Stop in to see the selection of posters available.

Jackson Hole Resort Store
50 N. Center St., Jackson
(307) 739-2767

If you don't ski or can't make it up to Teton Village, stop in at the downtown location of the Jackson Hole Resort Store, where you'll find a full selection of T-shirts, hats, clothing, and gifts bearing the resort's trademark logo. You can also buy winter lift tickets and summer tram ride tickets at the store, located on the east side of the Town Square.

Mountunes
265 W. Broadway Ave., Jackson
(307) 733-4514, (800) 982-2241
www.mountunes.com

Mountunes is Jackson's only full-service store for CDs, cassettes, and accessories. You'll find a great selection of music, from rock and reggae to country and classical. There's also a large section of regional and local artists, and Mountunes sells concert tickets for upcoming shows around the valley.

Tobacco Row
120 N. Cache St., Jackson
(307) 733-4385

You'll find the largest selection of cigars, cigarettes, and pipe and rolling tobaccos in the area at Tobacco Row, which also features handmade humidors and smoking accessories. In addition to tobacco products, there is also a nice selection of fine, locally roasted coffee. Tobacco Row opens at 10 A.M. daily.

The streets of West Yellowstone are lined with Western charm. PHOTO: DONNIE SEXTON/TRAVEL MONTANA

West Yellowstone

Accommodations
Restaurants
Nightlife
Shopping

West Yellowstone, or "West" as the locals call it, is a town that thrives on tourism associated with Yellowstone National Park. Perhaps more than any other gateway town, West depends on the influx of visitors during the summer and winter to fuel its economy, and it's been this way for nearly 100 years.

The town sprang up in 1908 when Union Pacific's Oregon Short Line brought the first trainload of passengers into the area. The train came south from Ashton, Idaho, over Targhee Pass to the West Entrance of the park, where visitors could enter the park on stagecoaches. Before that, the only way down to the west entrance was by horse or foot from Bozeman or Virginia City—a trip only a few hearty travelers made each year.

The Oregon Short Line would serve West Yellowstone for 52 years, but the introduction of the automobile signaled the railroad's end. Cars were allowed into the park for the first time in 1915, when they shared the road with stagecoaches (although that didn't last long). The following year one of the largest stagecoach companies called it quits, and more and more private cars were driving on the park's roads. In fact, the traffic was so great that most of the park's infrastructure had to be rebuilt. Since the mid 1930s when the roads were paved, West Yellowstone has attracted tourists from around the world.

Millions of tourists arrive in West every year, entering the park by car, snowcoach, or snowmobile. The town is still the starting point for many family vacations, and in the summer and winter it is bustling seven days a week. With this many visitors, the town has grown to accommodate them. Numerous hotels, restaurants, shops, galleries, and attractions make it a great spot for people to stay and enjoy the wonders of park and the surrounding area.

Not surprisingly, the local population is driven by the service industry. From snowmobile rental shops to pancake houses, gas stations to museums, and fly fishing shops to rafting companies, chances are that if you live here you're associated with something that serves visitors. Just under 1,000 people call West home year round and find it an exciting mix of commerce, recreation, and natural beauty. Centrally located between Bozeman and Jackson, West is not only great for tourists, but locals also flock here to enjoy the millions of acres of National Forests and hundreds of miles of trails and waterways to enjoy. And when West quiets down during the shoulder seasons, it is a peaceful, beautiful place to call home.

The difference between summer and winter in West basically comes down to one thing: snowmobiles. Chances are you've never seen anything like it. Snowmobiles buzz around town on the snow-covered roads, hopping from motel to restaurant and into the park. Trails start in the middle of town and head into the woods, giving snowmobilers instant access to unmatched terrain, scenery, and fun.

Snowmobiling in West will change, as the Clinton administration and the National Park Service have enacted a ban on snowmobiling in Yellowstone and Grand Teton National Parks, scheduled to take effect in the winter of 2003–04. This controversial issue has divided the town. Some say the ban will cause businesses to close up shop. After all, snowmobilers are a big part of the town's economy, and why would they come here if the park is off limits? Others argue that numbers will drop only slightly and that West's other attractions will keep visitors coming—just as they always have. It will still be one of the premier cross-country skiing destinations in the world, and people will still have the opportunity to enter the park on snowcoaches or snowvans. In addition, there are 580 miles of snowmobile trails around West Yellowstone, and only 180 of them are in the park. There will still be plenty of powder to go around.

Whatever happens, one thing will remain certain: West Yellowstone will always be a place people come to because of Yellowstone.

Just outside of West Yellowstone you'll find the communities of Ennis, Montana, and Island Park, Idaho, which will be included in this chapter. Refer to the map at the beginning of the book on their locations.

Accommodations

Hotels

Hotel Rates

Keep in mind that some rates are based on availability. This code indicates the average nightly rates for two adults. The hotels and motels in this chapter accept all or most major credit cards, unless otherwise noted in the listing.

$ . . . . $70 or less
$$ . . . . $71 to $90
$$$ . . . . $91 to $110
$$$$ . . . . $111 and more

Best Western Executive Inn
236 Dunraven St., West Yellowstone
59758
(406) 646-7681, (877) GEYSERS
$$$

There are four Best Westerns in West, but the 82-room Executive is the largest and the only one with an attached restaurant, a Western-style dining hall that serves breakfast, lunch, and dinner. There's an exercise room, outdoor pool, and a hot tub, and pets are allowed. The Executive also offers winter packages including snowmobile rentals.

Big Western Pine Lodge
234 Firehole Ave., West Yellowstone
(406) 646-7622, (800) 646-7622
www.wyellowstone.com/bigwesternpine
$$

This centrally located hotel offers just about everything you will need during your stay. Forty-five rooms feature new carpeting and furniture, cable television, and tub/showers. The three-bedroom, two-bath cottage is great for large parties and snowmobilers, and features a full kitchen, living room, laundry room, wood burning stove, hardwood floors, and maid service. There is also a cabin that sleeps 20, with two kitchens, two baths, and two televisions. The outdoor heated pool is only open during the summer, but a large hot tub and sauna is relaxing enough after a cold day of trail riding. The attached Rustler's Roost restaurant offers a wide variety of food, including a soup and salad bar, and specializes in wild game. You can get appetizers and pizza in the Lounge, where you'll find a pool table and several video gambling machines. The Big Western also serves as West Yellowstone's Greyhound depot, and pets are allowed.

The Brandin' Iron Inn
201 Canyon St., West Yellowstone
(406) 646-9411, (800) 217-4613
www.brandiniron.com
$$$

Two blocks from the west entrance to Yellowstone, the Brandin' Iron offers 79 remodeled king and queen suites, a spacious lobby with a stone fireplace, oversized Jacuzzis, and a laundry facility. The rooms are big and tastefully decorated with oak furniture. The Brandin' Iron also offers bus tours of the Park during the summer and winter snowmobile rentals.

City Center Motel
214 Madison Ave., West Yellowstone
(406) 646-7337, (800) 742-0665
$

This budget hotel offers 25 clean and comfortable rooms at a convenient location two blocks from Yellowstone's boundary. There's a nice hot tub room, in-room coffee makers, cable television, and a health club. The City Center also offers summer bus tours and winter snowmobile packages and has undergone a recent renovation.

Days Inn
801 Madison Ave., West Yellowstone
(406) 646-7656, (800) 548-9551
www.allyellowstone.com
$$$$

This 115-room hotel is worth mentioning because of the 100-foot water slide that empties happy kids into the indoor pool. Standard hotel rooms include double queen beds and cable television, although kitchenettes and suites with in-room spas are available. The attached restaurant—Trapper's Restaurant—has great food for families. The hotel is right across from All Yellowstone Motorsports and SnoVan Tours.

Gray Wolf Inn and Suites
250 S. Canyon St., West Yellowstone
(406) 646-4200, (800) 580-3557
www.graywolf-inn.com
$$$$

The Gray Wolf is one of West's newer hotels and offers 102 guest rooms, including 16 one- and two-bedroom apartment-sized suites. All rooms have 25-inch televisions, pay-per-use Nintendo gaming systems, and movies, clock radios, hair dryers, coffee makers, speaker telephones with data ports, voice mail, two vanity areas with sinks and mirrors, full bath with tub/shower combination, and individually controlled heat and air conditioning units. Suites include complete kitchens with microwaves, dishwashers, toasters, dishes, and utensils. Rooms are nicely decorated with soft colors and oak woodwork. The three-story building also houses an indoor pool, a sauna, hot tub, coin-operated guest laundry, and an indoor heated parking garage. A continental breakfast is served in the lobby.

The Hibernation Station
212 Gray Wolf Ave., West Yellowstone
(406) 646-4200, (800) 580-3557
www.hibernationstation.com
$$$$

Stepping into the rustic log cabins of the Hibernation Station might give you the impression of being in a remote resort in the middle of Yellowstone, not three blocks from its entrance. Since 1994, guests have been staying in these elegantly appointed cabins, which offer king-, queen-, and double-bed combinations. Each impressive cabin has a different theme, named for regional rivers and streams. The Madison's hand-crafted king bed, jetted tub, and fireplace will leave you warm and well rested. The Henry's Fork has three queen beds, a fireplace, full kitchenette, and a dining area for six people. Whichever cabin you choose, you'll get down comforters, extra soft bath towels, and an overall luxurious and rustic atmosphere. When you're done gaping at the incredible log construction of the cabins and furniture, you can relax in the center courtyard's Jacuzzi room while marveling at the largest bronze sculpture in Montana. Winter packages are available.

Insiders' Tip

Quake Lake, created by a massive earthquake in 1959 that took out an entire mountainside, is a short drive from West Yellowstone on U.S. Highway 87. The fatal quake dammed up the Madison River, creating this small lake just west of the larger Hebgen Lake. Stop in at the visitor's center for the interpretive display that commemorates a violent and tragic day in local history.

Kelly Inn
104 S. Canyon St., West Yellowstone
(406) 646-4544, (800) 259-4672
www.wyellowstone.com/kellyinn
$$$$

The Kelly Inn is a large hotel located on West's main thoroughfare, and features 78 large, nicely appointed rooms with one king or two queen beds. Standard rooms offer 25-inch televisions, pay-per-view movies, Nintendo, and electronic keyless entry. Specialty suites feature a wet bar, whirlpool, refrigerator, microwave, and hair dryer. There is an indoor, heated pool, a Jacuzzi, and a sauna. Enjoy the daily continental breakfast in the lobby. The Kelly Inn is located on the south side of town across from the IMAX movie theater and the Grizzly Discovery Center. The parking lot is large enough to accommodate snowmobile trailers. Winter packages are available.

Pony Express Motel
4 Firehole Ave., West Yellowstone
(406) 646-7644, (800) 323-9708
www.yellowstonevacations.com
$

Nothing fancy here, just nicely sized, clean rooms at a price that will leave you with plenty of cash left over for the area's numerous attractions. Rooms have a warm, knotty pine décor and winter snowmobile packages are available. This single-story hotel is right across the street from the Yellowstone entrance.

Stage Coach Inn
209 Madison Ave., West Yellowstone
(406) 646-7381, (800) 842-2882
www.yellowstonein.com
$$$

You can't miss the Stage Coach, which looks like a grand Swiss ski chalet. With 91 rooms and an underground heated parking garage, the Stage Coach is one of West's largest full-service hotels. The Coachman Restaurant and Lounge is one of the town's more popular eating and partying places, specializing in steak dinners and nightly live entertainment in the

Coachman and during the winter in the Barrel Bar, located downstairs.

West Yellowstone Conference Hotel
315 Yellowstone Ave., West Yellowstone
(406) 646-7365, (800) 646-7365
www.yellowstone-conf-hotel.com
$$$$

This deluxe Holiday Inn is West's largest hotel, with 123 rooms, including deluxe executive suites with stone fireplaces, king rooms with jetted tubs, and two-room family units. All rooms have mini fridges, coffee makers, hair dryers, and microwaves. There's also an indoor pool, hot tub, sauna, exercise room, and a conference center with 10,000 square feet and room for 500 guests. The popular Oregon Short Line restaurant serves up excellent grub, including bison kabobs, BBQ short ribs, and pan-fried trout. The Iron Horse Saloon offers video gambling and a large selection of Montana microbrews. If you have time, walk through the fully restored 1903 Oregon Short Line rail car, one of the best preserved train cars of its type in the world. Winter and summer packages are available.

Yellowstone Lodge
250 Electric St., West Yellowstone
(406) 646-0020, (877) 239-9298
www.yellowstonelodge.com
$$$$

Built in 1999, the deluxe Yellowstone Lodge is West's newest hotel. It features 80 rooms, with your choice of two queen beds or one king bed with a queen sofa sleeper. Suites that accommodate up to six people are available, too. Each room has a coffee maker, 25-inch cable television, telephone with data port, two vanity areas with sinks, and full baths with a tub/shower combination. Approximately one third of the rooms have small fridges. The three-story hotel also has an indoor heated pool, hot tub, coin-operated laundry, and ample parking for large vehicles.

Bed and Breakfasts, Lodges, and Cabins

Bed and Breakfasts, Lodges, and Cabins Rates

$ . . . . Less than $85
$$ . . . . $86 to $115
$$$ . . . . $116 to $150
$$$$ . . . . $151 and more

Bar N Ranch/Campobello Lodge
3111 Targhee Pass Hwy. 20
West Yellowstone
(406) 646-7229, (800) BIGSKYS
www.bar-n-ranch.com
$$$$

You'll get a complete Montana vacation at the Bar N, located southwest of West Yellowstone and five miles from the Park. The recently built main lodge is a breathtaking structure, with a three-sided fireplace and hand-hewn logs, and is full of family heirlooms and old-fashioned charm. You can listen to music from one of the 1890s pianos or watch the sunset from the hot tub on the wraparound porch. The Bar N's main lodge has eight rooms that accommodate two to six people, and seven private cabins for groups up to eight. All of the rooms, even in the main lodge, have a fireplace and each cabin has a private hot tub. Fly fishers take note: The Bar N has five miles of private access on the world famous Madison River. Rates include three hearty meals a day and all the Rocky Mountain scenery you can take in.

Cliff Lake Resort
844 MT Hwy. 87N
(406) 682-4611
www.clifflakeresort.com
$–$$$$

Located 15 miles west of West Yellowstone on scenic Cliff Lake, this resort offers three newer cabins and eight rustic cabins and plenty of nearby activities. Only the two log cabins, which sleep eight to twelve people, are available in the winter. The rustic cabins have no running water, shared baths, and wood cookstoves. If you enjoy hiking, you'll be happy to know that you are close to numerous mountain lakes and a stretch of the Continental Divide trail. Snowmobilers and cross-country skiers have plenty of options in the winter, and some of the best elk hunting in the state surrounds the resort.

Firehole Ranch
P.O. Box 686, West Yellowstone
(406) 646-7294
www.fireholeranch.com
$$$$

Nestled between the shores of Hebgen Lake and Coffin Peak, the Firehole Ranch caters to the fly fishers. The rustically elegant lodge was rated the number one Orvis-endorsed fishing lodge in 1996, and provides a complete Montana vacation for both seasoned and novice anglers. The ten cabins are tucked into the woods and are spaced far enough apart for privacy, but are really only made for two people, with the exception of a few adjoining ones that can accommodate larger groups. However, the capacity of the ranch is limited to 20 guests.

Reminiscent of an old hunting camp, the main lodge houses a huge stone fireplace and numerous animal racks. Meals are included and are as much a visual feast as a tasteful one. The dining room offers expansive views of the lake and surrounding mountains. The ranch is surrounded by some of the best trout fishing streams in the world, including the Madison, the Yellowstone, the Gallatin, the Henry's

Fork of the Snake River, the Gibbon, and the Firehole. Head guide Scott Ross leads a team of eight guides that will have you hooking the big ones in no time.

Parade Rest Ranch
7979 Grayling Creek Rd.
West Yellowstone
(406) 646-7217, (800) 753-5934
www.parade-rest-ranch.com
$$$$

Have yourself a real Western experience at the Parade Rest, which can be found by heading west on U.S. Highway 287 at the junction with U.S. Highway 191, eight miles from West Yellowstone. The ranch offers rustic log cabins with full bathrooms that accommodate two to ten people. The new R & R Lodge is an activity center for all ages, and you can play horseshoes, volleyball, and basketball on the premises. In the summer the ranch wrangler will guide novice horse riders on easy morning or afternoon rides, while advanced riders can take a challenging journey up to higher elevations. The price includes three meals, and the ranch will pack a lunch for you to take with you when you leave to explore. You'll know when it's time to eat at the Parade Rest—just listen for the old-fashioned dinner bell. Rates are discounted 20 percent from mid-September to mid-June, and include transportation to and from the West Yellowstone airport if needed.

The Pines at Island Park
3907 Philips Loop Rd.
Island Park, ID 83429
(208) 558-0192, (800) 455-9384
www.pinesislandpark.com
$$$$

Each immaculate log cabin at this luxury resort boasts 1,500 square feet of space, three bedrooms, two bathrooms, loft, living and dining rooms, fireplace, laundry facilities, satellite television, hot tub, and full kitchen. Leather and log furniture complete the Western atmosphere. Snowmobiling and fishing opportunities await you just outside your door.

Wolves frolic in the snow at West Yellowstone's Grizzly Discovery Center, a bear and wolf preserve that gives visitors a closer look at these remarkable animals. PHOTO: DONNIE SEXTON/TRAVEL MONTANA

Campgrounds and RV Parks

Campground and RV Park Rates

$	Less than $10
$$	$11 to $20
$$$	$21 to $30
$$$$	$31 and more

La Siesta RV Park
510 Madison Ave., West Yellowstone
(406) 646-7892
$$

La Siesta's 12 sites make it one of the smallest RV parks in town, but its downtown location also makes it one of the most convenient. Open all year, it offers cable TV, laundry, showers, electric hookups, flush toilets, drinking water, and plenty of shade trees for those hot summer days.

Madison Arm Resort Campground and Marina
South Shore of Hebgen Lake, West Yellowstone
(406) 646-9328
$$$

Summer is a busy time at Madison Arm, where the campgrounds and RV sites are nestled in a large stand of lodgepole pines and on the shore of scenic Hebgen Lake. Choose from 70 RV and 20 tent sites, and enjoy the lake by renting a boat, canoe, or kayak. Facilities include general store, laundry, showers, electric hook-ups, dump stations, and a full-service marina, where you'll find a boat ramp, docks, and fuel. Madison Arm is open from mid-May to mid-October. To get there, take U.S. Highway 191 north out of town for three miles, then take a left on Forest Service Road 291. The resort is five-and-a-half miles from the turnoff.

Super 8 Motel/Lionshead Resort
1545 Targhee Pass Hwy.
West Yellowstone
(406) 646-9584
$$$

The year-round Lionshead, with 194 RV and 48 tent sites, is the area's largest RV park. It's located about eight miles west of town on U.S. Highway 20, part of a large complex including a Super 8 and Alice's Restaurant. A favorite activity here is nightly square dancing in the summer, and

snowmobilers flock to the Lionshead for its proximity to the great riding near Targhee Pass and the Lionshead area. RV facilities include laundry, showers, drinking water, flush toilets, and electric hook-ups.

Yellowstone Grizzly RV Park
210 Electric Ave., West Yellowstone
(406) 646-4466
$$$$

This large RV park is located downtown and within walking distance of all services. Choose from 154 RV sites and 16 tent sites.

Yellowstone Park KOA
U.S. Hwy. 20, West Yellowstone
(406) 646-7606, (800) 562-7591
$$$$

Enjoy 360-degree mountain views from this KOA, located six miles west of town. Amenities include laundry, showers, dump station, indoor pool, and hot tub.

Insiders' Tip

Looking for something to do at night? Go see a show at the Playmill Theatre, which has provided entertainment for summer visitors for nearly 40 years. Shows are every night but Sunday, and usually include a rotating series of musicals, dramas, and comedies. The season typically runs from Memorial Day through Labor Day. Reservations are strongly encouraged and can be made by calling (406) 646-7757. Check out the theater's website at www.playmill.com for schedules and ticket information.

Restaurants

Restaurant Rates
Rates reflect the price a meal for two people, excluding beverages, tip, and tax.

$	$10 to $19
$$	$20 to $27
$$$	$28 to $35
$$$$	$36 and more

The Campobello Lodge
3111 Targhee Pass Hwy.
West Yellowstone
(406) 646-7229, (800) BIGSKYS
www.bar-n-ranch
$$$$

The Campobello, also known as the Bar N Ranch provides a fine dining experience at a reasonable price with true Western hospitality. The four dollar sign rating is a bit deceiving, as diners pay $29 per person for a three course country supper, complete with a complimentary happy hour with hors d'oeuvres, wine with dinner, dessert, and after dinner drinks in the lodge's Great Room. The chef cooks up a different meal each night of the week, with Thursdays being the lodge's popular Thanksgiving turkey dinner with all the trimmings. Other nights of the week include roast pork night, Italian night, ethnic night, seafood night, beef night, and country chicken night. Sleigh ride dinners are available in the winter for $44. Happy hour usually starts at 6 P.M., with dinner at the Campobello served at 7 P.M.

Canyon Street Grill
22 Canyon St., West Yellowstone
(406) 646-7548
$

The Canyon Street feels like a classic diner from years ago, right down to the shiny red vinyl chairs and booths, huge chocolate malts, big burgers, and 50s-era decorations. The walls are adorned with old advertising signs and pictures of hot rods. Food is standard American fare, including sandwiches, burgers, and fish and chips.

The Coachman Restaurant
209 Madison Ave., West Yellowstone
(406) 646-7381
$$

Located in the Stage Coach Inn, Chef Jack Cole serves up a diverse American menu in the Coachman. Choose from steaks, fresh seafood, chops, and pasta, or try a delicious Buffalo Burger—yes, we do eat bison around here—and enjoy your meal in the restaurant's casual atmosphere. Homemade desserts and a full wine list are available. The Coachman also serves breakfast from 7 to 11 A.M. and lunch from 11 A.M. to 2 P.M., and will also box your lunch so you can take it with you. Dinner starts at 5:30.

Eino's
8955 Gallatin Rd., West Yellowstone
(406) 646-9344
$

You won't see a lot of fancy advertisements for Eino's, one of West's best word-of-mouth eating establishments. In fact, only a small neon sign on a satellite dish lets you know where it is—north of town near the junction of U.S. Highways 191 and 287. You'll find the menu on the wall by the bar—steaks or burgers, cut to your liking, and priced by the ounce. When you order, you'll be given a slab of meat and shown the grill, because you're the chef here. Season your meat the way you like it and cook it over an open flame, then enjoy your meal with great views of Hebgen Lake. Eino's is a popular spot for snowmobilers, as you can eat and gas up.

The Gusher Pizza and Sandwich Shoppe
40 Dunraven Ave., West Yellowstone
(406) 646-9050
$

The Gusher is one of West's favorite places to grab a burger or a sandwich after a day in the park or on the trails. There are also steaks, shrimp, soups, salads, chili, and vegetarian dishes. The seven-ounce sirloin steak sandwich and the Gusher Special Pizza—beef, sausage, pepperoni, Canadian bacon, mushrooms, olives, green peppers, and onions—are popular and tasty items. Everything on the menu is available for take out and delivery, too. There's also a pub and game room with pool tables, video games, and Montana poker.

The Oregon Short Line
315 Yellowstone Ave., West Yellowstone
(406) 646-7365
$$$

After you tour the adjacent 1903 Oregon Short Line Railroad Executive Train Car, stop in for a fine meal at this restaurant in the West Yellowstone Conference Hotel. The signature dish here is the barbecued ribs, slow roasted in the restaurant's famous sauce and topped with grilled pineapple. If you want to taste something different, try the open range bison kabobs, draped in a mild Szechwan sauce and served with grilled vegetables and rice pilaf. Seafood lovers might want to try the pan-fried trout with toasted almonds, raisins, and white wine. All dinners include the large salad bar and fresh beaked bread. Meals are served daily.

Pete's Rocky Mountain Pizza and Pasta
104 Canyon St., West Yellowstone
(406) 646-7820
$

Pete's—a popular spot for locals and visitors alike—is known for its excellent and filling meals. You'll find traditional Italian dishes here, but the pizza ensures return customers. Choose from a variety of toppings—including sauerkraut and barbecue sauce—or try the Original Incredible Combination Pizza. There's also excellent salads, chicken, pasta, and homemade spaghetti. Pete's offers free delivery.

Running Bear Pancake House
538 Madison Ave., West Yellowstone
(406) 646-7703
$

The Running Bear serves up delicious breakfasts and lunch seven days a week from 7 A.M. until 2 P.M. It's no surprise that the house specialty is pancakes, but there are plenty of traditional breakfast favorites, homemade baked goods, and a full lunch menu, including burgers, sandwiches, soups, and salads. The Running Bear is closed during November and April.

Wolf Pack Brewing Company
111 S. Canyon St., West Yellowstone
(406) 646-7225
$

Enjoy hand-crafted German lagers and ales 365 days a year at the Wolf Pack, located next to the IMAX Theater and one block from the entrance to Yellowstone National Park. The Wolf Pack opens at 7:30 A.M. and serves up delicious baked goods and gourmet coffee. Lunch and dinner feature hot dogs, Polish sausages, and bratwurst steamed in the brewery's beer. Dinners are served until 9 P.M.

Insiders' Tip

The Bear's Den is West Yellowstone's only year-round, current-release movie theater. You'll find all the amenities of a larger theater, including a full-sized screen, surround sound, and hot buttered popcorn. The theater is located at 15 Electric St. Call (406) 646-7777 for current prices and showtimes.

Nightlife

The Coachroom Lounge
209 Madison Ave., West Yellowstone
(406) 646-7381

This is West's favorite seasonal bar, located in the Stage Coach Inn. It has a cozy feel, thanks to the large fireplace, offers a big screen television, gambling machines, and licensed poker dealers. During the winter and summer the

Coachroom offers live entertainment several nights a week.

Eino's Tavern
8955 Gallatin Rd., West Yellowstone
(406) 646-9344

If you're snowmobiling around the West Yellowstone area, a stop in at Eino's is a must. Near the end of the day, you'll start to see snow machines heading north along U.S. Highway 191 to Eino's, where the parking lot will slowly fill up. Inside, riders gather to talk about the trails that day and where they will go the next, then cook themselves up a burger or a steak on Eino's grill. It's a great atmosphere, and one of West Yellowstone's more interesting sights.

Grizzly Lounge
205 Yellowstone Ave., West Yellowstone
(406) 646-7475

Adjacent to the Three Bear Lodge, the Grizzly is a mellow place full of great old photos depicting Yellowstone's rich history. There is a big screen TV and a casino for you to try your luck in.

Rustler's Roost
234 Firehole Dr., West Yellowstone
(406) 646-7622, (800) 646-7622

The Roost is a casual and enjoyable lounge with a big-screen TV and electronic gambling machines. It's a favorite spot to go after a day of snowmobiling, where visitors and locals mix comfortably. There is an extensive wine list and plenty of beers to choose from.

Shopping

Book Peddler
106 Canyon St., West Yellowstone
(406) 646-9358

This is West's oldest and best bookstore, and specializes in books, maps, and related items of the West and Yellowstone National Park. There's a large selection of hiking, travel, tourism, and recreation books, as well as numerous titles by local and regional authors. Relax in the espresso bar with homemade baked goods and gourmet coffee and tea, or at one of the outside tables during the summer.

Eagle's Store
3 Canyon St., West Yellowstone
(406) 646-9300

Open year round, the Eagle's has been West Yellowstone's one-stop shop since 1908. You'll find a complete line of Western wear from brands like Stetson, Levi, Lee, Tony Lama, and Acme, as well as sportswear from Woolrich and Columbia. There's hiking and backpacking equipment and fishing tackle, and a gift section including Native American arts and crafts, t-shirts, and souvenirs.

Flying T Trading Post
311 Canyon Ave., West Yellowstone
(406) 646-7557

Looking for something old and Western? Try the Flying T (open year round), where you'll find a large selection of Western trappings, old toys, antique firearms, Native American artifacts and trade beads, dolls, china, and more. There is also a den of animal mounts and a gallery of Western art.

Madison Crossing
121 Madison Ave., West Yellowstone
(406) 646-7621
www.madisoncrossing.com

This is West Yellowstone's newest year-round retail complex, consisting of nine stores. The Gallery, (406) 646-4300, features the latest Western wildlife and landscape art; Treetop Toys, (406) 646-7621, has unique toys for all ages, including a large selection of stuffed animals; the Yellowstone Apothecary, (406) 646-7621, is a full-service pharmacy that carries gifts and cards; Homeroom, (406) 646-4338, has a variety of accessories, gifts, and home furnishings. You'll also find a one-hour photo store, a florist, a kitchen store, an activewear outlet, and an interior design shop.

Northern Bear Trading Post
109 S. Canyon, West Yellowstone
(406) 646-7150

Honoring the heritage of the American West, Northern Bear, which is open year round, features Yellowstone gifts and garments reflecting nature and wildlife. You'll find Christmas ornaments, metal art, handmade pottery, Native American artifacts, wood carvings, and t-shirts.

Rare Earth Store
111 Yellowstone Ave., West Yellowstone
(406) 646-9337

You can mine for gold, garnets, Montana sapphires, and other gems at the Yellowstone Mining Company, a working sluice that is part of Rare Earth. In the store, there is a dazzling array of rocks, fossils, and minerals, including the largest amethyst geode in Montana. There are

also postcards, souvenirs, apparel, and stuffed animals to choose from. Open year round.

Wolf Den Gift Gallery
29 Canyon St. #5, West Yellowstone
(406) 646-9760

At the Wolf Den you'll find animal-related things, including affordable wildlife art, contemporary art, and limited edition prints. You can also get an authentic wolf paw casting, leather art, and there is a large selection of Christmas items. The Wolf Den is open all year.

Yellowstone T-shirt Company
20 Canyon St., West Yellowstone
(406) 646-7722

The Yellowstone T-shirt Company has a large selection of silk-screened t-shirts, sweatshirts, and hats. Custom designing and silkscreening is available for groups and activities, and the shop recently added a full line of gifts and curios reflecting the Yellowstone region.

Bozeman

Accommodations
Restaurants
Nightlife
Shopping

With a history of agriculture and a present day economy that thrives on tourism, the scenic college town of Bozeman is one of the best examples of the inherent contrast present in Yellowstone Country. Like many Montana cities, its residents grapple with the displacement of farmland with roads and infrastructure, while at the same time promoting the town's booming high tech industry, and all the while touting the open space that surrounds the community.

Bozeman, elevation 4,795 feet, is located in the beautiful Gallatin Valley and is the county seat for Gallatin County. The city has a population of about 26,000, but the county's population of around 60,000 is a more accurate description of the number of people who live around the city. Many folks choose to live in one of the outlying towns—Belgrade, Three Forks, Manhattan, Big Sky, and Livingston—and make the commute to work in Bozeman.

The city sits at the intersection of Interstate 90 and U.S. Highway 191, offering two direct routes to Yellowstone National Park. Heading 90 miles south on Highway 191 will take you along the breathtaking Gallatin River, past Big Sky, and on to West Yellowstone. Heading east over Bozeman Pass will put you in Livingston, a mere 60 miles from the north entrance to the park on U.S. Highway 89. It is this reason that many visitors to the Yellowstone Region make Bozeman the starting and/or ending point of their journey, as they have for the past 130 years.

The best thing about Bozeman is the contrast. Historic Main Street boasts acclaimed art galleries, renowned restaurants, and upscale shops, while at the same time offering typical Montana taverns, hardware stores, and fly fishing shops. From sushi bars to T-shirt stores, Bozeman's Main Street is a place where you can spend the day just walking around and taking in the sights, sounds, and smells of one of Montana's finest cities.

While Main Street is still a hotspot for business, Bozeman is suffering the same symptoms of urban sprawl that many Montana cities have already gone through. Stores like Wal-Mart and Target have set up shop on the north end of town, and North 19th Avenue has seen its acres of farmland give way to housing developments, strip malls, shopping centers, and restaurants. This is a hot topic in Bozeman, and the city is doing its best to regulate business expansion while at the same time promoting the downtown district. So far, it seems to be working out, as even Bozeman's East Main Street has seen recent addition of restaurants and shops.

Bozeman is home to the nearly 11,000 students of Montana State University, which is located on College Street on the south side of Main Street. The beautiful campus is a great place to walk around, and the school contributes much to the city's thriving arts and cultural scene. Theater shows, art exhibits, and live music are continuously present on campus, and the competitive Division I sports teams are great fun to watch if you have the time. MSU is also home to the Museum of the Rockies, a world famous museum that offers exhibits in paleontology, geology, contemporary art, and more, as well as the Taylor Planetarium and museum gift shop. Check the local newspapers for listings and exhibits.

Of course, Bozeman is rich in history. Native American tribes including the Shoshone, Nez Perce, Blackfeet, Flathead, and Sioux date back several hundred years. Lewis and Clark traveled through the area in 1805, arriving at the three forks of the

Madison, Jefferson, and Gallatin Rivers, about 30 miles west of town. And it was 1863 when John Bozeman came through Wyoming, over a pass from the east and dropped into what the Native Americans called "Valley of the Flowers," and settled in the town that would bear his name. With him and leading the wagon train was legendary frontiersman Jim Bridger, who now has a mountain range, canyon, and numerous trails named after him. It wasn't long before the rest of the world discovered the same beautiful spot.

Bozeman's weather is typical for a higher elevation mountain town. Summers are often dry and hot, but are a little on the short side. June is hit or miss, and can be either a cold, wet extension of spring or a warm, dry beginning to the summer. Winters can be long and cold, with plenty of snow, but lots of blue sky to go around. Typically, winter runs from Thanksgiving to May, but it is not uncommon for snow in October or July. For the summer, July through September often brings the best weather, and snow lovers will want to be here January through March.

Look around Bozeman and you'll also notice the geographical contrast. The lush, wide valley gives way to rugged, snowcapped peaks—the Madison and Gallatin Ranges to the south, the Tobacco Roots to the west, and the Bridgers to the northeast. On a clear day, you can see far north up the valley into the Big Belt Mountains near Helena. It's no wonder they call Bozeman a "mountain town." And because of this, it is an outdoor lover's dream.

From blue ribbon trout streams and world class skiing to whitewater boating, rock climbing, and mountain biking, Bozeman offers something for every sport. Miles of hiking trails wind through the adjacent Gallatin National Forest, where even a novice hiker can summit a 10,000-foot peak. Championship golf courses abound, cross country skiing trails are everywhere and beautiful mountain lakes are close by, making Bozeman a hard place to leave.

In short, Bozeman is a mixture of Old West and New West, chic and country bumpkin, lively and liveable. It's a great Montana city, one full of a vibrant past and an exciting future, and a place that residents take pride in. You may leave Bozeman, but it will never leave you.

Insiders' Tip

Looking for something fun to do? Bozeman has a couple of free newspapers that will give you the inside scoop. The *BoZone* lists all of the enterainment, live music, art exhibits, festivals, and other activities going on. It comes out on the 1st and 15th of every month. The *Tributary* is a local literature and commentary magazine that comes out around the first of the month and includes an event calendar. Look for both of these at coffee shops around town. On Fridays the *Bozeman Daily Chronicle's* "This Week" section gives music, art, theater, and movie listings. The paper costs fifty cents, but many hotels leave copies of "This Week" in their rooms.

Accommodations

Hotels

Price Codes

Keep in mind that some rates are based on availability. The average nightly rates for two adults at the hotels and motels listed in this section are indicated by a dollar sign ($) ranking in the following chart. Also, the hotels and motels in this chapter accept all or most major credit cards.

$	$25 to $49
$$	$50 to $75
$$$	$76–100
$$$$	$101 and more

The Alpine Lodge
1017 E. Main St., Bozeman
(406) 586-0356, (888) 92ALPIN
www.alpine-lodge.com
$

This lower-priced hotel is located on the east end of Bozeman's Main Street, four blocks from the downtown district and within walking distance of antique shops, restaurants, and boutiques. The Alpine Lodge offers individual cottages with kitchens, three-bedroom units, suites, and single rooms for the budget-minded traveler. All rooms are nonsmoking and a continental breakfast is included.

Blue Sky Motel
1010 E. Main St., Bozeman
(406) 587-2311, (800) 845-9032
www.avicom.net/bluesky
$$

The Blue Sky's view from the courtyard is a good selling point, as the peaks of the Bridger Range loom in front of the hotel's courtyard. There are 27 rooms here, all on the ground floor and with queen beds. Other amenities include an indoor Jacuzzi, microwaves and refrigerators, suites and family rooms, individually controlled heat and air conditioning, winter plug-ins, and free local calls.

If you like to walk, the Blue Sky is a great choice. It is adjacent to Lindley Park, one of Bozeman's largest and prettiest parks, which connects to the Peets Hill trail system. The motel is also within walking distance of downtown shops and restaurants, and the Jackpot Casino and Grill is just across the street. You'll find the Blue Sky on East Main Street as you are heading out of town toward the interstate.

The Bozeman Inn
1235 N. 7th Ave., Bozeman
(406) 587-3176, (800) 648-7515
$$

This busy hotel is located on one of Bozeman's main commercial thoroughfares, and offers queen sized beds, free local calls, outdoor pool, hot tub, sauna, and a free continental breakfast. Attached to the hotel is Santa Fe Red's Restaurant, Lounge, and Casino, which offers excellent Mexican and American food at reasonable prices.

City Center Best Western
507 W. Main St., Bozeman
(406) 587-3158
$$$

The 63-room City Center has one of the best locations in town, situated on Main Street a few blocks from the center of activity. Rooms are bigger than average, and the two-floor hotel has an indoor pool, hot tub, and workout gym. Attached to the hotel is the Black Angus steakhouse and casino (587-0652), with good food and moderate prices for breakfast, lunch, and dinner. If you want a place where you walk from, the City Center is a good choice.

The Days Inn
1321 N. 7th Ave., Bozeman
(406) 587-5251, (800) 987-3297
www.bozemandaysinn.com
$$$

If you're traveling with a pet, the Days Inn accepts them with a deposit. The newly remodeled hotel offers courtesy airport shuttle, spa, sauna, fitness center, guest laundry, complimentary HBO, and local phone calls and a free, cooked-to-order breakfast every day. The Days Inn is located on the corner of Oak and North 7th Avenue, close by to any service you may need. Within walking distance are the shops in the Bridger Peaks Town Center, which offers everything from restaurants (Bennigan's, Kentucky Fried Chicken, A&W) and dry cleaning to brand name stores like the Gap, Pier 1 Imports, and Old Navy.

Gallatin Gateway Inn
U.S. Hwy. 191, Gallatin Gateway
(406) 763-4672, (800) 676-3522
www.gallatingatewayinn.com
$$$$

Featured in magazines like *Pacific Northwest* and *Travel & Leisure*, the historic Gallatin Gateway Inn is one of the premier lodgings around Bozeman. Located about 15 miles southwest of Bozeman in the small community of Gallatin Gateway, the massive Spanish-style building offers single, double, or two-room suites as well as a swimming pool, hot tub, and tennis court. After years of extensive restoration, the inn has managed to keep its colorful past (see Close-up) as a train depot, including the original railroad clock, Polynesian mahogany woodwork, and high, arched windows. The Gateway is also home to an award-winning dining room that serves contemporary American cuisine with an extensive wine list, as well the Baggage Room Pub, which has casual food in a lively atmosphere and often offers live music. The cozy Fireplace

Room also serves cocktails by the mammoth hearth. All room prices include a full continental breakfast.

Gallatin River Lodge
9105 Thorpe Rd., Bozeman
(406) 388-0148, (888) 387-0148
www.grlodge.com
$$$$

At the Gallatin River Lodge, you can fish, ride a horse, take a sleigh ride, and enjoy a fine dining experience all without leaving the property. Situated on a small trout pond and near the East Gallatin River, the upscale lodge has an elegant, cozy feel. The lodge is especially suited for anglers, who can find world-class fishing just out the door. Owners Steve and Christy Gamble offer complete packages with meals, lodging, and guide services included. The outstanding restaurant offers creative American cuisine, from seafood to game dishes (the duck is excellent here). Each rustic but elegant suite features a Jacuzzi tub, a fireplace, and outstanding view of the mountains and rivers surrounding the lodge.

The Hampton Inn
75 Baxter Ln., Bozeman
(406) 522-8000, (800) 426-7866
$$$

The Hampton Inn is located in the hotel district just off of North 7th Avenue exit from I-90. The tastefully decorated rooms offer coffee makers, hair dryers, and irons, and business travelers will appreciate the phones with data ports. On-site amenities include an indoor pool and spa, fitness facility, laundry, and winter automobile plug-ins. The Hampton also offers a free airport shuttle and a deluxe breakfast bar, served in a Western style eating area with views of the magnificent Spanish Peaks.

Holiday Inn
5 Baxter Ln., Bozeman
(406) 587-4561, (800) 366-5101
www.bznholinn.com
$$$

This is Bozeman's largest full-service hotel, with 179 rooms furnished with queen or king-size beds, and free cable television with a premium movie channel. A large indoor pool and Jacuzzi are offered, and Cantrell's Food and Spirits boasts a nightly happy hour with complimentary hors d'oeuvres and a locally famous Sunday Champagne Brunch that will leave you stuffed for around $10 per person. The hotel was given a significant facelift in the summer of 2000. Free airport transfers are available.

The Imperial Inn
122 W. Main St., Bozeman
(406) 587-4481
$$

The budget-priced Imperial Inn is perfect for those who don't want to spend a fortune on a room and still be in the heart of the action. Taking up almost an entire block between Willson and Grand Avenues on Bozeman's Main Street, the two-story, 37-room hotel is within walking distance of restaurants, shops, and services. Directly across the street is Bozeman's historic hotel and highest building, the Baxter (no longer a hotel), which houses a bar and three restaurants. Diagonally across the street is the Leaf and Bean coffee shop and a bank. The United States Post Office is two blocks away.

International Backpacker's Hostel
405 W. Olive St., Bozeman
(406) 586-4659
$

If you want to save some bucks and shack up with a few other folks, this large hostel is the perfect place. It's located within walking distance to downtown Bozeman and the university, and is open year round. Rates are $14 per night, and there is one private room available for $32 per night. The hostel has a lively atmosphere and is a great place to meet travelers from all over.

Bed and Breakfasts

Bed and Breakfast Rates

$	Less than $85
$$	$86 to $115
$$$	$116 to $150
$$$$	$151 and more

The Chokecherry House
1233 Story Mill Rd., Bozeman
(406) 587-2657
$$$

The Chokecherry House is Bozeman's most unique guesthouse. Owners Rick and Kimberly Pope have renovated the sixty-year-old Quonset house, which was once part of the Story Mill Schoolhouse, into a charming, eccentric, and private getaway. With its checkerboard floor, original artwork, and curvaceous lines, the Chokecherry is a unique and fun place to stay. Amenities include two bedrooms, fully equipped kitchen, living room, smoking porch, outdoor hot tub, private phone, TV, VCR, a fly tying bench, and a well-stocked library.

Rick and Kimberly live next door, and both are professional artists. Kimberly is a metalsmith and jeweler, and Rick is an art professor at Montana State University as well as a licensed fishing guide. The house is 13 miles from Bridger Bowl ski area and a short walk from the 18-hole Bridger Creek golf course and the good fishing of Bridger Creek. Rates are $140 per night for up to six people, with a two-night minimum stay.

Close-up

The Gallatin Gateway Inn

It's hard to miss the Gateway, as the locals call this grand old hotel, when you're driving south from Bozeman to West Yellowstone on U.S. Highway 191. The 42,000 square foot, Spanish-style building sits back from the road but commands a view, with its well-kept lawn, semi-circular driveway and large, overhanging porch.

The Gateway was built in 1927 by the Milwaukee Railroad, which had only recently carved a line across Montana to the West Coast. A spur line was also built to carry adventurous passengers to Yellowstone National Park, generating more traffic than anticipated. Plans were made for the first railroad hotel outside a national park, and Salesville—now Gallatin Gateway—was chosen as a location, at the head of the Gallatin Valley. Ground was broken on February 18, and the inn opened on June 17 to a reported crowd of 20,000 excited visitors. The 35-room hotel was considered one of the most luxurious of its time, boasting advanced fire protection systems and telephones in every room, and was the talk of the town for many years.

As highway travel gradually began to replace railroads, the Gateway was left behind and sold by Milwaukee Railroad in 1951. Since then it has passed through several owners, eventually falling into disrepair. Luckily, the original building was hardly modified and many of the ornate details were preserved. It was listed on the National Register of Historic Places in 1980, and underwent years of renovation before reopening in 1987.

Walking into the main lobby of the Gateway can't be much different than it was almost 75 years ago. Huge east and west facing windows light up the grand room. A mammoth chandelier hangs from the high, arched ceiling. To the left is the Fireplace Room, a cozy gathering place with a ten-foot fireplace and doors leading to a sun-drenched porch. To the

Thanks to a historically accurate renovation, the Gallatin Gateway Inn has retained its railroad roots and early-20th-century-charm. PHOTO: GALLATIN GATEWAY INN

right is the Baggage Room Pub, a quaint grill that serves casual fare and cocktails with occasional live music. Through the Fireplace Room is the 72-seat main dining room, serving superb contemporary American cuisine. Selections from Executive Chef Eric Stenberg and Sous Chef Ian Troxler include Shellfish Risotto, Rosemary Roasted Pork Loin, Red Wine Braised Lamb, and Fettuccine with house-made Italian sausage. An extensive wine list and impressive dessert tray compliment your meal.

Today the Gateway is a year-round destination for travelers, offering an outdoor pool, tennis court, casting pond, and a hot tub. The rooms offer the flexibility of single, double, or two room suites, and the hotel is 12 miles outside of Bozeman and within a short drive of everything Montana and the Yellowstone Region have to offer. If you don't stay here, at least stop in and take in the sights and see why the Gallatin Gateway Inn is a marvel of elegance, history, and preservation.

Fox Hollow Bed and Breakfast
545 Mary Rd., Bozeman
(406) 582-8440, (800) 431-5010
www.bozeman-mt.com
$$–$$$

This newer bed and breakfast is located midway between Bozeman and Gallatin Field, near the town of the Belgrade. Fox Hollow offers a country setting with spectacular views of the Bridgers and Tobacco Roots from its wraparound deck, which houses a hot tub for soothing soaks after your day of exploring the area. Guests can choose from five nonsmoking rooms, three of which are located in the main house and two in an adjacent building. Each room offers a queen size bed, private bath, and breathtaking views. A gourmet breakfast is served each morning and guests can relax by the fire in the family room. Owners Nancy and Michael Dawson operated their own travel agency for ten years and pride themselves on understanding the needs of travelers, so don't hesitate to inquire about what to do during your stay. Nancy's parents also own the Cason Gallery in Helena, and the walls at Fox Hollow are peppered with original, contemporary, and Western art.

The Lehrkind Mansion
719 N. Wallace St., Bozeman
(406) 585-6932, (800) 992-6932
www.bozemanbedandbreakfast.com
$$–$$$$

When Julius Lehrkind, owner of Bozeman Lager Beer, built this magnificent mansion in 1897, he had each brick soaked in large vats of beer before setting them, making it truly "the house that beer built." Situated in Bozeman's historic Brewery District, where classic Queen Annes mingle with gritty industrial buildings, the Lehrkind offers guests an elegant reminder of Montana's Victorian past. The Thoreau Room was the mansion's original nursery and features an antique brass bed; The Muir Room lets

Insiders' Tip

If you are planning on being in Bozeman during the three-day Sweet Pea Festival of the Arts, held each year during the first full weekend in August, book your hotel room extra early. The city swells with visitors from around the region, and most plan far in advance.

the sun in from a south-facing stained glass window; The Leopold Room includes a private bath and a high-back oak bed, writing desk, and reading chairs; the plush Audubon Suite includes a private bath and a tower sitting room with a direct view of the Bridger Mountains. Guests can also rent the Carriage House, which is perfect for families or groups. The large space includes vaulted ceilings, lodgepole pine furnishings, and an extra bedroom if needed. Rounding out the immaculate décor is the mansion's music parlor and library, complete with a rare, seven-foot tall 1897 Regina music box and a large book collection highlighting the area's spectacular national parklands. Incidentally, owners Jon Gerster, Jr. and Christopher Nixon worked as rangers in Yellowstone and Grand Teton National Parks, so most questions won't go unanswered. A complimentary full breakfast and late afternoon tea are included.

Mountain Sky Guest Ranch
P.O. Box 1128, Bozeman, MT 59715
(406) 587-1244, (800) 548-3392
$$$$

Driving up the rocky Forest Service road will make you feel as if you are in the backcountry, but the truth is that guests of Mountain Sky do not rough it. All the details from food to fun are taken care of here. Tucked into the Gallatin Range, south of Livingston, this dude ranch combines luxury with simple western style. The charming rustic cabins are tucked into groves of lodge pole pines, and are secluded though they are only a short walk from the main lodge.

Dining at Mountain Sky is an event on its own. Whether it's poolside barbecues featuring steaks and chicken or seafood or an inside meal of gourmet continental cuisine, you won't want to miss it. Breakfasts range from light to hearty, depending upon your preference. Lunch, served outside buffet-style after the morning ride, may include homemade soups, deli sandwiches, pasta salads, stir fries, or other specialties. Don't worry, you won't go hungry here.

Hiking and horseback riding, designed for any fitness level, are the Ranch's main activities. The children's program is educational and very active, catering to all ages so the folks can get some guilt-free adult time. Tennis courts, a pool, sauna, volleyball, horseshoe pits, and Ping-Pong tables should keep you busy if simply relaxing becomes tiresome.

Silver Forest Inn
15325 Bridger Canyon Rd., Bozeman
(406) 586-1882, (888) 835-5970
www.silverforestinn.com
$$–$$$

Skiers will appreciate the Silver Forest Inn's convenient and scenic location, north of Bozeman and a quarter mile from the Bridger Bowl Ski Area and at the base of the Bridger Mountain Range. Originally built as an artist's retreat in 1932, the National Register historic log-hewn home offers six guest rooms, a large outdoor deck with hot tub and delicious gourmet breakfasts, as well as a beautiful sun room with Bridger views. Guests can also rent the entire inn by the night or week. Some rooms have private Jacuzzis, and a day on the slopes wouldn't be complete without a relaxing, quiet evening by the fireplace in the Great Room.

The Voss Inn
319 S. Willson Ave., Bozeman
(406) 587-0982
www.bozeman-vossinn.com
$$

Located on one of Bozeman's most historic and architecture-rich streets, the Voss Inn offers six Victorian style rooms in an elegant, late-nineteenth-century brick home. Proprietors Bruce and Frankee Muller have taken great pride in keeping the Voss Inn true to its Victorian roots. Each room has a private bath and its own décor, including the nine-foot brass headboard of the Chisholm room and the private deck of Robert's Roost to the oversized clawfoot tub in the Pease Room and the private sitting area of the Elliott Room. The parlor on the first floor offers a quaint area for relaxation and socializing, and a full breakfast is pre-

Bozeman is home to the world-class fishing of the Gallatin River. PHOTO: DONNIE SEXTON/TRAVEL MONTANA

pared for guests to enjoy in the comfort of your own room or in the guest parlor. An afternoon tea is also served. Willson Avenue is full of Dickensian charm, and the Voss Inn is only a five-minute walk from downtown Bozeman.

The Wildflower Guest House
201 N. Bozeman Ave., Bozeman
(406) 586-6610
$$$

This is not your average bed and breakfast, simply because you rent the whole house for a flat rate of $950 per week or $150 per night. The house is also located in the heart of Bozeman's downtown North Side, two blocks from bustling Main Street, home to numerous restaurants and shops. The house sleeps seven, and offers a fully-appointed kitchen, woodburning stove with brick hearth, laundry, cable TV, and a Montana-inspired library and a fenced yard. The house is beautifully decorated in hues derived from the local wildflowers. The yard also boasts numerous flowers in a natural setting.

Campgrounds and RV Parks

Campground Rates

$	Less than $9
$$	$10 to $16
$$$	$17 to $23
$$$$	$24 and more

Bear Canyon Campground
4000 Bozeman Trail Rd., Bozeman
(406) 587-1575 (800) 438-1575
$$$

This campground and RV park is located four miles east of Bozeman, just off the Bear Canyon exit of I-90. There are spaces for tents and RVs, a heated pool, electrical outlets, dump sites, showers, restrooms, laundry, and a convenience store. Rates are $15 to $20 for two people, and weekly, monthly, and group rates are available. The campground has picnicking shelters, public phones, and is close to hiking trails.

Bozeman KOA
81123 U.S. Hwy 191
(406) 587-3030
$$$–$$$$

A campground with your own hot springs? Well, not quite, but Bozeman's KOA is located right next to Bozeman Hot Springs, where a few bucks will get you a good soak and full spa services are available. This KOA has more than 100 RV and tent sites, and 15 one and two bedroom cabins. Cabins run between $40 and $50, and there are on-site showers and laundry facilities. The campground is located about 10 miles southeast of Bozeman, adjacent to the hot springs (586-6492).

Fort Three Forks Motel and RV Park
10776 Hwy. 287, Three Forks, MT 59752
(406) 285-3233, (800) 477-5690
$$

This modern facility is located at the junction of I-90 and U.S. Highway 287 in Three Forks, about 30 miles west of Bozeman and 60 miles south of Helena. It's also the site of Fort Three Forks, also known as Old Fort Henry, one of the first trading posts between the Mississippi and the Pacific Ocean. Established in 1810 by John Colter and Andrew and Pierre Menard at the headwaters of the Missouri River, the post was abandoned a year later due to the perilous nature of leaving the camp to do what the men set out to do: trap beaver. These days, you'll find a large, full service motel and a RV park with full hookups, pull-thrus, laundry facilities, showers, and playground equipment.

Sunrise Campground
31842 E. Frontage Rd., Bozeman
(406) 587-4797
$$

This campground and RV park is east of Bozeman next to Dick Walter's Auto Center, and is close to the interstate. It's open from April 15 through November 15, and offers water, electric and sewer hookups, restrooms, laundry, ice, and grills. Leashed pets are welcome.

Restaurants

Restaurant Rates

For two people, excluding beverages, tip, and tax

$	$10 to $19
$$	$20 to $27
$$$	$28 to $35
$$$$	$36 and more

Aunt Sophia's
101 E. Main St., Bozeman
(406) 582-0393
$$

This popular Italian restaurant serves up pasta more than 40 ways and also offers nightly steak and seafood specials, an extensive wine list, and a low-key atmosphere. The Penne Looie (with gorgonzola cream sauce), the Patriciana Capricinia (linguine with cream sauce), and the homemade meatballs and sausage make Aunt Sophia's cooking seem like mom's. Sophia's also serves lunch, where many of the same dinner items are available at a reduced cost.

Bagelworks
708 W. Main St., Bozeman
(406) 585-1727
$

If you're on the road early to the ski slopes or the river, a stop at Bozeman's only true bagel shop is mandatory, quick, and convenient. You can choose from about 15 varieties of fresh baked bagels, and have them fixed to your liking. Especially tasty are the breakfast bagels, prepared with an egg and your choice of meat or cheese. One of these and a coffee or juice won't even set you back four bucks and is filling enough to last until lunch. You can dine in or take it with you, and Bagelworks is open every day but Sunday, starting at 6 A.M. Monday-Friday, and at 7:30 A.M. on Saturdays.

The Bay Bar and Grille
2825 W. Main St., Bozeman
(406) 587-0484
$-$$

The Bay has become a popular Bozeman restaurant because of its wide variety of options. From typical bar fare like burgers, salads, and sandwiches to incredible steak and seafood entrees, the Bay can be a great place for the family or a romantic spot for two. There's a large selection of appetizers (the shrimp wontons are excellent) and the sandwiches are some of the most creative in town. The restaurant also has a gaming room, occasional live music, and is located in the Gallatin Valley Mall.

Boodles
215 E. Main St., Bozeman
(406) 587-2901
$$$$

The atmosphere is a little different at Boodles than most Bozeman restaurants. It's somewhat dark and free from the raw wood look popular in many local establishments. Instead, Boodles has the look and feel of an out-of-the-way Irish pub,

Insiders' Tip
Unless specified, don't worry about dressing up for dinner. Bozeman is a place where you can go to the most expensive restaurant in town in jeans and sneakers—and see someone else wearing the same thing. This is "Montana casual," as we like to call it.

with its beautiful mahogany bar, dim lighting, and brick walls. The food here—steaks, seafood, and wild game—is some of the best around. The service is always great and the occasional live jazz is welcoming. If you like crab cakes, Boodles has some of the best. The restaurant is open for lunch, and after dinner hours, the causal atmosphere at Boodles becomes a little bit more like a bar, but never too loud or rowdy.

Burger Bob's
39 W. Main St., Bozeman
(406) 585-0080
$

You'll find some of the best burgers in town at Burger Bob's, a popular downtown restaurant and classic burger joint that doesn't take itself too seriously. In fact, owner Bob Fletcher tongue-in-cheekly proclaims his restaurant as being a "semi-classy eating establishment with dishwater coffee and questionable atmosphere." The food speaks for itself, though, and you can choose from several varieties of burgers—third and half pounders—as well as chicken sandwiches, salads, hot dogs, and sausages. Seafood lovers should try the Jamaican Tuna Steak, and the hot wings will have anyone running for the water fountain. The walls of the restau-

The dining room at the Gallatin Gateway Inn is renowned for its excellent continental cuisine. PHOTO: GALLATIN GATEWAY INN

rant, which housed an ammunition factory in the basement during World War II, are adorned with old pictures of Bozeman and the Gallatin Valley.

Café 131
131 W. Main St., Bozeman
(406) 587-5100
$

This bright, eclectic corner café serves excellent homemade sandwiches, soups, and salads 7 A.M. to 10 P.M. daily. There is a great selection of teas, tempting desserts, and vegetarian food, as well as espresso and juice bars, and there is outdoor dining during the summer. A relax-

ing sitting area gives the 131 a coffee shop atmosphere.

Café Internationale
207 W. Olive St., Bozeman
(406) 586-4242
$$

This small restaurant has all the look and feel of a more expensive place, which is one reason why it's popular with locals who want a night out without the hefty price tag. The other reason is the food, a mixture of American and international flavors. The menu offers stir-fry items with a variety of sauces, steaks, seafood, and pasta. The delicious appetizers regularly include crab cakes, shrimp wontons, and escargot. Café Internationale is also open for lunch and has outdoor dining in the summer. It is located inside the Emerson Cultural Center, an old school converted into art galleries, shops, and studios.

The Daily Coffee Bar
1013 W. College St., Bozeman
(406) 585-8612
$

If you're over near the university or want a quick snack, the Daily serves up Starbucks coffee (the closest thing Bozeman has to a national chain coffee shop) and a variety of brownies, scones, croissants, and cookies. Interested in something other than coffee? Check out the juices, ice cream, and milkshakes. There's always local art on the walls, and lively conversation going on inside.

Ferraros
726 N. 7th Ave., Bozeman
(406) 587-2555
$$$

Ferraros offers fine Italian dining in a smoke-free environment seven days a week. The restaurant boasts the largest Italian wine selection in Montana, so ask your server for a recommendation if you're unfamiliar with some of the names and regions of wines. A variety of pasta, chicken, and seafood selections is on the menu, as well as beef and lamb. Seafood fans will love the scallops served with linguine and the restaurant's trademark Pink Floyd sauce—a delicious combination of tomato and alfredo sauces that will leave a lasting impression. Salads are served house style—one big bowl for everybody, a fitting example of an authentic Italian meal.

Fred's Mesquite Diner
451 E. Main St., Bozeman
(406) 585-8558
$$

It's a favorite local pastime in the summer: Head to Fred's for a cold beer and a big burger on the outdoor patio. This little establishment serves up mesquite-grilled seafood and steaks, too, cooked over an open flame right in front of you, and also offers pasta and chicken dishes. Particularly satisfying are the steak sandwiches, the chicken parmesan, the sauteed vegetables and the huge gourmet burgers. Sandwiches are served on delicious, fresh-baked ciabatta bread. The ribs are the house specialty, but you wouldn't know it because everything on the lunch and dinner menus is so good.

Grum's Gourmet Market and Deli
2107 N. 7th Ave., Bozeman
(406) 585-3023
$

Grum's has excellent hot and cold sub sandwiches, soups, salads, and a variety of fresh deli items. Sandwiches come on fresh-baked French and ciabatta bread, and a half (8 inches) is plenty big enough for one person. The gourmet market has many unusual and hard-to-find foods, as well as a large selection of wine and imported specialty beers. The deli also serves up great desserts, and you can order ahead for sandwiches, which you can enjoy on the patio in the summer.

It's Greek To Me
16 N. 9th Ave., Bozeman
(406) 586-0176
$

Bozeman's only Greek restaurant serves up traditional favorites including gyros, souvlaki, spanakopita, baklava, and tyropita—cheese baked in filo dough—from its somewhat hidden location just behind the Safeway supermarket on West Main Street. There's also American-style food with Greek flavor—Greek cheeseburgers, grilled cheese, pita melts, and even a pita dog. If the kids don't like the Greek choices, they can order a small pizza.

John Bozeman's Bistro
125 W. Main St., Bozeman
(406) 587-4100
$$$$

Named after the legendary pioneer who founded the city in 1864, this wonderful bistro is one of Bozeman's most popular fine dining establishments. Although the

Close-up

The Bozeman Trail

People labeled John Bozeman as foolhardy or brave when he set out in 1863 to find a better route to the Bannack and Virginia City gold mines from Fort Sedgwick, near the Nebraska/Colorado border. Bozeman, a native Georgian who moved west in search of gold in 1861, was living in Bannack (Montana's first territorial capital) at the time and set out in the spring with fellow pioneer John M. Jacobs and Jacobs' daughter, 11-year-old Emma. The three of them traveled to Three Forks, across the Gallatin Valley and over its eastern pass to the Yellowstone River, the same route William Clark took in 1806.

Bozeman ignored the fact that his route would violate a treaty and slice through land sacred to the Sioux, Crow, and Cheyenne Indians, figuring that conflict could be avoided. Although the party had a few run-ins, the three of them arrived alive at the North Platte River near the Oregon Trail few months later. They would regroup there and try to return to the mines with a wagon train.

The route Bozeman wanted to take back left the Oregon Trail near present day Douglas, Wyoming, crossed the Powder and Tongue Rivers, continued on the Bighorn and the Yellowstone Rivers to the pass he had come through a few months before. The planned route would cut more than 800 miles and six weeks off the Oregon Trail route up through Idaho to the Montana mines. In July of 1863, 46 wagons and 89 people set out from the North Platte to try what was called the Bozeman-Jacobs cutoff.

They got as far as what is now Buffalo, Wyoming, before running into a large party of Sioux and Cheyenne, who wouldn't let them pass. After realizing they weren't going to get by, most of the wagon train returned to take the longer, safer Oregon Trail route to the mines. But Bozeman and a few others were determined.

The men loaded up their horses and raced across Wind River Country and down the Clark's Fork of the Yellowstone, traveling at night, until they reached the pass into the Gallatin Valley—now dubbed Bozeman Pass—in early August. They arrived at the mines safely, but Bozeman deemed the attempt a failure since the wagon train didn't make it. Nonetheless, Bozeman and Jacobs knew that future trains could be successful, and returned to the North Platte via Salt Lake City for another run at it.

Over the next three years the trail was heavily used as settlers and miners moved west. It went by many names, including the Montana Road, the Bonanza Trail, the Big Horn Road, and the Powder River Road. But for most parties, the Indians made sure it was a bloody excursion, thus the nickname: The Bloody Bozeman Trail.

The Army established three forts along the popular trail—Fort Reno and Fort Phil Kearney—and fortified them at the same time government officials were in the field assuring the Sioux this was not taking place. Needless to say, this did not go over well. In 1866, William Fetterman and his party of 80 men ignored orders not to leave the trail and were ambushed by a band of Indians led by Red Cloud. He and his entire party were killed.

After the Fetterman Massacre, as it was called, use of the trail dwindled and two years later the route was deemed unsafe and illegal by the Fort Laramie Treaty of 1868. Although it was popular for only a few short years, Bozeman had indeed found a faster route. And he did manage to get a pass, a trail, and a town named after him (and eventually one of his namesake town's best restaurants). As for Bozeman himself, he was killed by Native Americans in 1867.

The actual route of the Bozeman Trail is not well marked and on private land, but numerous monuments and informational signs are located where the trail intersects public roadways.

food remains high-end, the atmosphere is casual and lively. The ever-changing menu offers a hearty selection of seafood, wild game and pasta dishes, an extensive wine list, and Montana microbrews served on tap. If you can't shell out the bucks for dinner, the Bistro's lunches offer the same quality at lesser prices, about $10 per person. Either way, save room for the restaurant's signature homemade tiramisu; it's worth the price of the meal alone. Unfortunately, the restaurant is closed Sunday and Monday.

La Parilla
1533 W. Babcock St., Bozeman
(406) 582-9511
$

Absolutely Bozeman's best bang for the buck is this pint-sized restaurant that makes some of the fattest wraps around. Choose from traditional fajita and burrito-style Mexican wraps or the restaurant's signature wraps, including the Wrap of Khan (Thai spices), BBQ smoked chicken, ceasar salad, jambalaya, blackened salmon, and fettuccine alfredo wraps. La Parilla also offers tacos and kids' choices, dessert wraps, and outdoor patio dining in the summer.

The Leaf and Bean
35 W. Main St., Bozeman
(406) 587-1580
$

This eclectic coffee shop is a great way to begin your day of strolling around Bozeman's downtown shopping district with a hot cup of coffee or tea, or a great way to end the day by stopping in for a decadent dessert. The bright, cozy atmosphere is perfect for warming up on a chilly evening, listening to the live acoustic music playing several nights a week (the schedule's on a chalkboard in the back). You can also look through a selection of gifts and whole bean coffee to go. Try the homemade hot chocolate or the delicious milkshakes if you're not a coffee drinker, and if you're in a hurry for lunch, stop in and grab a pre-made sandwich or salad.

Looie's Down Under
101 E. Main St., Bozeman
(406) 522-8814
$$$$

There's actually three restaurants in what's known in Bozeman as the Looie's Complex, with the downstairs restaurant being the most exclusive. Upstairs you'll find more than 40 lesser-priced pasta and seafood dishes of Aunt Sophia's (582-0393), which also serves up a mighty fine lunch, and adjacent to Looie's Down Under is Jadra's Sushi Bar (522-8814), authentic as any you'll find. Looie's, however, is the most tantalizing, offering everything from gourmet beef tenderloin meatloaf (not your mom's) to delicious steak and seafood entrees. If you've never had bison, this is the place to try it, and the mashed potatoes are more than a side dish. Dinner is complemented with a terrific wine list and excellent, gourmet desserts. Looie's also has a great bar, perfect for enjoying a glass of wine or a cold beer with one of the many outstanding appetizers. Owner Paul Grossman has also recently opened up the Baxter Grille (105 W. Main St., 586-1314), which serves up even more elegant seafood and steak selections.

MacKenzie River Pizza Co.
232 E. Main St., Bozeman
(406) 587-0055
www.ueatpizza.com
$

This is Bozeman's most popular lunch and dinner place for pizza, and its gourmet, deep dish pies are what people come here for. With signature items like the Flathead, the Brandin' Iron, and the Bobcat, MacKenzie River offers gourmet pizza with traditional and nontraditional sauces and toppings. Smoked trout on a pizza? No problem. Want a pizza with Thai spices and a peanut sauce? Try the Thai Pie. The pizzas are made with a choice of five fresh sauces (Tomato, Pesto, BBQ, Alfredo, and Extra Virgin Olive Oil), marinated and grilled meats, and chunky-fresh vegetables, then topped off with a three-cheese blend. The restaurant has become a staple throughout Montana and has stores in several cities, including Belgrade, eight miles west of Bozeman. Bozeman's was the first in 1992, and the restaurant's rustic, lodgepole interior is a great example of Montana-inspired architecture. MacKenzie also offers great sandwiches and huge, mouthwatering salads (try the house dressing, a specialty) as well as wine and several beers on tap. The kids will love this place as they can choose their own personal size pizzas. MacKenzie River also delivers.

Montana Ale Works
611 E. Main St., Bozeman
(406) 587-7700
$$

This popular grill and pub opened during the summer of 2000 in the old Montana Transportation depot and has quickly become one of Bozeman's dining and social hotspots. The bar features more than 40 beers on tap, and the food ranges from casual fare like burgers and chicken sandwiches to grilled salmon and prime rib. It's also a great place to go for appetizers, and diners have the choice of eating in the pub or the separate lounge, although there is only one menu. Montana Ale Works also offers pool tables by the hour.

The Pickle Barrel
809 W. College St., 209 E. Main St.
Bozeman
(406) 587-2411, (406) 582-0020
$

Big and cheap. That's what the sandwiches at Bozeman's oldest sandwich shop are. You can get a half or a whole, but don't be fooled: A half is about as big as other whole sandwiches and is plenty for one person. Local favorites include the Bobcat (named for the university's athletic mascot), Ken's Special, and the Mushroom Steak. The College Street store delivers and, of course, every sandwich includes a signature pickle—plucked right from the barrel.

The Point After Bar and Grill
15 N. Rouse Ave., Bozeman
(406) 587-7982
$

Sports fans will love the Point After, where owner Phil Schneider has assembled a great collection of Montana State University memorabilia, which you'll see hanging on the walls of this restaurant on the main floor of the old Bozeman Hotel building. Big burgers, sandwiches, salads, and appetizers appear on the menu, and portions are usually bigger than your appetite. With six televisions, chances are the game you want to watch will be on. If not, the friendly staff will try to find it for you.

Ruppert's Tap House
2711 W. College St., Bozeman
(406) 522-8960
$$

Ruppert's, one of Bozeman's newer restaurants, has become popular since it opened in 1999. Although the nonsmoking establishment doesn't brew its own beer, it offers a large selection of Montana microbrews, imports, and domestics. The food here is creatively American, with great burgers, sandwiches, salads, and pasta. Ruppert's serves lunch and dinner, and offers a late night bar menu after 9 P.M. and occasionally has live music.

Spanish Peaks Brewing Company
Corner of N. Church and Main Sts.
Bozeman
(406) 585-2296, (800) 810-CHUG
www.spanishpeaks.com
$$

Spanish Peaks, established in 1991, maintains its place as Bozeman's first brew pub. A new location in the American Bank Building in downtown Bozeman manages to get everything right: the food, beer, and atmosphere. The cuisine is a bit more upscale than most brew pubs, but the surroundings remain casual: high, exposed ceilings with lots of windows, dark woodwork, an upstairs dining area, and an open grill. The nonsmoking restaurant offers mostly Italian style dishes, from tasty brick oven pizzas to excellent scampi, ravioli, and calzones. There's always seafood and steak specials, and the pork tenderloin in a currant bourbon sauce is especially good. Signature beers include Black Dog Ale (the real dog on the brewery's label, Chug, is a popular local icon), Sweetwater Wheat and an outstanding porter. T-shirts and other clothing with the Spanish Peaks logo are popular items and available at the restaurant.

Sweet Pea Café and Bakery
19 S. Willson Ave., Bozeman
(406) 586-8200
$–$$

This quaint little spot serves up fresh baked goods and coffee for breakfast, delicious homemade soups and sandwiches for lunch, and a variety of gourmet entrees for dinner. For lunch and dinner, choose from a wide variety of croissants, baguettes, pastries, and vegetarian dishes. Choices you are apt to see on the menu include broccoli and red potato soup, a chicken salad sandwich served on a croissant, and a mushroom risotto served atop a portabello mushroom. Beer and wine are also available, as well as a healthy, or not so healthy, selection of amazing desserts.

The Western Café
443 E. Main St., Bozeman
(406) 587-0436
$

If you gaze at the walls of the Western, you'll see magazine and newspaper articles highlighting the café's celebrity guests and longtime local patrons. Farm and ranch old timers give the Western its namesake atmosphere. Nothing is fancy here, just like all the great diners, but the servings are hearty and the mood is relaxed. Breakfast is the main staple, where you'll often see college kids mingling with the regulars, and the Western is usually a busy place for lunch. If you're staying in Bozeman, a meal at the Western is a satisfying tradition that anyone can take part in.

The Wok
319 N. 7th Ave., Bozeman
(406) 585-1245
$$

The Wok is one of Bozeman's better Chinese restaurants, and its selections are pretty much standard Chinese fare. The Mongolian Beef is especially good. You can also choose from a healthy number of seafood entrees. If you don't want the food delivered to your door, you can eat in The Wok's delightfully casual atmosphere.

Nightlife

The Belgrade Lounge and Karaoke Club
32 E. Main St., Belgrade, MT 59714
(406) 388-6098

This popular spot is located in Belgrade, about eight miles west of Bozeman on the Frontage Road. The Frontage Road turns into Belgrade's Main Street, and you'll find the lounge on the left as you come into town. Karaoke is entertaining here, and live country and rock music is featured on the weekends. Bill's Grill (388-8840), serving up good breakfasts, lunches, and dinners, is attached to the lounge.

The Cat's Paw
721 N. 7th Ave., Bozeman
(406) 586-3542

This large bar has live music from local and national acts every weekend, as well as some performances during the week. Choose from a large selection of tap beer and packaged liquor to go. Also, there are plenty of gambling machines as well as a card room in the back for those feeling lucky.

The Crystal Bar
123 E. Main St., Bozeman
(406) 587-2888

This downtown fixture is a mix of locals and college students and is a classic Montana bar, complete with cowboy boots and the occasional scuffle. Don't let that discourage you, though, as the Crystal can be a great place to hang out, especially in the summer when the upstairs patio serves up great burgers, sandwiches, and drinks.

The Haufbrau
22 S. 8th Ave., Bozeman
(406) 587-4931

This is where old tables go to die. Walk in the Haufbrau, look up, and you'll see old wood table tops nailed to the ceiling, full of initials, names, and phrases that people carved in long ago. There's a few booths and tables here, a pool table, and a small stage in the corner. The bar hosts an open mike or a local singer/songwriter every night of the week, with Tex Tucker being the one-man house band. Tex is local

icon, and can belt out just about any tune you request. The Haufbrau also serves up a good—and cheap—lunch.

Little John's
515 W. Aspen St., Bozeman
(406) 587-1652

Variety is the theme at Little John's, where you'll find country and western dancing, blues bands, and DJs all in the same week. A local swing dance instructor is usually on hand once a week to give you a few lessons, and weekends often feature live music. Little John's has a casual atmosphere and a clientele of college students and younger business professionals.

The Mint Bar and Café
27 E. Main St., Belgrade, MT 59714
(406) 388-1100

Just across the street from the Belgrade Lounge (see above) you'll find the Mint, a great spot to soak in some real Montana atmosphere. You'll often find cowboys sipping martinis here, as the Mint offers more than 30 different styles, from classic

Insiders' Tip

After many years of trying, Bozeman skateboarders and inline skaters finally got the skate park they were asking for. With money mostly from private donations, the park opened in the summer of 2000 and is already a popular gathering spot for the local skating community. The park isn't that big, but it's super fun with rails, boxes, hips, and a bowl. It can get a little crowded at times, and there's likely to be lots of younger kids. The park can be found on North 20th Avenue, one block from West Main Street, and is open from dawn to dusk. No BMX bikes are allowed (if you're on your bike, head to the dirt track at the corner of Tamarack Street and North 5th Avenue). If you need equipment, stop in and say hello to the friendly folks at World Boards (601 W. Main St., (406) 587-1707) and they'll set you up and suggest other places to skate.

to eccentric. The restaurant in the Mint offers excellent steaks and seafood, and there is usually live acoustic music once or twice during the week.

Montana Ale Works
611 E. Main St., Bozeman
(406) 587-7700

This bar/restaurant is on the east end of town, which has seen a resurgence of building over the past few years. The large, nonsmoking establishment is one of the most popular places in town from happy hour (4 to 6 P.M.) until closing. You can get food late, and there are hourly and coin-operated pool and snooker tables. The bar doesn't offer liquor but instead serves up its own brand of beer, specially brewed by Helena's Blackfoot River Brewing Company. But your choices aren't limited to that you can also choose from more than 40 tap and bottled beers, as well as a good selection of wine. It's open until midnight Sunday through Thursday and 1 A.M. on Saturday and Sunday.

The Robin Lounge
105 W. Main St., Bozeman
(406) 586-1314

This newly remodeled lounge, located on the main floor of the historic Baxter Hotel building is a great place to go for happy hour and is one of Bozeman's more popular after-work bars. There are great appetizers to choose from (you won't be able to finish the nachos) and a good selection of beer, wine, and cocktails. There's usually live jazz at the Robin on the weekends, and the bar is part of three restaurants in the Baxter. The Bacchus Pub (586-1314) serves casual fare and breakfasts, while the excellent Baxter Grille (586-1314) specializes in steaks and seafood. All three are connected to the elegant, two-level main lobby of the Baxter.

The Zebra Cocktail Lounge
321 E. Main St., Bozeman
(406) 585-8851

The cocktail lounge, located in the basement of the old Bozeman Hotel building, is actually part of a network of three bars located in the same area. You'll find live music on the weekends and DJs during the week here (it can get quite loud), and right next store is the more quaint and quiet Colonel Black's, where there are two pool tables and plenty of comfy chairs. Upstairs, on the main floor, is another bar (587-2339) where you'll usually find a laid back atmosphere and core group of locals vying for the lone pool table.

Shopping

The Big R Ranch and Home Supply
2275 N. 7th Ave., Bozeman
(406) 586-8466

Let's say you're staying in a cabin with a wood stove. You're outside chopping wood, and somehow you break the axe and rip your brand-new flannel shirt. After that you notice Fido's food is gone and the truck's low on oil. At the Big R, you can replace your axe, grab a new flannel, pick up some dog food, and fill your truck up with oil all in one stop. There's a big selection of Western wear as well as designer clothes from Ralph Lauren, and plenty of pet supplies—and just about everything in between. It's a popular store that is spreading to different cities around the state.

Bob Ward's Sporting Goods
2320 W. Main St., Bozeman
(406) 586-4381

This Montana chain store offers everything from hunting and fishing licenses and equipment to ice skates, inline skates, skis, and snowboards. Not to mention swimsuits, shoes, golf clubs, sleeping bags, backpacks, sunglasses, books, and clothing. Get the picture? If you need something, chances are Bob and the boys have it.

Highway 10 on local Bozeman maps is almost always referred to as the Frontage Road. The road runs alongside I-90 and is used by locals instead of the interstate. You'll notice these roads while driving alongside just about any Montana highway, as they were often primary roads until the four-lane interstate system took over.

Bridger Peaks Town Center
North 19th Ave. and Oak St.

This strip mall type shopping center is an example of the development taking place on North 19th Avenue near the interstate. It's a nice looking structure that blends into the New West environment, and offers an excellent variety of shops, services, and restaurants. Among these are Pier 1, Old Navy, the Gap, Kentucky Fried Chicken/A&W, Benningan's Restaurant, a dry cleaner, a Christian Science Reading Room, a toy store, bank, and many others.

Cactus Records
29 W. Main St., Bozeman
(406) 587-0245

At Cactus, you'll find a healthy selection of bluegrass, world, rock, folk, pop, local, and used CDs, as well as an eclectic selection of t-shirts, candles, cards, knick-knacks, and novelty items. You can also buy tickets here for local concerts, which are advertised on the chalkboard behind the counter. Cactus will let you listen to any album before you buy it.

Community Food Co-op
908 W. Main St., Bozeman
(406) 586-1023

This is the place to go for organic produce, dairy products, meat, and groceries. The Co-op is a popular Bozeman spot with reasonable prices and a selection that would satisfy most shoppers. There's also a great deli that serves delicious soups, salads, and sandwiches for lunch. The Co-op also carries beer and wine, and has a large selection of bulk grains and other items.

The Emerson Cultural Center
111 S. Grand Ave., Bozeman
(406) 587-9797

The two-story Emerson, as you'll often hear it called, is a former school that has been converted into more than 40 art galleries, shops, and studios. There's often music, dance, or theater going on in the main auditorium, and there's an espresso bar as well as the Café Internationale restaurant on the first floor. The Emerson is part of a nonprofit organization that offers art and related classes as well as exhibits, concerts, and films.

The Gallatin Valley Mall
2825 W. Main St., Bozeman
(406) 586-4565

This small shopping center, located on the west end of town near the Main and College intersection, has undergone a $1.8 million facelift and added more nationally known stores since ownership exchanged hands in 1997. Anchor stores include the Bon Marche and JC Penney. Some of the newer stores include Eddie Bauer, Bath and Body Works, and Victoria's Secret. There's also a variety of restaurants, a game room, flower and framing shops, a post office, and a bank—plenty to keep you busy on a rainy afternoon.

Montana Gift Corral
237 E. Main St., Bozeman
(406) 585-8625

If you want to pick up something from your trip that says Montana, this is the place. From antler candle holders to moose-laden dishcloths and sweatshirts, Montana Gift Corral has a large selection of unique items for the home. There is also a Montana Gift Corral store in Big Sky.

Northern Lights Trading Company
1716 W. Babcock St., Bozeman
(406) 586-2225

This store is representative of Montana's active lifestyle. Here you'll find gear for backcountry skiing, rock and ice climbing, canoeing and kayaking, and everything in between. Northern Lights also has a great selection of casual wear, sweaters, shirts, pants, and shoes, and rents kayaks and canoes during the summer and skis and snowshoes in the winter. There's also a large topographic map and book selection, and a basement that offers closeout deals on brand-name gear.

Osco Drug
1600 W. Main St., Bozeman
(406) 587-9252

Osco has everything that a typical drug store has and more. There is a pharmacy and wine shop (one of the biggest selections in town), as well as film developing and selected food items. Osco also has a Made In Montana section, where you'll find things like huckleberry jams, regional travel books, and knickknacks.

Poor Richard's News
33 W. Main St., Bozeman
(406) 586-9041

This classic downtown newsstand has just about any magazine you could want, as well as local and national newspapers and books of regional interest. Poor Richard's also sells cigars, pipe tobacco, and a variety of imported and specialty cigarettes. It closes at 9 P.M.

The Round House Ski and Sports Center
1422 W Main St., Bozeman
(406) 587-1258

The Round House has a great selection of outerwear and equipment for just about any form of outdoor recreation. Specializing in skiing, snowboarding, backpack-

ing, and biking, the Round House is a full service sports center. In the summer, Larry Merkel's staff will tune your bike and in the winter they'll tune your skis. They also rent rafts and bikes in the summer, and skis and snowshoes during the winter, and have a second location at the Bridger Bowl Ski Area north of Bozeman.

Vargo's Jazz City and Books
6 W. Main St., Bozeman
(406) 587-5383

This downtown fixture has a great selection of new and used books and a large selection of jazz CDs and hard-to-find records. There's a large regional author section, highlighting some of Montana's more well known writers, including David Quammen, William Kittredge, Rick Bass, Tim Cahill, Thomas McGuane, Annick Smith, Mary Clearman Blew, and more. Vargo's also has many rare and older books for sale.

Insiders' Tip

Traveling Bozeman's side streets in the winter can be a treacherous affair. Most of them don't get plowed—designated snow routes are plowed first and main thoroughfares second, leaving side streets a distant priority. When it snows, the streets become sloppy, rutty, and hard to navigate, especially when cars are parked on both sides, so go slow and avoid them if you can.

Golfing in Big Sky with Lone Mountain looming in the background. PHOTO: BIG SKY RESORT

Big Sky

Accommodations
Restaurants
Shopping
Nightlife

This year-round resort community was founded in 1973 by the late NBC newsman Chet Huntley and sits in a small valley between Bozeman and West Yellowstone, surrounded by the Gallatin National Forest and the Spanish Peaks Wilderness Area. Big Sky is a popular spot in the summer and winter, when most visitors come to play in the shadow of Lone Mountain, a cone-shaped 11,166-foot peak that dominates the horizon.

Big Sky's location—about 20 miles from the Yellowstone Park border and along the Gallatin River—makes it a tourism-driven place, and because of that there is plenty to do. Summer visitors to the Park often spend time in Big Sky, taking advantage of horseback rides, hiking and biking trails, fly-fishing, rock climbing, and whitewater rafting just outside your doorstep. Big Sky also is home to rustic dude ranches and posh guest lodges, excellent restaurants, and a world-class golf course. The Big Sky Association for the Arts also puts on classical, bluegrass, and country concerts at their outdoor pavilion, and past performers include Willie Nelson, Randy Travis, Del McCoury, and the Bozeman Symphony. Check the organization's web site www.bigskyarts.org for schedules.

Powder-hungry skiers and snowboarders from all over the world flock to Big Sky Resort in the winter, hoping to catch some of the annual 400 inches of snow. The European-style ski area boasts more than 120 trails on three mountains, 3,600 acres, a high-speed lift system, and a total vertical drop of 4,350 feet, making it one of the premier destinations in the Rockies. Lone Mountain Ranch is a world-class Nordic resort, offering 75km of beautiful trails, professional instruction, gourmet cuisine, Yellowstone tours, lodging, and sleigh rides. Snowmobiling is the other popular winter activity, with hundreds of miles of trails accessible from the Big Sky area. For more on these activities, see the Winter Sports chapter in this book.

Big Sky is different than other ski towns in that there is no quaint little village like Aspen, Telluride, or Crested Butte, and since it is fairly new, development has been scattered around the mountain, dividing Big Sky into three distinct parts: the Canyon area, the Mountain Village, and the Meadow Village. The Gallatin Canyon area at the entrance to Big Sky refers to the shops and services located along the Gallatin River at the junction of U.S. Highway 191 and the Big Sky Spur Road, which heads west toward Lone Mountain and the ski resort. The Canyon area has many shops, restaurants, hotels, and other services, and is about nine miles from the mountain.

After driving two miles on the Spur Road you'll come to the Meadow Village. This is really the center of town for the

Insiders' Tip

When people refer to the Big Sky entrance, they are talking about the junction of U.S. Highway 191 and the Big Sky Spur Road. The road heads west from the highway toward the ski resort. Also, if you hear Gallatin Road mentioned, that means Highway 191.

locals, and where you'll find grocery stores, galleries, banks, restaurants, shops, and a post office. You'll see plenty of condos along the Arnold Palmer-designed golf course, and lots of new construction. Big Sky is a booming place, with multimillion-dollar homes, shopping centers, and condominiums sprouting up all over. You'll also hear people refer to Westfork, which is the area on the south side of the Spur Road across from the golf course. Westfork also has restaurants, lodging, and shops. You'll often hear people refer to all of these locations with just one word: Mountain, Meadow, and Westfork.

The Mountain Village refers to everything that is around the base of the ski resort. To get to the village, turn left off the Spur Road by a well-marked sign. This will take you past Lake Levinski and numerous condo complexes. There is a turnaround loop at the main cluster of buildings, which include the Huntley Lodge, the Summit Hotel and the Shoshone Condominium, and there is a $10 day parking lot for guests here. Summit guests have the option of underground valet parking, and other condos have their own parking. If you're just skiing for the day, a free skier parking lot is located a short walk from the Mountain Village. In the Mountain Village, you'll register for resort rooms and condos and find guest and skier services, shops, galleries, restaurants, and real estate offices. Driving past the Mountain Village on the Spur Road will take you toward the Moonlight Basin area, where there is a newly constructed lodge and even more places to stay. There are also chairlifts to Moonlight Basin, providing some of the many ski-in, ski-out lodging opportunities available at Big Sky.

Big Sky has an interesting and colorful history. Shoshone and Crow Indians inhabited the area before trappers arrived in the early 1800s and were followed by gold prospectors who left their mark on nearby towns like Virginia City and Nevada City. Early homesteaders lived off the land, which even today is full of wildlife and natural beauty. In the early 1900s, numerous dude ranches sprang up in the remote Gallatin Canyon to give Big Sky its first tourists. Many of these historic places, including the 320 Ranch, the Covered Wagon Ranch, and Lone Mountain Ranch, are still in full operation today—a testament to the way the area draws visitors in droves to experience a piece of true Western history. The original Crail Ranch house, named after early pioneer and cattle rancher Frank Crail, can be seen by the golf course in the Meadow Village.

In 1969, well known newscaster Chet Huntley teamed up with a group of investors to buy the old Crail Ranch, and began his dream of putting a ski area in this once-remote, incredibly stunning stetting. In 1973, Big Sky Resort opened its doors, but Huntley died of cancer shortly before his dream was realized. Boyne U.S.A., which owns several resorts around the country, bought Big Sky in 1976 and has developed the area into a world-class summer and winter destination.

Today, Big Sky really is a place where people come and create their own vacation. If you want to be pampered, Big Sky has everything you want: Spas, five-star restaurants, luxurious hotels, and guided recreation. This is the New West version of Big Sky. If you want the Old West, you can stay in a rustic cabin and hike back into a mountain lake, or take a horseback ride for the day and cook out over a campfire. And if you're the adventurous type, you'll be in paradise. Run the Gallatin in a raft or kayak, climb the Gallatin Tower or mountain bike down from what seems like the top of the world. Big Sky is also a place where more and more locals are calling home, becoming a hodgepodge of ski bums, entrepreneurs, retired folks, and adventure seekers.

Obviously, Big Sky is a place driven by the seasons. In the summer and winter, it can be a busy place, but quiet compared to most resorts. In fact, most people come to Big Sky because of its laid back, relaxing atmosphere, and to get away from the crowded resorts of the East and West. Around 4,500 people make the busiest day on the slopes, and most days are half that. That's a far cry from the most popular destinations in Colorado, Utah, California, and Vermont, and it's also one of the reasons why more and more people are discovering the area.

In the spring and fall, typically referred to as "shoulder seasons," the town can seem deserted. There are great deals on lodging and other activities during these times, making for an uninterrupted, peaceful vacation. Some of the resort services close for a period during the off-season, so check closure dates before you plan your trip.

Traffic on the highway between Bozeman and West Yellowstone (and all the way to Jackson) can be heavy during the summer and winter, and this is also a trucking route. Be especially alert on the often winding, narrow road, which can turn icy and snowy during the winter.

Big Sky's summer doesn't get going until mid-June and typically is fairly dry and warm. The high mountains can sometimes trap clouds, leaving Big Sky socked in with rain, hail, and even snow. (In fact, Willie Nelson played in a storm with driving, dime-sized hail.) Temperatures drop considerably when the sun goes down, so bring warm clothes. Big Sky truly is one of the prettiest places in Montana, and a place well worth visiting any time of the year.

If you don't have a car or don't want to drive, the free Snow Express shuttle service (995-6BUS) makes regular winter stops around Big Sky from mid-December to mid-April, from about 7 A.M. until 11 P.M. Stops in the Big Sky area are marked by a big blue sign—similar to a city bus stop sign—in front of local businesses, condo complexes and shops. Call for schedule information.

Accommodations

Hotels and Condominiums

Hotel and Condominium Rates

Keep in mind that some rates are based on availability. The average nightly rates for two adults at the hotels and motels listed in this section are indicated by a dollar sign ($) ranking in the following chart. Also, the hotels and motels in this chapter accept all or most major credit cards.

$ . . . . $50 to $75

$$ . . . . $76 to $100

$$$ . . . . $101 to $150

$$$$ . . . . $151 and more

Best Western Buck's T-4 Lodge
P.O. Box 160279, Big Sky, MT 59716
(406) 995-4111, (800) 822-4484
www.buckst4.com
$$$

Buck and Helen Knight established Buck's T-4 in 1946 as a hunting camp, but it was converted to the present day lounge bar four years later and became a popular spot for visitors heading down the canyon to Yellowstone. Buck and Helen sold the establishment in 1972, and Mike Scholtz has since turned the T-4 into a full service resort complex. The grill and gameroom were added in 1975, a new dining room was constructed in 1977, and a Best Western lodge was added in 1979. The hotel unit features 75 deluxe rooms, two outdoor hot tubs, and a complimentary hot breakfast buffet every morning. There is great food in the lounge, and even better food in the renowned dining room, which has been featured in *Ski Magazine*, *Gourmet Magazine*, *Mountain Living*, and the *Chicago Tribune*. The wine list consistently wins awards, and entrée selections include a long list of seafood and game dishes. Buck's is located one mile south of the Big Sky entrance.

Insiders' Tip

If you are an advanced skier and can't find suitable skis at the resort's rental shop, try one of the local ski shops on the mountain or in the canyon. You can pick from a variety of advanced equipment and rent it for the duration of your stay.

Big Sky Chalet Rentals
P.O. Box 160058, Big Sky, MT 59716
(406) 995-2665, (800) 845-4428
www.bigskychalets.com
$$$–$$$$

You can rent condos and guest houses in the Mountain and Meadow Villages through Big Sky Chalets. Accommodations in the Mountain Village include both two to four bedroom ski-in/ski-out condos as well as regular two to five bedroom condos, townhomes, and two to four bedroom homes. You can choose from the Beaverhead, Big Horn, Saddle Ridge, Sky Crest, and Cedar Creek condominiums. In the Meadow Village you can choose from one to four bedroom condos and townhomes as well as homes with two to four bedrooms. These include the Crail Creek, Glacier, Hidden Village, Silver Bow, Yellowstone, and Blue Grouse condominiums. Check the website for photos and locations of the properties, as well as the availability of private guest homes.

Castle Rock Inn
65840 Gallatin Rd., Gallatin Gateway, MT 59730
(406) 763-4243
$

Situated next to the Gallatin River and beneath the towering rock spires that line the Gallatin Canyon, the Castle Rock Inn is one of the few establishments on Highway 191 from Bozeman to Big Sky. You can choose from eight medium sized riverside cabins that sleep up to six people comfortably, and you'll find groceries, propane, gasoline and camping supplies at the small store. There's also a family style café and a 10-unit trailer court with full hookups and modern bathrooms.

The Comfort Inn
P.O. Box 161095, Big Sky, MT 59716
(406) 995-2333. (877) 466-7222
www.comfortinnbigsky.com
$$

The main feature of the Comfort Inn is the indoor, 90-foot water slide, which

Close-up

All play, no work

Get in the snowcat. Enjoy the warm ride up. Put on your skis or snowboard. Follow the powder all the way down. Repeat.

That's the object at **Montana Backcountry Adventures** (406) 995-3880, www.skimba.com, a guided snowcat skiing operation that has been giving fresh tracks on the north side of Lone Mountain since 1997. For $225, you can enjoy up to 12,000 vertical feet of skiing on more than 1,800 acres of excellent terrain. MBA is one of Montana's few backcountry operations, and you'll get primed on avalanche conditions and safety before you head out.

The best part about it? Tell owner Kyle Hockenstein or one of his experienced guides where and what you want to ski and you'll most likely be led right to it. If it's a full-on powder day you'll be in heaven, and even if it hasn't snowed in a few days there will be plenty of powder. This happened to our group once, and Kyle simply took us to a secret spot he was saving just for this occasion. Lucky for us.

You'll stop just long enough to enjoy a lunch at MBA's backcountry hut, and continue until your legs burn as if you've just run a marathon. But you won't care, as you'll be too busy wiping that powder mustache off your face.

Call ahead to check on availability and conditions. Only 12 people can go at a time, and a large group can reserve the snowcat for around $2,000 per day. Skis, snowboards, helmets, and avalanche equipment are available for rental.

makes the hotel a great place for families. Amenities include king suites with spa and fireplace, complimentary ski lockers, continental breakfast, triple queen suites with private bedroom, pool, and hot tub. The 62-room hotel is located just south of the Big Sky entrance in the Canyon Area.

The Corral Bar, Café and Motel
42895 Gallatin Rd., Gallatin Gateway, MT 59730
(406) 995-4249, (888) 995-4249
www.corralbar.com
$

This eight-unit log motel is located on U.S. Highway 191 about five minutes south of the Big Sky Spur Road. It's one of the most affordable places to stay in the area, and rooms include phones and use of an outdoor hot tub. The grub at the popular café is legendary—big burgers, great steaks, and a salad bar, as well as huge breakfasts to get your day started right.

Golden Eagle Lodge and Management
P.O. Box 160058, Big Sky, MT 59716
(406) 995-4800, (800) 548-4488
www.bigskylodging.com
$$–$$$$

Golden Eagle, a ResortQuest company, offers everything from economy lodging to luxury condominiums and homes, mostly located in the Meadow Village, but also in the Mountain Village and the Canyon area. When you call Golden Eagle, simply explain what you are looking for and chances are they will find something to match your needs and your budget.

The recently completed Summit at Big Sky hotel complex provides European luxury with Western hospitality. PHOTO: BIG SKY RESORT

The Huntley Lodge and Shoshone Condominium Hotel
P.O. Box 160001, Big Sky, MT 59716
(406) 995-5000, (800) 548-4486
www.bigskyresort.com.
$$$

The Huntley and Shoshone were the main base area lodging facilities until the completion of the Summit in the summer of 2000. The Huntley offers 200 rooms, lofts, and suites, and the Shoshone has 95 one-bedroom and loft units with kitchens. There are also tennis courts, heated indoor/outdoor pools, a health club, retail shops, restaurants, and lounges. All rooms are within walking distance to the chairlifts.

The Summit Hotel at Big Sky
P.O. Box 160001, Big Sky, MT 59716
(406) 995-5000, (800) 548-4486
www.bigskyresort.com
$$$$

The impressive Summit is one of the most recent additions to the lodging at the base of the ski area, and its ten stories tower over the Mountain Village. The 222-room structure is also one of the most luxurious in Big Sky, designed in an elegant, Euro-Western style with leather couches, finely crafted furniture, and mammoth rock fireplaces. You'll find restaurants, boutiques, fitness center, spa, underground valet parking, outdoor soaking pools, and hot tubs all within a few hundred feet of the chairlifts. Rooms are designed so they can be interchanged as studios and one-, two-, and three bedroom units, and feature kitchens, fireplaces, balconies, and hot tubs in many units.

Insiders' Tip

It is not long distance to call from Big Sky to Bozeman, West Yellowstone, Livingston, and Gardiner, even though that represents a large geographic area. This makes it convenient when planning day trips or other activities.

Guest Ranches and Lodges

Guest Ranch and Lodge Rates

$	Less than $85
$$	$86 to $115
$$$	$116 to $150
$$$$	$151 and more

320 Guest Ranch
205 Buffalo Horn Creek, Big Sky, MT 59730
(406) 995-4283, (800) 243-0320
www.320ranch.com
$$$

The 320 Ranch has a rich history as one of the first guest ranches in the Big Sky Area, beginning in 1898 when two homesteads were combined to total 320 acres. The ranch was purchased in 1936 by Dr. Caroline McGill, Montana's first woman physician, and has been a working ranch and a favorite spot for visitors since. Accommodations range from cozy, one-bedroom cabins to large, three-bedroom guest homes.

The 320 has several activities to keep you busy, including horseback riding, fly-fishing (you can fish two miles of the Gal-

The 320 Ranch near Big Sky, Montana, still has working wranglers. PHOTO: DONNIE SEXTON/TRAVEL MONTANA

latin without leaving the property), snow-mobiling, sleigh riding, and skiing. The old West steakhouse at the 320 offers superb dining and is open to the public.

Cinnamon Lodge
37090 Gallatin Rd., Big Sky, MT 59716
(406) 995-4253
$–$$

The newly restored Cinnamon Lodge is located 11 miles south of the Spur Road, and features individual log cabins, some of which are on the Gallatin River and include full kitchens. The full service bar and restaurant offer the area's best Mexican cuisine as well as Montana steaks, burgers, chicken, homemade desserts, and vegetarian dishes served daily from 5 to 10 P.M. The Cinnamon Loge also offers horseback rides, and nearby you'll find fishing, hunting, river rafting, hiking, biking, skiing, and snowmobiling.

Covered Wagon Ranch
34035 Gallatin Rd., Gallatin Gateway, MT 59730
(406) 995-4237
www.coveredwagonranch.com
$$$$

The Covered Wagon has provided mountain dude ranch vacations since 1925 and prides itself on a true Western experience without the glitz or glamour associated with many resorts. At the CW, you'll find comfortable one- and two-bedroom rustic log cabins with private baths, and a spacious, stunning main lodge where you'll be fed ranch-style meals three times a day.

The ranch, which sits at 6,700 feet above sea level, is located about 18 miles south of Big Sky on U.S. Highway 191, three miles from Yellowstone National Park and adjacent to the Taylor's Fork of the Gallatin River. Nature is just out your door, and in the summer you can partake in guided horseback rides and hikes, fly-fishing, mountain biking, and evenings are capped with a bonfire outside the main lodge. The CW is open year round (rates are significantly cheaper in the winter) and also offers snowshoe and cross country ski tours, and is close to snowmobile trails and downhill skiing.

Lone Mountain Ranch
P.O. Box 160069, Big Sky, MT 59716
(406) 995-4670, (800) 514-4644
www.lmranch.com
$$$$

Lone Mountain Ranch is a renowned destination resort for cross-country skiers, but even if you don't hit the 75km of groomed trails there is plenty to do. There are two options for staying here: the individual, cozy guest cabins or the Ridgetop Lodge, an incredible six bedroom guest lodge perfect for families or large groups. The cabins are warm and comfortable, and each one has a private bath, wood burning stove, or fireplace and electric heat. None of them have phones or a TV, making sure nothing distracts you from enjoying the area. The smaller cabins have one bedroom/living area and bath and the larger cabins have a separate living room and two to three bedrooms. The main lodge is a breathtaking structure that exemplifies Montana-style architecture and features one of the best restaurants in Big Sky.

In summer, activities include horseback riding, naturalist tours, fly-fishing, guided Yellowstone Park trips, and programs for kids. During the winter, enjoy the snowshoe trails and sleigh rides, and Big Sky Resort is only five miles away. Lone Mountain Ranch is located about halfway between the Meadow and Mountain Villages on Spur Road.

Rainbow Ranch
Gallatin Canyon, Big Sky, MT 59716
(406) 995-4132, (800) 937-4132
www.rainbowranch.com
$$$$

The Rainbow Ranch has been voted one of the 25 best American lodges by *Travel & Leisure* magazine, and is located about 10 miles south of Big Sky on U.S. Highway 191. The ranch was first occupied by the Lemon family in 1919, when few people lived in the area. After realizing that cattle ranching on the land was too difficult, the family built the Halfway Inn (named for the inn's location halfway between Bozeman and the entrance to Yellowstone) offering meals and cabins for rent. The Lemons sold the ranch in 1946 and since then it has gone through several different owners and names. The barn down by the river is the only building that remains from the Lemon family's days at the ranch.

These days, the Rainbow Ranch is a year-round vacation spot that offers guests luxurious accommodations and gourmet dining. Guest rooms include lodgepole beds, fireplaces, whirlpool tubs, handcrafted duvet covers over stuffed comforters, and private decks overlooking the Gallatin River. The Rainbow offers horseback rides from its own stables and fly-fishing right out your back door. The ranch's restaurant is one of Montana's finest. (See the Restaurants section of this chapter for more information.)

River Rock Lodge
3080 Pine Dr., Big Sky, MT 59716
(406) 995-2295, (800) 995-9966
www.riverrocklodge.com
$$$

The small, luxurious River Rock Lodge provides European-style service in a relaxed, warm atmosphere. The lodge, located three miles from the Spur Road turnoff, features 29 secluded guest rooms and an executive suite, each with a stocked mini-bar, VCR, and designer bath, as well as personal touches such as natural toiletries, fresh cut flowers, and comfy bathrobes.

The rooms are decorated in typical Western fashion, and the Vista Suite includes a fireplace, private balcony, and Jacuzzi tub. The River Rock has custom packages to suit your needs, and fly-fishers will want to take advantage of the guided trips offered by 1997 Orvis Fly-Fishing Guide of the Year Gary Lewis.

Restaurants

Restaurant Rates

Prices include cost of meals for two people, excluding beverages, tip, and tax

$	$10 to $19
$$	$20 to $27
$$$	$28 to $35
$$$$	$36 and more

Big Horn Café
47995 Gallatin Rd., Big Sky, MT 59716
(406) 995-3350
$

The Big Horn is located in the Big Horn Center, a large log structure just north of the Big Sky entrance that houses a few other shops as well, and serves breakfast and lunch all day until 3 P.M. The majority of the café's delicious food is homemade, right down to the potato chips served with your gourmet sandwich. Favorites here include the huevos rancheros, the potato platter, the Cuban sandwich, and

the hot pastrami. The Big Horn also has great coffee and espresso, and you can dine in or take out.

Café Edelweiss
Meadow Village, Big Sky, MT 59716
(406) 995-4665
$$$

A little bit of Europe in Big Sky, as this cozy restaurant serves authentic Austrian cuisine like schnitzels, bratwurst, and knockwurst, as well as traditional meat, game, and seafood dishes. Try the Sauerbraten Platter, Mountain Trout Almondine, or

Whitewater rafting the Gallatin River is a popular summer activity for Big Sky visitors. PHOTO: DONNIE SEXTON/TRAVEL MONTANA

the Pepper Steak Austria for something different. Every Wednesday and Friday Café Edelweiss hosts a Fondue Stube, featuring full course dinners with a variety of fondues. The food isn't the only Old World thing here—the interior's hand-carved wood décor lets you think you could be in downtown Vienna.

The Corral Bar, Café, and Motel
42895 Gallatin Rd., Gallatin Gateway, MT 59730
(406) 995-4249, (888) 995-4249
$–$$

If you're staying in Big Sky and don't make the short drive down U.S. Highway 191 for a meal at the Corral, you'll be missing out on some of the best grub from Bozeman to Jackson. Breakfasts here are legendary—big, greasy omelets, chicken fried steak, and homemade biscuits and gravy—and a favorite of early morning skiers, snowmobilers, and hikers. A burger at the Corral for lunch or after a day of skiing is a delicious and fill-

ing local tradition. For dinner, the restaurant is famous for its monster mouthwatering steaks, but the menu also offers seafood, sandwich, and pasta selections. There's also an all-you-can-eat salad bar, and the chili here will have you shedding layers in no time.

Dante's Inferno
Mountain Mall, Big Sky, MT 59716
(406) 995-3999
$–$$

Dante's location at the base of the ski area makes it a popular lunch and aprés ski spot, where you can feast on hearty appetizers, burgers, pizza, and sandwiches and water it down with one of the 10 beers on tap. The dinner menu in this big, open, barn-like structure features New York strip steak, pastas, calzones, seafood, and nightly specials, and a children's menu. You can often find music here after a day of skiing and on weekend nights, and Dante's is well known for its large selection of single malt scotches.

Close-up

Dining out—literally

Everyone likes to eat out, but how about eating *outside*? In the middle of winter, a few miles back in the woods? Well, in Big Sky it can be done, as many restaurants and outfitters offer sleigh ride, horseback, or snowcat dinners and lunches. It's a romantic and family favorite for locals and visitors alike.

Montana Backcountry Adventures (406) 995-3880, www.skimba.com) offers guided snowcat skiing and snowboarding as well as snowshoe tours to Ulrey's Lakes. The company also offers moonlight dinners, where guests are transported to MBA's backcountry dining lodge by snowcat, then feast on a delicious dinner prepared on the spot. After dinner guests will enjoy live music until it's time to go back—which always seems to come too soon.

Sleigh Ride Dinners at the **Lone Mountain Ranch** (see above) are extremely popular and offer a true Western experience not found in many places. Horse-drawn sleighs take diners out to the ranch's remote North Fork cabin, where a prime rib dinner is cooked on an old-fashioned wood stove and served by the light of the lantern. Western guitar music and songs by well-known area musicians round out the evening. Dinner is available six nights a week (the other day is reserved for ranch guests) and cost $69 per person during the 2000–01 season. Call (406) 995-2783 for reservations, which are strongly encouraged.

At the **320 Ranch** (see above), beautiful Percheron draft horses pull an old-fashioned sleigh along the Gallatin River every winter evening to a campsite where guests can warm themselves by the crackling fire, enjoy cowboy chili and hot beverages, and listen to stories of the ranch and the Western lifestyle. Rides begin at 5:30 P.M. and 7 P.M., and cost $29 per adult, $18 per person under 12 during the 2000–01 season. Reservations are required.

A little further drive down the highway is the elegant **Bar N Ranch** (800-BIGSKYS, www.bar-n-ranch.com) where a sleigh ride dinner is included with a three-night minimum stay. You'll be wrapped up in cozy blankets and taken along a 30-minute ride through the ranch's moonlit trails before returning to enjoy an authentic Western meal next to a warm fire. The Bar N is located southwest of West Yellowstone on U.S. Highway 20.

First Place
Meadow Village Center, Big Sky, MT 59716
(406) 995-4244
$$$

First Place is open for dinner seven days a week from 6 P.M. to 10 P.M., and offers a fine dining experience in a casual atmosphere. A large and varied menu will satisfy most every appetite, and popular favorites include baked Montana trout with lemon and herbs, lightly salted veal with morel mushrooms, king salmon, charbroiled tenderloins, and charbroiled rack of lamb with rosemary and garlic. The bar at First Place opens at 5 P.M., and reservations are suggested.

Gallatin Gourmet
Meadow Village, Big Sky, MT 59716
(406) 995-2314
$

The Gallatin Gourmet, located in the Meadow Village plaza on the north side of the Spur Road, serves up made-from-scratch soups, sandwiches, salads, and desserts for lunch and dinner 11 A.M. to 9 P.M. daily. There are also burgers, pasta, chicken, fish, and steak on the menu, and a full bar is available.

Huckleberry Café
Meadow Village, Big Sky, MT 59716
(406) 995-3130
$

This cute and cozy restaurant is located in the American Bank building in the Meadow Village and is open every day but Wednesday from 7:30 A.M. to 2:30 P.M. This local favorite, known for big portions and friendly service, has many vegetarian and Southwestern specialties (the huevos rancheros are excellent) and a different soup every day. You can also grab a cup of coffee or espresso to go.

Lone Mountain Ranch
P.O. Box 160069, Big Sky, MT 59716
(406) 995-4670, (800) 514-4644
www.lmranch.com
$$$$

The beautiful log dining lodge at the Lone Mountain Ranch is a spectacular sight. Huge elk chandeliers dangle from the high ceiling and a massive stone fireplace warms the room on cold winter nights. When you sit down at your table here, the food will be equally spectacular. Dinner (reservations required) is served between 6 P.M. and 8:30 P.M., and the menu includes nightly selections of beef tenderloin, seafood, venison, trout, and pasta. Bison, duck, lamb, pheasant, and elk also make regular appearances on the menu. Chef T. R. Romagnuolo's self-described "New American Ranch" cuisine has been featured in magazines like *Town and Country*, *Travel & Leisure*, the *New York Times* and the *Los Angeles Times*. There's also a great saloon in the main lodge that opens at 3:30 P.M.

Milkie's Pizza and Pub
Westfork Meadows, Big Sky, MT 59716
(406) 995-2900
$

This lively local hangout has great food at reasonable prices served in a pub-style atmosphere. The pizza here is top-notch and a big hit with hungry skiers after a day on the mountain. Other fare includes standard selections of burgers, salads, appetizers, and sandwiches. Milkie's is also a popular nightlife spot.

Mountain Top Pizza Pies
Mountain Mall, Big Sky, MT 59716
(406) 995-4646
$

Mountain Top is a tasty and inexpensive place to stop in for lunch if you're skiing, as the thin-crust pizza is sold by the slice and by the pie. Choose from a variety of toppings or specialty pizzas like the Omnivore (vegetables) or the Carnivore (meat), as well as huge, mouthwatering calzones. Mountain Top also delivers to the Mountain Village and is located at the base of the ski area.

M.R. Hummers
Mountain Mall, Big Sky, MT 59716
(406) 995-4543
$$–$$$$

This popular Mountain Village establishment has served up great lunches and dinners since 1983. If you stop in for lunch, try the hot pastrami sandwich or Joe's Famous Chili, and steak lovers should make it a point to head here for supper. You can get a filet mignon, sirloin, New York strip, prime rib, or T-bone steak any way you like it. Hummers also

---

Insiders' Tip

When parking in the free skier parking lot during the winter, a skier shuttle—a big Ford truck pulling an even bigger trailer with benches—will come around every five minutes or so and take you up to the resort and back to the parking lot. It's not a far walk but the convenience is nice, especially after a tiring day on the slopes.

has crab, lobster, and surf and turf specials, and is open for lunch 11 A.M. to 3:30 P.M. and dinner from 5:30 P.M. on.

Peaks
Mountain Village, Big Sky, MT 59716
(406) 995-8076
$–$$$

This is one of Big Sky's newest restaurants, opening for the 2000–01 ski season in the new Summit Hotel at Big Sky. Beautifully decorated in Euro-Western fashion —lots dark wood, black, and chrome—and a great view of Lone Mountain out the windows, Peaks is a great place to come for an après ski appetizer or a romantic dinner. The homemade, big-enough-for-two pizza is made with a whole wheat crust and is a great choice for lunch. If it's a warm day, enjoy your food or drink out on the patio, which is only about 50 yards from the slopes. Peaks recommends making reservations for dinner.

Rainbow Ranch
Gallatin Canyon, Big Sky, MT 59716
(406) 995-4132, (800) 937-4132
www.rainbowranch.com
$$$$

The public restaurant in this well-known lodge (see above) has been featured in magazines like *Bon Appetit* and *Outside*. Chef Michael McAulliffe combines local, regional, and international cuisine to create a unique and imaginative menu, which features wild game, fresh fish, and vegetarian items. Sample entrees include Black Quinoa Tabouleh with Leek and Carrot-Wrapped Enoki Mushrooms, Caramelized Spaghetti Squash and a Haitian Pepper Sauce; Pan-Seared Chilean Sea Bass with Thai Sticky Rice, Grilled Fingerling Potatoes, and a Saffron & Vanilla Bean Sauce; and New Zealand Rack of Lamb Crusted with Tobacco Mushrooms with a Pomegranate Mustard Glaze, Chestnut Lima Bean Succotash, and Buffalo Mozzarella. The wine list boasts more than 500 selections, and is consistently recognized for excellence by *Wine Spectator* magazine. The ranch recommends reservations.

The ranch also offers summer barbecues on Tuesday, Wednesday, and Thursday nights on the banks of the Gallatin River, with ribs, burgers, and chicken served on the deck of the property's old barn.

Rocco's
Meadow Village, Big Sky, MT 59716
(406) 995-4200
$–$$

In the mood for Mexican or Italian but can't decide which? Head to Rocco's, a restaurant that serves up both varieties every night, including enchiladas, rellenos, pasta, fajitas, veal, and seafood. It sounds like an odd combination, but locals appreciate Rocco's for its variety, reasonable prices, and big portions.

Sun Dog Café
Mountain Village, Big Sky, MT 59716
(406) 995-2439
$

If you are staying in the Mountain Village and need a good cup of coffee, stop in the Sun Dog and say hello. It's a favorite morning meeting spot for locals heading for the slopes, who often grab a fresh-baked bagel, croissant, or muffin on the go. These same locals come back for lunch, too, for the Sun Dog's steamed tortilla wraps, hearty soups, chili, and Montana-sized sandwiches. There's also a large vegetarian selection and ice cream for dessert or a quick snack. You'll find the Sun Dog directly to the right of the lift ticket office in the Snowcrest Lodge.

Timbers Restaurant, Bar, and Deli
Moonlight Basin Lodge, Big Sky, MT 59716
(406) 995-7777
www.moonlightbasin.com
$–$$$$

The new Moonlight Basin Lodge, constructed for the 2000–01 ski season, is situated at the base of the Powder River ski run and the Iron Horse chairlift on the north side of Lone Mountain. It is a magnificent structure, with huge picture windows, massive pine pillars, leather furniture in the lobby, and a 37-foot stone fireplace. The bar at Timbers serves fresh soups, bleu cheese burgers, and excellent chicken sandwiches for lunch and dinner, and the spicy fries are delicious. Chef Scott Méchura runs the Timbers restaurant, which specializes in a wide range of American classics with a metropolitan accent, including beef tenderloin topped with a wild mushroom tomato confit, herb and juniper crusted lamb loin, oven steamed salmon, grilled yellowtail tuna, and venison. The restaurant serves lunch and dinner.

The deli at Timbers serves lighter fare for breakfast, lunch, and dinner, including sandwiches, soups, salads, and cheeses, and it carries a few grocery staples as well. A big, south-facing patio is perfect for sunny, warm days when taking a break from skiing at the lodge. If you are driving to the lodge, continue on the Spur Road past the entrance to the ski resort and follow the signs to the Moonlight Lodge, about two miles.

Twin Panda
Arrowhead Mall, Big Sky, MT 59716
(406) 995-2425
$

Big Sky's only Chinese restaurant has all the favorites—egg rolls, chow mein, beef and chicken stir-fries, Szechuan dishes—in a casual atmosphere great for families or groups of friends. It is located on the third floor of the Arrowhead Mall in the Mountain Village.

Shopping

Big Sky Boardroom Snowboard Shop
Mountain Mall, Big Sky, MT 59716
(406) 995-5840

Located in the lower level of the Mountain Mall at the base of the ski area, this is Big Sky's only true snowboard shop.

You'll find equipment and apparel from Burton, Sims, Lib Tech, K2, and Salomon, and a full-service repair shop will put your board in top condition. The shop is also a Burton test center and demos are available. The shop is open daily from 9 A.M. to 6 P.M.

The Country Market
Meadow Village Center, Big Sky, MT 59716
(406) 995-4636

The Country Market is Big Sky's largest grocery store and it has been since 1983. It's not what you'd really call a supermarket, but it has everything you need. There's fresh produce, a bakery, and a deli, as well as a large selection of beer and wine. You'll also find Montana made gifts and souvenirs. The Country Market offers a winter delivery service, too, and is open from 8 A.M. to 8 P.M. daily.

Grizzly Outfitters
Meadow Village, Big Sky, MT 59716
(406) 995-2939
www.grizzlyoutfitters.com

With a new location next to the post office in the Meadow Village Center, Grizzly Outfitters offers equipment for downhill skiing, touring, ski mountaineering, snowboarding, telemarking, snowshoeing, backpacking, climbing, and mountain biking. You can also rent downhill and cross-country skis, snowshoes, mountain bikes, and camping gear, and a repair shop offers complete ski, snowboard, and bike tune-ups.

J.P. Woolies
Mountain Mall, Big Sky, MT 59716
(406) 995-4542

The hand-knit wool ski hats at J.P. Woolies have been keeping Big Sky skiers warm for 16 years. You'll also find a big kid's selection, jewelry, gifts, candles, bath supplies, home furnishings, clothing, and toys. Many items are handcrafted by artists from around the Northwest.

Lone Mountain Ranch Outdoor Shop
P.O. Box 160069, Big Sky, MT 59716
(406) 995-4734

Located in the historic Lone Mountain Ranch (see Lodging section), this shop (open daily from 8 A.M. to 7 P.M.) has a full selection of cross-country equipment, accessories, and apparel, as well as Mon-

tana-made gifts and unique Native American jewelry. You can also rent cross-country skis and snowshoes and get your dinged skinny skis repaired.

Lone Mountain Sports
Arrowhead Mall, Big Sky, MT 59716
(406) 995-4471

This full-service Mountain Village ski shop has a retail area upstairs and a rental and repair shop downstairs, specializing in performance shaped skis. You can rent skis or snowboards by the day or week, and the friendly staff will set you up with the proper equipment for the conditions. A full selection of clothing, equipment, and accessories is available in the retail shop upstairs. This shop is open 8 A.M. to 6 P.M. daily during the winter.

The Lone Spur
Shoshone Lobby, Big Sky, MT 59716
(406) 995-3980
www.lonespur.com

If you want to pick up some real Western wear during your stay, stop in at the Lone Spur and get done up the cowboy way. Pick out a nice hat and a pair of boots, and choose from a variety of leather and traditional apparel. There's also stuff for kids and a unique selection of gifts.

Moose Rack Books
P.O. Box 160039, Big Sky, MT 59716
(406) 995-4521, (406) 995-2551

This quaint little bookstore has two locations, one in the Big Horn Center in the Canyon area and one in the Mountain Village at the base of the ski area. Moose Rack has a large selection of regional and travel books, USGS topographic maps, out of print and rare books, books on tape, stationery, greeting cards, gifts, shipping service, and more. The Big Horn shop also has a coffee/espresso bar and baked goods.

Paparazzi Fur and Leather
Huntley Lodge and Mountain Mall
Big Sky, MT 59176
(406) 995-4705, (406) 995-4605

This upscale furrier has been selling designer furs, wearable art, leather fashions, and accessories since 1985. Prices start at $100 for certain headwear, but this stuff is not cheap. A fur coat from Zuki and other famous designers runs from $2,500 to $80,000. Paparazzi specializes in the latest, trendy fashions, or what co-owner Craig Swick calls "fun furs." These are often found in magazines such as Vogue and appeal to much of the high-dollar crowd at Big Sky. Stopping in just to look is OK.

Plum Logo
Mountain Mall, Big Sky, MT 59716
(406) 995-4141, (406) 995-2155

If you're looking for something that says Big Sky, this is the place—literally. At Plum Logo, you'll find fleeces, sweatshirts, hats, mugs, keychains, and stickers, all with the Big Sky logo on them. You'll also find a great selection of other clothing, jewelry, gifts, and plenty of stuff for the kids.

Spirits of Big Sky
Canyon Area, Big Sky, MT 59716
(406) 995-4343

This is Big Sky's only retail liquor store and is located next to Buck's T-4 Lodge on U.S. Highway 191, just south of the Big Sky entrance. There is also a large selection of wine, beer, gifts, huckleberry products, and local artwork. Stop in from 10 A.M. to 8 P.M. Monday through Saturday, or choose to have your items delivered.

Willow Boutique
Meadow Village Center, Big Sky, MT 59716
(406) 995-4557

You'll find designer clothing, jewelry, gifts, furniture, and accessories for the home at the quaint shop, located in the Meadow Village next to the post office. There is a large selection of Western-style knit sweaters and hats to choose from to complete the Big Sky look.

Wilson's Video
Westfork Meadows, Big Sky, MT 59716
(406) 995-4046

Want to chill out with a movie after a rough day of skiing? Wilson's is Big Sky's only video store and offers a wide selection of new releases and kids' videos. You can also grab some popcorn, candy, ice cream, and soda to complete your viewing experience.

Nightlife

Big Sky is not really known for its nightlife, but as the area grows, more and more spots are popping up. Most après ski places are in the Mountain Village and become more mellow the later it gets. There are a few genuine party bars, although you may have to head down into the Meadow or Canyon to find that atmosphere.

The Carabiner
Mountain Village, Big Sky, MT 59716
(406) 995-8078

This new lounge is on the terrace level of the 10-story Summit Hotel and is a great spot to end your day on the slopes. A fireplace keeps the small space toasty and the chairs and couches are extra comfy. You can order from a nice selection of appetizers, and there are plenty of liquor, beer, and wine choices. Après ski entertainment usually consists of acoustic music performed by a local tunesmith.

Chet's
Huntley Lodge, Big Sky, MT 59716
(406) 995-4253

Chet's is a mellow place named after Big Sky's founder, Chet Huntley. It is a popular après ski spot, and there is regularly scheduled live music, usually a solo guitar player or duet, in the evenings. A menu of hearty appetizers should satisfy most appetites after a day of playing around the area.

Cross-country skiers flock to the trails of Lone Mountain Ranch in the winter. PHOTO: DONNIE SEXTON/TRAVEL MONTANA

Dante's Inferno
Mountain Mall, Big Sky, MT 59716
(406) 995-3999

Dante's is a happening place on the weekends, when live music is often heard until the bar closes at 2 A.M. The crowd is a pretty good mix of tourists and locals, and the big, barn-like structure can hold plenty of people. You'll usually find a solo performer during the aprés ski scene, generally from about 3:30 P.M. until 6 P.M.

Lolo's Saloon
Mountain Village, Big Sky, MT 59716
(406) 995-3455

This loud and lively bar is located on the lower level of the Mountain Mall at the base of the ski area and is popular with the under-30 crowd. The atmosphere can range from quiet to rowdy—mostly the latter—and is where many of the ski resort employees hang out after work. Lolo's also serves decent appetizers and sandwiches and has pool and foosball tables, as well as occasional live music.

Milkie's Pizza and Pub
Westfork Meadows, Big Sky, MT 59716
(406) 995-2900

This is the Meadow's little hotspot, although it depends on the night. Some nights you'll find a real party crowd here, full of locals celebrating a powder day, and other nights the bar will be better suited for quiet conversations. Either way, Milkie's is a hoot, with a pool table, a few dart boards, and great food served late.

Rooster's
Arrowhead Mall, Big Sky, MT 59716
(406) 995-4933

This Mountain Village bar and grill—formerly known as Scissorbill's—is mostly an aprés ski spot, but occasionally folks stay well into the night. It's a small place with a tasteful décor, tables, and booths under exposed beams and lots of windows. There are standard burgers, appetizers, and sandwiches to eat and an outdoor patio to enjoy them on. Rooster's usually has live music a few times a week on the small, corner stage.

Livingston

Accommodations
Restaurants
Shopping

If there is such a thing as a "new Montana," Livingston is it. Here, writers, artists, and Hollywood movie stars mingle with ranchers, railroad workers, and miners. With a population of 7,500, the town is a little bit blue collar, a little nouveau riche, a little outdoorsy, a little glitzy, a little Old West.

Livingston is a community where old and new generations co-exist and intermingle and thrive in their own unique ways. A stroll down historic Main Street reveals the melding of the town's diverse interests. In the six blocks of the neatly restored downtown you will find art galleries, cowboy boot makers, fly fishing shops, interior designers, and hardware stores next door to each other. This is authentic small town USA, where a handwritten sign on the door of any retail shop reading "gone fishing" or "back in 10 minutes" seems perfectly acceptable in the context of good business.

One thing that residents, both old and new, share is a pride in the town's heritage. Just ask the 1,500 citizens who made national headlines when the U.S. Postal Service tried to move the historic Livingston post office from downtown—it took just four days for them to compile a petition, contact their congressman, and stop the move. Residents have also worked hard to meticulously restore the Livingston Depot Center, a tribute to the town's original 1882 railroad roots. This community's spirit is evident in so many places, from the Carnegie Library to the artfully designed Sacajawea Park with its fishing bridge, lagoon, and river path.

Livingston's location makes it seem like paradise. Sitting on the big bend of the legendary Yellowstone River and surrounded by three mountain ranges—the Absaroka, Crazy, and the Gallatin—Livingston is just 55 miles from Yellowstone Park's northern entrance. The quality of life also makes this an appealing community. Living here means embracing the wondrous natural beauty and appreciating a lifestyle that is removed from the fray of a large metropolis. Visiting here means adjusting to the easy-going pace and taking things as they come.

Like many Montana towns today, Livingston struggles with a changing economy that has moved from dependence upon the railroad and natural resource industries to tourism and high technology. Although most residents would never call their town a bedroom community to Bozeman, nearly 35 percent of the population commutes to jobs in the "big city," just 23 miles to the west on I-90. The Livingston Rebuild Center—a longtime headquarters for repairing locomotive engines— is still a major employer, as is Montana Rail Link.

Although the actual population of Livingston has remained steady for the last 20 years, it is not undiscovered. Robert Redford's film, *The Horse Whisperer* and local resident Dennis Quaid's TNT movie, *Everything That Rises,* as well as parts of *A River Runs Through It* were filmed here. Singer Jimmy Buffet also wrote the hit song, "A Livingston Saturday Night," about this town's raucous nightlife. And judging by the number of bars, saloons, and casinos within a three-block radius—12 in all—you can see why. You could do your own kind of pub crawl, moving from the old-timer's cowboy clique at The Stockman, to disco night at The Sport Next Door, to the rowdy biker sanctum of the Hyatt House, or to the sound of blues at The Murray. On a weekend night during the summer, don't be surprised if you find folks sipping wine at gallery walks or two-stepping in the streets for the annual Fourth of July celebration.

Close-up

The Ghost of Chico Hot Springs

Chico Hot Springs Lodge is famous for its hot water and gourmet cuisine. Tucked into a corner of Paradise Valley just south of Livingston, the historic resort could even call itself other worldly thanks to stories of a resident ghost.

Some folks believe that Chico's first proprietor, Percie Knowles, is still alive, at least in spirit. Since her death more than 75 years ago, there have been reports at the hotel of a floating old woman, mysterious rattling of pots and pans, and a rocking chair that always returns to the spot where Knowles spent some of her last days gazing out at Emigrant Peak.

Most of the ghost stories come from Chico employees, but there was one report of a New Year's Eve occurrence almost twenty years ago. A group of teenagers were diving into the hot springs pool from the roof of the locker rooms when a mysterious white light appeared. It reportedly began moving along the eaves of the building from where the swimmers had been jumping. Spooked by the unexplainable experience, the kids stopped partying and went inside.

"I don't know if there is a ghost at Chico," says Eve Art, the current owner. "A lot of people believe they've seen something and say it was Percie or someone else. But I have never seen a ghost."

She and her husband, Mike, bought the dilapidated Chico in 1973 and have restored it to its glory.

"I can tell you that in the early days this was a very spooky old building," Art continues, "and things happened that I can't explain—doors slamming, curtains blowing for no reason when the windows weren't open, all kinds of scary noises. But Chico is really a place to enjoy and if people believe in ghosts, they'll just have to come and see for themselves."

The natural mineral pools at historic Chico Hot Springs Lodge in Pray, Montana, are perfect for soaking after a long day of play in Yellowstone. PHOTO: SEABRING DAVIS

In the late 1890's Bill and Percie Knowles operated a boarding house near the hot springs for gold miners who'd staked their claims in Emigrant Gulch. Bill was known in the community for his gregarious nature and love of the outdoors. His prim wife, Percie, was remembered for her strong opinions against drinking and gambling. Together they saw their dream come true with the opening of Chico Warm Springs Hotel on June 20, 1900.

Their business boomed. Guests raved about the luxurious accommodations and soothing natural waters of the adjoining pools. Against his wife's wishes, Bill Knowles soon opened a saloon and dance hall on the property. Percie spoke adamantly against the use of liquor and wanted it nowhere near the hotel. Nevertheless, the addition only improved business and Chico Hot Springs Resort continued to flourish.

After her husband died from cirrhosis of the liver in 1910, Percie shut down the saloon and transformed Chico into a sanitarium/hospital. She hired Dr. George Townsend to run a hospital wing and touted the natural hot springs as the cure for everything from "rheumatism to kidney troubles." For sixteen years the health care center thrived, until the doctor retired. In his absence business dwindled and Percie's health began to suffer under the pressures of running her business alone.

Later her family cared for her and she was kept in room 349 on the third floor of the old hotel. It's said that she would sit in a rocking chair during her waking hours and stare out the window at Emigrant Peak. As she deteriorated mentally and physically, Percie was sent to the Warm Springs state mental hospital where she died four and a half years later. Her son brought her body back to Chico to have her buried in the old cemetery.

Although modern day Chico has seen many changes, the original hotel is structurally very much as it was during Mrs. Knowles' day. Ironically the third floor is where many haunting encounters have occurred, such as one night when former security guard Larry Bohne was working.

"It was the third week of January 1990, and I was used to being alone in the old hotel," Bohne said. "During the winter months there are usually only a few guests at any one time and on this night they were in rooms on the main floor just off the lobby. Besides them and me, the only other person in the hotel was the night auditor in the main office.

"Even though no one was staying on the second and third floors, it was still my job to make routine fire checks in these areas," Larry went on. "On one of my rounds, at about 2:30 A.M., I was walking along the second floor hallway. As I passed the stairwell leading to the third floor I could sense that someone was at the head of the stairs. I stepped back a few paces and looked up to see a matronly lady standing at the top landing looking down at me.

"That seemed unusual because I was sure there were no registered guests above the first floor," Larry explained. "The lady appeared to be about five feet four or so and approximately forty-five to fifty years old. Her face, though clearly defined, seemed real pale and expressionless. It was obvious she was looking at me, but she didn't acknowledge me at all. She wore a full-length light blue dress with a high collar and long sleeves and the material looked like it was printed with tiny white flowers. Her hair was up in a tight bun and she had her hands clasped in front of her.

"I thought she was a guest who'd gotten lost, so asked if I could help her. When I spoke she moved back into the darkness of the third floor hall. I say 'moved', because she didn't look like she was walking—more like she just drifted away without any movement in her upper torso or any kind of leg movement under her long dress.

"I went up to the main hall on the third floor, but everything was dark except for dim light coming from the courtyard. Since all the guest rooms are locked, I figured the lady must have gone into one of the bathrooms in the hall. But as I walked in that direction I smelled a sweet fragrance in the vicinity of rooms 346 through 350. I went and checked the bath-

(Continued)

rooms, which were empty and dark, then backtracked until I got a whiff of that sweet smell again. It reminded me of jasmine or lilac and it was strongest near room 349," Bohne said.

"I knocked, then opened the door with my pass key. The room was dark and silent. I shined my flashlight around. Nothing. Then I noticed that the rocking chair in the corner was moving back and forth gently. My heart jumped, I flipped on the light switch quickly and saw the chair stop rocking instantly. I checked the window. It was closed tightly. But even if it had been open, it wasn't windy that night and if it had just been the wind the movement wouldn't have stopped so suddenly. I felt like there had been someone in that room, but I also noticed that the sweet scent had faded away . . . The whole thing took five or six minutes," Bohne said.

There have been countless reports of other phenomena related to Percie's ghost: On another night two security guards attempted to take a photograph of an apparition that hovered in the lobby for several minutes; from outside the dining room two figures were seen sipping drinks at 2:30 in the morning, but when someone went to investigate, they found no one there; housekeepers hear footsteps and doors slamming on a supposedly deserted third floor; there's an inexplicable cold feeling and the sense of some presence in a room. And no matter where a certain antique rocking chair is moved in room 349, it is always mysteriously returned to the same window with a view of Emigrant Peak.

Accommodations

Price Code

Keep in mind that some rates are based on availability. The average nightly rates for two adults at the hotels and motels listed in this section are indicated by a dollar sign ($) ranking in the following chart. Also, the hotels and motels in this chapter accept all or most major credit cards.

$	$25 to $49
$$	$50 to $75
$$$	$76–100
$$$$	$101 and more

Chico Hot Springs Lodge
1 Old Chico Rd., Pray
(406) 333-4933, (800) HOT WADA
$$

Not far from the river, just south of Livingston and 30 miles north of Yellowstone National Park is Chico Hot Springs Lodge, an oasis in the rough.

Rooted in history, the resort has been a secret getaway spot since its opening in 1900. Most people come to soak in the natural hot springs, but it's the true rustic charm and unpretentious glamour that draws visitors again and again. Without the modern distractions of telephones or TVs in the rooms, this destination resort provides sheer relaxation instead. Guests can explore the wonders of Yellowstone on a day trip, enjoy hiking or mountain biking, horseback riding, or choose the simple luxury of doing nothing at all.

Although the many locals who frequent Chico would like to keep the place their little secret, the turn-of-the-century Victorian-style inn attracts visitors from around the world.

Choose from a variety of accommodations on the property, ranging from the cozy antique rooms in the main lodge to private cabins on the hillside, a room in the comfortable motel addition, or the option of beautifully decorated new rooms in the lower lodge. Wherever you lay your head, Chico's amenities will win you over.

The Murray Hotel
201 W. Park St., Livingston
(406) 222-1350
$$

According to a *New York Times* article, "The historic Murray Hotel appeals to celebrities and to a certain Western disorder."

It is true that the turn-of-the-century hotel rented a permanent room to the late actor Warren Oates—the room is still decorated with some of his lamps and pictures.

Located in the historic district, within walking distance of museums, restaurants, and fishing, the 30 comfortable rooms are inspired by the Western tradition. The elegant lobby, with Victorian and art deco décor, invites you to lounge with a good book and hot cup of tea. A roof-top spa has views of all three mountain ranges and the Murray Bar downstairs features music throughout the week.

Insiders' Tip

Livingstonites refer to Paradise Valley, located south of town on your way to Yellowstone, as "The Valley." Since there are quite a few valleys around, it can be confusing if you're new to the area.

Yellowstone Inn
1515 W. Park St., Livingston
(406) 222-6110, (800) 826-1214
$$

New owner Tom Vincent has upgraded this 100-room modern hotel for the business traveler. Focusing on attracting conferences and large events, Vincent says service is the key to keeping guests happy.

Consequently, the Yellowstone's staff will readily arrange activities for visitors to the area with advance notice. They also provide shuttles to Bozeman airport and Bridger Bowl Ski area. An on-site restaurant and lounge can keep you happy, but if you'd like to enjoy other areas of Livingston, you might want to drive or call a taxi.

Bed and Breakfasts

Price Code

$	Less than $85
$$	$86 to $115
$$$	$116 to $150
$$$$	$151 and more

Greystone Inn Bed and Breakfast
122 S. Yellowstone St., Livingston
(406) 222-8319
$$

Gary and Linda Lee have restored this Colonial Revival Style stone house to its near 1900 perfection. One of only five homes in Livingston made of hand-cut local sandstone, this stately house is a landmark. Rich interior furnishings and maple floors lend the rooms an elegant coziness.

Guests can get a sense of what it is like to live in this quaint town as they lounge in the hammock and watch neighborhood children play. The location is just slightly removed from downtown's bustle, but still within walking distance to all of the community's sites. The Inn's neighborhood features many fine, restored historic residences.

The River Inn
4950 U.S. Hwy. 89 S., Livingston
(406) 222-2429
$$

Sitting on the edge of the Yellowstone River, just four miles south of Livingston, this little Inn looks up to the Absaroka Mountain range. Dee Dee Vanzyl and her family share this exquisite spot by renting two cabins on their property. The Victorian-era house resembles homesteads of old and feels like a step back in time. Both cabins are newly refinished with western influences, hardwood floors, and covered porches overlooking the river. Each has a kitchenette and requires a three-night minimum stay. Just a stone's throw from the river, you are minutes from hot fishing spots and cool shady spots to wade in on warm summer day.

Campgrounds and RV Parks

Campground Rates

$	Less than $9
$$	$10 to $16
$$$	$17 to $23
$$$$	$24 and more

Paradise Valley/Livingston KOA
$$ 163 Pine Creek Rd., Livingston
(406) 222-0992, (800) 562-2805
$$

There may not be a better located campground than this one along the shady banks of the Yellowstone River. A heated indoor pool, ice cream socials, outdoor pancake breakfasts, and Sunday evening chapel are only half of why this place has been running for 22 years. Experienced guides and support staff make it seem if you are an old friend, and they will make you want to come back year after year.

Accommodations include cabins with river-front porches, RV hook-ups, and tent sites. Bike and raft rentals are available here, as well. Reservations are a must, however, and it's a good idea to book at least six months in advance.

Restaurants

Price Code

For two people, excluding beverages, tip, and tax.

$	$10 to $19
$$	$20 to $27
$$$	$28 to $35
$$$$	$36 and more

Chatham's Livingston Bar and Grille
130 N. Main St., Livingston
(406) 222-7909
$$$$

Renowned landscape artist Russell Chatham combined his passion for food and wine with his painting in this fine dining restaurant. He can often be seen rambling through the restaurant in painter's overalls, sipping a glass of Bordeaux or Spanish wine, and stopping to greet customers during dinner. Chatham prides himself on a menu which offers fresh catches from both coasts regularly, as well as an unusual wine list, hand selected from his own cellar. His stunning lithographs, depicting the sunsets, snowstorms, and hayfields of Montana, are showcased throughout the restaurant's two rooms.

The stately bar and the captivating, warm, and luxurious atmosphere make this a popular spot with the after-work crowd. The cuisine has European influences, with rich sauces and classic preparations of duck confit, Poisson, and seviche.

The building was erected by local businessman George Carver in 1882. The space was originally a grocery store, but since then has seen many transformations. It became the Livingston Bar and Grille in the early 1970s. Unfortunately the restaurant closed and stayed that way until 1983, when Chatham purchased the property. His dream was to open a restaurant that would appeal to locals' gourmet

Insiders' Tip

The Livingston Farmer's Market is held every Wednesday July through October from 4 P.M. to 7 P.M. at the Depot and Rotary Park, rain or shine. You'll find a sweet offering of home-baked pastries, breads, crafts, and gorgeous wildflowers.

palettes. What he didn't know was how badly dilapidated the building truly was. What was intended to be a simple remodel wound up being a million-dollar restoration.

Chico Hot Springs Lodge
1 Old Chico Rd., Pray
(406) 333-4933
$$$$

People began raving about the restaurant at Chico Hot Springs Lodge over 100 years ago.

It started with a bowl of strawberries during the height of the Montana gold rush. A young couple named Bill and Percie Knowles opened a modest boarding

also an element of refinement that has been integrated to bring out the richness of those basic foods: a pork loin chop stuffed with sun-dried cherry, walnut, and cornbread stuffing; grilled venison served with a Merlot vin rouge; pine nut-crusted halibut finished with a fresh fruit salsa and port wine butter sauce; baked brie served over lingonberry and hollandaise sauces. The result is a menu that is uniquely Montana—as appealing to a local rancher or a Hollywood celebrity as it is to the bon vivant.

Coffee Crossing
104 N. 2nd St., Livingston
(406) 222-1200
$

Located across from the post office and next to the movie theater, this funky coffee shop is a great people-watching spot. Owner John Rawlins and his crew serve up the espresso drinks with friendly smiles and wry humor. To pass the time the guys who work here think up witticisms to paste on the paper go cups. "Wherever you joe, there you are" and "Don't joe there!" are some of the favorites, but they change weekly.

Java Bean
113 W. Park St., Livingston
(406) 222-8472
$

Formerly called The Leaf and Bean, this is Livingston's oldest coffee shop. But that doesn't necessarily mean it's a landmark since lattes and cappuccinos only hit this cow town about 10 years ago. The convenient location on Park Street in the downtown area make this a great spot to grab espresso as you hit the road out of town.

Mark's In and Out
801 W. Park St., Livingston
(406) 222-7744
$

The opening of Mark's In and Out every March (it's open from March 1 to November 1) is a sure sign that spring is coming in Livingston. The neon lights go on, the

house near a natural hot springs and catered to fortune-seeking miners weary of campfire meals and washing their clothes in the creek. They promised a slice of luxury amidst a rugged way of life. What they offered was a clean bed, a hot bath, and fresh strawberries with every meal.

What they learned is that folks will travel far for a good soak and a fine meal.

That's still true today, as Chico has been written up in *Bon Appetit*, *Gourmet*, and *The New York Times*. And for the last three years the restaurant has received the *Wine Spectator*'s award of excellence for its well-rounded wine list.

Over the decades the melding of culinary styles have improved upon those comfort food roots. Chef Jack Hall and his crew still rely on fresh ingredients from the year-round greenhouse and garden, as well as on the local offerings of the area—Montana beef, farm-raised fowl, wild game, and regional trout. Signature dishes on the menu reflect the traditional hearty tastes: Rosemary Rack of Lamb, Beef Wellington, Grand Marnier Roasted Duckling, and Smoked Trout. But there is

open sign goes up and a life-size cut-out of Marilyn Monroe beckons you to slurp up a malt with her.

There are no car hops to serve the shakes, burgers, and fries as there were when this cute drive-up opened in 1954, but otherwise not a lot has changed. Home of the Super Cheese—two patties with two slices of cheese and your choice of toppings for less than $2—it's hard to beat the nostalgia served up here. If there ever is a perfect time to have dinner on the hood of your car, it would be in July when Mark's sponsors the Old Car Show. American flags line the streets to guide a parade of several hundred vintage cars. It's a step back in time that is a must see.

Martin's Cafe
108 W. Park St., Livingston
(406) 222-2110
$

This is a regular's joint that packs 'em in for breakfast every day and doesn't take reservations for the sold out $8.99 Prime Rib Night. It is the kind of place where you expect the waitresses to be named Flo

Insiders' Tip

Make your reservations a year in advance if you plan on visiting Livingston on Independence Day. Fourth of July is bigger than Christmas in Livingston. The whole town kicks off a three-day celebration with a downtown parade and the first night of the Livingston Round-up Rodeo. The rodeo is held July 2, 3, and 4, ending with fireworks every night.

and Vera, wearing horn-rimmed glasses, smacking gum, and callin' you "honey" as they take your order. Signature mint green vinyl seats and chrome edging says 1950s diner culture all the way. The vintage Formica counter is faded from the scrape of thousands of coffee mugs and the stools are worn from old timer's ordering "the usual" over the years

Martin's used to be the all-night diner catering to railroad workers and truckers. Located next to the historic train depot, the building is so close to the tracks that it literally rattles when a train passes. The restaurant still clings to its roots with railroad memorabilia displayed on the walls.

You won't find gourmet frills here. But you can order breakfast anytime of day, get a cup of joe for 50 cents and always choose from five home-baked pies. The milkshakes are great, too. Like the rotating neon sign in the parking lot reads, this is "just good food."

The Pickle Barrel
131 S. Main St., Livingston
(406) 222-5469
$

This place has the biggest sandwiches in town. This corner restaurant is casual and clean, serving hot and cold subs, as well as locally made Wilcoxson's ice cream. The food is consistent, quick, and filling. Their signature is that you will never feel like you need to ask for a second helping of anything.

Founded about 20 years ago by a local ski bum in Bozeman, the Pickle Barrel is a long-time success. This is the ideal spot for the entire family to grab a good lunch or quick dinner to stay or eat on the go.

Rumours
102 N. 2nd St., Livingston
(406) 222-5154
$$

How this unpretentious little café got its name is a very long story, one that involves several prominent figures in town. Still, the bottom line is that the food is excellent. Dubbed "yada yada cuisine" by owner Barbara Pritchett, you can get breakfast, lunch, and dinner with a surprising flair of the exquisite tossed in here and there.

The menu is soul food meets Cordon Bleu, only much more fun. You'll find the seafood selections such as seared ahi or shrimp risotto are fresh and tasty. But the specialties of the house are the oatmeal creme brulee at breakfast—it's worth the splurge of essentially eating dessert first thing in the morning—and the sweet potato ravioli appetizer is sinfully rich enough to be your whole dinner. Also, absolutely any dessert item here is toothsome, as the owner has formal training as a pastry chef.

With a breezy decor offset by mismatched china and a window seat perfect for watching the small town bustle, this is a very pleasant spot to enjoy a meal or leisurely cup of coffee. And true to its name, this is also the spot to catch up on local gossip.

The Sport/Sport Next Door
114 S. Main St., Livingston
(406) 222-3533
$$

The walls of this western bar and restaurant have stories to tell about fortunes won and lost in all-night poker games, bar room brawls, hard luck, hard work, and hard-earned money spent on rounds of drinks. But this once-rowdy saloon is pretty tame these days; the last brawl here was a staged scene for a TNT movie in 1997 directed by Dennis Quaid. He and fellow celebrities Robert Redford and Peter Fonda belly up to the bar every now and then.

Owner Suzanne Schneider has operated The Sport since 1983 and renovated the adjacent space in 1997 for The Sport Next Door. She and her son Eric have carefully restored the space that was originally dubbed The Beer Hall in the late 1800s. The walls give glimpses of history from photos of Livingston's unpaved Main Street to cowboy memorabilia. The original molded tin ceilings and richly painted walls retain that turn-of-the-century charm.

The menu offers a reasonably priced array of salads and sandwiches from teriyaki chicken burger to a vegetarian burrito. There are rumors that the famous Sport Burger is as good as it gets. They proudly serve local meat for lunch and dinner. There is something for everyone here and families are welcome.

The Stockman Bar
118 N. Main St., Livingston
(406) 222-8455
$$

For the past 50 years this old timer's bar and restaurant has been serving unforgettable burgers. It's the place to go to for a slice of Americana Old West style with French fries on top. Sure, the salads are strictly iceberg lettuce and the table clothes are red-checked vinyl, but folks don't come here for the greens or the atmosphere.

There's nothing fancy about this restaurant, but it is a Livingston mainstay. Its greatest strength is consistency—whether it's the rib eye or the New York steak, you can count on the quality. The food is simple and the service is fast. Although smoking is acceptable, this is a fine family restaurant. On weekend nights there may be a 30- to 45-minute wait, so plan ahead and come hungry. They do not accept reservations.

Insiders' Tip

For fly fishers who are hitting the Yellowstone River without a guide, there are several businesses that offer river shuttles to take the logistics hassle out of your day. Contact any of the local fly shops.

Downtown Livingston has many shops, galleries and restaurants housed in beautiful old buildings, framed by the impressive Absaroka Mountains. PHOTO: DONNIE SEXTON/TRAVEL MONTANA

Shopping

Books & Music, Etc.
106 S. Main St., Livingston
(406) 222-7767

Offering everything from autobiographies to science fiction and Sinatra to Santana, this is a shop with something for everyone. You'll find comfy chairs tucked away throughout the store to promote browsing. Owner Tim Gable is very knowledgeable on a broad number of topics and his shop contains a notable travel section.

Catherine Lane Interiors
103 S. Main St., Livingston
(406) 222-7166

Cowboy chic never looked so glamorous as it does here. Catherine Lane is a noted interior designer who has a showroom that doubles as a retail shop. Fabulous wool rugs, plush leather couches, and rich home accents are only part of what you'll find here. You'll feel like you walked onto the set of a home magazine photo shoot and wish you could ship it all home as is.

Golden Bear Trading
122 N. Main St., Livingston
(406) 222-3911

Whether it's an outfit for the Academy Awards ceremony or the PTA picnic, this highly tasteful women's boutique has got it with its selection of silk capris with matching jackets, suede riding skirts, pashmina shawls, sequins, and beads. It's high fashion meets the West. Owner and local ranchwoman Courtney Gannon adds just enough cowboy flair in the style of clothes here to be appropriately glamorous, but not over the top.

Prairie Renaissance
326 S. Main St., Livingston
(406) 222-7605

Take a piece of Montana's beauty back with you in the form of a wildflower candle. This retail/wholesale candle factory romanticizes the necessities of the old West, making you wish you lived in a time where candles lit your way at night. The shop is easily missed because it is at the very end of Main Street near the high school and separate from other retail shops. But it would be a shame to pass it up, since the enticing variety of beautifully made candles, soaps, and other relaxing luxuries are so fine. The shop also takes custom orders for weddings and parties.

Sax and Fryer Company
109 W. Callendar St., Livingston
(406) 222-1421

This quaint bookstore opened in 1883 and is Livingston's oldest business. Inside not a lot has changed, although there are a lot more magazines to choose from now. Owned by John Fryer, who took on the shop from his father, who'd worked it with his own father, this is a great source for books written by local and western authors, Fryer's specialty. Here you'll find signed copies from local novelist Tom McGuane, Missoula author James Welch, or international adventure writer Tim Cahill, who also lives in town.

Timber Trails
309 W. Park St., Livingston
(406) 222-9550

It's hard to miss this hip outdoor shop at the edge of the historic district—there is a bicycle mounted on the rooftop. Though the retail space is small, the selection is vast. The shop sells clothing and equipment for rock climbing alpine/cross country skiing, cycling, mountaineering, snowshoing, and backpacking. Owner Dale Sexton is a do-everything kind of outdoorsman and his store reflects that. He has made the shop a priceless resource for equipment rental and advice on local recreation spots.

Wild West Custom Clothing
116 E. Callendar St., Livingston
(406) 222-8716

This corner boutique offers sassy women's and children's clothes. You'll find the outfit that's just right for a summer barbecue or your victory ride through the arena as Rodeo Queen. The clothing isn't something you'd find at a large western chain store; it is uncommon finery. Alterations and custom fitting are also offered here.

Wilson Boot Company
1014 W. Park St., Livingston
(406) 222-3842

The only problem with a pair of cowboy boots from this landmark boot maker is that they will never wear out. Established in the 1950s, Sterling and Dixie Bowman have seen their business grow from the local cobbler's shop into a booming international product. They do custom fitting in their Livingston shop, but the major factory is in San Antonio, Texas.

Gardiner

Accommodations

Restaurants

Shopping

No other town has boasting rights that include the words, "located right across from Yellowstone National Park." Gardiner, however, has had this distinguished honor since its founding days in 1880. It sits only paces away from Yellowstone's northern entrance, the park's first official entrance and only gate open year round.

Ever the service town, this little burg originally cropped up to feed and shelter miners searching for gold in nearby Jardine. Later it catered to soldiers when the U.S. Army managed the national park services from Mammoth's Fort Yellowstone. It boomed as a tourist town in 1883 when the Northern Pacific Railroad routed its Park Branch Line as far as Cinnabar; reportedly there were six restaurants, two dance halls, four houses of ill-repute, one milkman, and 21 saloons all catering to the thousands of visitors who came to see the wilds of Yellowstone at that time. In 1903 Gardiner hosted president Theodore Roosevelt when he dedicated the Roosevelt Arch, officially marking the gateway to "America's gem."

Since those beginnings, the town's 200 year-round residents have cultivated their love-hate relationship with the park. Just five miles from Mammoth, where park employees reside all year, Gardiner shares its public school, but borrows Mammoth's medical clinic. It is home to the warehouses of AmFac Resorts, Yellowstone's largest concessionaire. It is still the supply town, with an economy reliant upon tourism, mining, and Yellowstone employee needs.

Encircled by the Absaroka-Beartooth Wilderness, Gallatin National Forest, and National Park land, there isn't a lot of potential for Gardiner to grow. It is arguably one of the most scenic locations in North America, with the Yellowstone River running through the center of town, but also the most limited. People either love it or leave it for this reason. Its beauty is double-edged, because as gorgeous as it is here, it can't ever really be much more than a quiet stopover for workers or tourists or wanderers.

As a result, the folks who do call this cul de sac home are hearty, dedicated, and real. It is a tight community that looks out for its neighbors and relies on them in times of need. Everyone here truly knows everyone else's business, although ties loosen up in summer when the number of "parkies"—Yellowstone employees—doubles the town's population. Many of the residents claim their heritage of old mining families, their experiences in Yellowstone, and their love of nature as the reasons they remain in Gardiner. They are stickers and if you want to live here, you'll have to show 'em you're a sticker, too.

What is most genuine about Gardiner is that you won't find any paved streets gussied-up for the tourists or any promotional stunts to make you stay a little longer. It makes a great base to explore

Insiders' Tip

It's not rare to see elk or bison lazing or grazing on the front lawns of Gardiner residences, particularly in winter. The herds loll across park borders in search of the town's lower elevation and warmer temperatures.

Yellowstone. This town offers a quiet, homey perch above the river to re-fuel, relax, and maybe even re-think your tightly scheduled trip. If you do this you might hear the quiet whisper that says, "If you like what you see, stay a while."

Accommodations

Price Code
Code reflects the average nightly rate for two adults.

$	$25 to $49
$$	$50 to 75
$$$	$76 to $100
$$$$	$101 and more

Absarokee Lodge
$$ U.S. Hwy. 89, Gardiner, MT 59030
(406) 848-7414, (800) 7557414

With a balcony overlooking the Yellowstone River and Yellowstone National Park in every room, it is hard to beat the Absarokee's location. Owners Dick and Irene Herriford keep their lodge clean, comfortable, and cozy, considering the place bustles year round. Each room offers all the modern conveniences you could imagine with a friendly crew to back it all up. In addition to rooms with a view, the hotel also has picnic tables on a nice lawn on the banks of the river.

Best Western by Mammoth Hot Springs
$$$ U.S. Hwy. 89, Gardiner, MT 59030
(406) 848-7311, (800) 828-9080

Ask the locals where the action is: where to get in a good steak, a little dancing, and a slick room, they'll tell you it's at the Best Western. The hotel houses the Yellowstone Mine Restaurant and the Rusty Nail Lounge to make everything simple for its guests. Sitting on the banks of the Yellowstone River, this local Best Western combines modern amenities with rustic influences. All 85 rooms offer the usual modern conveniences, along with a laundry facility just off the lobby. The hotel was recently renovated and has a large indoor pool for the kids to romp in after a long drive through the park.

Dome Mountain Ranch
$$$ 2017 U.S. Hwy. 89, Emigrant, MT 59027
(406) 333-4361

Maybe you have already toured through Yellowstone Park and now you want to find out what the western pace of life is really like. Dome Mountain Ranch is the place to experience the quiet of life in Big Sky country, from feeding the cattle in the winter to hiking wildflower-covered trails in the summer. Tucked in the Absarokee Mountains on 5,000 private acres with over four miles of Yellowstone River frontage, Dome Mountain Ranch is a million miles away from any urban distractions. From family reunions to corporate retreats, this dude ranch has a little something for everyone. Accommodations range from a bed and breakfast-style house, to rustic cabins, modern houses, to wilderness camps. The options are limitless here, and the staff will happily arrange horsepack trips into the park, floats on the river, or point you in the right direction for finding the secret spots in Yellowstone on your own. Just 20 minutes from the park's northern entrance, staying here gives you the opportunity to daytrip into Yellowstone and at the same time offers a really unusual place to stay.

Close-up

Yellowstone's Bison Controversy

If having the first official entrance to Yellowstone National Park wasn't enough to put Gardiner, Montana, on the map, the controversy of Yellowstone's bison was.

A government sanctioned killing of the park's bison in 1996 brought national attention to Gardiner once again. The clashing politics of the National Park Service, environmental groups, Montana Department of Livestock officials, and even President Clinton were put to the test over the how to manage the nation's last free-roaming bison herd. It was an issue that landed protesters in prison and sparked a nation-wide debate that still continues today.

In the winter of 1996–97, heavy snows and limited food supplies drove Yellowstone's bison over park borders (primarily to areas north and west of the park in Montana) onto public and private lands where domestic cattle graze in spring and summer. Fearing the transmission of brucellosis from the buffalo to their cattle, livestock producers objected.

Brucellosis is an organism transmitted through birth material left from bison on land where cattle later graze. It can cause cows to abort their calves. Montana has been a "brucellosis-free" state since 1985, which means the state's ranchers do not have to test their herds for the disease before selling them out of state.

Although there is no documented case of Yellowstone bison transmitting brucellosis to cattle, wildlife biologists estimate that nearly half of the park's herd carries the disease. There is no vaccine to prevent the transmission of brucellosis. Montana rancher's felt the risk was too great to be ignored and demand that the bison not be allowed to roam freely out of Yellowstone.

As a result, during the winter of 1996–97, 1,100 bison were shot or sent to slaughter after exiting the park. Another 300 to 400 animals died naturally due to harsh winter conditions, bringing the herd numbers down to 2,400. Native American tribes, animal rights activists, and environmentalists were in an uproar. And though government officials listened to protests, the interim-management solution of eliminating the bison to protect cattle continued.

Bison management in Yellowstone has been an issue since the park's inception, when national herd numbers had dwindled down to just 1,000 animals from the former population of 65 million in North America. Market hunting and poaching nearly eliminated the majestic creatures, prompting the National Park Service to restore their numbers in 1902 with the instigation of the "Buffalo Ranch" in the Lamar Valley. Buffalo were raised like domestic cattle until the 1930s when the herd finally grew to a healthy number. The government saved America's last free-roaming bison herd, but with that intervention began the on-going question of what is the best method to manage them: as wildlife or livestock?

After much debate, in September of 2000 the government released a Final Environmental Impact Statement regarding the Yellowstone bison. Under this plan the NPS is to maintain the overall herd population at 3,000. If bison leave the park, officials will test for brucellosis. Those testing positive would be sent to slaughter and those testing negative will be moved back into park boundaries. The plan was still denounced by many conservation groups.

So the controversy remains. The issue tests the very principles upon which Yellowstone was founded in the Congressional act of 1872, when it was designated as both a place to "preserve all natural wonders and curiosities within" and a place for "the benefit and enjoyment of the people."

Bed and Breakfasts

Price Code

$ . . . . Less than $85

$$ . . . . $86 to $115

$$$ . . . . $116 to $150

$$$$ . . . . $151 and more

Arch House Bed and Breakfast
$$$ 320 Park St., Gardiner, MT 59030
(406) 848-2205

This building was built in 1910 for Harry Childs, president of the Yellowstone Park Improvement project, because he wanted to be the first person to drive a car into the park (a Minnesota tourist beat him to it on July 31, 1916). Tucked into the line-up of shops and restaurants on Park Street, this stone building looks unassuming, but it has seen a lot of changes since its construction. It was a long-time studio and retail store for Yellowstone photographer Robert Haynes, before becoming a general store. It was renovated about four years ago and has been transformed into a condominium-style hostelry.

The little sandstone building was designed by Seattle architect Robert Reamer, who is best known for designing the park's Old Faithful Inn and Lake Hotel, as well as the Roosevelt Arch marking Yellowstone's first official gateway. Located directly across from that famous arch, you can't get a room any closer to the park's northern entrance. This fully equipped house sleeps six people comfortably and includes a daily continental breakfast from Electric Peak Espresso next door. Ask about the extended-day discount.

North Yellowstone Bed and Breakfast
$ 172 Jardine Rd., Gardiner, MT 59030
(406) 848-7651

Located two miles outside of Gardiner on Jardine Road, this feels more like a dude ranch or a summer camp than a B & B.

You are sure to have a piece of Montana wilderness nearly to yourself here, with only two log cabins on the property. Owners Peggy and Bill Hoppe will make you feel like it's your little piece of paradise. A fifth generation Montanan, Bill might even tell you some stories about his ancestors—he claims that his great-grandfather was "the first white child born in Montana Territory circa 1864." He has lived and guided in Yellowstone for 25 years and offers a wealth of knowledge on the area. Ask about extended-stay discounted rates. Other meals, including picnics, can be arranged.

Insiders' Tip

The Gardiner Chamber of Commerce provides a weekly community newsletter that includes local advertisements, upcoming events, and pertinent local news articles. It is distributed on Wednesdays at Chamber member locations. The Sinclair Station and The Food Farm are the easiest places to pick up a copy.

Yellowstone Suites Bed and Breakfast
$ 506 4th St., Gardiner, MT 59030
(406) 848-7937 (800) 948-7937

The white picket fence around this charming sandstone house tells the whole story of this bed and breakfast: home sweet home. Built in 1904, by famous Yellowstone architect Robert Reamer, the house is located in a peaceful residential neighborhood. The four bedrooms are decorated in a non-fussy Victorian style, with antiques and good taste. A private verandah and garden make for pleasant dining in the mornings, while the library is ideal to curl up with a book. The bed and breakfast is open year-round.

Campgrounds and RV Parks

Price Code

$ . . . . Less than $9
$$ . . . . $10 to $16
$$$ . . . . $17 to $23
$$$$ . . . . $24 and more

Canyon Campground
No charge U.S. Hwy. 89, Gardiner, MT 59030
(406) 848-7375

Half-way through Yankee Jim Canyon, just 18 miles north of Gardiner, this tiny campground's 12 units are separated by massive boulders. Located at the base of the canyon wall, across the highway from the Yellowstone River and traces of the old toll road, the first into Yellowstone National Park, this campground has two toilets but no other facilities. The old railroad bed and the Yellowstone Trail, the first automobile route into the park, are on the far side of the river as well. The campground is open year–round. RVs are limited to 48 feet.

Eagle Creek Campground
Jardine Rd., Gardiner, MT 59030
(406) 848-7375
$

It's tough to find a bad campsite in this loosely formed campground, but cruise through the entire area from top to bottom before you choose your spot. At the top you'll find designated tent spaces tucked into the trees. At the bottom there are open spaces with mowed grass. To the east are the corral and plenty of room to pull through with a fifth-wheeler. Don't be alarmed if you end up sharing your morning coffee with a couple resident elk or deer. They like this spot because of the fine grazing, sweet creek, and the fact that it is a little off the beaten path. To find it, head straight for the "CAMP" sign of the Rocky Mountain RV Camp, but don't turn in. Bear left past the entrance instead and drive north approximately 1.5 miles until you see a Forest Service sign for the campground on the left. The services are limited here: there are two toilets, one that is wheelchair accessible. But bring your own water and pack out your garbage.

Rocky Mountain RV Camp
14 Jardine Rd., Gardiner, MT 59030
(406) 848-7251
$$$

Overlooking Gardiner and Yellowstone National Park, Rocky Mountain RV Camp has one of the lower 48 state's most breathtaking views. Follow the neon CAMP sign to this communal oasis after touring the hot, dusty roads of the West. This campground offers 50 RV sites and 21 tent spaces with grass. For the wayward camper, whether RVing it or roughing it, this is an ideal spot to rest or use as a base to sightsee in the park. With public showers, coin-operated laundromat, RV dump station, and garbage drop (just toss it into the back of the 1948 dump truck parked by the office), this is your one-stop shop. If you roll in during the wee hours of darkness, there is an after-hours registration for your convenience by the office door. The campground is only open May 1 to November 1.

Timber Campground
No charge Jardine Rd., Gardiner, MT 59030
(406) 848-7375

Spring rains and winter snow will seem dreamy in this open meadow encircled by a wonderfully isolating stand of Douglas fir and lodgepole pines. But summer brings a spread of wildflowers with every color imaginable. With the small creek gurgling by your tent, camping will never

seem better. Open from June 15 through December 1, Timber Creek campground is about nine miles north of Gardiner and four miles north of Jardine. Bring your own water, as there is none here. RVs are limited to 48 feet.

Insiders' Tip

The beginning of November is ideal for viewing elk in Gardiner. Each year 11,000 of the ungulates amble through town, since it is in the center of the Northern Yellowstone herd's winter migration route.

Restaurants

Price Code

These prices include cost of meals for two people, excluding beverages, tip, and tax.

$	$10 to $19
$$	$20 to $27
$$$	$28 to $35
$$$$	$36 and more

Corral Drive Inn
U.S. Hwy. 89, Gardiner
(406) 848-7627
$, no credit cards

Owner and local character Helen Gould has been serving up her legendary buffalo burgers here for nearly 40 years. This is a Gardiner staple and a greasy spoon that shouldn't be passed up. There are also regular beef burgers served, half-pounders

that come sizzling from the grill to the table with a basket of handcut french fries. The burgers are famous and Helen is infamous for offering straightforward, gruff, unsolicited advice.

Any time of year is a good time for a Helen burger, but summer offers a pleasant spot out on the patio. The rest of the year it's indoor dining at a handful of tables.

K-Bar and Cafe
Main St., Gardiner
(406) 848-9995
$$

It's hard to beat the thick-crust pizza here. Inspired by Chicago-style pies, the ingredients offered may be basic, but they're all good. With the kitchen located just to the left of the actual dining room, the staff makes your order right in front of you. This is the kind of bar that has that "it's a small world feeling," the kind of place where you'd run into an old friend whom you haven't seen in years. The pool table and juke box see a lot of action, particularly during long winter months. It's a big Monday night football spot in town.

Park Street Grill and Cafe
204 Park St., Gardiner
(406) 848-7989
$$$

Opened in 1998 by veteran chef Steve Petalino, this upscale eatery has gained quite the local following. Serving a number of regional microbrewed beers and a decent wine list, there is nothing else like it in Gardiner. Folks will drive from Livingston, some 50 miles away, to feast on this continental cuisine with western influences. Pasta dishes are the specialty of the house, but seafood and beef selections are also available.

Petalino has spent most of his Montana career in Big Sky at Lone Mountain Ranch, but his affinity for Yellowstone brought him to Gardiner. Being business savvy, he also saw an unfulfilled niche in the tiny town that had yet to target the gourmet tastebuds of travelers and residents alike.

The restaurant is decorated with a typical modern western theme: logs and antlers. But it's not overdone here and the atmosphere is charming. Several cozy booths provide an intimate setting in the otherwise wide-open log interior. The restaurant is open June through September.

Shopping

Flying Pig Camp Store
511 Scott St., Gardiner, MT 59030
(406) 848-7510

Snow in July, 10 days of rain in June, stifling heat in November during your trip to Yellowstone? Layering your clothes is the way to prepare for the temperamental weather flashes this area is notorious for, and this store has the perfect clothing for all conditions. It's a kind of everything outdoor store selling cameras, equipment, knives, and even jewelry. There's even a computer here with Internet access if you feel you need to get back in touch with the outside world or if you must check e-mail. For a good chuckle, ask a clerk to tell you the story behind the store's name.

Kellem's Montana Saddlery
U.S. Hwy. 89, Gardiner, MT 59030
(406) 848-7776

The glitzy, red-fringed leather riding gloves and platter-sized belt buckles may be the bait that lures customers into this

Insiders' Tip

Locals refer to Gardiner's Park Street as Front Street, since it was the first avenue built in town and it faces the entrance to the park.

Western shop, but it's Les Kellem's artistry that keeps them coming back. Though you can buy your cowboy duds here, the selection of Western wear is limited. Saddles are the specialty of the house, as customers as far away as Europe will attest. As an artisan, Kellem makes his custom saddles to last a horse's lifetime and then some, with prices ranging from $1,700 to $10,000. His wife Carol makes beautiful chaps (pronounced "shaps"). They have owned the store for more than a decade and have built such a following that they don't even need to advertise.

Parks' Fly Shop
U.S. Hwy. 89, Gardiner, MT 59030
(406) 848-7314

Owner Richard Parks grew up in Gardiner and has been guiding the Yellowstone area all his life. He has plenty of opinions on park management policies and isn't afraid to express them with gentle conviction. An old-time Gardiner business, the shop itself is simple compared to others, but the basics are here. Parks offers a wealth of knowledge to the curious fisher.

Cooke City

Perched high in a crook of the rugged Beartooth Mountains, Cooke City is surrounded by four national forests, two wilderness areas, and Yellowstone National Park. The eight "blocks" of this mountain village are small and quaint reminders of bygone days when gold miners staked their claims in the 1800s. What this translates to is that, though the area is gorgeous, only people with ulterior motives (striking it rich, in this case) would dream of settling here.

Today's residents live here for a different kind of treasure: high mountain trails, abundant wildlife, pristine wilderness, and silence. The mountains here rise up just beyond the edge of the road, seemingly close enough to reach out and touch. Sitting at 7,651 feet, you don't fight the lights of a city to see the stars or watch the moon rise over Mount Republic. You don't have to worry about traffic jams. Things are simple up here. Life is quiet and probably a little quirky when the cabin fever kicks in sometime during the long, dark winter nights. This is literally the end of the road come October when they stop plowing the Beartooth Scenic Highway (U.S. Highway 212) to Red Lodge, Montana. In November Wyoming highway crews stop plowing the Chief Joseph Scenic Byway to Cody. Cooke is snowbound until April and can only be accessed via Yellowstone National Park to the west.

With the founding of the New World Mine, Shoo Fly changed its name to Cooke City in honor of Jay Cooke, Jr. in 1883. Cooke planned to promote the area's development and bring a branch line of the Northern Pacific Railroad to town, but he ran into financial difficulties and never made good on his promises. As a result, the area remained relatively isolated, preserving the region's beauty.

In Silver Gate, just three miles down the road from Cooke, it's evident that the founding fathers had big plans for the area. Meant to be an Old West attraction, it was platted in the 1930s with covenants that dictated rustic architecture and log construction. The notion never really took, although today Silver Gate services many summer visitors with lodging and meals. However, the town shuts down when winter rolls in.

Cooke City is best known as a stopover en route to Yellowstone National Park (the northeast entrance is only four miles away) or to Red Lodge along the Beartooth Pass. But the mid-1990s saw the community recognized as a hotbed of political controversy when the New World Mine proposed an open-pit gold mine in hopes of tapping the largest gold deposit known in North America. The act threatened to change the face of Cooke City and Yellowstone Park forever. In an unprecedented move, President Clinton stopped the development and persuaded Congress to buy out shareholders' mining rights.

Rather than returning to its mining roots, today's economy is reliant on tourism. One clue to this is the 15 lodging facilities between here and Silver Gate. But don't let this fool you; Cooke City is no

Insiders' Tip

The Absaroka-Beartooth Wilderness is home to a greater concentration of high-altitude alpine lakes than anywhere else in the world.

tourist trap. It's a genuine alpine hamlet just trying to make a living. The friendly locals are less guarded to tourist traffic than any other place in the state. A stronghold for ski bums, recreationists, and lifetime Yellowstone Park devotees, Cooke City has a culture unto itself. The town's 90 hearty year-round residents welcome winter visitors who snowmobile, backcountry ski, or snowboard. During summer months the population swells to about 300 people who join tourists in a love for hiking, backpacking, fishing, hunting, and hiding-out in summer getaway cabins. Instead of a dead end, you can see it as a starting point for exploring the outdoors or a simpler lifestyle.

Accommodations

Price Codes

Some rates are based on availability. Price includes the average nightly rate for two adults. The accommodations in this chapter accept all or most major credit cards.

$	$25 to $49
$$	$50 to $75
$$$	$76 to $100
$$$$	$101 and more

Alpine Motel
U.S. Hwy. 212, Cooke City
(406) 838-2262
$$

It's a good idea to make your reservations as early as possible at this popular, 25-unit, high country motel. Located right in the middle of town, it's easy to walk from one end of Main Street to the other. The Alpine has sparkling clean rooms ranging from singles to suites with kitchens. Most of the rooms, though, have single or double beds. You'll find newer rooms in a two-story complex built in 1993. The Alpine is open year round.

Cooke City Yurt Hostel
18 W. Broadway, Cooke City
(406) 586-4659, (800) 364-6242
$

The only difference between this permanent "tent" and camping is the wood burning stove that warms the canvas walls in here. Although there are skylights in the ceiling, this is a semi-primitive place to stay. With bunk-style sleeping arrangements (bring your own sleeping bag), the Cooke City Yurt is an alternative to forest service campgrounds and more expensive

Insiders' Tip

Cooke City is a winter haven for backcountry skiing and snowboarding. For a small fee Bill Blackford, owner of the Cooke City Bike Shack, offers snowmobile rides to the popular Daisy Pass, seven miles east of town, where you can ski all day. But after the first run, you do have to hike back up.

hostels. Just a block off Cooke City's Main Street, it's a convenient and easy option. There is sleeping room for six people, but unless you are traveling with a large group remember that this is a hostel, so you may be sharing the space with other travelers. Owned by Jim Marshal, an avid backcoun-

Main Street in one of Montana's oldest mining towns, Cooke City. PHOTO: DONNIE SEXTON/TRAVEL MONTANA

try skier, the yurt is frequented by fellow powder hounds during winter and hikers in the summer. Heated only by the wood stove, snowy mornings can be a little chilly, but at least it gets you up and going early. Guests have access to a simple cooking area with a Coleman stove and a heated bath house with a nice shower.

Edelweiss Cabins
106 Main St., Cooke City
(406) 838-2304
$

This little cluster of cabins sits at the western edge of town. All five of them have tiny decks, perfect for sitting with a hot cup of coffee in the early morning. The five cabins range in sizes, and some have showers, while others have bathtubs. All have kitchenettes and one is wheelchair accessible. When you call for reservations, ask to stay in one of the three new units. Cabins sleep two to four people and are situated in the shady cover of a lodgepole pine forest. Summer is the best time to stay here, since that's the time when the owners are sure to keep the place open. Winter is another story and depends on whether or not they are in town.

High Country Motel
U.S. Hwy. 212, Cooke City
(406) 838-2272
$

Winter and summer, the High Country offers cabins and motel rooms to weary travelers and wayward snowmobilers. In summer, High Country's 15 units fill fast, often months ahead of time between mid-June and mid-August, so be sure to call ahead. You'll find an assortment of carpeted, wood-paneled rooms with either one queen-size or two double beds. Montanans love to come here, and Christmas, New Year's, and Presidents' Day weekend are booked almost a year in advance.

Soda Butte Lodge
U.S. Hwy. 212, Cooke City
(406) 838-2251, (800) 527-6462
$$

Soda Butte Lodge is the closest thing to a resort that you will find in Cooke City. Open all year, the lodge has everything you might need during your stay here, including an indoor pool and spa, laundromat, fax, and snowmobile rentals. The Lodge's 32 rooms range from those with one dou-

ble bed to king suites. Built in 1959, Soda Butte Lodge is simple and functional.

Locals and tourists gather here for Monday Night Football and happy hour in the Ore House Saloon. An on-site restaurant, The Prospector, complete with a picture window overlooking a creek, serves three square meals a day. Soda Butte Lodge is a hopping place throughout the year. Call for details on snowmobile packages.

Campgrounds

Price Code

$	Less than $9
$$	$10 to $16
$$$	$17 to $23
$$$$	$24 and more

Colter Campground
U.S. Hwy. 212, Cooke City
(406) 848-7375
$

Just a mile and a half east of Cooke City, this campground offers a rare scenic view over 8,000-foot Colter Pass. Burned in the Yellowstone fires of 1988, this campground was cleared and now has a thick growth of new young trees. While those

little trees don't do much in the way of providing a barrier between you and other campers, you will find campsites are far apart. From here you have easy access to hiking up Lulu Pass Road (a mile to the east), which leads to Grasshopper Glacier. Open from mid-July to mid-September, Colter Campground is a popular spot for Yellowstone visitors. Campsites fill quickly each morning with campers who were unable to find room at park campgrounds. The grounds include several toilets, drinking water, and trash cans. The RV length limit is 48 feet.

Soda Butte Campground
U.S. Hwy. 212, Cooke City
(406) 848-7375
$

This is the first campground to fill up with overflow of campers from Yellowstone National Park's northeast entrance. The campground is a good staging spot for wolf-watching in Yellowstone's Lamar Valley, if you can get up that early. Set under the heavy cover of forest, dawn comes late here and night falls quickly. That means it stays cool most of the time

Insiders' Tip

All terrain vehicles are a popular way to see some of the area's wilderness. Several roads in town lead up to deserted turn-of-the-century mining camps and outstanding mountain views.

Close-up

Beartooth Mountains

Encircling Cooke City, Montana, and tipping the northeastern edge of Yellowstone National Park, the Beartooths are renowned for their pristine moonscape beauty. Some of the world's oldest rocks, dating back 2.5 to 3 billion years ago, were found in the Beartooth Mountain range, a finding that solidified a reverence for this craggy, jagged formation that its admirers have felt for decades.

There are a number of different theories that attempt to explain how these skyscrapers formed. However, geologists generally agree that the range emerged when a giant block of Precambrian volcanic rocks were uplifted 25,000 feet through the course of 70 million years, then carved by glaciers and streams. Imagine radical geologic changes much like what we see in the geothermal region of Yellowstone—erupting, solidifying, and eroding through the centuries.

Today, driving along the heralded Beartooth Highway, you'll witness a series of plateaus averaging about 10,000 feet high, glaciated spires, and layers of sedimentary rock indicative of an ancient sea that once covered the region. The Beartooths make up the highest continuous region in the U.S. and are home to the highest point in Montana, 12,799-foot Granite Peak. At 10,947 feet, the striking Beartooth Pass is encased in snow for most of the year, but from June through October thousands of visitors traverse it by car, bike, and motorcycle.

Although the horn-shaped Pilot and Index Peaks were used as landmarks by early travelers to the Yellowstone region, few people actually penetrated the Beartooths before the nineteenth century. Even today, the 600,000 acres of alpine terrain are home to unexplored lakes, basins, and waterfalls. Even without knowing their geological history, to see them jutting up from the prairie on the eastern side, they are clearly magnificent, vast, and ancient.

in here and it's hard to roust yourself from that cozy sleeping bag on a cold morning. Don't be surprised to be eating watermelon in the snow on Fourth of July, as it's not unusual to hear of snow during any month of the year at this campground. You'll find water and trash pickup here. There are 21 campsites. RVs are limited to 48 feet.

Beartooth Pass

Chief Joseph Campground
U.S. Hwy. 212
(406) 848-7375
$

With access to two outstanding trails, this six-unit campground is a find. The trailheads for Kersey Lake and Clarks Fork Trail begin here and lead you along difficult, but rewarding hikes. With just a small number of campsites available, this campground is often occupied by large groups traveling together. It's a favorite spot for family reunions and group vacations, because of its proximity to Cooke City (four miles to the west) and of course the Beartooth Highway. But if you're lucky you might be able to get a site in here. The campground is open from July 1 through September 30.

Crazy Creek Campground
U.S. Hwy. 212
(307) 754-7207
$$

Just inside the Wyoming border, this campsite is a surprise of lush green grass and purple lupines within the Shoshone National Forest. It's about six miles off the Highway 212 junction and worth the short detour from the main route. Tucked into a stand of lodgepole pines, you'll find 19 campsites with water and restrooms available. A short trail begins at the campground and leads to Crazy Creek's small waterfall. RVs are limited to 32 feet.

Island Lake Recreation Area
U.S. Hwy. 212
(307) 754-7207
$$

This might be as close as you can get to camping on top of the world (at least from your car). Sitting at 9,600 feet, Island Lake Recreation Area is in the Clarks Fork District of the Shoshone National Forest. Sites in this beautiful and well-used campground are scattered among big round boulders, behind conifers, below and above the winding road, and back in the trees. Adjacent to the campground you'll find a boat launch leading into the icy waters of Island Lake, a popular float-tubing lake full of pan-size brook trout. Trail #620 will lead you to alpine meadows brimming with wildflowers and numerous lakes in the Absaroka-Beartooth Wilderness.

Island Lake has 20 campsites. Depending on snow conditions, this campground is open from June 1 until September 15. Prepare to see snow and ice in September and possibly during summer months when you're up this high.

Chief Joseph Highway

Wyoming Highway 296, also known as the Chief Joseph Scenic Byway, offers several camping possibilities, including the following campground.

Hunter Peak Campground
WY Hwy. 296 (Chief Joseph Hwy.)
(307) 754-7207
$

This small Forest Service campground is secluded, well shaded in heavy timber, and an ideal stopover between Cody, Wyoming, and Cooke City, Montana. This quiet resting place lies next to the Clarks Fork River, where the fishing should be fine. Since grizzlies frequent the river, you should be on the watch for bears and store your food appropriately. There are only nine campsites here. If you are traveling during peak tourist season, plan to get here early. You'll find full service amenities here, including water and garbage pickup.

Restaurants

Price Code

Price code covers meals for two people meal, excluding beverages, tip, and tax.

$	$10 to $19
$$	$20 to $27
$$$	$28 to $35
$$$$	$36 and more

Beartooth Cafe
Cooke City
(406) 838-2475
$$

From this café's deck view 9,000-foot snow capped mountains. You'll feel like you are dining in the Swiss Alps. The menu is sophisticated enough to be in Switzerland, too, with gourmet dishes featuring pastas, meat, and seafood. Winter recreationists pack into this log building after a day of backcountry skiing, snowboarding, or snowmobiling to slurp down a couple of the trendiest microbrewed beers. During summer months, the outdoor seating gives you the best view of Cooke City's main street and people watching.

Joan and Bill's Family Restaurant
Cooke City
(406) 838-2280
$

You can get breakfast all day at Joan and Bill's. The platter-size sourdough pancakes or chicken fried steak will stave off hunger for a week. You can also have homemade pie for breakfast if you like it, and you just might need to do that since Joan's apple, peach, blueberry, or huckleberry pies get snatched up early. This homey old place is a third-generation business, serving breakfast, lunch, and dinner to folks for the last 59 years.

Nightlife

Miner's Saloon
Main St., Cooke City
(406) 838-2214

Sooner or later everyone in Cooke City ends up at the Miner's Saloon. In the center of town, it's practically the only place that is open after 10 P.M. It's the gathering place for drinks, billiards, video poker, and friends. Because the town is so small, it's not unusual to see families hanging out here. You might have to share a pool table with a group of ten-year-old kids, but it's still the happenin' spot in town.

Range Rider's Lodge
U.S. Hwy. 212, Silver Gate
(406) 838-2359, (801) 468-3211

Like a roadhouse or juke joint, this big, old log building rocks with live bands most nights of the week during the summer season. People come from all over the area to this spot to hear country music and to shake off all that quiet isolation. It's where you can learn to do the two-step or the jitterbug or sip your drink while watching the crowd on the dance floor. The Range Rider also offers lodging and serves lunch and dinner.

Red Lodge

Accommodations
Restaurants
Shopping
Nightlife

Nestled at the base of the Beartooth Mountains, Red Lodge's historic main street is what remains of the raucous little settlement that once housed outlaws, miners, wild west legends, gamblers, and prostitutes in its heyday. Named for the red dirt painted on teepees, Red Lodge was originally considered Crow Indian country until massive coal deposits were discovered here in 1866. The mines brought hundreds of Finnish, Scottish, Irish, Italian, Slavic, and Scandinavian immigrants and their families, adding to the town's colorful heritage. Founded in 1888, most of the brick buildings on Broadway—the town's main thoroughfare—proudly speak of a time when this was a thriving community on the grow from the influx of coal mining money. Most of the downtown buildings, which are listed on the National Historic Register, have been nicely restored to showcase their intricate turn-of-the-century architectural details. During the summer months Yellowstone Park visitors flood the streets of Red Lodge, but during the long winters this is largely a weekend ski playground for residents of Billings and Cody.

You won't find big box retail outlets or a strip of fast food chains anywhere in Red Lodge. This little mountain town is as close to undiscovered as the West can be these days. It is easily the most breathtaking gateway to Yellowstone via the 11,000-foot view from the Beartooth Scenic Highway; the late journalist Charles Kuralt called it America's most beautiful drive. Given its location bordering thousands of miles of spectacular wilderness, proximity to Yellowstone National Park, excellent skiing, and access to a well-serviced airport (an hour away in Billings), it's hard to believe that Red Lodge hasn't blossomed into a chi-chi resort community akin to Aspen or Vail, Colorado. Despite national magazine articles that dubbed this quiet burg "America's Last Great Place" and "The West's next great boomtown," Red Lodge has stayed small. Although population numbers have jumped a bit county-wide with newcomers buying up agricultural acreage for second homes, the town itself has maintained a steady population of about 2,000 people.

Still, Red Lodge has its legitimate struggles with growth and the ever-expanding shift from a natural resource economy to one based predominantly on tourism. High-paying jobs are scarce here (the average annual per capita personal income in Carbon County is $18,000), which is most likely what keeps the population numbers down. The community is almost evenly divided between families and business owners who work hard to preserve Red Lodge's small-town integrity and the transient recreationist residents who come here to labor through a season of skiing or mountain biking. Teetering on the edge of whether to keep this great spot a secret or to shout the area's attributes from the top of the Beartooth Pass, Red Lodge folks are keenly aware of how good life is here.

Accommodations

Price Code

Keep in mind that some rates are based on availability. The average nightly rates for two adults at the hotels and motels listed in this section are indicated by a dollar sign ($)

ranking in the following chart. Also, the hotels and motels in this chapter accept all or most major credit cards.

$ . . . . $25 to $49

$$ . . . . $50 to $75

$$$ . . . . $76 to $100

$$$$ . . . . $101 and more

The Pollard Hotel
2 N. Broadway, Red Lodge
(406) 446-0001
$$$

From the outside, this three-story brick building on the corner is unassuming, but as you step through the double-glass doors into the lobby of The Pollard Hotel you experience the elegance of a bygone era. Decked out with classic oak-paneled walls, jewel-colored floral carpets, and plush furniture, the lobby is only the beginning of the tasteful restoration. Built in 1893, this was the first brick building in Red Lodge, at a time when the town was on a steady roll as a result of mining in the area. The hotel serviced the regular folk, as well as the famous and infamous. Everyone from salesmen and ranchers to names such as Buffalo Bill Cody, Calamity Jane, Liver Eatin' Johnston, and William Jennings Bryan signed the guest register. The Pollard was known for its gambling, billiards, and fine accommodations and cuisine. In its heyday it was the place to see and be seen in Red Lodge.

Though today's Pollard has been pared down a bit—catering more to skiers and Yellowstone visitors than to the famous—the focus is still on quality and service. Owner David Knight completed a major renovation of the entire facility in 1994, restoring the historic integrity and beauty of the place. His influence shows in the hotel's detailed finery. You'll notice the *Wall Street Journal* and *The New York Times* are available every morning in the History Room, just off the lobby. Each of the 50 hotel rooms are decorated with modern, but classic furnishings inspired by Victorian period decor. You can choose from rooms with two queen beds and a mountain view or a suite with a Jacuzzi tub and an interior balcony overlooking a sitting area and soothing fireplace. All the rooms are tastefully finished and the hotel's location makes it possible to walk all over town to restaurants and shops.

You don't even need to leave the premises for food. Greenlee's Restaurant inside the hotel is a formal dining room with excellent service and food. Lavish breakfasts, lunches, and dinners are served daily.

Red Lodging
424 N. Broadway, Red Lodge
(406) 446-1272, (800) 673-3563

If you plan to stay in the Red Lodge area for a week or more, this vacation rental company can arrange accommodations ranging from creekside cabins and golf course townhouses to quaint Victorians in the heart of town. With 35 area homes to choose from, you should be able to find something to suit your needs. Rates begin at $78 per night and $550 per week. Monthly rates are also available. Most of Red Lodging's rentals are upscale with fireplaces and Jacuzzis and sleep from four to ten people, and some allow pets.

Rock Creek Resort
HC49 U.S. Hwy. 212, Red Lodge
(406) 446-1111, (800) 667-1119
$$

When Olympic skier Pepi Gramshammer (of Colorado's famed Beaver Creek Ghast Haus Gramshammer) bought Rock Creek in the 1970s, it was anything but a resort. First he fixed up the property's existing Grizzly Condos to be used as lodging for students participating in his summer ski clinic on the west side of the Beartooth

Pass. Next he put an addition on the historic Piney Dell restaurant (it was once a fur trapper's cabin) and things snowballed from there. Today it is an 88-room complex with accommodations ranging from the unbelievably romantic Stoney Honeymoon Cabin (it has a fireplace in the bedroom and a private Jacuzzi next to the creek) to vaulted-ceiling condos and small ski-chalet-inspired rooms with decks overlooking the stream. Since there are countless configurations connecting rooms both upstairs and down, the resort has become popular for large family reunions, weddings, and conventions. The property sits along the banks of Rock Creek and features two restaurants, a massive convention facility, health club, indoor swimming pool, kids' trout fishing pond and playground, a soccer field, tennis courts, and hiking trails. The lobby of the Beartooth Lodge, with its river rock fireplace, antler chandeliers, and comfortable chairs invites you to lounge with a good book.

The Old Piney Dell, well known for its fine dining and select wine list, serves breakfast and lunch in the Kiva Dining Room. The only things that might lure you away from this all-purpose vacation spot are Red Lodge Mountain's skiing and the shopping in Red Lodge (just 5 miles away). Although, with the on-site Twin Elk Fine Collections boutique you may even forego that trip to town. En route to the Beartooth Scenic Byway, Rock Creek is popular with Yellowstone visitors and makes a great base for exploring the area.

The Yodeler Motel
601 S. Broadway, Red Lodge
(406) 446-1435
$$

This funky chalet-inspired motel reflects some of Red Lodge's early influences from German, Swiss, and Austrian immigrants who came to the area to work in nearby coal mines. The Yodeler is not a historic motel, of course, but that's the connection. Sitting at the south edge of Red Lodge's main street, you can easily walk to downtown restaurants and shops. Across the street is a picnic area sitting along the banks of Rock Creek and skiing at Red Lodge Mountain is only a short drive away. What the Yodeler prides itself on are the very clean rooms and sincere hospitality. They also advertise in-room data port phones for business travelers and high quality mattresses for guaranteed comfort. Ground floor rooms are spacious with front and back doors. The main level rooms are half-basement units with large daylight windows.

Insiders' Tip

Just eight miles east of Red Lodge you'll see the long-abandoned buildings of Smith Mine just before you drive into the tiny settlement of Belfry. The remarkably preserved skeleton of the mine stands as an eerie memorial to the largest disaster in Montana's mining history. In 1943 the coal mine exploded and killed 74 men. A commemorative plaque marks the site and details the tragic event that brought an end to coal mining in the area.

Close-up

Kevin Red Star

In the art world, the mention of Red Lodge, Montana, is synonymous with premier Native American artist, Kevin Red Star. Through his dynamic, soulful depictions of the proud and powerful Crow Indians it's as if he is asserting the original Crow Indian ties to the land surrounding Red Lodge. He has gained praise and acclaim all over the world as an artist preserving a rare culture. On exhibit at The Kevin Red Star Gallery in downtown Red Lodge, his paintings demand respect and admiration.

The museums holding Kevin Red Star originals in their permanent collections include the Smithsonian Institution; Institute of American Indian Art in Santa Fe; Denver Art Museum; the Heard Museum in Phoenix; the Pierre Cardin Collection in Paris; the Eiteljorg Museum of American Indian and Western Art in Indianapolis; The Whitney Museum of Western Art in Cody; and museums in Belgium, China, Germany, and Japan.

Born in Lodge Grass, Montana, on the Crow Indian Reservation, Red Star now lives just outside of Red Lodge. The artist calls himself a "romantic" because his bold portraits of Crow warriors and dancers, mystical animals, teepees and proud women are realistic but also exaggerated. Brilliant colors jump from his oil canvases and speak of bravery, sadness, war, joy, and wisdom. Red Star uses his heritage for inspiration as he records the Crow Nation's culture.

While Red Lodge, Montana, seems an unlikely place to find such an acclaimed painter, Red Star is responsible for inspiring an unprecedented art movement in the community. He recently returned to his home state after spending years in the competitive art scenes of Santa Fe, New Mexico, and San Francisco, California. Back in Montana he has found the place that feeds his creativity.

Though Red Star does not consider himself a political artist, his work does make a statement that commands you to realize he is recording a vanishing culture. His paintings preserve the pow-wows, the magnificent dress and physical features of his ethnicity, and a people who impacted Western history.

Bed and Breakfasts

Price Code

$	Less than $85
$$	$86 to $115
$$$	$116 to $150
$$$$	$151 and more

Bear Bordeaux Bed and Breakfast
302 S. Broadway, Red Lodge
(406) 446-4408
$$

Sharon and Joe Torcaso aren't afraid to say that their B & B looks horrible on the outside (that's a direct quote). But you can't judge a book by its cover, because inside Bear Bordeaux you'll find a romantic getaway spot filled with small luxuries and abundant attention to detail. And actually, the place doesn't look bad from the outside, just cozy. Built in 1917, this three-bedroom house offers unique accommodations with amenities like two-person Jacuzzis, fireplaces, lodgepole pine beds, and luxurious linens. Each room follows the "Bear" theme, though loosely, with cutesy names: the Grizzly, Brown Bear, and Polar Bear (if they added rooms they would have to resort to Panda and Koala). One room has a king-size bed, a cast iron stove, and a two-person shower. With a modern touch for decorating, Sharon used western accents and boldly painted walls to create an inviting little hideout within walking distance of downtown Red Lodge.

The Torcasos have thought of everything you might need during your stay here, including a library with 3,000 book titles and over 850 video selections. There is even space to store your motorcycle if you are one of the many Harley Davidson voyagers who pass through town on the way to the Beartooth Scenic Highway. To top that off, a professional chef prepares a four-course breakfast each morning. But the best thing about Bear Bordeaux is the concierge—Winston, the four-year-old resident golden retriever, who is responsible for wake-up calls and the delivery of your morning paper (Arthur, his younger sidekick, is in-training). Sharon says that some guests make a return visit just to see Winston again.

Campgrounds and RV Parks

Price Code

$	Less than $9
$$	$10 to $16
$$$	$17 to $23
$$$$	$24 and more

Basin Campground
U.S. Hwy. 212, Red Lodge
(406) 446-2103, (800) 280-CAMP
$

Drive just one mile south of Red Lodge and you'll see a brown Forest Service sign marking a campground. From there, head west for 7 miles on Forest Road 71 to Basin Campground. This pretty campground has 30 tent and camper sites, picnic tables, public toilets, and fire pits. A hand pump provides water and there is a dumpster for trash. Remember that this area is bear country, so take care you store food properly. Campsites are tucked into a heavily forested area, but if you take the nearby Basin trailhead you can hike to incredible views of the Beartooth Mountains.

Insiders' Tip

Take a self-guided walking tour of Red Lodge's historic buildings, most of which are on the National Register of Historic Places. Brochures for the tour are available at the Red Lodge Area Chamber of Commerce and Peaks to Plains Museum.

M-K Campground
U.S. Hwy. 212, Red Lodge
(406) 446-2103, (800) 280-CAMP
$

About 7 miles south of Red Lodge you'll find one of the few free camping facilities in the region, the M-K Campground. A brown Forest Service sign marks the turn-off for this campsite. Originally a field camp during the construction of the Beartooth Highway in the 1930s, this secluded spot offers incredible views of the mountains above and the Rock Creek Valley below. Although both picnic and camping sites are available here, the area is considered a "reduced services" site—meaning that you will need to pack out your trash and provide your own water. Though the amenities are spare, the M-K is a wonderful spot to experience the feeling of camping in the backcountry while only paces from the convenience of your vehicle.

Parkside Campground
Rock Creek Rd. #421, Red Lodge
(406) 446-2103, (800) 280-CAMP
$

On the west side of U.S. Highway 212, about 12 miles south of Red Lodge, Parkside Campground is the largest of three Forest Service campgrounds clustered within a mile of each other. All part of the Red Lodge Ranger District of the Custer National Forest, sites here are easily accessible for travel on the journey along the Beartooth Highway. (The elevation here is 7,200 feet.) At Parkside you'll find conifers, grass, wild flowers, and cool mornings along the banks of Rock Creek. The access roads are paved, and sites have back-in spurs. The RV limit is 40 feet. Of the 26 sites here, 15 can be reserved through the National Recreation Reservation System.

Perry's RV Park and Campgrounds
P.O. Box 3500, U.S. Hwy. 212, Red Lodge
(406) 446-2722
$$

The only sounds you'll hear at Perry's Park and Campground are the creek, the shivering of aspen leaves, and the muffled voices of content campers. This location, just two miles south of Red Lodge is cozy, comfortable, and packed with amenities. Situated along the banks of little roaring Rock Creek, you'll find plenty of aspens and cottonwood trees for shade at your campsite. You'll also find showers, electrical and water hook-ups, laundry facilities, a convenience store, and dump station at Perry's. Guest can also take advantage of the picnic area's barbecue grills. Perry's has 20 RV units and space for 10 tent camps.

Restaurants

Price Code

Price code covers meals for two people meal, excluding beverages, tip, and tax.

$	$10 to $19
$$	$20 to $27
$$$	$28 to $35
$$$$	$36 and more

Bear Creek Saloon and Steakhouse
U.S. Hwy. 308, Bear Creek, MT
(406) 446-3481
$

Also known as Bear Creek Downs, this could very well be the only place in the world where you can have dinner while watching the pig races. Round and round the track the little piglets go, cheered on by spectators grazing on thick steaks and hefty burgers (Thankfully, there are no pork items on the menu.) While you wait for your dinner to be served, you can place a bet on the pig of your choice—part of the winnings go to a local education fund. Just a short drive six miles east of Red Lodge, this tiny saloon in the middle of nowhere once serviced the coal miners from the nearby Smith Mine. Well-worn, wide-plank pine floors and walls give the Bear Creek an Old West atmosphere. Old black and white photos and countless magazine clippings about the famous swine hang on the walls. During summer months the races are held outside on a larger track. This spot is open Friday, Saturday, and Sunday from Memorial Day to Labor Day and Christmas until Easter.

Bogart's
11 S. Broadway, Red Lodge
(406) 446-1784
$$

Bogart's claim to fame is the margaritas. In fact, the margaritas are so popular that when the doors open at 11:30 A.M., Bogart's staff is ready with a 15-gallon batch of margarita mix. Owners Tom Leatherberry and Judy and Jody Christensen won't tell you what the secret ingredient is, but after years of taste tests they know what they've made is the good stuff. The mix will soon be sold commercially along with Bogart's canned salsa, Ruggie's Rocky Mountain Salsa, and their fajita marinade.

The menu at Bogart's is sort of a mishmash of Mexican and Italian dishes, hand-tossed pizzas, and sandwiches. We recommend sticking to the south of the border theme and going with anything Mexican at Bogart's—if you're not counting calories, definitely try the sour cream enchiladas. There is a comfortable, fun atmosphere here, complete with Humphrey Bogart posters and lots of plants. Bogart's is popular with the after-work crowd, who order pitchers of the oh-so-drinkable margaritas.

Bridge Creek Backcountry Kitchen and Wine Bar
116 S. Broadway, Red Lodge
(406) 446-9900
$$$

Owner Peter Christe knew just what the Red Lodge restaurant scene was lacking when he opened the Bridge Creek Backcountry Kitchen in the summer of 2000. The restaurant is casual and elegant at the same time, with an inviting atmosphere. As you enter, a small bar beckons you to sit down for a pre-dinner glass of wine. You can keep yourself busy looking at regional topographic maps of the nearby wilderness (remember the word "backcountry" in the restaurant's name.) Since Christe is a wine enthusiast extraordinaire, the restaurant's extensive list includes rare finds from his "private collection." A wine storage area divides the wine bar from the formal dining area in the center of the restaurant.

Bridge Creek puts a casual spin on upscale gourmet cuisine, and features steak, seafood, and pasta entrees. After an exhausting day of skiing, you might want to sit in front of the fireplace with a Montana microbrew and indulge on something from the large appetizer list—we recommend the spicy beef quesadilla. The menu changes seasonally and utilizes fresh local ingredients as much as possible. Look for the organic beef provided by a local distributor, the Lazy E-L Ranch. But save room for dessert—they serve a creme brûlée of the day, a decadently smooth custard that may be infused with tasty flavors like rosemary, coffee, or huckleberries. Don't worry if this doesn't interest the kids, as the kid's menu features a variety of options. During summer months, enjoy the outdoor dining on the sidewalk.

Coffee Factory Roasters
6½ S. Broadway, Red Lodge
(406) 446-3200
$

With a light, airy atmosphere and a big window looking out on Red Lodge's main street, the Coffee Factory is an easy spot to while away the morning watching the town come to life. A wall-size chalkboard lists the selection of pastries, bagels, juices, smoothies, and sandwiches. Large jute bags of coffee beans are piled against the far wall, where the actual roasting is done in-house—take home some of the Beartooth Blend. Kids are welcome at this cafe, as clearly evidenced by the overflowing basket of toys and small shelf of children's books. If you need more reasons to stay, there is also a computer here with Internet access for checking e-mail or surfing the web, if you really must on your vacation.

Greenlee's
2 N. Broadway, Red Lodge
(406) 446-0001
$$$$

Chef Scott Greenlee's dining room feels much the way it did a century ago when the likes of Buffalo Bill Cody and William Jennings Bryan dined here. The atmosphere is sheer old-fashioned luxury, with crisp white linen and fresh flower arrangements on the tables. Plush drapes filter light through ceiling-high windows that look out to Red Lodge's historic district. Along with ambiance and an impressive seasonal menu, the staff here offers exquisite service with knowledgeable suggestions about the restaurant's award-winning wine list.

Greenlee opened the restaurant in the historic Pollard Hotel after it was rigorously restored to its former glory. With his ever-changing gourmet cuisine, he helped put the place back on the map as a Red Lodge landmark. You'll find a European influence added to wild game items. Signature dishes include huckleberry duck breasts and elk medallions with a port wine butter sauce. Reservations are recommended here, summer or winter. Greenlee's serves breakfast, lunch, and dinner. Don't pass up the outstanding Sunday brunch.

Shopping

In the last decade there has been a visible shift from a downtown that catered to locals to one that has focused on snagging tourist dollars. The grocery, hardware, and lumber stores all moved off Broadway to be replaced by high end shops peddling espresso drinks, expensive knickknacks and Western art. Everything from Harley Davidson motorcycles to handmade quilts can be found in the local shops. With everything clustered downtown, it's easy walking to the little shops bustling with people during the summer and winter.

Elk Ridge Cabin Furnishings
3 N. Broadway, Red Lodge
(406) 446-4246

You might think the word "cabin" in the name Elk Ridge Cabin Furnishings implies something simple and rustic. But between the decadent French bath products, the gourmet espresso, and designer doggy treats, the only thing rustic in this stylish shop are the logs used to stoke the fire in the native stone fireplace. The word "cabin" is redefined here (read: luxury). A seemingly odd combination—part coffee shop, part gift shop— Elk Ridge exudes a warmth that invites you to linger. The store is filled with fineries that will keep your senses heightened because there is so much to see, taste, smell, and touch. Handmade jewelry and other accessories, lavender linen water, wood furniture, unique Western clothing—you can sip your latte and take your time perusing it all.

Kibler and Kirch Furniture and Design
22 N. Broadway, Red Lodge
(406) 446-2802

Divided like rooms of a house, each section of the store is magnificently decorated with overstuffed armchairs and ottomans, leather sofas, and down-fluffed beds. Houseware items range from pieces influenced by Native American culture to cowboy regalia. This store oozes a new western elegance. Clearly this high-end furniture store is a response to the recent influx of wealthy part-time residents. Pieces here range from trendy to elegant, most with high price tags, but also with definitive high quality. There is more to ogle upstairs, where you can meet with a professional designer to help with projects as simple as matching your living room drapes with the pattern on your sofa or as elaborate as decorating a 10,000-square-foot vacation home. As you top the stairway, a soothing fountain and a shelf filled with several dozen samples of rich fabric greet you. Turn the corner and venture down the tiny hallway outside to the deck, where bird feeders and windchimes will make you feel like you are right at home.

Magpie Toymakers
115 N. Broadway, Red Lodge
(406) 446-3044

You won't find the latest selection of Play Station games or anything battery operated here. Magpie Toymakers is an old fashioned shop that carries toys powered by your imagination—Lincoln Logs, boomerangs, hula hoops, dominoes, jack-in-the-box, and children's books. You'll find Betty Boop dolls and Curious George lunch boxes tucked alongside collectable hand-carved wooden toys and yo-yos. Owner Wayne McClane, a toy aficionado, can tell you who invented the Slinky and which wooden tray puzzle is developmentally appropriate for a toddler. He is the resident toymaker, crafting one of a kind works from wood that are more for whimsical adults than for playful children. (Some cost several thousand dollars.) Whatever your fancy, this is the place where you'll encounter some favorite old toy that brings back memories of childhood.

Montana Candy Emporium
7 S. Broadway, Red Lodge
(406) 446-1119

Even if you don't have a sweet tooth, the volume of confections in Montana's oldest and biggest candy store will dazzle you. At the Montana Candy Emporium, in addition to 22 kinds of fudge made while you watch, they carry 2,300 kinds of candy. Bushel baskets line the walls of this turn-of-the-century shop, each one filled with mouthwatering caramels, taffy, mints, chocolates, and every kind of hard candy imaginable, from basic to extravagant. One of their biggest sellers is the huckleberry bark, but the fudge is a close second. This main street shop is a picture right out of Willie Wonka's Chocolate Factory, only better because it's real.

Nightlife

The Roman Theater
110 S. Broadway, Red Lodge
(406) 446-1942

Films at this historic movie house seem better somehow. It could be because there is more leg room between aisles than most modern twin-plex theaters or that the once-exclusive recital hall still holds onto a certain elegance. It could be that in addition to the regular buttery popcorn you can also buy freshly made caramel corn. It could definitely be that you can sit and watch the movie on a sofa (one of four, in fact), slouch down, put your feet up on the coffee table, slurp your drink, and enjoy the big screen. It's better than renting a video at home. The Roman has a niche as a funky hometown theater where you can get comfortable. They don't charge an arm and a leg for refreshments, either.

The Round Barn
HC28 U.S. Hwy. 212, Red Lodge
(406) 446-1197

You'd never know this homey, old round brick building was once a dairy barn. Originally built in 1941 by the Kent family, current owner Marcee Farrar has fixed it up as a restaurant and dinner theater. Dinner is served buffet style with four entrees (a range of meats and fish), homemade mashed potatoes, a fresh vegetable,

> ## Insiders' Tip
> During summer months the high country above Red Lodge is home to a ski race camp. Details are available at the local Chamber of Commerce.

such as steamed snow peas, and dessert. A 15-foot salad bar features fresh salads, homemade soups, and bread just out of the oven. You don't have to eat to get into the theater upstairs in the hayloft, but we recommend it. June through September Farrar books professional actors, singers, musicians, and comedians to perform in her "theater in the round." The schedule changes depending on the season, so call ahead. The Round Barn is closed in January and February.

Silver Strike
609 N. Broadway, Red Lodge
(406) 446-3131

With advertising that touts "Tons of TV," the Silver Strike is primarily a bowling alley. But you can also enjoy the sports bar, a game of billiards, and a video poker casino. Local bowling leagues are competitive and meet here every Tuesday and Thursday. You might have to sign up on a waiting list to get a slot on a team. (Obviously the winters are long in Red Lodge.)

Snow Creek Saloon
124 Broadway, Red Lodge
(406) 446-1100

There is nothing historic or nostalgic about the Snow Creek Saloon, but you can catch live music here every weekend. It is the place to be when you say you're going to have a night out on the town in Red Lodge. Eventually everyone ends up here before 2 A.M. on a weekend night. The bar welcomes you with a party atmosphere—neon beer signs, shot glasses, and patron names carved into wooden tables. It's dark and smoky and a little seedy. The band plays in the back of the house just a little above a dirty, well-scuffed dance floor. Usually you can count on good old rock and roll, sometimes a little country, maybe some rhythm and blues. The Snow Creek is everything a small-town watering hole should be.

Cody

Accommodations
Restaurants
Shopping
Nightlife

William Frederick "Buffalo Bill" Cody left an indelible mark upon western history, and nowhere is it more alive than in his namesake town of Cody. In this historic western community Buffalo Bill is the beginning, middle, and end. He played the role of everything from visionary, fundraiser, negotiator, marketer, to celebrity in order to put "Cody City" on the map in 1896.

In his day, while traveling with his Wild West Show, Buffalo Bill was an authentic western hero. He was famous as a Pony Express rider, scout, hunter, entrepreneur, and a showman who became a friend to presidents and kings, senators and governors, and many of the country's most influential businessmen. With his connections, he was included in economic developments that would later shape the West. It was no mistake that the Burlington Northern Railroad led to Cody in 1901 or that Yellowstone National Park's East Entrance was opened around that time as well. When the world's first national park was founded in 1872, Buffalo Bill smelled the potential fortune in an area he came to know during his youth. As a result, he built his own lodge, Pahaska Teepee, just yards from Yellowstone's eastern boundary—a place that still bustles with tourist traffic both summer and winter. In anticipation of the visitors who would come on the railroad, W.F. Cody built the now historic Irma Hotel, with a restaurant and saloon to cater to all his guests' needs.

Yes, Buffalo Bill had an image, and he was never too shy to use it in order to further himself. He made investments throughout the West, but none were quite as successful as the town of Cody. As a result, his influence often overshadows the sweat equity that fellow Cody citizens put into making the town a success. There were others, of course, who built the lively town, which was once uncharted territory—the streets of downtown Cody bear their names and echo through the city's foundation. But it was Buffalo Bill who truly saw the potential and shaped this corner of the Western frontier into a thriving place to live and work.

Today's Cody still upholds and reaps the benefits of Buffalo Bill's legacy, using his name, his image, and his business savvy to market itself to tourists. Located just 50 miles from Yellowstone, the town has much to sell, with its rivers, mountains, wildlands, and history. One million visitors annually flood the streets and mountains and establishments of this town with a regular population of around 8,000 residents. Folks here put on nightly rodeos and shoot-outs for entertainment, and the community proudly builds upon the unprecedented collection of art and artifacts at the Buffalo Bill Cody Historical Center. In the summer Cody is alive with festivals, gatherings and attractions that fill up the nights and days. Winter is much sleepier here, although there is no

Insiders' Tip

In and around the city of Cody you'll find a series of trails for walking, in-line skating, or jogging. Some of the paths are wheelchair accessible and most are geared toward recreationists of any ability.

Portrait of William F. Cody, c. 1895. PHOTO: PARK COUNTY TRAVEL COUNCIL

shortage of recreationists who come to enjoy Yellowstone and the Shoshone National Forest trails. But in town it's more of a time to rest and regroup for the next season of tourists.

If Cody lacks in any way, it is because it has perhaps sold itself too much and catered all too often to the needs of visitors rather than its bona fide citizens. Some of that is changing, however, as more voices in the community speak this sentiment. In 2000, the city started building a new recreation center, ice arena/convention facility, and a city pathway system, signaling the locals' desire to see some return for their entertaining and showboating efforts.

As a retail, medical, and entertainment hub for the entire Bighorn Basin, Cody has witnessed drastic changes to the face of its historic town with major retail chains popping up on the west end. Commonly referred to as the "West Strip," this part of Cody was never zoned with historical integrity in mind. Several major national hotel chains and various gas stations dominate the landscape here on the highway that leads to Yellowstone's East Entrance. Although the Cody Nite Rodeo Grounds and Old Trail Town are located at this end of town, there have been community disputes about whether the type of growth seen on the west side is a positive addition. Regardless, major national businesses have boosted the local economy by attracting many outlying residents for shopping, though partially at the expense of the "Mom-and-Pop" stores which were once the backbone of the town. It is the classic struggle that faces many small American communities. Cody struggles with finding a way to grow a healthy diverse economy, but so far it's doing pretty well. With the oil and gas industry continuing to be Wyoming's greatest industry, Cody is not entirely reliant on tourism dollars.

Categorically, the town has been a city of strong traditional values, never a place for rabble-rousing or dissent. A good old boy mentality that says a handshake is still enough to seal a deal and that most people are just plain honest folk is what largely governs the mentality of the body politic here. In turn, Cody is a nice place to raise a family, a fine location to retire, and a great spot to plant your roots.

Accommodations

Price Code

Some rates are based on availability. The average nightly rates for two adults at the hotels and motels listed in this section are indicated by a dollar sign ($) ranking in the following chart. Also, the hotels and motels in this chapter accept all or most major credit cards.

$ . . . . $25 to $49
$$ . . . . $50 to $75
$$$ . . . . $76 to $100
$$$$ . . . . $101 and more

Americinn Lodge & Suites
5908 Yellowstone Ave., Cody, WY
(307) 587-7716, (800) 634-3444
$$$

Cody's newest hotel is a short distance from the center of town, but worth it. This modern log and stone lodge is located just west of the Buffalo Bill Historic Center and about a 15-minute stroll to the Cody Nite Rodeo grounds. The warm, welcoming lobby with its large river rock fireplace and cozy, over-sized furniture is the hotel's best attribute. A practical breakfast area is tucked into a corner near the staircase for the morning's continental breakfast. All 42 rooms—decorated in a subtle western motif—feature lodgepole pine beds and all the modern amenities. An indoor pool, Jacuzzi, and sauna are pleasant extras. Additionally, the staff members go out of their way to offer directions and extra hospitality.

Cody Guest Houses
1401 Rumsey Ave., Cody, WY 82414
(307) 587-6000
$$$$

If you want to test-drive how it feels to live in a Cody neighborhood, stay at one of the seven Cody Guest Houses. There is no minimum stay required, and you can rent just one room or a whole house in one of the cottages, duplex suites, and homes in Cody's historic residential neighborhood. The Mayor's Inn and the Victoria House, both operated like bed and breakfasts without the breakfast or the innkeeper, are meticulously decorated with antiques. In fact, owner Kathy Singer has decorated all her vacation rentals with great style and expense. The four-bedroom Western Lodge is richly decorated with a masculine influence showing in its massive log furniture. Rates for the Cody Guest Houses are competitive with hotels and range from $80 to $205 nightly for two people.

Insiders' Tip
Every Friday night in July and August, musical performers from string quartets to bluegrass bands play at the City Park Bandshell at 6 P.M. Get there early, and bring a picnic and some lawn chairs.

Days Inn
524 Yellowstone Ave., Cody, WY 82414
(307) 587-6604, (800) DAYS-INN
$$$

If the words "rustic, cozy, or quaint" accommodations don't appeal to you, then you'll be happy to find the Days Inn, which features basic, clean, new, spacious rooms with queen or king-size beds. Lounge in the massive lobby, relax in the indoor pool and spa, use the guest laundry, and enjoy a complimentary continental breakfast.

Elephant Head Lodge
1170 Yellowstone Hwy.
Wapiti, WY 82450
(307) 587-3980
$$$ (American plan)

These cabins are so comfy that you may not even want to venture the whole 11 miles down the road to Yellowstone National Park. Owners Phil and Joan Lamb have taken care to modernize all 12 historic cabins without sacrificing any of their Old West charm. While each cabin is decorated differently, they all come with a heavy old-fashioned quilt and the luxury of pastoral peace. Although most of the cabins are smaller, one sleeps nine and a few have kitchenettes. The Lodge, restaurant, and "Honeymoon" cabin were built in 1910 by Buffalo Bill Cody's niece, Josephine Thurston, and her husband in 1910.

While most guests use Elephant Head Lodge as a base for exploring Yellowstone and Cody, technically you don't ever have to venture beyond the lodge's property. Everything you need is right here, from horseback riding, hiking, rock climbing, and biking to children's activities. In the evenings you can even catch a movie in the old lodge living room or enjoy a family card game in the lounge.

Phil and Joan even take care of the meals, serving up hearty breakfasts, lunches, and dinners every day. You won't be able to resist the aroma of fresh baked bread and homemade pies wafting over from the main lodge, only 100 yards or so from your cabin. You can savor the tastes

The Irma Hotel, built in 1902 by Colonel William F. "Buffalo Bill" Cody and named after his daughter, Irma. PHOTO: PARK COUNTY TRAVEL COUNCIL

of grilled steaks and Joan's wonderful potato salad at one of five tables covered with red gingham tablecloths.

While overnight guests are welcome, most folks stay from three to five days to relax and enjoy the area. A European Plan in which guests pay a flat rate for their cabin, then extra for meals and activities is the best alternative unless you plan to do quite a bit of riding. The American Plan includes lodging, three meals a day, and up to four hours of riding daily.

Irma Hotel
1192 Sheridan Ave. Cody, WY 82414
(307) 587-4221, (800) 587-IRMA
$$

When Buffalo Bill Cody was certain the railroad was coming to town, he built a luxury hotel to receive the wealthy visitors who would travel so far to see Yellowstone National Park. The Irma Hotel, named for his youngest daughter, went up in 1902 and became what some referred to as the last outpost of civilization. With its steam heat, gas lighting, and telephones in every

room, The Irma was mighty fancy. Catering to a guest's every need, the hotel had an elegant bar, billiards, a telegraph office, a barber shop, and baths. In the dining room, weary eastern travelers enjoyed fresh produce and meat from the hotel's farm. A livery stable chartered every kind of rig and horse possible for forays into Yellowstone Park.

Today's Irma is still a landmark, but not so much a luxury hotel. On the National Historic Register, it commands attention and still stands as a cornerstone gathering place in the community. After so many years and so many visitors, The Irma is a little worse for wear, but a stay here is worth the experience. As you enter the hotel, a dozen mounted deer, elk, and big horn sheep—reminders of Buffalo Bill, the great hunter—stand watch in the main hallway. A wide staircase leads upstairs, where most of the rooms are located. Accommodations range from simple to elegant, with a number of different sleeping combinations. All of the rooms have private baths and telephones.

The main street looking west, Cody, Wyoming. PHOTO: PARK COUNTY TRAVEL COUNCIL

Pahaska Teepee
183-CCC Yellowstone Hwy., Cody, WY
82414
(307) 527-7701, (800) 628-7791
$$

Buffalo Bill Cody built his hunting lodge on this spot at the turn of the century, when big game hunting was actually allowed in Yellowstone Park. When automobiles became the popular mode of travel into the park during the mid-1920s, Pahaska became a hub with its enticing Teepee Tavern for cocktails and the Lodgepole restaurant for hearty western fare. Today, situated on the edge of Yellowstone's eastern entrance on U.S. Highway 14/16/20, Pahaska Teepee remains a bustling center for tourists looking to refuel, buy souvenirs, or grab a bite before continuing their drive.

There is, of course, Buffalo Bill's historic lodge, which has scarcely changed since 1910. The stone fireplace spans up to high vaulted ceilings and draws guests to circle around on cool evenings. There is also endless opportunity for horseback riding and the appeal of that Old West atmosphere. But what Pahaska is best known for is its cross-country skiing and snowmobiling. Winter recreationists have access to 110 miles of groomed roads in the park, which run all the way to West Yellowstone, Montana. Large groups can stay in one of 48 older A-frame houses. This is the perfect spot for a family vacation or large family reunion. Additional fees are required for all activities. Pahaska is open when Yellowstone Park is open.

Rainbow Park Motel
1136 17th St., Cody, WY 82414
(307) 587-6251, (800) 341-8000
$

With reasonable prices and clean rooms, this 40-unit motel fills up during the summer months. Its location at the east end of Sheridan Avenue, Cody's main thoroughfare, makes it ideal for strolling to downtown shops and restaurants.

This single-story motel is well maintained and even has a safe grassy area that is fenced in for kids. Rooms with or without kitchenettes are available, and there is an area for barbecuing on the grounds. Adjacent to the motel is Cody Coffee Company, where you can get a good cup of joe and baked goods each morning.

Insiders' Tip

If you've got a hankerin' to taste-test buffalo, the Wyoming Buffalo Company in downtown Cody will tempt you with a morsel of bison jerky. After that you might move on to another one of their numerous buffalo-meat concoctions.

Bed and Breakfasts

Price Code

$	Less than $85
$$	$86 to $115
$$$	$116 to $150
$$$$	$151 and more

Close-up

Heart Mountain's Sad Legacy

Just west of Cody the remains of a chimney spire and a few lonely buildings at the base of Heart Mountain are reminders of a tragic moment in American history.

On February 19, 1942, President Roosevelt signed an executive order approving the evacuation of more than 100,000 Japanese Americans from the West Coast to 10 relocation centers throughout the U.S. Heart Mountain Relocation Camp was one of those centers.

In turn, the action that followed forcibly removed people from their homes, schools, and communities and placed them in a desolate camp encircled by barbed wire and guarded with armed military personnel. The camp included 468 barracks, two mess halls, two laundry-toilet buildings, and two auxiliary buildings, as well as a fire station, water and sewage treatment plants, power station, a hospital, and several administrative buildings. Internees were restricted from leaving the camp. At its peak nearly 11,000 Japanese were contained here and it was the third largest community in Wyoming.

During its three-year existence Heart Mountain Camp saw the birth of 552 babies and 185 deaths. Despite the unjust confinement, the camp's residents organized themselves and established a school system, newspaper, and internal government. Life went on here as the world was at war. Many internees resorted to low paying jobs as agricultural hands and kept the camp "self-sufficient," as ordained by the federal government. The camp gave the communities of Cody and Powell an economic boost during wartime hardships.

Finally, in 1945, President Roosevelt proclaimed the internees could go free. Each person was given $25 and a train ticket to the destination of their choice on the West Coast. In theory, this was good news, but in practice it left thousands of Japanese Americans homeless. During the internment most had their homes foreclosed and lost all their possessions. They didn't know where to go and the government offered no further assistance. While the rest of the nation celebrated America's victory, Japanese Americans suffered their own defeat.

The order which created Heart Mountain Relocation Camp was signed under the guise that it was for the "protection" of the Japanese, but later it was verified that the establishment of these camps was an act of paranoia and prejudice, resulting in a gross violation of human rights. Although many of the camp internees were American citizens, all were suspected to be disloyal to America based on their race. In the mid-1980s, Congress conceded this shameful fact, granting compensation to internees and their families who lost property as a result of their internment. Later, a memorial plaque was placed at the site, which is now on the National Historic Register. It reads: "May the injustice of the removal and incarceration of 120,000 persons of Japanese ancestry during World War II, two-thirds of whom were American citizens, never be repeated."

Visible from most any point in town, Heart Mountain is a foreboding sentinel of a sad moment in history. Although the camp's activities are finished, the affront to loyal American citizens has not been forgotten; in 2000 Wyoming Senator Mike Enzi helped push legislation through the U.S. Senate to approve a $500,000 federal economic development grant to be used toward the future Heart Mountain Interpretive Learning center. The goal is to have the center open to the public in three years.

Heart Mountain is located just 15 miles west of Cody. Take U.S. Highway 14-A to Road 19 and continue ½ mile to the small memorial sign.

Lockhart Inn Bed and Breakfast
109 W. Yellowstone, Cody, WY 82414
(307) 587-6074, (800) 377-7255
$

This large, turn-of-the-century home offers seven different rooms to choose from. Located in the heart of Cody's historic residential area, the Lockhart Inn is just removed enough from the bustle of town to be relaxing yet convenient. All the neatly decorated rooms have private baths. Innkeeper Cindy Baldwin serves a lavish breakfast and lunch upon request. She can also help arrange activities in the area. All the rooms are non-smoking and children are welcome.

Parson's Pillow
1202 14th St., Cody, WY 82414
(307) 587-2382, (800) 377-2348
$

What you'll find in the steeple of Cody's first church is a cowboy-style bathroom with a plunge tub for soaking. That's only one of the thoughtful accents that innkeepers Lee and Elly Larabee have added to this converted house of worship. Each one of the four guest rooms is uniquely adorned with vintage furniture and elegant style. Built in 1902 as a Methodist church, the Larabees have meticulously restored and converted the building into an unforgettable hostelry. Tall, narrow windows stretch to the ceiling and let in wonderful natural light. Guests can enjoy the large parlor and the daily abundant breakfasts.

> **Insiders' Tip**
> Cody residents alpine ski at the mountain in Red Lodge, some 80 miles away. But Sleeping Giant Ski Area, a tiny hill 40 miles east of town is a shorter trip.

Campgrounds and RV Parks

Price Code

$	Less than $9
$$	$10 to $16
$$$	$17 to $23
$$$$	$24 and more

Camp Cody
415 Yellowstone Ave., Cody, WY 82414
(307) 587-9730, (888) 231-CAMP
$$$

With all 50 state flags plus Canada flying above this campground, you can't miss it at the north end of Yellowstone Avenue. Hook up your RV at one of the 63 sites or choose from 15 cabins and 15 tent spaces. The grounds are shady and pleasant with a heated pool, free cable TV, restrooms, and guest laundry.

Eagle Creek Campground
U.S. Hwy. 14/16/20, Cody, WY 82414
(307) 527-6921
$

Just 44 miles west of Cody you'll find 20 RV spaces and tent camping along the North Fork of the Shoshone River. Conifers shade the paved spurs and drinking water is available The North Fork offers great fishing, while just a half mile away you have access to a trailhead and horse corrals.

Old Trail Town—23 authentic historic buildings reassembled on the original townsite of Cody, Wyoming.
PHOTO: PARK COUNTY TRAVEL COUNCIL

Gateway Campground
203 Yellowstone Ave., Cody, WY 82414
(307) 587-2561
$$

Staying at the Gateway Campground puts you in the perfect position to enjoy three of Cody's best things. You're just an easy stroll away from the Cody Nite Rodeo and Old Trail Town (see our Attractions chapter) and across the street from Cassie's Supper Club, giving you no excuse not to enjoy a full night of dinner, dancing, and rodeo.

This campground—only a mile west of downtown—is surrounded by a broad sweeping lawn and mature trees, making it feel like a little spot in the country. Next to the campground, owner Lura Showman's father offers horseback riding along the river. The quiet lawn behind the motel accommodates 87 tent spots, along with 29 electric hook-ups and 13 full hook-up sites. You'll find laundry, clean restrooms with showers, a pay phone, UHF television reception, and free coffee in the mornings. The Gateway is open from April through October.

KOA Kampground of Cody
5561 Greybull Hwy., Cody, WY 82414
(307) 587-2369
$$$

Staying at the Cody KOA feels more like staying at a dude ranch than a campground. The daily pancake breakfasts and nightly chuckwagon dinners make up for this campground's distance from town. Take the free shuttle to the Cody Nite Rodeo and the campground is a pick-up point for Powder River Tours.

With 200 RV hook-ups and 100 tent sites, this KOA begins to feel like a village during peak season. Enjoy the swimming pool, playground, hot tub, laundry, and showers. The campground is open May through October.

Fall foliage and snow-covered mountains near Cody, Wyoming. PHOTO: PARK COUNTY TRAVEL COUNCIL

Shoshone River Float—companies offer scenic river float trips through beautiful red rock canyons, frequent rapids, and tranquil pools. PHOTO: PARK COUNTY TRAVEL COUNCIL

Cody Nite Rodeo—professional cowboys perform every night June through August. PHOTO: PARK COUNTY TRAVEL COUNCIL

Newton Creek Campground
U.S. Hwy. 14/16/20, Cody, WY 82414
(307) 527-6921
$

This U.S. Forest Service campground along the North Fork of the Shoshone River comes complete with bear boxes—containers provided on site to make it simple for you to lock up your food. The Shoshone National Forest is in the thick of bear country, and the Wapiti Ranger District works hard to avoid bear-human confrontations. This campground closes each spring when the bears come out of hibernation and wander the river banks in search of food. Other than that, these 31 campsites offer running water and a pleasant place to picnic.

Three Mile Campground
U.S. Hwy. 14/16/20, Cody, WY 82414
(307) 527-6921
$

Because this is a grizzly bear corridor into Yellowstone Park, only hard-sided campers are allowed here. Most of the 33 sites here are equipped with user-friendly bear boxes for food storage—use them, as this area is known as a favorite spot for grizzlies during the night, particularly in spring and fall. Four sites are situated along the North Fork of the Shoshone River and are for day use only. Because this campground is only three miles from the East Entrance of Yellowstone, this campground is a popular overnight spot for park visitors.

Restaurants

Price Code

Price code covers meals for two people meal, excluding beverages, tip, and tax.

$ . . . . $10 to $19
$$ . . . . $20 to $27
$$$ . . . . $28 to $35
$$$$ . . . . $36 and more

Franca's
1421 Rumsey Ave., Cody, WY 82414
(307) 587-5354, (888) 806-5354
$$$$ no credit cards

Franca Franchetti makes a piece of Italy come alive every night at her tiny restaurant. Located in a 1920s French Colonial house, Franca slaves over stove and oven all day and then greets her faithful customers with a smile in the evening. Bringing her love of food and wine, Franca whips out traditional Northern Italian dishes. Each meal is served with focaccine (an Italian specialty bread) and (depending on what night of the week you come to dine) you might have the chance to try her homemade crab ravioli topped with fresh tomatoes or Tortelloni Verdi al Mascarpone (spinach pasta stuffed with an Italian cream cheese). The prix-fixe menu changes nightly. With write-ups in *Gourmet Magazine* and *Wine Spectator,* this unlikely Cody restaurant has made quite a name for itself. Franca has hand selected more than 100 different wines to make your meal that much better.

Insiders' Tip

Fine dining in Yellowstone country doesn't mean you have to dress to the nines. Casual dress is accepted almost everywhere.

But along with the food comes the ambiance and the fact that you are encouraged not to worry about the time here—just come hungry and ready to linger over a romantic four-course meal. Each table is set with linen, its own antique china pattern, and antique crystal. The work of Franca's artist husband, Joseph, hangs in the restaurant; a stroll from the back of the house leads to his studio.

Franca's is open Wednesday through Sunday May 15 through January 15. With just 24 seats in the house, reservations are a must.

The Irma
1192 Sheridan Ave., Cody, WY 82414
(307) 587-4221
$$

You can't come to Cody without dining at The Irma. Built at the turn of the century by Buffalo Bill himself and named for his youngest daughter, the restaurant and bar still draw the locals. Still a cornerstone of the downtown area, it exudes a nostalgic Western charm. Standing at the long, intricately carved cherrywood bar (a gift to Bill Cody from the queen of England), listening to the steady din of voices from people sitting at the round tables scattered throughout the room as smoke wafts up to the high pressed tin ceilings and the saloon doors swing open, you're almost transported into another era. Most people come for the prime rib dinners, but the menu also features barbecued ribs, chicken fried steak, trout, shrimp, and a variety of chicken dishes. Serving breakfast, lunch, and dinner, you can make reservations in the winter. In the summer months reservations are not accepted.

Maxwell's Restaurant
937 Sheridan Ave., Cody, WY 82414
(307) 527-7749
$$$

Start your day off with the morning paper, a fresh baked chocolate-filled croissant, and espresso in the bakery of Maxwell's. But be sure to return for lunch to try the unforgettable meatball sandwich or certainly to indulge in the Steak Formaggio—a 6-ounce tenderloin pressed in cracked peppercorns, grilled, then topped with gorgonzola cheese and a cream sauce. This old Victorian home (moved to this spot from the outskirts of town) at the end of Cody's historic downtown houses this comfortable and airy eatery. Maxwell's—a favorite with locals and tourists alike—is known for the wonderful array of fresh baked specialty breads and pastries that accompany a mouthwatering menu of dishes. Best of all, however, is savoring the fine food with a glass of wine at an outdoor table in the summer time.

Mustard's Last Stand
1276 Sheridan Ave., Cody, WY 82414
(307) 527-4147
$, no credit cards

It's hard to beat a good old hot dog—especially at a place where nothing on the menu is over $3.95. Mustard's serves up 21 different all-beef, quarter-pounder Oscar Mayer Wieners. If you're feeling bold, try the Hombre Dog—dressed with avocado, salsa, onions, and jalapeño slices—wow! Located in the heart of downtown, this new joint keeps the vittles simple, but packs in the hungry customers for lunch and dinner.

The Proud Cut Saloon
1227 Sheridan Ave., Cody, WY 82414
(307) 527-6905
$$

With a long list of juicy steaks, including a 22-ounce porterhouse and 14-ounce prime rib, The Proud Cut also serves Rocky Mountain Oysters (breaded bull calf testicles). Either way you won't leave hungry. The restaurant is full of old local characters, and the walls are lined with cowboy memorabilia as well as black and white photos.

By the way, if you think "Proud Cut" refers to the steaks, you are mistaken. Filled with the supposed machismo of the West, the proprietors will tell you the name refers to castrated stallions that can't quit acting like studs because the procedure was botched. Let's just say that just enough of the male equipment remains to make the stallion "think" he's still a stud.

Children are not welcome here. During the height of tourist season reservations are suggested for both lunch and dinner.

Shopping

True to its pioneer heritage, most of the stores in downtown Cody offer different angles to Western wear and Native American sundries. The other influence that shapes the retail scene here is, of course, the outdoors. You'll find shops specializing in every mountain sport imaginable.

Cody Newsstand
1112 13th St., Cody, WY 82414
(307) 587-2843

Open since 1988, the Cody Newsstand features an entire wall of magazines— 4,000 titles, to be exact. The store carries 20,000 book titles and showcases a wonderful collection of children's books. You can also buy a fine cigar to accompany your *Wall Street Journal*.

Buffalo Bill Historical Center, exterior view. PHOTO: PARK COUNTY TRAVEL COUNCIL

Whitney Gallery of Western Art, Buffalo Bill Historical Center. PHOTO: PARK COUNTY TRAVEL COUNCIL

Plains Indian Museum, Buffalo Bill Historical Center. PHOTO: PARK COUNTY TRAVEL COUNCIL

Cody Firearms Museum, Buffalo Bill Historical Center. PHOTO: PARK COUNTY TRAVEL COUNCIL

Buffalo Bill Museum, Buffalo Bill Historical Center. PHOTO: PARK COUNTY TRAVEL COUNCIL

Cody Rodeo Company
1291 Sheridan Ave., Cody, WY 82414
(307) 587-5913

The sheer peculiarity of seeing a pair of legs sticking out of a VW bug displayed in the window will draw you into this shop. The car (which came from the wrecking yard) has been in a couple of demolition derbies, but here it is stuffed with clowns (only mannequins, of course). Even if you don't venture any further than the front door, the display will make you smile. But you must come inside; your curiosity won't let you walk away once you get a glimpse of Buford, the bucking Brahma bull (he's stuffed in an eternal bucking pose). Once you've gotten an eye-full of these sights, you'll notice the unique cowboy clothes, furniture, housewares, and accessories. You might even walk out of the shop wearing a ten-gallon Stetson hat on your head.

Look for owners, Susan and Ev Diehl, at their Cody Nite Rodeo shop. You can also shop from their mail-order catalog when you get home.

Museum Selections, Buffalo Bill Historic Center
720 Sheridan Ave., Cody, WY 82414
(307) 587-3243, (800) 533-3838

Authors frequently make appearances for book signings at the Buffalo Bill Historic Center. The store has a small collection of titles aimed at art and Western history. You'll also find posters and reproductions of paintings featured in the museum's collection, gifts, and a coffee bar.

Prairie Rose Northern Plains Indian Gallery
1356 Sheridan Ave., Cody, WY 82414
(307) 587-8181

The intricately beaded clothing that adorns this shop's walls are true works of art. Each seed bead has been hand stitched onto feather-soft leather in designs that have been passed down through generations of Northern Plains Indians. In here you'll find peculiar utilitarian objects that Native Americans use to make these beaded masterpieces, including seed beads, eye beads, trade beads, coyote and wolf knuckles, bear claws, porcupine quills, elk hide, moose hair, and feathers. Prairie Rose also carries Native American music, jewelry, and books.

Sunlight Sports
1251 Sheridan Ave., Cody, WY 82414
(307) 587-9517

After 29 years of serving Cody residents and their outdoor addictions, Sunlight Sports is still on top. Inside you'll find gear for backpacking, climbing, skiing, snowboarding, snowshoeing, rock and ice climbing, and all the right apparel to go with your recreational pursuits. Sunlight's ample stock suits all ages and levels of expertise.

During winter months the ski shop offers rentals and beefs up its cold-weather clothes to get through the long season. This hometown sporting goods store is also the place to go for tips on great local trails and climbing spots.

Timber Creek Interiors Furniture and Design
1371 Sheridan Ave., Cody, WY 82414
(307) 587-4246

There's so much to "ooh" and "aah" over in this richly furnished store. Overstuffed couches and heavy hand-hewn harvest tables invite you to have a seat, but you wouldn't dare. This high-end furniture store exudes the new upscale Western motif. With rooms arranged like a house, Timbercreek welcomes you to imagine your own home so tastefully done. Antler chandeliers and sophisticated household accessories conjure up the possibilities of redecorating to the hilt. Let the store's expert designers advise you on how to bring a little bit of the West into your house without overdoing it.

Traditions West
1131 Sheridan Ave., Cody, WY 82414
(307) 587-7434

From dainty lace antique hankies to turn-of-the-century steamer trunks, owner

Mary Lou Bunting has searched high and low for the treasures in her "antique mall." Beautifully worn armoires, charming children's wagons, porcelain wash basins, and vintage clothes—there is so much to pore through in this large shop that you are sure to walk away with at least a little purchase. Many of the items at Traditions West are large pieces of stately furniture, both unique and common. Should you find furniture you can't live without, the store ships anywhere in the U.S.

Wind River Hat Company
144 W. Yellowstone Hwy., Cody, WY 82414
(307) 527-5939, (800) 899-5939

Country singers Tanya Tucker and Ray Price will tell you that master hat maker Gary Anderson makes the best hats west of Nashville. Like true cowboys, they know the key to a fine fitting hat is to have it made just for you. A true artisan, Anderson custom fits hats and makes them on site. Prices range from $125 to $1,200, depending on the amount of braiding, burning, and beading. He has made a name for his company and shows his wares each year at Cody's Western Design Conference.

Nightlife

Cassie's Supper Club
214 Yellowstone Ave., Cody, WY
(307) 527-5500
$$$

You don't need line dancing lessons to enjoy the foot stompin' country-and-western music that pipes out of Cassie's dance hall. Owner Steve Singer, a Cody native, played music on the road for 20 years before he returned home to liven up the town's music scene. He plays music seven nights a week during summer months and Wednesday through Saturday in the winter.

Cassie's, owned in the 1920s by Cassie Waters, the renowned madam of Cody's other former nightlife attraction, has always been the place to go for fun and dancing. As a boy Singer grew up down the street from the place; he played piano for the bar regulars. Since then he's become an avid collector of Cassie memorabilia. Look for her fur lap robe displayed in the entryway and the parrots above the bar.

Singer has made a name for Cassie's as the place to go for dinner and dancing. The menu consists of steak and seafood items. Lunch is also served here and reservations are recommended.

Cody Nite Rodeo
421 W. Yellowstone Ave., Cody, WY 82414
(307) 587-2992

The folks in Cody know what you came looking for in the West: cowboys. The old time legend is alive and well here with bull riders, rodeo clowns, and barrel racers showing off their skills. The rodeo runs for 90 consecutive nights from Memorial Day until Labor Day. It has become the town's number one nighttime activity and attracts 90,000 spectators each summer. Originally started in 1938 as a gimmick to lure Yellowstone tourists into Cody to stay the night, it still works. But the Cody Nite Rodeo is no tourist trap. It's the real thing with the cowboys and stock putting their hearts into every performance.

Attractions

Yellowstone National Park

Of course Yellowstone National Park in and of itself is an attraction. But the world's first national park is a complex place. Like any living thing, it has many different sides. At a glance you will see its astounding beauty, its vast wildness. Scrutinize it and you will notice flaws; examine it closely and you will recognize nature's intricate links to past, present, and future. Yellowstone is truly like no other place on earth. And to offer up a handful of highlights labeled "the best" or "the most interesting" or "the most dynamic" does not do the place justice. It is a place you must return to again and again to grasp its significance and to realize its importance and rarity. For some people it is worth moving here just to be near this natural wonder and to experience it on a regular basis. For others it's a one-time whirlwind tour that will linger in memory. This chapter highlights just a few of the places you must see if you will only come here once and a couple others that you might lure you back for a return visit.

Grand Canyon of the Yellowstone

Renowned painter Thomas Moran may have been the first to fall in love with the Grand Canyon of the Yellowstone. He accompanied the 1871 Hayden Expedition, and his paintings helped convince Congress to create the world's first national park. In particular, his depiction of the canyon's richly layered colors from his perch at what is now called Artist's Point captured the area's uncommon grandeur and unparalleled beauty. Today, you can still see it through his eyes from this same spot on the canyon's southern rim. You can also view the Lower Falls, which is the highest waterfall in Yellowstone (308 feet) from the North Rim Drive. At sunset, Inspiration Point sets off a wild display of pinks in the canyon's rock layers. Walking and cross country ski trails also wind along both rims of the canyon.

No matter where you stand, this canyon—24 miles long and 4,000 feet wide in some places—will leave you speechless. Its walls are colored in hues of red, brown, white, and orange layers where the Yellowstone River has, over centuries, cut through rock down to 800 or 1,200 feet below.

Yellowstone Lake

Whether it is from the perch of your canoe, a lakeside trail, the comfy seat in your campsite, or the elegant veranda of Lake Yellowstone Hotel, there isn't a bad view of Yellowstone Lake. Its pure, icy waters stretch 20 miles long and 14 miles wide across the cradle of the Yellowstone Plateau at 7,333 feet. On stormy days the water churns in ocean-like waves and looks foreboding. The largest high-altitude lake in North America, you will find more than 110 miles of shoreline where you can sit and peer into the deep, frigid blue. But unless you have a dry suit, don't think about swimming in here—the average temperature is 41 degrees (brrrrrrr).

Fishing is encouraged, however. Yellowstone Lake is home to the largest inland population of wild cutthroat trout in North America. Unfortunately, it also contains a growing population of lake trout, a non-native species that preys upon cutthroats and has depleted their numbers significantly since 1994.

During summer months, the pristine blue waters span out into a crystalline plain. From the shore you can watch small sailboats, tour boats, and fishing rigs in designated areas or take a cruise around the lake yourself. At Bay Bridge Marina, regularly scheduled scenic cruises depart throughout the day from June through September. You can also rent outboard motorboats and canoes, or charter a guided fishing trip. A favorite land-lubber ride is the Sunset Tour on a historic replica of a 1937 white touring bus. The bus leaves from Lake Hotel and Fishing Bridge RV Park and motors through scenery around the lake to the breathtaking views at Lake Butte Overlook. On a clear day you can see layers of snow-capped mountains ringing the surrounding plateau. By walking along one of the many designated hiking trails you can also get a closer look at geyser and fumaroles and hot springs that seep and steam into the lake's chilly water. Ask at the visitor center for details.

Even below the surface Yellowstone Lake offers another intriguing world, but most of us don't get to experience it. Since 1999 researchers have been exploring the mysterious lake bottom and have unearthed a whole other system of geothermal features. Thirty to 40-foot high spires have been found, sprouting from the bottom of the lake like an underwater forest. Scientists discovered that the formation contains the same minerals found in the geyser basins, dating back 12,000 years. Look for new discoveries about Yellowstone Lake when you visit and keep an eye out for research ships equipped with scuba diving scientists.

Lamar Valley

In one morning it is feasible to see bear, wolves, fox, coyotes, bison, and deer in Yellowstone's Lamar Valley. Located in the northeastern corner of the park, this is the wildlife-watching mother lode if you are patient enough to watch and wait with your binoculars or a spotting scope. Called the Serengeti of North America, Lamar is a grassy, broad sweeping drainage that provides ideal habitat for more animal species than any other place in Yellowstone. It is probably best known as the stage for the 1995 re-introduction of the wolves, which were initially released here. Since then the wolf packs have grown and claimed other territories, but it is still possible to glimpse these ellusive creatures (early mornings in spring or fall are the best times.)

Lamar Valley is historically known as the home of the Buffalo Ranch. By 1902 Yellowstone's bison were nearly extinct due to early market hunting by settlers and later poachers within park boundaries. The U.S. government was moved to action and saved the last free-roaming bison herd by raising bison like domestic cattle until the 1930s when the herd finally grew to a healthy number. Today Buffalo Ranch is the headquarters for The Yellowstone Institute, a non-profit educational group which conducts field courses on topics ranging from park ecology to plein air painting.

Even without the wildlife or the history, Lamar is beautiful. Its vast landscape is captivating in a gentler, subtler way than some of the more dynamic attractions in Yellowstone. You can enjoy it from nearby Cooke City, Montana (3 miles past the northeastern gate), or from Slough Creek and Pebble Creek campgrounds.

Mount Washburn

From the summit of Mount Washburn you will see the Grand Canyon of the Yellowstone River to the east; to the south it's Hayden Valley and Yellowstone Lake. On a clear day you will also get a look at the Tetons, Absarokas, and the Gallatin Range. With a view like this, there's no question why this is Yellowstone's best-known mountain. Rising 10,243 feet above the west edge of Yellowstone's Grand Canyon, this mountain was named after Gen. Henry Dana Washburn, who led the 1870 expedition to the area. Since the park's creation, the mountain has been a popular hiking spot; historic photos even show early travelers stepping out of stagecoaches at the summit (this should be your first clue that the hike is a moderate one.)

Walking the three miles to the top you will gain 1,500 feet in elevation and perhaps a friend's admiration should you decide to call from the pay phone at the summit. If you're lucky, you might also catch a glimpse of a few bighorn sheep. But regardless of which of the three trails you take, the walk is paved with wildflowers of every color. There is also a fire lookout at the summit where you can take shelter in bad weather.

Specimen Ridge

Near Tower Junction, Specimen Ridge holds the remnants of one of Yellowstone's greatest mysteries. Here scientists have discovered as many as 27 separate petrified forests, one on top of the other. Some of the trees are still standing and indicate that at one time the climate was much warmer. Among the identified species are redwood, pine, magnolia, dogwood, oak, maple, hickory, and walnut. The best way to see Specimen Ridge is through a tour led by one of the park's naturalist-guide rangers. Check at any visitor center to find out when you can catch one of these tours.

The Big Burn

The fires of 1988 were the greatest natural event to happen in the greater Yellowstone area since the massive caldera-forming volcanic eruption more than 600,000 years ago. We are still seeing the effects of the flames that covered 793,880 acres (35 percent) of the park. Though to many people, the fires seemed like a tragic loss, biologists and ecologists saw the burn as a natural function of a healthy ecosystem. As new trees grow and forest underbrush replenishes the burnt areas, researchers are gaining new information on how a forest recovers from an event like this.

You can learn more about the long-term results of the Yellowstone fires, too. It's worth a walk and talk from a park ranger who will take you on a "Fire Hike" through burnt area to see how the forest has regenerated more than a decade after the fires. A scheduled two-hour hike leaves from the Lake Overlook Trailhead in the West Thumb Geyser Basin parking lot afternoons in July and August. You must make a reservation to participate, call (307) 242-2650.

Geothermal Features

To early explorers, the eerie spouting, steaming, sulfurous areas of the Yellowstone region were unlike anything they had ever seen. The sight inspired the creation of Yellowstone National Park, but it wasn't easy to convince people of this natural curiosity. In 1807, when John Colter returned home with accounts of the area's geothermal activity, people laughed at him. In fact, until the Hayden expedition of 1871 returned with photographs and paintings of Yellowstone's geysers and mud pots, people doubted their existence.

Yellowstone's geothermal features still enthrall visitors today. Geysers that shoot up hundreds of feet from the depths of the earth and pools that boil at temperatures beyond 450 degrees have the power to remind us that we are part of a planet that is alive and ever-changing. They are fascinating and strange and magic. With seven geyser basins accessible by car, it's possible to see some of the most spectacular specimens. There are more hot spots in Yellowstone's backcountry. It's not possible to list them all, but here are a few. We haven't given specific directions to these locations because they are clearly marked on the map you'll get when you enter the park and on road signs.

Firehole Lake Drive

This level, one-way, paved road begins from Old Faithful-Madison Road eight miles north of Old Faithful and takes you through much of the Lower Geyser Basin. Active, ever-changing mud pots, constant geysers, and hissing fumaroles make it a worthwhile stop. There are also a number of colorful, bubbling hot springs to see just off the road if you are willing to stroll a little. As this is the largest basin in Yellowstone National Park, you'll find a dozen geyser groups here.

The most interesting group are the Fountain Paint Pots, with bubbling, creamy mud that resembles latex paint. Among this group is the Great Fountain Geyser, which was the first geyser seen by the Cook-Folsom-Peterson Party (see our History chapter to learn more about these explorers). This group is the largest in the Lower Basin, and the activity here increased dramatically after the 1959 earthquake. Great Fountain Geyser, one of Yellowstone's most spectacular, erupts about every 11 hours. It will overflow for about 70 minutes prior to erupting, so if the crater is full and you see water seeping out, definitely wait to see the eruption. Just beyond that is White Dome Geyser with its very large and impressive geyserite cone. White Dome erupts fairly frequently—about every 30 to 60 minutes.

Beyond White Dome you continue to pass thermal features, such as Pink Cone Geyser, which is known to erupt infrequently, and Firehole Lake, which deserves an exploration along its boardwalks. The Firehole Lake area is surrounded by large meadows where you might spot coyote, bison, or sandhill crane, particularly in the early mornings.

Mammoth Hot Springs

You could come back to the cascading terraces of Mammoth Hot Springs and never see the same thing twice. The unusual travertine limestone terraces are a living sculpture, growing and changing minute by minute. These springs, with their source in a hillside above park headquarters, discharge about 500 gallons of hot water per minute. Almost 2 tons of travertine (calcium carbonate) are deposited every day. But these cascades of minerals don't just flow and grow, they show off bright colors and ornate formations. There is no other formation like it anywhere else in the park.

A walking trail through the Lower Terraces and a one-way drive through the Upper Terraces offer views of these fascinating formations.

Mud Volcano

Discover turbulent and explosive mud pots, including Mud Volcano and

Dragon's Mouth. View—and smell—Sulfur Caldron from the overlook just north of the Mud Volcano area. It is located on the road between Lake and Canyon, six miles north of Fishing Bridge Junction.

Old Faithful

The world's largest concentration of geysers (300 in all) is located here in the Upper Geyser Basin, with Old Faithful among its most famous. But there is much more to explore in this area. Several miles of trail begin at the visitor center, winding past geysers and hot springs too numerous to count. Names such as Beehive Grotto, Castle, Spasmodic, Grand, Giant, Riverside, and Morning Glory only hint at the wonders you will see. Stop at the visitor center for orientation and geyser information.

After a walk along nearby nature trails, we encourage you to check out the Old Faithful Inn. Completed in 1904, this massive building is still the largest log structure in the world. Beyond the sheer size of it, however, is the attention architect Robert Reamer placed on the aesthetics of the place. As you walk into the 80-foot high lobby, knotted pine balconies perch above. Notice the wrought iron detail on door handles, hinges, room numerals, and the one-of-a-kind tower clock which clings to the huge stone fireplace (see this chapter's Close-up). In its day, Old Faithful was the height of luxury. Regular guided tours are available to the public every half hour, check at the front desk.

Steamboat Geyser

In May 2000 the world's tallest geyser roared up to 400 feet in the air, spewing steam and debris for several hundred yards. It has a history of this—when it first became active in 1878, it hurled huge rocks into the air with such force that it killed nearby trees and plants with its burning mud. Still, an eruption from this legendary geyser happens so infrequently that word of it blowing draws park employees and geyser enthusiasts from 30 miles away. But you could get lucky—who knows when this geyser will go off again. In the 1980s, Steamboat erupted 23 times in one summer.

Steamboat is only one of many geysers you can check out in Norris Geyser Basin, which is the home of the hottest geothermal features in the park. An elaborate trail system starts at the Geyser Basin Museum and winds around to Porcelain Basin. This ever-changing group of geysers sits in open terrain with hundreds of densely packed geothermal features. The features in the Back Basin are more scattered and isolated.

West Thumb Geyser Basin

Take a stroll down one of the prettiest boardwalk trails found anywhere in the park through West Thumb Geyser Basin (named for a thumb-shaped bay on the southwestern end of Yellowstone Lake.) Situated on the shore of Yellowstone Lake, the boiling springs in this basin, including the famous Fishing Cone, discharge their waters into the icy lake. This odd-looking gray mound used to erupt regularly to heights of up to 40 feet. Nearby you'll find the jewel colored greens of Abyss Pool and Black Pool. With the Absaroka Mountains as a backdrop to the east, you won't forget this view.

> ## Insiders' Tip
> During the bronc riding event at any given rodeo you might hear a zealous fan in the crowd yell "Put 'em east and west, boy!" The expression means for the rider to spur the horse's shoulders with toes pointing outward.

Old Faithful Clock Strikes Again

Thousands of visitors set their watches by the clock at the Old Faithful Inn.

Little did they know that the historic clock had been missing time for decades and its pendulum had been silent for 80 years. When it was finally restored in September of 2000, people noticed its new life echoing through the grand hotel.

Tick-tock-gong.

That sound was like music to the ears of Dave Berghold, owner of the Last Wind Up in Bozeman, Montana, and machinist Mike Kovacich, of Anaconda, Montana, who restored the historic 15-foot tower clock to its glory.

"It was like all clocks when I build them—the first time you let the pendulum go, it's like bringing something to life," said Kovacich.

Constructed in 1903-1904, Old Faithful Inn is a national historic landmark and is the world's largest log structure. The clock is an essential part of that history. Mounted to the massive stone fireplace, it is a focal point of the Inn, anchoring the cavernous 85-foot high lobby. Yet most people took it for granted as just a decorative relic. Each season resident tour guides repeatedly note the clock for its craftsmanship, without understanding its uniqueness.

Old Faithful employees said the clock was actually considered a nuisance by many visitors before the restoration. When it ticked it was fine, but when it tocked it woke up everyone in the west wing. Guests complained about the awful racket and so the staff just turned it off. Over the decades maintenance crews had done patch-up jobs to fix various malfunctions, but what the old thing needed was a complete overhaul.

AmFac Resorts and Hotels, the concessionaire responsible for lodging in the park knew the clock needed to be fixed. The Inn is a living usable museum and the clock is an integral part of that history. What AmFac didn't know was how complicated the process of restoring the clock would be. They discovered the tower clock was a rare piece in this part of the country and rebuilding it wasn't a job just anyone could accomplish. An expert was what they needed. That's where Berghold came in.

He was elated at the opportunity to work on a turn-of-century clock, and to study the mechanism that ran the timepiece before electricity was utilized. But what he found inside the body of the clock was a 1920s electric Seth Thomas wind-up timepiece, which made the hands tell time, albeit inaccurately. Berghold said he looked inside the clock and found that it was a hodgepodge of fixer uppers and patch jobs that had reduced the valuable timepiece to not much more than face, hands, and pendulum.

To a watchmaker, this is akin to blasphemy. It meant that over the years the original, intricate mechanism had been disassembled, repaired, removed, and finally replaced with something merely functional. Berghold realized that he was looking at a great challenge, especially since no one affiliated with the park seemed to know what the original clockworks looked like. A whole new clock mechanism had to be constructed with special attention to historic integrity.

Not much is known about the original Old Faithful clock. It seems that Livingston blacksmith George W. Culpitts forged the dial, pendulum, and connecting hardware. But even this is hearsay, since there is no mention of this work in the Yellowstone Park archives. Culpitts was the artisan responsible for all the ironwork throughout the Inn—door knobs, room numbers, and light fixtures. Later in his life he was applauded for his skill and good taste, but it's unclear whether he designed the intricate system that ran the actual timepiece.

Clock enthusiast and historian Dick Dysart researched the clock's history and helped with the installation. He pored over old photos and postcards of the Inn in local museums, searching for clues of original construction. Despite the fact that the National Park Service and local historians provided very little information about the clock, the project continued. In some ways the clock's vague history gave Berghold and Kovacich more artistic freedom. Like an intricate science project, the two men struggled with problems in constructing the guts of the clock. They had to decipher factors like friction, height, length, and aesthetics. All new gears, pinions, and plates were cut based on designs he knew existed in that era.

Their efforts resulted in a majestic original time piece. Although the current motor used to wind the clock is modern, the appearance of the clock and its actual time-keeping mechanism are historically correct. The new clock is an endless free-wind mechanism with a jeweled face that is very similar to timepieces built at the turn of the last century; the 156-inch pendulum ticks every two seconds and strikes on the hour. The bulk of the project cost AmFac $5,000.

Finally, after months of work, on September 13, 2000, Berghold, Dysart, and Kovacich climbed the three-stories of scaffolding to install the clock. The process was frustrating and lengthy. But it was worth the work when the first sounds of this rare timepiece resounded through Old Faithful once again. Now, walking through the Inn during the quiet of the night you hear the incredible sound echo on different levels of the building.

Tick...one-thousand-one...tock...one-thousand-two...gong.

The Old Faithful Inn offers regular tours of the entire lodge throughout the day from Memorial Day to Labor Day.

Grand Teton National Park

Snake River Overlook

This overlook on the northeast route between Moran and Moose junctions is widely considered the best spot to see the panorama of the majestic Teton range. Framed by the slow-moving water of the Snake River, the overlook is also a popular wildlife watching spot. Look for moose, beavers, river otters, and birds. In addition, it's also a lesson in history. The willow thickets that flank the river and its tributaries were home to the beaver that attracted the first fur traders to the Jackson Hole valley. Further up the road past the Moran Junction is the Oxbow Bend Turnout, where you can catch equally impressive views of towering Mount Moran.

Jenny Lake

Probably the most popular lake in the park, Jenny Lake looms beneath the three Tetons and Mount Owen, making it a great spot for photos or a lunch break. An easy, flat, 7.7-mile hike starts at the Jenny Lake turnout or the South Jenny Lake trailhead and circles the lake, making for one of the park's favorite routes. You can also take ranger-led trips across the lake to Inspiration Point. These depart from the Jenny Lake boat dock every summer morning at 8:30 A.M. A shuttle will also take you across the lake for $4 round trip, where you can access the Cascade Canyon Trail and numerous other trails that lead into the Teton backcountry.

Grand View Point

This appropriately named spot produces one of the most dramatic views in the park. To get to the beginning of the 1.1-mile trail, make the first turn on the east side of U.S. Highway 89 north past Jackson Lake Lodge. The road is fairly rough, so low clearance vehicles may need to park at one of the turnouts on the dirt road. The trailhead isn't far, less than one mile from the turnoff.

The trail to the point starts out flat, but soon you'll come to a steep hill. Don't fret, the climb will be short and you'll be at Grand View Point—elevation 7,586 feet—when you reach the top. And once you get there, you'll get a fantastic look at Mount Moran and the rest of the mighty Tetons, as well as a sweeping vista of Two Ocean Lake and the Teton Wilderness. Round trip is 2.2 miles, and it's downhill all the way from the top.

Jackson, Wyoming

National Elk Refuge
(307) 733-9212

You'll pass by this 23,754-acre refuge as you head toward Grand Teton from Jackson. The territory serves as the annual winter range for as many as 10,000 elk, which migrate to the feeding grounds of the refuge as winter encroaches on the Yellowstone ecosystem. At the end of the winter season, local Boy Scout troops gather and auction the elk antlers that are naturally shed every spring, donating 80 percent of the profits to buy supplemental winter feed for the elk. Many buyers come from Asia, where antlers are considered to have medicinal value. In the winter, stop in at the interpretive center located in the National Museum of Wildlife Art.

National Museum of Wildlife Art
2820 Rungius Rd., Jackson, WY 83002
(307) 733-5771
www.wildlifeart.com

The 51,000 square-foot National Museum of Wildlife Art houses more than 2,000 works of art, including pieces by American explorer artists, landscape artists, contemporary wildlife artists, and sculptors. Media include oil, bronze, stone, acrylic, watercolor, gouache, pastel, pencil, lithography, photography, and charcoal.

Since it opened in 1987, the nonprofit museum has become an important educational center and meeting place for the Jackson Hole region. The new building, completed in 1994 at a cost of $10 million, sits perched on a hill across from the National Elk Refuge on U.S. Highway 89, two miles north of Jackson. The museum houses the interpretive center for the refuge during the winter months.

Interesting exhibits include the second-largest public collection of work by Carl Rungius, which features the only two bronzes he completed, and the American Bison Collection, more than 100 images

Insiders' Tip

You can be your own expert guide to Yellowstone along the park's system of boardwalks and paths that meander through steep canyons and scenic thermal areas. Trail guides and signs display informative explanations of the sights and lead you through most of the locations.

which portray the bison's relationship with humans and nature. Other artists represented include John J. Audubon, John Clymer, Karl Bodmer, Eugene Delecroix, and Charles Russell.

Museum facilities include 12 galleries, a 200-seat auditorium, two classrooms, a conference room, gift shop, and a café. Hours are daily from 8 A.M. to 5 P.M. in the summer, and 9 A.M. to 5 P.M. in the winter. Spring/Fall hours are 9 A.M. to 5 P.M. Monday through Saturday and 1 P.M. to 5 P.M. on Sunday. Admission is $6 for adults, $5 for students and seniors, $14 for a family, and children under five are admitted free.

Grassy Lake Road
Flagg Ranch, WY to Ashton, ID

If you are driving from Jackson to West Yellowstone (or vice versa) and don't want to go through Yellowstone National Park, the scenic Grassy Lake Road is a great option. From Jackson, head north through Grand Teton National Park, along the John D. Rockefeller, Jr. Memorial Parkway to Flagg Ranch, a few miles from the south entrance to Yellowstone. Turn left at the ranch and follow the signs for the Grassy Lake Road.

The 50-mile stretch of dirt road passes through numerous lowland meadows and the charred remains of 2000's Flagg Ranch Fire. Keep your eye out for deer, elk, and moose in the creek-filled meadows. You'll come to the huge Grassy Lake Reservoir and continue on a one-lane section of the road toward Ashton. A short side trip can be made to the Lake of the Woods, appropriately named for its timbered shores deep in the heart of the Targhee National Forest. On the way out you'll pass Indian Lake and a trumpeter swan refuge, and you'll see great views of the Tetons. One of the best times to drive this road is in the fall, when plentiful stands of aspens turn bright gold, highlighting the contrast between the green pines, blue skies, and white-capped peaks of the Tetons.

As the dirt road turns to pavement, you'll drive through the rolling potato fields of eastern Idaho into Ashton. Turn right onto U.S. Highway 20 toward West Yellowstone. The road closes for the winter months and is not recommended for large trailers or RVs. Call Grand Teton National Park at (307) 739-3399 for road information.

Jackson Hole Aerial Tram
Jackson Hole Mountain Resort, Teton Village

You can ride the Tram at the ski resort 2.4 miles up to the 10,450-foot summit of Rendezvous Mountain for one of the most spectacular views in North America. Bring your sweatshirt and jacket, as the wind can blow quite hard and the temperatures can dip into the 20s. While at the top, walk around and soak in the views of the Tetons to the north and the mountains of Wyoming and Idaho in every other direction. You can also access trails in Grand Teton National Park and the Bridger-Teton National Forest from the top, and grab a snack or a souvenir in the café. Rides cost $15 for adults. Keep your eye out for the black bears and other wildlife that roam the mountain on the way up. Grand Targhee Ski and Summer Resort and Snow King also offer scenic rides to the top of their respective summits.

Idaho

Yellowstone Bear World
6010 S. 4300 West, Rigby, ID
(208) 359-9688

This drive-thru wildlife park has plenty of animals to see, including elk, reindeer, fallow deer, mule deer, bison, white-tailed deer, wild turkeys, wolves, pheasants, grizzly bears, and black bears. Look up and you're likely to also see ducks, geese, and swans. Bear World accommodates all vehicles, even travel trailers, motor homes, and tour buses. If you're on a motorcycle, you can tour the park in a loaner car.

At the Photo Den, you can have your picture taken with a bear, wolf, or bull elk, and the Hungry Bear Café has cold drinks, burgers, ice cream, and more. There's also a petting zoo where kids can feed the ducks and fish from the overlook deck.

Admission is $8.50 for adults, $7.50 for seniors, $5.50 for children ages three to twelve, and free for kids under three. Yellowstone Bear World is located just off U.S Highway 20, about halfway between Idaho Falls and Ashton.

Cody, Wyoming

Buffalo Bill Dam Visitor Center
4804 N. Fork Hwy., Cody, WY
(307) 527-6076

The Buffalo Bill Dam transformed the geography of the Bighorn Basin. By blocking the conjunction of the south and north forks of the Shoshone River, it gave new life to the dry lands and changed the area into a fertile valley for agricultural practices that continue to thrive. One of the first three major dams built by the newly formed Bureau of Reclamation, the Buffalo Bill Dam was the highest in the nation (328 feet) when it was built in 1910. It was raised to 353 feet in 1992.

Six miles west of Cody, the little visitor center/rest area depicts the story of the dam's construction. Standing on the walkway above the dam, you get the spectacular views of the canyon and lake; you also get a sense of how dramatically it changed the river. This visitor center is open from May through September. There is no admission charge.

Buffalo Bill Historical Center
720 Sheridan Ave., Cody, WY
(307) 587-4771

The West may be wild, but it is not uncivilized. You'll find proof of this in the 237,000-square-foot Buffalo Bill Historical Center filled with its art, artifacts, and interactive history exhibits. Dubbed the Smithsonian of the West, within these museum walls you can experience the inspiration of Yellowstone as seen through the eyes (and paintbrush) of famous Hayden Expedition artist, Thomas Moran; you can glimpse Buffalo Bill Cody's visionary presence in the history of the American West; or experience the inside of a Hidasta Plains Indian lodge.

What the BBHC is famous for is an artful retelling of the American West through its collection of original paintings by western artists in the Whitney Gallery; the Cody Firearms Museum (the world's largest collection of American firearms); the Buffalo Bill Museum, which, of course, chronicles this legendary figure in one of our country's most exciting periods of growth; and the Plains Indian Museum, with its exhibits of the rich cultural objects and spiritual practices of the many Native American tribes who inhabited this land before the nineteenth century. Inside this massive museum you will feel the formality of that characteristic look-don't-touch aura, but there is something else here. The BBHC is also an interpretive center, where you can experience the West through the eyes and ears of a Pony Express rider or a Sioux warrior. This place is alive with culture clashes, hardships, and triumphs of the West.

When we visited in the fall of 2000 ground had been broken for the Draper Museum, an extensive fifth wing of the BBHC, which will open in April 2002. This $17 million addition will focus on the influence of nature on humans and humans' affect on the environment using interactive exhibits. You won't be able to overlook the larger-than-life statues of a bison herd marking this new attraction in front of the main BBHC. Geared toward all ages, this exhibit will teach about the ecology, geology, and biology of the American West along with contemporary influences such as logging, oil development, ranching, and the reintroduction of the wolves. But don't mistake this part of the museum as just another bunch of old things behind glass—when you walk through the doors you'll embark on a virtual expedition through the four ecosystems of the western environment, from the alpine tundra to the sweeping plains.

You'll want to spend at least a couple days here, as a quick run-through doesn't do it justice. Your museum ticket is good for two consecutive days and costs $10 for adults, $4 for kids, and children under 5 are admitted free. Museum hours during summer are 7 A.M. to 8 P.M. daily. Hours vary the rest of the year.

Cody Murals Visitor Center
Wyoming Ave. and 18th St., Cody, WY
(307) 587-3290

When you walk into the Cody Murals Visitor Center you will get a history lesson of a different kind. The Cody Murals depict the story of the Latter-day Saints' colonization of Wyoming's Big Horn Basin. Their presence here spans 70 years, beginning with the great immigration of settlers from the east coast to this region of the west. The early Latter-day Saints overcame hardships on the difficult trip westward in hopes of finding a new life and home to build upon with their faith. Their story is all here in the 18-foot-high mural, which spans the 36-foot-wide dome of Cody's Church of Jesus Christ of Latter-day Saints. Viewing of the Cody Murals is free and it is open from June 1 to September 1.

Cody Nite Rodeo
Stampede Park Rodeo Grounds, Cody, WY
(307) 587-2992

Every summer night in Cody is rodeo night. Since a rodeo is a reason to have a party in this part of the country, the town has its own kind of constant festive atmosphere. It's been that way for the past 60 years, when the community rallied together in hopes of luring Yellowstone Park visitors (and their wallets) to town in the 1930s. The idea stuck and today that means you get to see a rodeo with real live cowboys and rough stock that twist, twirl, buck, and spin. The Cody Nite Rodeo is one big attraction that runs nightly from Memorial Day through Labor Day. Grandstand seating for adults costs $10 ($4 for children). Seats in the Buzzard's Roost above the chutes cost $12 for adults and $6 for kids. For more information see our Annual Events chapter.

Colter's Hell National Historic Site
WY Hwy. 120, Cody, WY
(307) 587-2777

John Colter, a fur trapper and explorer fresh from the Lewis and Clark expedition, traipsed through the area back in 1807. His estimated 500- to 600-mile trek took him through the heart of what would become Yellowstone National Park and to a site on the edge of present-day Cody. Today, this site is listed on the National Register of Historic Places as "Colter's Hell," a region of almost extinct geysers that once spewed odious gases and cauldrons of boiling water and mud, and thundered as if possessed by angry spirits. Yet when Colter returned to St. Louis in 1810, no one believed his tall tales. Yellowstone National Park is often mistakenly referred to as Colter's Hell, but the real site is located along Wyoming Highway 120 on the banks of the Shoshone River heading toward Heart Mountain and Red Lodge, Montana. The area is marked with a sign telling the story of John Colter's discovery.

Old Trail Town
Yellowstone Hwy., west of Cody, WY
(307) 587-5302

Just outside of Cody, the Old West is alive and well. Old Trail Town gives you a glimpse into frontier life, as you walk along the boardwalks where outlaws Butch Cassidy and the Sundance Kid strolled, where Buffalo Bill strutted, where Jeremiah "Liver Eatin'" Johnston bellied up to the bar. Imagine when times were simpler in these parts, when there were good guys and bad guys, when people didn't have the modern conveniences of electricity, indoor plumbing, or cars. This cluster of 200-year-old buildings stands as a monument to the frontier era. Walking through the dusty main street, you'll feel like you were almost there.

Owner Bob Edgar began collecting historic buildings and relics of the west in the 1960s, when he realized that if these remnants of the western settlement deteriorated, so did an important piece of history. The project began as a labor of love for Edgar, who is an archeologist and western historian. He and his wife Terry gathered homestead cabins, livery stables, general stores, and homes with the help of local ranchers and historians. Gradually, his collection began to take the shape of a town on a piece of property where the original "Cody City" had been platted by Buffalo Bill Cody in 1895.

Today, Old Trail Town consists of 25 buildings dating from 1879 to 1901. With over 100 horse-drawn vehicles and frontier memorabilia, it is the largest collection of its kind in Wyoming. Old Trail Town is open daily from mid-May until mid-September. Admission is $3 and free for children under 6.

Gardiner, Montana

Roosevelt Arch
Park St., Gardiner, MT
Today the Roosevelt Arch stands in stark contrast to the quiet sloping land around it. But it was once the focal point of the Gardiner train depot, where it stood welcoming visitors to Yellowstone National Park. Standing 50 feet high, with 12-foot high walls at its edges, it curved around a beautifully landscaped pond and garden. The stately arch was the idea of Captain Hiram M. Chittenden of the U.S. Army Corps of Engineers (he and his troops managed the park and subsequent road improvements until 1916) who thought Yellowstone needed a "proper" entrance to dazzle visitors about to embark on a "grand tour of wonderland." Chittenden and architect Robert Reamer came up with the plans to construct the arch out of local columnar basalt. President Theodore Roosevelt dedicated the majestic arch marking the official entrance into Yellowstone National Park on April 24, 1903. In his speech he said Yellowstone was set aside, "For the Benefit and Enjoyment of the People." These words are inscribed on the top of the arch's face.

Livingston, Montana

Farmer's Market
Rotary Park on W. Park St., Livingston, MT
(406) 222-0850
Homemade breads, magnificent wild flowers, fresh vegetables, crafts, and pottery are just a few of the wonderful local items you'll find at this quaint market along the main thoroughfare in town. The vendors and wares sold here change every week, as the summer season ebbs and flows. One week you'll be able to find five different kinds of heirloom tomatoes and the next the hot item will be brilliant purple delphiniums. The market is held rain or shine on Wednesdays from 5 to 7 P.M. May through September.

Natural History Exhibit Hall
120 E. Park St., Livingston, MT
(406) 222-5335
Giant prehistoric raptors and mastodons are part of the Hall's world-class exhibits.

The Livingston Depot Center hosts a variety of cultural events. PHOTO: DONNIE SEXTON/TRAVEL MONTANA

This unassuming building (originally home to a bottling plant) is home to a sort of dinosaur factory, because this is where many of the extinct creatures' skeletons are cast to create displays that appear in museums around the world. The exhibit hall has hosted shows featuring prehistoric mammal skeletons from both China and Argentina and a history of the grizzly bear using fossil bear skulls. Admission costs $3.

Park County Museum
118 W. Chinook St., Livingston, MT
(406) 222-4184

The hundred year old Northern Pacific Railroad caboose on the front lawn of the Park County Museum is just the beginning of the journey through the past offered here. Located in the historic Northside School, this little museum offers three floors of exhibits featuring memorabilia from life on Montana's frontier and the early railroad days. The museum is open from Memorial Day to Labor Day.

Livingston Depot Center
200 W. Park St., Livingston, MT
(406) 222-2300

Livingston was founded in 1882 as a base for Northern Pacific Railroad workers who ran railways and maintained repair shops in the region. Later, the town became a jumping-off point for Yellowstone travelers. To accommodate them, the railroad built a three-building brick complex for its depot. The Italianate architectural design of the building even showcases tiny red and black Northern Pacific Railroad logos throughout the ornate decorative exterior. Today it has been restored and is the home of the Livingston Depot Center, a combination museum, meeting hall, and convention and cultural center. On permanent display is the "Rails Across the Rockies," an extensive exhibit on railroading. The depot is also a destination for the Montana Rockies Railroad, which originates in Sandpoint, Idaho, stays the night in Livingston, and buses guests to Yellowstone National Park for the day before continuing on to Billings. While the Depot is an interesting stop for tourists, it is also a community gathering place that hosts an annual Christmas tree lighting, craft fairs, and parties.

Red Lodge, Montana

Beartooth Nature Center
Red Lodge, MT
(406) 446-1133

The Beartooth Nature Center in Red Lodge offers an alternative for countless animals that are displaced by human activity, injured, or abandoned as babies and are not able to return to the wild. This nonprofit organization cares for black bears, moose, mountain lions, fox, bobcats, sand hill cranes, and wolves. The kind staff fills in a gap that can often not be fulfilled by the U.S. Fish and Wildlife Department. It provides educational experiences with the resident animals, offering the public a chance to see them up close and learn about habitat, history, and lifestyle. Each spring staff members also raise a number of young animals and return them to the wild. If you're lucky you might get a glimpse of these babies before they are released. The kids will enjoy meeting domestic animals in the on-site petting zoo, where they'll find goats, sheep, and a miniature horse. The best time to see the animals is in the morning when the staff feeds them. Located at the north entrance of town, the center is open from 10 A.M. to 5:30 P.M. from Memorial Day to Labor Day and 10 A.M. to 2 P.M. at other times of year or by arrangement. Donations are welcome.

Peaks to Plains Museum
S. Broadway, Red Lodge, MT
(406) 446-3667

Red Lodge has seen the booms and busts of trapping, coal mining, railroads, and prohibition. The town has been a stronghold for celebrities, outlaws, and immigrants. It has ridden the highs and lows of wars, the Great Depression, and develop-

ment. At the Peaks to Plains Museum, you can experience and learn about these rich beginnings.

Inside the newly restored 1909 Labor Temple brick building, the Carbon County Historical Society has assembled a variety of exhibits that offer glimpses of Red Lodge's history. Most interesting is a simulated coal mine you can walk through to see a collection of old mining tools and photographs. You'll also find a collection of cowboy and rodeo memorabilia from the local Greenough family, who became world-renown rodeo riders; a restored 1890s Yellowstone National Park stage coach; and, oddly, an electroshock therapy machine from the more recent past. Traveling exhibits and classes are also scheduled each year. Contact the Red Lodge Chamber of Commerce for a current schedule.

The Peaks to Plains Museum is open daily throughout the year. Admission is $3 for adults; $2 for children six to 17 years old; it is free to Historical Society members and children under six.

Beartooth Scenic Byway
U.S. Hwy 212, Red Lodge, MT

Along the Beartooth Highway out of Red Lodge, you will gain more than 5,000 feet of elevation to the highest drivable points in both Montana and Wyoming. The spectacular 65-mile drive is an extremely scenic route into Yellowstone National Park through the northeast entrance near Silver Gate, Montana. Charles Kuralt dubbed this the most beautiful drive in America and the hundreds of motorcyclists who travel the narrow winding road to the "Top of the World" summit of 10,942 feet will agree.

Opened in 1936, this road seems to switchback up to impossible heights. From many points along the drive you can pull over to see broad sweeping mountain meadows and endless peaks. Allow for at least three hours to enjoy the ride, or longer if you intend to set out on a hike on one of several difficult trails that begin up here. The snow never melts up top, as you'll notice driving through a mini canyon of bluish drifts along the roadside toward the summit. Because of this, hard core snowboarders and skiers pack their boards and hike up the snowy headwalls of the Beartooth Pass and bomb down the slopes to celebrate Fourth of July.

At the summit you will find the Top of the World Store, open only in summer. The owners, former schoolteachers, return each June to dig their store out of the snow. In 1997, they found the store buried under a 23-foot snowdrift. Depending on the time and amount of snowfall, this road is open from mid-May to mid-October. It can snow any month of the year here.

Bozeman, Montana

Museum of the Rockies
600 W. Kagy Blvd., Bozeman, MT
(406) 994-2251
www.museumoftherockies.org

A walk around the Montana State University-affiliated Museum of the Rockies is a journey through the 4.5 billion-year-old history of the Northern Rocky Mountains. The museum has permanent exhibits detailing the geology, archaeology, history, and paleontology of the region, as well as revolving displays of contemporary and historic regional artwork. The Taylor Planetarium, also housed in the museum, shows interpretive programs, such as "Native American Skies" and "Winter Skies." The planetarium also specializes in laser shows for kids and adults. In the summer, the Living History Farm gives visitors a glimpse of a working farm of the past, and a café serves lunch on the museum's terrace.

Summer hours are 8 A.M. to 8 P.M. daily, and winter hours are 9 A.M. to 5 P.M. Monday to Saturday and 12:30 P.M. to 5 P.M. Sunday. Museum admission is $7 for adults, $4 for students ages five to 18. Kids under five are admitted free. Laser shows are $5, and regular planetarium shows are $3. Combo tickets are available. Call the museum for current shows and exhibits.

The American Computer Museum
234 E. Babcock St., Bozeman, MT
(406) 587-7545
www.compuseum.org

Also known as the Compuseum, the American Computer Museum is an interesting place that appeals to more than just technology buffs. The museum traces more than 4,000 years of navigating and computer technologies, including hundreds of historical devices from the abacus to the microchip. There are displays on cave painting, the Pony Express, the telegraph, the telephone, cash registers, typewriters, radios, televisions, room-sized computers, and the first personal computers. The museum's slogan fits well: "See the information highway when it was a dirt road."

Summer hours are Monday through Saturday from 9 A.M. to 5 P.M., and winter hours are Tuesday, Wednesday, Friday, and Saturday from noon until 4 P.M. Admission is $3 for adults, $2 for children ages six through twelve, and free for kids under six.

Gallatin Country Pioneer Museum
317 W. Main St., Bozeman, MT
(406) 522-8122

This free museum is housed in the old Gallatin County Jail and is listed on the

See live grizzly bears in at the Grizzly Discovery Center in West Yellowstone, Montana. PHOTO: DONNIE
SEXTON/TRAVEL MONTANA

National Register of Historic Places. Inside, you'll find a railroad photo display, a display on Bozeman's Chinese community from the nineteenth and twentieth centuries, Native American leather and beadwork, a cowgirl photo exhibit, and the historic Big Horn Gun. The Solveig Sales Memorial Library is open to the public and contains books, papers, and genealogical records of the county, and the photo archive contains more than 10,000 images from the past. The bookstore sells current history books, hard-to-find pamphlets, and maps relating to the Gallatin Valley and Montana.

Summer hours are 10 A.M. to 4:30 P.M. Monday through Saturday. Winter hours are 11 A.M. to 4 P.M. Tuesday through Saturday, and 1 to 4 P.M. on Saturday. Donations are appreciated.

Palisades Falls
Hyalite Canyon

This is an easy, short hike that anybody can take up to an impressive, 120-foot waterfall cascading off the rocky cliffs of the Hyalite Canyon area. The quarter-mile trail is actually paved and wheelchair accessible and winds through tall timber stands to the base of the falls. Experienced hikers can make the short but steep climb to the top of the falls, producing great views of the Gallatin and Hyalite mountain ranges. To get to the Hyalite area, take South 19th Avenue out of Bozeman until you see the Hyalite Canyon turnoff. Turn left here and take the road back to and around Hyalite Reservoir (popular for boating and swimming) and follow the signs to the falls. The road turns to dirt just before the reservoir but is in excellent condition.

The 'M' Trail
Bridger Canyon Rd.

It doesn't take much driving around Montana to notice the large, white letters that appear on various hillsides. Usually associated with the nearest town, the letters can be seen from miles away and often have trails leading up to them. In

Bozeman's case, the gigantic letter M sits on a steep hill on the north side of the road leading into Bridger Canyon. It's the most popular trail in town, a spot where locals, dogs, and tourists climb to the top for tremendous view of the Gallatin Valley and the surrounding mountains. From the trailhead there are two routes to the top. One goes straight up and is recommended for hikers who are in good shape. The other, however, is suitable for anyone, as it slowly meanders its way up in the span of about two miles. If you're still feeling good at the top, the trail continues as far as you want to take it, and in fact traverses the entire ridge length of the Bridger Mountains. There are benches at the top where you can sit and rest, watching the sun set over the Tobacco Root Mountains to the west. There will often be other people enjoying the view with you, many of them Bozemanites getting exercise after a hard day at the office.

To find the M, take North Rouse Avenue out of town. This will turn into Bridger Canyon Road and the trailhead will be about three miles on your left, across from the fish hatchery. You can't miss it, as there are often many cars parked there.

Lewis and Clark Caverns State Park
MT Hwy. 2
(406) 287-3541

Located about halfway between Three Forks and Whitehall on the scenic Jefferson River, this underground cave was Montana's first state park. Although in 1908 President Theodore Roosevelt named these caverns in honor of the famous explorers, Lewis and Clark never actually saw the caverns. In fact, whites only discovered the hole in the ground in the late 1800s, while Native Americans knew about its existence for centuries.

The caverns are accessible by taking a two-hour tour that begins and ends at the park's visitor's center. The tour starts with a three-quarter mile walk to the mouth of cave, then descends 326 feet into the earth. The path is lighted and features 600 steps down into 12 different rooms filled with magnificent stalactite and stalagmite formations. Outside the caverns, the park has 3,000 surface acres to explore. There's a campground with showers and flush toilets, RV dump sites, three camping cabins for rent, and plenty of nature trails. The fishing and floating on the nearby Jefferson is great, too.

The park is open Memorial Day through Labor Day. To get here, exit I-90 at Three Forks and follow Montana Highway 2 and the signs to the caverns.

West Yellowstone, Montana

Yellowstone IMAX Theatre
101 S. Canyon St., West Yellowstone, MT
(406) 646-4100, (888) 854-5862
www.yellowstoneimax.com

See the splendors of Yellowstone on a six-story screen with digital surround sound. This IMAX specializes in nature films, with *Yellowstone* and *Wolves* being two of the more popular films often showing here. *Yellowstone* is a great introduction to the history, wildlife, and geothermal features of the park, allowing you to view some of its most famous features up

close. Each movie lasts about 45 minutes and there are shows every hour on the hour. Call or stop in for current IMAX movies and showtimes.

Grizzly Discovery Center
201 S. Canyon St., West Yellowstone, MT
(406) 646-7001, (800) 257-2570
www.grizzlydiscoveryctr.com

If you want to get a first hand view of real, live grizzly bears and wolves, this is the place. You'll see numerous big bears and gray wolves living in a natural setting, and

The Museum of the Yellowstone, located in West Yellowstone, Montana, features exhibits on bears, Western histroy, Native American artifacts, forest fires, and regional wildlife. PHOTO: DONNIE SEXTON/TRAVEL MONTANA

receive firsthand knowledge of their social and playful behaviors. The center also presents a broad range of interactive and educational exhibits, films, and presentations, and kids and adults will love the gift shop with a wildlife theme.

The center is a nonprofit bear and wolf preserve and is open all year round from 8:30 A.M. until dusk. Admission is $7.95 for adults, $7.50 for seniors, $3.50 for kids five to 15, and children under fives are admitted free.

Playmill Theatre
29 Madison Ave., West Yellowstone, MT
(406) 646-7757
www.playmill.com

The Playmill has been West Yellowstone's only live theater for nearly 40 years, producing high-quality comedies, dramas, and musicals each summer season from Memorial Day to Labor Day. Shows are at 6 and 8:30 P.M. every day but Sunday, and typically feature three revolving productions, so you could actually see all three within the span of a week. Past productions include *Joseph and the Amazing Technicolor Dreamcoat, Fiddler on the Roof,* and *Annie Get Your Gun.* Call the theater or visit the website for current shows and prices. Reservations are recommended.

Quake Lake
U.S. Hwy. 87

On August 17, 1959, one of the biggest earthquakes in North America struck the Yellowstone region with a magnitude of 7.8 on the Richter scale. In a span of 30 seconds, the massive quake left 28 people dead, a path of destruction, and a new lake. Twenty-foot waves caused by the quake swelled up over Hebgen Dam and swept down the Madison Canyon, destroying everything in its path. The walls of the canyon were made of strong, vertical layers of dolomite that supported loose, unstable schist underneath. The shock waves fractured the dolomite, and a million tons of rock, timber, and debris came crashing down. It was as if an entire side of a mountain fell off. This debris from the slide stopped the surging water and created Quake Lake.

At the visitor's center along the highway you'll find lots of incredible photos from the earthquake and a detailed description of the tragic events that took place.

Pinedale, Wyoming

The Museum of the Mountain Man
P.O. Box 909, Pinedale, WY 82941
(307) 367-4101, (877) 686-6266
www.museumofthemountainman.com

Learn about the romantic and rugged life of the Mountain Man through an interpretive and visual experience that details the era of the Western fur trade. Pinedale and the surrounding Green River Valley was the hub of the Rocky Mountain Rendezvous system, where fur traders in the early 1800s gathered once a year to sell their wares to wagon trains going back

east. The 15,000 square-foot museum—part of the Sublette County Historical Society—houses exhibits on the fur trade, western exploration, and early settlement of western Wyoming. You can also take a look at famed Mountain Man Jim Bridger's rifle, watch living history demonstrations, and listen to lectures. The museum opens around May 1 and closes on September 30. Admission is $4 for adults, $3 for senior citizens, and $2 for children ages six through 12.

Old Faithful is Yellowstone National Park's most famous geyser. PHOTO: NATIONAL PARK SERVICE

Annual Events

The Yellowstone Region is chock full of all kinds of annual events and activities. Many of them celebrate the area's rich and colorful history, in some cases with live re-creations of life back in the days of the Old West. Still others celebrate the area's vibrant arts and cultural scene or the outdoor recreation opportunities that bring visitors here. As you get to know our area, you'll realize that just about every town has something going on every weekend. And although you may be staying in one of the larger gateway communities, by visiting the smaller, outlying towns you can get a great slice of our life here in Yellowstone Country.

This is just a partial listing and dates for many events change within a few days every year. Contact local chambers of commerce for more information.

January

International Rocky Mountain Stage Stop Sled Dog Race
Jackson, WY
(307) 733-3316
www.wyomingstagestop.com

If you've never seen a sled dog race up close, this is the one to see. Each 30–80 mile stage begins in a different Wyoming town, starting in downtown Jackson and ending up in Teton Village 13 days later. Unlike a marathon race where dogs pull for extended periods of time, the stage stop is run in stages like cycling's Tour De France. Spectators are encouraged. The race is gaining in popularity and is drawing top mushers from around the world, who hope to snag a share of the $100,000 purse. If watching the race gives you the urge to mush, several Jackson companies offer sled dog tours. The opening banquet and closing awards ceremony are also open to the public, but reservations are required.

February

Waterfall Ice Round Up
Double Diamond X Ranch, Cody, WY
(307) 587-0629

For most people frozen waterfalls are just a nice view, but there is that rare breed who sees climbing said ice a blatant challenge of their skills: They must climb it; they must conquer it. "Cody Ice" is quite vast with some 150 known pitches and many more being discovered every winter. Ice climbing in the area (about 40 miles from Cody up the south fork of the Shoshone River) is not for novices. When the best known climbs go by names like "Broken Hearts" and "Smooth Emerald Milk Shake" you know there is work involved in scaling them. Bison Willy's Bunkhouse operator Ken Gasch is doing his best to promote ice climbing in the Cody area. He hosts the late February event each year (depending on cold weather), which features expert climbing competitions. Bring your winter camping gear and an ice ax.

Cowboy Ski Challenge
Jackson, WY
(307) 733-3316
www.nasja.com

Ever wonder what cowboys do in the winter? Well, many of them continue to ride horses—or get pulled by them on skis. It's called skijoring, and the Cowboy Ski Challenge is one of the six sanctioned events of the North American Skijoring Association (in fact, all but two take place around the Yellowstone Region in Bozeman, Cody, Red Lodge, and here). Contestants, made up of teams of two, must navigate a course of jumps and gates for the fastest time. It's competitive, and a kick in the chaps to watch.

Buffalo Bill Birthday Ball
Cody Auditorium, Cody, WY
(307) 587-2777

Of course they celebrate Buffalo Bill's birthday in Cody—he's the fuel for this town's engine. So if you happen to be in town on the Saturday before Buffalo Bill's February 26 birthday, it's a great reason to get gussied up to go out and kick up the dust in honor of the Western legend. Contact the Cody Chamber of Commerce for the exact date. The only thing you need to get into this annual bash is a turn of the century costume, since you wouldn't want to break tradition. The gala attracts almost 500 people for dinner and dancing. In years past, the event has raised more than $70, 000 for new exhibits and educational programs at the museum.

Montana Winter Fair
Gallatin County Fairgrounds, Bozeman, MT
(406) 585-1398

Bozeman's Winter Fair has been a great family event for more than 50 years. You'll find exhibits, crafts, and animal displays, but the real action lies in watching the skijoring contestants test their skills. To get to the fairgrounds, head east on Tamarack St. from North 7th Avenue. The grounds will be on your left; you can't miss them.

March

National Finals Skijoring
Red Lodge Rodeo Grounds, Red Lodge, MT
(406) 446-1718

Long winters cause some folks to resort to strange ways to pass the time. Skijoring is a case in point. The zany sport requires a strong, fast horse harnessed to pull a skier through an obstacle course of gates and jumps. It's not a pretty sport, but it does entail a certain amount of skill and horse training to insure the teams finish the 250 yard course in record time. Just to place in the event competitors must land upright with at least one ski touching the ground when crossing the finish line. Sounds simple, unless the pony is a wild one. Racing against the clock, teams compete for purses of up to $7,000. This annual competition draws more than 100 teams from across the country (Yes, there

Insiders' Tip

Yellowstone's gateway communities have many acclaimed local artists in residence. Look out for summer art walks hosted by local gallery associations. Galleries open their doors after hours and offer select showings of new artists along with refreshments.

are that many people who do this) to the Red Lodge Rodeo Grounds. Admission is about $3.

Rendezvous Ski Race
West Yellowstone, MT
(406) 646-7701

The Rendezvous has been the region's premier cross-country ski event for more than 20 years. More than 600 skiers compete in courses ranging from 5 to 50 kilometers. It's not just for hardcore racers; anybody can join in on the fun. Registration fees include the race, T-shirt, feed stations, and an awards ceremony. Prizes are awarded in both gender and age categories. The event has a real festival atmosphere and is great if you just want to watch when you're in town for the weekend.

U.S. National Powder 8s
Jackson Hole Mountain Resort, Jackson, WY
(307) 733-3316

This is the stuff ski movies are made of. Teams of two skiers float down a slope in perfect unison, creating a figure eight with each careful turn. The prettiest line wins, and it's a big deal to those who make the journey each year. Teams are invited to register for the qualifying competition in hopes of joining twelve other teams from around the country. Winners head to Canada for the world championships. The contest is held in Cody Bowl, south of the resort, but can be viewed from the top of Rendezvous Bowl within the ski area boundary. The Jackson Hole Powder 8s, held in January, determine who represents the ski area at the nationals.

Clean Snowmobile Challenge
Jackson, WY
(307) 733-3316

Check out the future of snowmobiles at the annual Clean Snowmobile Challenge, where students from American and Canadian universities participate in an engineering design competition aimed at solving the problem of noise and air pollution from snowmobiles in environmen-

tally sensitive areas. Engineering students bring their team's modified sleds to Jackson and compete against each other in a variety of events, including noise, emissions, acceleration, hill climb, fuel economy, design, and cold start. This event has attracted national recognition since the controversial issue of snowmobiling in the national parks has been front-page news in regional newspapers.

World Championship Snowmobile Hill Climb
Snow King Resort, Jackson, WY
(307) 733-6433

It sounds crazy, but people have been doing it for more than 25 years. Thrill-seeking snowmobile riders charge up a 1,500-foot hill at the Snow King ski area, all in the name of competition. Inclines are as steep as 45 degrees and, you guessed it, some of them peter out and don't make it all the way to the top. Winners are crowned King and Queen of the Hill. The event is held on the fourth weekend in March and is sponsored by the Jackson Hole Snow Devils.

Red Lodge Winter Carnival
Red Lodge Mountain, Red Lodge, MT
(406) 446-2610

Enduring seven or eight months of winter in Red Lodge isn't a bad thing. Most folks just equate it to more time spent skiing and the best time for the annual Winter Carnival. For two decades most of the town has come up to Red Lodge Mountain to watch at least some of the goofy competitions held here. The two-day event has a different theme each year, so everything from the snow sculpture contest to the races is based on the theme. In past years some of the themes were "Under the Sea," "Under the Big Top," "Back to the Future," and "Wild Wild West." The main event is the Cardboard Classic—contestants have to build a vehicle out of cardboard boxes and race down a ski slope to see who crosses the finish line first—optimally the "vehicle" cruises downhill fast enough that the cardboard doesn't have time to start getting soggy. Some contestants spend weeks designing and assembling their entries only to see them blown to pieces as soon as they hit the snow. Other events take place throughout town, but don't miss your chance to be crowned the carnival's King and Queen at the Snow Ball, where you can dance the night away with your very own royal court of Snowflakes.

World Snowmobile Exposition
West Yellowstone, MT
(406) 646-4383, (800) 736-5276

This is an event that diehard snowmobilers wouldn't want to miss, held on the third weekend in March. There are numerous vendors who let you check out all the latest equipment, but the highlight is the adrenaline-pumping SnoWest Snocross Challenge. Competitors race around a tight track with banked turns, jumps, and moguls. This event certainly is not for novices, but extremely exciting for sideline sledders.

Insiders' Tip

If you enjoy cycling, plan a trip to West Yellowstone and Yellowstone National Park between April 1 and 20 for Cycle Only Days. The park is closed to snowmobiles, cars, and buses, so riders have the roads to themselves and there is no entrance fee. From West Yellowstone, you can bike to Madison Junction, Canyon, or Mammoth, but the road between Madison and Old Faithful is closed. Side trips to Hebgen and Quake Lakes west of the park are encouraged, too. It's a great time to take in the splendor of the wildlife and scenery without any other noise—except your own breathing. Call (406) 646-7701 for more information.

April

Sweet Corn Ski Festival
Daisy Pass, Cooke City, MT
(406) 838-2412

For the last decade Cooke City has hosted this spring ski competition which takes place in a popular backcountry spot. The event used to draw only the heartiest of local powder hounds. Today, however, it draws spring breakers from all over the state in search of the sweetest snow away from high speed trams and crowds at most resorts. Held up at Daisy Pass, just 5 miles west of town, snowmobiles shuttle racers to the top of the run. More than anything, though, Sweet Corn Festival is a great excuse for a spring party. Call Cooke City Bike Shack at the number above, and speak to Bill Blackford, who organizes the event.

Pole-Peddle-Paddle
Jackson, WY
(307) 733-6433

For more than 25 years this has been an original Jackson event, where individuals and teams race on alpine and cross-country skis, bicycles, and boats. Hard-working athletes show up every year to test their endurance, but so does the local flavor: Many don hilarious costumes and run the river in less-than-seaworthy contraptions, making the event popular with spectators. It's also a fundraiser for the Jackson Hole Ski club's local youth skiing and racing programs.

May

Old West Days
Jackson, WY
(307) 733-3316
www.jhchamber.com/oldwestdays.htm

For a taste of the real Wild West of the 1800s, the place to be on Memorial Day weekend is Jackson, where thousands of visitors join the locals for the area's annual "Old West Days" celebration. The long weekend of activities includes a parade, a chuckwagon dinner and concert, bed races, the Mountain Man Rendezvous, a rodeo, and daily events on the Town Square and Glenwood Street. Cowboy hats and boots, black powder guns, and Indian trade beads reign during this whooping Western weekend.

Although events start Friday morning, the real kickoff is the first "shoot out," which is held in the town square on Saturday. Here, gunslingers give Western re-enactment that pits the good guys against the bad, giving onlookers a taste of frontier justice. Old West Days include the first regular rodeo of the season on Saturday night, live country music throughout the weekend, and historic walking tours of Jackson. At the Mountain Man Rendezvous, you'll find a historically authentic camp, from teepees to campfire-cooked grub. The event concludes on Sunday with the often-hilarious bed races, a local favorite.

June

Annual Beartooth Run
Beartooth Hwy., Red Lodge, MT
(406) 446-1718

When the snow finally melts off of America's most beautiful highway, you know

it's time for the Annual Beartooth Run. An unofficial celebration of the highway's yearly opening, this 8.2-mile race begins 14 miles south of Red Lodge at 7,000 feet and switchbacks up U.S. Highway 212 to the finish line at 9,000 feet. A true test of mind and body, the course covers some of the most scenic (and breathtaking) high altitude terrain in the region. Runners are congratulated with a picnic and awards ceremony at the finish line.

Cody Gunslingers
Irma Hotel, Cody, WY
(307) 587-4221

You'll see them slink out from the shadows of the building, their spurs jingling, their eyes slanted, hands ready to pull out the six shooters. Every summer the Cody gunslingers transform the modern streets of town into a Wild West stand off. The fastest shots in the West, they get a lot of practice each evening Monday through Saturday from Memorial Day to Labor Day on the steps of Buffalo Bill Cody's historic Irma Hotel. The show is surprisingly realistic; the 13 actors research and represent authentic Wild West characters such as Bill Hickok, Flatnose George, and Calamity Jane. There's no admission fee.

Cody Nite Rodeo
Stampede Park Rodeo Grounds, Cody, WY
(307) 587-2992

Every summer for the past 60 years Jim and Cathy Ivory have been giving people what they want: a rodeo with cowboys and rough stock that twist, twirl, buck, and spin. Fans sit on the edge of their seats until the buzzer sounds and the judge's, scores are announced. And not just for one night, but every night from June 1 until Labor Day. Though this rodeo is geared toward tourists (the guy driving up and down Sheridan Avenue with a blow horn advertising the night's event is your first clue to this), that doesn't mean it's just a show. The Ivorys raise calves, bulls, and broncs renown for their feisty character; many of them are destined for the pro rodeo circuit. But more than that, the cowboys at this rodeo are the real thing. Sure some of them are tired old timers, but their heart and soul are into the sport. Other competitors here are in training for professional careers in rodeo.

The Ivorys make the Cody Nite Rodeo very accessible; a rodeo bus will pick you up at your campground or motel. Grandstand seating for adults costs $10 ($4 for children). Seats in the Buzzard's Roost above the chutes cost $12 for adults and $6 for kids. Tickets for the 8:30 P.M. show can be purchased at the gate after 7 P.M., at the ticket booth wagon in City Park, at many Cody businesses, and at the chamber of commerce office.

Festival of Nations
Downtown Red Lodge, MT
(406) 446-1718

Don't miss the chance to find cannoli, lederhosen, Guinness beer, and cloggers all together at Red Lodge's Festival of Nations in July. This remote mountain town is an unlikely place to encounter such an array of cultural diversity, but its heritage stems from Scandinavian, Finnish, Italian, Slavic, German, Swiss, Austrian, and Scottish ancestors. Brought to the area in the 1800s with coal mining and railroad jobs, these immigrants were initially at odds with one another. Neighborhoods in town were segregated into their own Little Italy, Finn section, and the High Bug District for more affluent Brits. Cultural barriers were scarcely crossed until about 70 years ago when the Festival of Nations was conceived to encourage some friendly intermingling. Because it was started during the Great Depression, it seemed that Red Lodgians knew they needed to rely on their neighbors, regardless of their nationality. So the idea stuck. Presently the eight-day event is packed with parades, dancing, music, and food. There is no admission fee.

Cody Old West Show and Auction
Cody Community Center, Cody, WY
(307) 587-5994, (307) 587-9014

Collectors of western memorabilia and fans of the Old West have made this show one of the most successful events hosted in Cody. Renowned saddle, boot, hat, and spur makers fall over themselves to show their wares here, while antique collectors hoard their best stuff for this annual auc-

Outdoor concerts in Big Sky's Meadow Village Pavilion are a great way to enjoy music in the mountains.

tion. In 1999, a Colt Single Action gun with "Wyatt Earp 1879" engraved on it sold for $37,500—most experts considered that a bargain. The auction offers around 400 high quality, rare Western antiques on the block. But buyer beware, because this is no place to barter for bargains—a pair of R.T Frazier batwing chaps brought in $26,400 and G.S. Garcia spurs went for $17,600. The show is coupled with the Annual Winchester Gun Show and attracts enthusiasts from all over the country. Admission is $5 for the show on Friday and Saturday. There is no fee for the auction.

Paradise Valley Skydive Weekend
Chico Hot Springs, Pray, MT
(406) 333-4933, (800) HOT WADA

The long road that leads to Chico Hot Springs Lodge doubles as an air strip for this Skydive rally (insider's call it a "boogie") which takes place the third weekend in June (weather permitting). Several planes taxi about 100 experienced sky divers into the air near the summit of 11,000-foot Emigrant Peak so they can jump out into the expanse of Paradise Valley. Some say it's worth it just for the view on the plane ride up. But most take the second half of the trip and jump, landing with flying colors and stunts in the cow pasture just north of Chico. The two-day event includes a barbecue, soaking in Chico's natural hot spring pools, and an altogether different kind of "boogie" later on to live music in the saloon. Even if you are not an expert it's fun to watch the jumpers pull their chutes. But if you feel pretty brave, you can try it yourself on a tandem jump with an experienced sky diver for a fee.

Plains Indian Powwow
Robbie Powwow Garden, Buffalo Bill
Historical Center, Cody, WY
(406) 587-4771

Beads, feathers, buckskin, and leather move to the rhythm of the Northern Plains Indian powwow drums each June in Cody. Sponsored by the Buffalo Bill Historical Society, the Plains Indian Pow-wow has been held for the past 17 summers. Native American performers from Crow, Shoshone, Sioux, and Bannock nations compete in dance and musical contests. The atmosphere is a festive and enthralling celebration of many different cultures all at once. Adults and children alike will be mesmerized by the movement and color of the dancers' traditional garb as they compete for prize money. Admission is $3 for adults and $2 for kids ages six to 18. Children younger than six can attend free.

Upper Yellowstone Roundup
Gardiner Rodeo Grounds, Gardiner, MT
(406) 848-7971

This may be an "amateur" rodeo, but the hometown cowboys have been doing this stuff all their lives—rodeo is in their blood. You won't see any high-powered professional riders from Florida racking up the prize money here, but you will see a good ol' fashioned rodeo with genuine hometown spirit. Sanctioned by the Northern Rodeo Association and held on Father's Day weekend, the Roundup is known for a long line-up of bull riders. Typically considered the most exciting

event (and saved for the finale), here you'll see 30 to 60 riders. Admission is $10 and the seats are exposed to the elements, rain, shine, or snow.

> ## Insiders' Tip
> In rodeo the majority of contestants compete in the "slack" events, held after, before, and between the scheduled rodeo. Every rodeo producer wants to keep the regular show short and engaging, so only a handful of cowboys compete in front of packed stands. Watching the slack competition can be just as intense and interesting as the main rodeo and can get you closer to the cowboys.

July

Mountain Man Rendezvous
U.S. Hwy. 212, North of Red Lodge, MT
(406) 446-1718

Walk into the 1800s fur trading era at the Mountain Man Rendezvous near Red Lodge. Held in the first week of July, the event is a modern-day re-enactment of the Rocky Mountain gatherings that brought trappers, Native Americans, buffalo hunters, whiskey runners, and horse traders together for trading and festivities. This 10-day event attracts over 10,000 people who come to re-live this tradition that was once so integral to life in the nineteenth century. Mountain man enthusiasts come to sell their wares—

buckskin clothes, blankets, knives, beads, buffalo robes, quilts, and artwork; black-powder gun clubs come together for shooting competitions; and still others come to read cowboy poetry and play music. Admission is $3 for adults, $1 for kids under 12, and children under six are free.

Grand Teton Music Festival
Jackson, WY
(307) 733-1128
www.gtmf.org

This world-renowned music festival has been bringing in contemporary and classical music to Jackson for more than 30

Close-up

Bozeman, Montana's Sweet Pea Festival

It was not so long ago that southwestern Montana's Gallatin Valley was known as "the sweet pea capital of the nation."

At the turn of the century, sweet peas grew so prolifically here that it's said there were once 17,000 acres growing in the valley. Local farmers grew the crops and sold them to the Bozeman Canning Company, which later processed peas for the government to feed U.S. troops during World War I. In the end, 16,334 cases rolled off the production line during that period.

Capitalizing on the prolific, fragrant blossom, local businessmen in Bozeman hatched the idea of a local Sweet Pea Carnival to celebrate summer and the area's prosperity. The citizens of Bozeman rallied together to organize a fun-filled event that brought people from throughout the state.

In 1906 an unpaved Main Street was the thoroughfare for some 200 floats decorated with thousands of sweet pea blossoms in the city's first parade. Trumpets heralded the start of the parade, followed with floats pulled by showy white horses, marching bands, and, as a finale, the Sweet Pea Queen in her carriage.

"Amongst all the flowers which grow in such perfection and profusion here, there is one flower which seems as though nature herself has designed it to be grown at this particular spot where it has reached a perfection of growth, of form and color never before attained. That flower is the sweet pea, which has been selected as emblematic of the productiveness of the valley and the beauty of the city of Bozeman...." said the Lord High Chancellor J.A. Luce in an opening speech at that first Sweet Pea Carnival.

By the second year of the Sweet Pea Carnival, local merchants welcomed 10,000 visitors and their pocketbooks to town. To advertise the summer's Carnival, boxes of the fragrant flowers were sent to neighboring communities. In town, well-dressed young women passed out bouquets of sweet peas to female passengers on trains coming through town, a tradition that lasted long after the carnival.

But by 1914 the annual event lost its gusto when blight wiped out the sweet pea crop. Townspeople complained that they were tired of the dusty Main Street and that it did not impress visitors, and enthusiasm for a summer carnival faded. Two years later, the 1916 Sweet Pea Queen was crowned for a long reign at the last festival.

It wasn't until 1977 that the perfumed sweet pea was honored again in a revival of the celebration. The first Sweet Pea Festival was organized by local artists seeking a voice in the community. Since then, the week-long event has added dancing, painting, theater performances, competitions, parades, and food throughout the town. When 2,500 people showed up for the event, it was considered a success. Today Bozeman doesn't need to advertise the festivities outside of town, since it draws more than 20,000 Sweet Pea patrons each year. The series of lively shows and activities are now organized by an army of people who work throughout the year on an entirely volunteer basis. Sweet Pea has become an event that celebrates not only the arts, but also the spirit of community.

years. Most of the 42 concerts take place in the Walk Festival Hall in Teton Village. The music lasts eight weeks from July through August, with at least two festival orchestras and two chamber music recitals per week, plus a 200-member resident company comprised of players from all over the country. The festival also includes numerous open rehearsals and children's programs.

Ennis Rodeo
Ennis, MT
(406) 682-4700

This annual rodeo is one of the most exciting and challenging rodeos in the state and is sanctioned by the Northern Rodeo Association. It includes standard events and attracts top cowboys and cowgirls from around the region. The fact that it takes place on Fourth of July weekend gives the two-day event a party atmosphere, and there are many other activities going on in town as well. Rodeo hours are 8 to 11 P.M. Saturday, and 2 to 5 P.M. Sunday.

Insiders' Tip

If you can't make it to one of the larger rodeos, stop in at Jackson's JH Rodeo, held at the rodeo grounds on Snow King Avenue every Wednesday and Saturday at 8 P.M. throughout the summer. It features all seven main events, reserved grandstand seating, and plenty of up-close views along the arena fence. Any family can get in for $28, and there's free parking. Call (307) 733-2805 for advance tickets and information.

Music in the Mountains
Big Sky, MT
(406) 995-2742
www.bigskyarts.org

The nonprofit Big Sky Association for the Arts puts on great summer concerts, one in July and one in August, at their outdoor pavilion in the town's Meadow Village. These are a great way to see world-class performers in an intimate, beautiful setting, with majestic Lone Mountain as the backdrop. Performances are usually bluegrass or country, and you can bring in anything you want to the concert, except glass. Grab a cooler and a picnic lunch and enjoy music in the mountains under the big sky. The organization also help sponsor Big Sky's Community Celebration Day on July 4th, with music, an ice cream social, and fireworks in a spectacular mountain setting.

Gallatin County Fair
Gallatin County Fairgrounds, Bozeman, MT
(406) 582-3270

This week-long event is fun for all ages and is representative of small town Montana life. No beauty contest here, but ranchers love the livestock competitions and shows. Most of the fair centers around the area's rich history of agriculture, and there are numerous animal displays, commercial exhibits, arts and crafts, and music activities. There is also a four-wheel drive mud bog, auto racing, theater, dancing, and storytelling. Youngsters love the wild carnival rides, too. Fair hours are Wednesday through Saturday 10 A.M. to 10 P.M. and Sundays 10 A.M. to 5 P.M.

To get to the fairgrounds, head east on Tamarack Street from North 7th Avenue. The grounds will be on your left; you can't miss them.

Montana Motorcycle Rally
Red Lodge Rodeo Grounds
Red Lodge, MT
(406) 446-1718, (406) 664-3241

Every summer hundreds of Harley Davidson motorcycle enthusiasts pass through Red Lodge to tour the scenic Beartooth

Highway. But during the third week in July the town resounds with the distinct rumble of countless bikes for the Montana Motorcycle Rally. The weekend is highlighted by the Plains to Peaks U.S. Highway 212 Run, a race that begins in Red Lodge and continues to Cooke City, then over the Chief Joseph Highway and comes roaring down to Belfry at the Bearcreek Downs (home of the famous pig races). The purse for the event is $2,000 and attracts racers from all over the country. Next is the Iron Horse Rodeo (held at the Home of Champions Rodeo) where riders compete in barrel racing, obstacle courses, and other events. But you don't even need to own a "hog" to take in the live music and festive atmosphere in local bars and businesses. Everyone is welcome.

Home of Champions Rodeo
Red Lodge Rodeo Grounds
Red Lodge, MT
(406) 446-1718

Red Lodge is the small town with the big rodeo. After more than 70 years, the Home of Champions Rodeo boasts some of Montana's most notable rodeo heroes and heroines, including the well known Greenoughs and the Lindermans. Sisters Alice and Marge Greenough, raised on a ranch outside Red Lodge, were champion bronc riders who went all the way to Madison Square Garden in New York. Their brother, Turk, and Alice rode into fame from the 1920s clear into the 1950s.

Taking place over Independence Day, Home of Champions is a Professional Rodeo Cowboys Association event and is part of what competitors refer to as the "Cowboy Christmas" circuit—there are so many professional rodeo events during this three day period that it's considered better than Christmas. If you watch carefully you'll see cowboys arriving by private plane on the runway adjacent to the arena. They show up just in time to compete in their individual events before flying off to another rodeo. Few places take their rodeo so seriously; in Red Lodge that means it's

a great party. Admission ranges from $8 to $16. The rodeo is held July 2, 3, and 4.

Livingston Roundup Rodeo
Park County Fair Grounds, Livingston, MT
(406) 222-0850

In 1883 the town of Livingston was the first in Montana Territory to hold an Independence Day celebration with a parade and rodeo. The party was a hit and the Livingston Roundup Rodeo, which takes place on July 2, 3, and 4, is still around. Events kick off on the first day with a quaint hometown parade through historic downtown and then at 8:00 P.M. the Professional Rodeo Cowboy Association events begin. You'll see some of the best in the business compete in bareback, saddle bronc, calf roping, steer wrestling, bull riding, team roping, and barrel racing. The Roundup is one of three Gateway Rodeos held over the Fourth of July weekend and offers cowboys the opportunity to make more prize money at once than at any other time of the year. Competitors travel between Livingston, Cody, and Red Lodge, chartering private planes in order to squeeze in as many events as possible. Prize money for the Livingston Roundup alone is more than $60,000. Every evening begins with skydivers swooping into the arena and ends with an impressive blast of fireworks. Admission is $12 for reserved seats, $8 for general admission, and $4 for children ages six to 12.

Railroad Blues Festival
Livingston Depot Center, 200 W. Park St., Livingston, MT
(406) 222-2300

From across town the sounds of guitar riffs, harmonica solos, and winsome voices belting out blues songs resonate from the Livingston Depot. Inside several hundred people crowd around the small stage to hear the raucous songs that begin in the Mississippi delta and ride the rails throughout the country collecting sad stories. The historic Depot, with its high arched windows and inlaid marble floors is a beautiful venue for this rough genre of music. It's when a freight train passes on the tracks only 100 yards from the building and rattles the glass in the windows that the music and the setting all seem to come together best. This music festival is part of a series of events hosted by the Depot, which has become a regional stronghold for alternative entertainment.

Green River Rendezvous Pageant
Pinedale, WY
(307) 367-2242

This annual event celebrates the region's rich fur trade history and attracts modern day mountain men and women from all over the country. The pageant is a colorful re-creation of the fur trade rendezvous of the nineteenth century, when trappers would meet the supply wagons from back east to trade the fruits of year's worth of work in the wilderness. There's also a rodeo each night at 7 P.M. The site of the celebration is only a few miles from the original rendezvous site on the Green River. Pinedale is about 88 miles south of Jackson on U.S. Highway 191.

Teton Valley Balloon Fest
Teton Valley, ID
(208) 354-2500
www.tetonvalleychamber.com/balloon.html

Three towns—Driggs, Victor, and Tetonia—make up the Teton Valley, which you'll find at the west end of Teton Pass going from Jackson into Idaho. The Balloon Fest takes place at the Teton County Fairgrounds, where balloonists from around the country converge to float giant, magnificently colored hot air balloons over the valley, with the striking Tetons as their backdrop. The event occurs on Fourth of July weekend, and coincides with Victor's annual Old Time Fiddler's Contest in Victor and the Mountain Arts Celebration.

Stampede Rodeo
Stampede Park Rodeo Grounds, Cody, WY
(406) 587-5155

If you don't believe that Cody is the "Rodeo Capitol of the World," then you haven't been to the Stampede. The excitement starts with a wild-horse race, where a team of cowboys chases down a wild horse and tries to saddle it. And if that doesn't impress you, then consider the fact that this is the richest rodeo a cowboy can win on July 4. Each year the rodeo's purse is $300,000, which is important in a sport where the cowboy with the most winnings qualifies for the National Finals Rodeo at the end of the year. This kind of money is like high stakes poker—it draws the best players to the table. Most of the top hands on the national circuit show up here over Fourth of July (at least for one event before they fly off in a private jet to take in another competition in Red Lodge or Livingston.). Even with more than 700 contestants, the Stampede is a fast-moving, top-notch rodeo with world-class stock.

Admission is $14 for each of the July 1 to July 3 shows and $15 for the July 4 show.

August

Fiddler's Picnic
South of Livingston, MT
(406) 222-0850

For 20 years the Old Time Fiddlers Association has been gathering on Doc Allison's ranch for a weekend of music. Hundreds of people come to listen and dance to some of the best country and blue grass tunes around. It's a straight-playing, non-competitive gathering that draws musicians from all over the Rocky Mountains to play fiddles, guitars, and banjos together for good old fashioned fun. Bring the family, and pack a picnic and some lawn chairs for this afternoon of fun.

West Yellowstone Rod Run
West Yellowstone, MT
(800) 426-3148
www.wyellowstone.com/rodrun

This event marked its 30th anniversary in 2001, making it the oldest Rod Run in the Pacific Northwest. Street rods, custom cars, and special interest vehicles cram the streets of West Yellowstone for four days. Participate in poker runs, tours, games, and other events that lead up to the big car show on the final day.

Quilting in the Country Outdoor Quilt Show
5100 S. 19th Ave., Bozeman, MT
(406) 587-8216
www.quiltinginthecountry.com

Quilts are displayed everywhere here—on barns, fences, trees, or wherever there is room. Jane Quinn runs this quaint little quilt shop on her family ranch, making for a great setting for this annual small town event. The show gets bigger each year and as many as 400 handmade quilts are displayed. There's also quilt demonstrations, trunk shows, and workshops. Hours are 10 A.M. to 5 P.M., and the event is free.

Wild West Balloon Fest
Mentock Park, Cody, WY
(307) 527-7120, (307) 587-6122

Seeing a dozen hot air balloons tethered together at dusk in Cody's Mentock Park during early August, you will wonder if there has ever been a more beautiful sunset. The colorful silk balloons hover over town and cast a festive glow in anticipation of the two-day Wild West Balloon Fest. For the last six years balloonists have come from throughout the region to participate in races and other fun competitions, but mostly just to show off their rigs. You can watch the crews inflate and launch their balloons, then track their skyway path across town. The best part, however, is when you get to take a ride and see Cody from up high. Balloon rides are available for a fee.

Sweet Pea Festival of the Arts
Lindley Park, Bozeman, MT
(406) 586-4003

The first Sweet Pea Carnival was held on August 11, 1906, as a way to publicize Bozeman and the Gallatin Valley. The sweet pea flower was chosen as a symbol for its beauty, fragrance, and availability, and locals now compete for the best-looking one. Nearly 100 years later, the annual event has evolved into one of the biggest festivals in Montana, drawing upwards of 18,000 people each day. Held during the first full weekend of August, the Sweet Pea Festival of the Arts now spans three days and is a showcase for local and national artists, musicians, and thespians. The festival kicks off with the annual Sweet Pea Run on Friday morning (participants must register ahead). After the parade on Saturday, the action moves to East Main Street's Lindley Park. More than 100 artisans show their wares, while numerous stages present programs for kids and adults. Things get going around 10 A.M. Saturday and Sunday, with headlining national bands performing in the Bowl during the evening. There's tons of food, lots of kids, and an overall family atmosphere. You need a Sweet Pea button to get in, and you can purchase them at various locations around town or at the door. Admission is $7, good for all three days. Motel rooms fill up early this weekend, so plan ahead.

Buffalo Bill Celebrity Shoot Out
Cody Shooting Complex, Cody, WY
(307) 587-2777

In a town that houses the largest collection of American firearms in the world, it seems appropriate to have a celebrity shoot out. Naturally, in Cody, that shootout would be named after Buffalo Bill. (Is there anyone else?) This bang-up event at the end of August attracts celebrities who compete with amateurs and professionals in a series of shooting events. Admission is free.

Close-up

Small Town Shakespeare

Ahhh, the joys of summer. Floating and fishing on the river, lying in the sun, backpacking and . . . Shakespeare?

Well, us folks in Yellowstone Country are lucky enough to have Montana Shakespeare in the Parks, a professional Montana State University-based troupe that brings the Bard's plays to numerous towns around the region. Even Birney—a small town in southeastern Montana with a population of 17—gets into the act.

The Shakespeare Festival is a summer tradition for many of us. Grab a picnic dinner, a blanket, and a bottle of wine and enjoy an evening of outdoor theater at its best. When the sun sets behind the stage on a beautiful Yellowstone evening, there aren't many better places to be, and it reminds us how lucky we are to live here.

Artistic Director Joel Jahnke has been with the touring company for 26 of its 29 years, and the works never lose their excitement. "Every time I do one, I gain more admiration for his work as a playwright," he says. "Working with gifted actors and designers, unlocking the magic there, his genius folds out for me anew."

Montana Shakespeare in the Parks has been performing plays in Greater Yellowstone since 1974.

PHOTO: STEVE WINSLOW PHOTOGRAPHY

Jahnke picks two plays a year and hires actors from as far away as Seattle and Chicago. Many return each year, citing the incredible experience of bringing theater to small towns that don't exactly have many cultural activities. Up to 30,000 people see the shows each year.

Performances begin in Bozeman at the university around mid-June, and then travel from town to town through Montana, Wyoming, and Idaho. All performances are free, with the exception of the shows at Bozeman's Sweet Pea Festival of the Arts in early August.

For information on summer shows and schedules, call (406) 994-3901 or check out www.montana.edu/wwwmtsip.

Buffalo Days
Downtown Gardiner, MT
(406)848-7971

This event is like an old, small town block party, with dinner and dancing on main street. The music starts at noon and so do the vittles—barbecue, cole slaw, potato salad, and all the good stuff. The whole town dances until the wee hours and takes part in a host of kids' activities, such as the potato sack races and a dunking booth where local celebrities get drenched again and again. A combination end-of-the-season celebration and fundraiser for the Gardiner Ambulance Service, the event is weather-dependent. If all goes well, the fun begins the Saturday of Labor Day weekend. Admission fees vary.

Targhee Bluegrass Festival
Grand Targhee Ski and Summer Resort, Alta, WY
(800) TARGHEE
www.grandtarghee.com

This popular three-day music festival is fast becoming one of the premier blue-grass festivals in the country and is a yearly weekend journey for many of the region's bluegrass and folk lovers. Friday night typically features a regional band in one of the bars at the base of the ski resort, while Saturday and Sunday the music goes all day and into the evening. Part of the allure of the festival is the backdrop—beautiful alpine meadows and the peaks of the Tetons. Grand Targhee is located about 42 miles west of Jackson over the pass.

Christmas in August, Yellowstone National Park
All Yellowstone Park Lodges

Every year the staff at the Old Faithful Inn celebrates Christmas on August 25—complete with elaborately decorated trees, mistletoe, and holiday carolers. The tradition was spurred by a freak snow storm that stranded a group of visitors at the Inn during the early 1900s. Reveling in their "misfortune," the group decided to have a "Christmas party."

September

Western Design Conference
Cody Auditorium, Cody, WY
(307) 587-2777

At the end of September each year, Cody becomes a hotbed for furniture, fashion, and accessories with a Western flair. Top Western designers, buyers, magazine editors, architects, and artists gather here to display their work and decide what the next big trend will be in their field. Seminars ranging from historical theory to architectural influences in modern culture are offered throughout this three-day event. Admission to art exhibits is $5 per day; tickets to the fashion show held at BBHC cost $17; Sunday's awards banquet costs $20; and entrance into each of the six seminars is $25. A $200 registration fee for exhibitors entitles them to attend all events.

Buffalo Bill Art Show, Sale, and Quick Draw
Buffalo Bill Historical Center, Cody, WY
(307) 587-2777

Held in conjunction with the Western Design Conference, this art show and sale with both live and silent auctions is a fundraiser for the Buffalo Bill Historical Center. The show features local and regional artists. Tickets for Friday's live auction cost $60; Saturday's lunch and Quick Draw, in which about 25 artists work in different mediums, costs $20. A ticket for both events costs $75.

Patron's Ball
Buffalo Bill Historical Center, Cody, WY
(307) 587-2777

You never know who you might see at this gala event: Ted Turner and Peter Fonda have both attended in past years. The grand black-tie affair includes dinner and dancing inside the BBHC and draws more than 600 guests. Coupled with the Western Design Conference, this finale is another fundraiser for the museum. Tickets are $175 each for museum patrons and $200 for everyone else.

Jackson Hole Fall Arts Festival
Jackson, WY
(307) 733-3316

This much-anticipated event shows off the top 100 entries of the national Arts for the Parks competition, along with shows, programs, workshops, and cultural events. The festival lasts ten days, beginning in mid-September. This popular festival, which was started in 1985 as a way to showcase Jackson Hole's world-class art scene, also includes a silent auction, music, and chances to meet the artist who designed the annual poster you'll see hanging around town.

October

Yellowstone National Park/Old Faithful Fall Cycle Tour
West Yellowstone Chamber of Commerce, West Yellowstone, MT
(406) 646-7701

When the tourist traffic thins and the aspens line the winding roads with a golden hue, nearly 100 cyclists roll through Yellowstone. The bike ride begins in West Yellowstone and ends at the Old Faithful Inn. This is an easy cruise covering about 20 miles of rolling hills (nothing too steep). This ride has sag wagons carrying water and medical support. Riders should carry their own sack lunch and snacks. The fee is $25.

Bridger Raptor Festival
Bridger Bowl Ski Area, Bozeman, MT
(406) 522-2520

Not your average festival. No carnival rides, cotton candy, or parades here, just the peace and tranquility of trying to spot some of the 17 different species of birds of prey that make their home in the Northern Bridger Range. Witness the largest known migration of Golden Eagles in North America soaring over the range's knife-edge ridge as they head south. Festival activities include slide shows on raptor identification, kids' programs, and a birds of prey presentation with ambassador eagles, owls, and hawks from Big Sky Wildcare Raptor Center. There's also a two-mile hiking trail with prime viewing locations. This event is usually held in late September or early October; be sure to call ahead for specific dates.

November

Town Square Lighting Celebration
Downtown Jackson, WY
(307) 733-3316

Jackson's famous town square—you know, the one with the antlers—comes alive in the winter as snow blankets the ground and the lights go up. On the first Friday after Thanksgiving, townsfolk gather in the square to celebrate the season with refreshments, caroling, and plenty of Western holiday cheer.

December

Christmas Stroll
Main St., Bozeman, MT
(406) 586-4008

No matter how cold it is or how much snow is on the ground, Bozeman residents take to the streets in droves for this popular event, usually held the first Saturday in December from 4 P.M. to 7 P.M. The city closes Main Street's downtown section and vendors and artisans line the streets. Shops stay open into the evening, hoping to lure buyers in to purchase Christmas gifts. More than anything, this is one of Bozeman's premier social events, as it is a great way to run into people, wish them holiday cheer, and warm up with a cup of hot chocolate.

Kidstuff

When Yellowstone National Park was first opened to the public at large, it was dubbed "wonderland." Back in the 1800s the area's geysers, mountains, and animal life were unimaginable. Well, all the wonder of the place is still here. And today with the wide-open spaces, wildlife, Wild West shows, and wilderness to experience, there couldn't be a better vacation spot for kids. Out here, folks know that visiting Yellowstone and Grand Teton National Parks is a family affair. There are countless activities, celebrations, and contests to keep the kids having fun and enjoying this place as much as their parents. The following suggestions are listed in alphabetical order rather than geographical, but most communities are extremely kid-friendly and will happily refer you to additional activities.

A is for Art and Acting

Every August in downtown Bozeman, Montana, kids cover the sidewalks with drawings for the annual "Chalk on the Walk" as part of Sweet Pea Festival. Also in Bozeman check out Beall Park Art Center and the Emerson Cultural Center, 111 South Grand Avenue, (406) 587-9797, where kids (ages six and up) can learn to sculpt, paint, or make their own paper in summer art workshops.

You'll have to learn to think on your feet at Bozeman's Equinox Theatre Camp, 2304 N. 7th Ave., (406) 587-0737, a summer program for kids ages eight and up where instructors use improvisational acting to encourage self-expression and general silliness. At the Livingston Art Center, 119 South Main Street, (406) 222-5222, children ages four and up can practice painting, writing, drawing, and native craft skills throughout the year.

B is for Bears

If you aren't lucky enough to see the native grizzly or brown bear in the wild, try the West Yellowstone Grizzly Recovery Center and Wolf Preserve, 201 S. Canyon St., (406) 646-7001, (800) 257-2570. Here, you'll see eight grizzlies searching for food and playing in a somewhat natural habitat of the 1.8-acre area. Across from the bears is a 1-acre wolf exhibit where these other elusive creatures live all year. Most of the animals in captivity here were abandoned as babies or would have otherwise been destroyed. A wildlife biologist is on hand to answer questions. A visit to the Grizzly Discovery Center helps to preserve grizzlies in the wild through the non-profit international Grizzly Fund.

In Red Lodge the Beartooth Nature Center, (406) 446-1133, provides educational experiences with black bears in captivity. You will also see moose, mountain lions, fox, bobcats and wolves here; most of the animals are unable to return to the wild because of injury or human-related problems. You might even have the opportunity to pet some of the orphaned native animals in the petting zoo. The best time to see the animals is in the mornings when the staff feeds them. Check out our Attractions chapter for additional information.

C is for Climbing

. . . rocks and trees, walls and mountains. Learn from the pros at Bozeman Climbing Center, 1408 Gold Avenue, Bozeman, Montana, (406) 586-0756. The Center offers regular monthly classes for beginning climbers. With classes of about 10 students, instructors introduce kids to the sport on an indoor, artificial wall. Depending on the time of year, classes also travel to outdoor rock climbing areas. Special rates are offered for parent-child climbing teams on Sundays.

During the regular school year Cody, Wyoming, kids hurry to the Cody Rock Gym, 1260 Sheridan Avenue, (307) 587-5222, to try out the challenging indoor climbing walls. In the summer, the gym is not very busy, but makes for a great rainy day activity and a safe environment to learn this new sport.

The indoor wall at Teton Rock Gym, 1116 Maple Way in Jackson Hole, Wyoming, (307) 733-0707, can accommodate more than a dozen climbers at a time, with artificial holds and vertical and over-hung walls. Climbing holds are arranged differently every few weeks. Lessons and equipment rental are available during afternoons and evenings throughout the year.

D is for Dinosaurs

Some of the world's largest dinosaur deposits have been unearthed in Montana and Wyoming. To view a life-size skeleton of a T-Rex go to the Museum of the Rockies in Bozeman, Montana, 600 W. Kagy Boulevard, (406) 994-2251. There you will find a fun and educational interactive exhibit that teaches children about these prehistoric creatures. Short videos, presentations, and life-like dinosaurs will keep them fascinated. At the Natural History Exhibit Hall in Livingston, Montana, 120 E. Park St., (406) 222-5335, you can gaze upon the 50-foot skeleton of a mastodon or marvel at the 20-foot wing span of a prehistoric bird.

If you've ever wondered what it would be like to work a dinosaur dig, several actual sites throughout Wyoming will let you play paleontologist for a day. Warfield Fossils in Thayne, Wyoming (12 miles west of Cody), (307) 883-2445, is the closest one in the Yellowstone area. For a fee you can learn how to dig carefully for real fossils dating back 100 million years. They provide the tools and you provide the manpower. You do get to keep all the fossils you find, unless you happen to discover a rare middle Cretaceous-period dinosaur, of course. You'll need to call and make a reservation. See our Attractions chapter for more details.

E is for Elk Habitat

The Greater Yellowstone Area is home to about 40 percent of North America's majestic ungulates. (That's how wildlife biologists refer to them because they're hooves are split.) Approximately 900,000 elk living between the U.S. and Canada prefer higher elevations in summer and move to mountain meadows when the snows drive them down to the lowland. You can see about 12,000 Rocky Mountain Elk at the Jackson Hole National Elk Refuge from October through April. The state of Wyoming feeds the animals due to harsh winters and because prime grazing land has been developed for towns or agriculture. For a closer look at the herds, take a sleigh ride. Rides leave every 20 minutes from the National Museum of Wildlife Art, 2820 Rungus Rd., (307) 733-5771. There are other sanctioned feeding areas throughout the Jackson, Wyoming, area and also one just north of Gardiner, Montana, where it is common for elk to walk down any street in the tiny town or to lie on the front lawn of the high school.

F is for Fishing

Whether fishing to you means dropping a worm on a hook into a lake or learning the entomology of the Yellowstone River, you'll find plenty of places to cast your line on your vacation. The bridge in Livingston's Sacajawea Park is a favorite fishing hole for local kids. You are almost guaranteed to catch something since the pond is stocked with rainbow and brown trout each August for the Livingston Kids Trout Derby; call the Livingston Chamber of Commerce (406) 222-0580 for registration details. If you throw your line into the Bozeman Ponds on the west end of town next to the Gallatin Valley Mall, 2825 W. Main St., chances are good that you'll hook a rainbow, brook, or brown trout.

Teton Valley, Idaho, and Jackson, Wyoming, both have kids-only fishing spots. In Jackson Hole it's Flat Creek, which meanders quietly across town and is reserved just for kids within city limits. In Teton Valley, it's the Trail Creek Pond at the base of Teton Pass, fenced safely away from Idaho Highway 33, surrounded by blooming yellow mules' ears and bright green picnic tables. Wherever you are, call a local fishing shop. The folks there will know where to send you and can also arrange for a guide. Our Fishing and Watersports chapter details other locations.

> ## Insiders' Tip
> In Yellowstone National Park fishing permits are required for kids older than 11.

G is for Golf

... miniature golf, that is. In Cody, Wyoming, the lush Cody Mini Golf Course, (307) 587-3685, is right across from the Chamber of Commerce on Sheridan Avenue. Owned by the city, this golf course is open from Memorial Day until Labor Day. In summertime in Jackson, Wyoming, you can play miniature golf at the base of Snow King Mountain, call (307) 733-5200.

H is for Hot Springs

Summer or winter, the hot water is soothing and fun to play in. Look for cool pools, too, at public swimming facilities throughout the region. But the hot spots are truly unique in this area, ranging from commercial pools to natural "hot pots" within Yellowstone's boundaries.

Inside Yellowstone National Park you'll be thrilled by the chance to soak in the Boiling River, about 10 miles past Mammoth Hot Springs from the Northern Entrance. After a short mile-long stroll on a flat path, you'll see steam rising on your left and a thermal stream that flows into the Gardiner River. In the natural pools here you can feel the freezing currents of the river blend with the scalding thermal flow to equal a just-right temperature for soaking. Jump into the Firehole River Swimming Hole in Yellowstone. Pack a picnic and steer your parents toward Firehole Canyon Drive (you'll see it on the Yellowstone National Park map they give you at the entrance gate). The road is just south of Madison Junction on the west side of the Madison-Old Faithful Road. Keep on going until you come to the Firehole River Swimming Hole. The only way you'll miss it is if your eyes are shut.

> ## Insiders' Tip
> Fish hatcheries are great places to learn more about trout. Some hatcheries also have feeding ponds where you can purchase a handful of fish food and attract trout as long as your arm.

At Astoria Hot Springs, (307) 733-2659, outside of Jackson, Wyoming, children can play in their own wading pool while grown-ups soak in a relaxing 95-degree pool. Just 30 miles north of Gardiner, Montana, is Chico Hot Springs Lodge, (406) 333-4933, where two naturally heated pools glisten in the cool mountain air, waiting for you to enjoy a game of volleyball or tag. Between Bozeman and Big Sky, Montana you'll find Bozeman Hot Springs, (406) 586-6492, which houses seven pools of different temperatures under one roof. While you romp in the water, Mom and Dad can enjoy a spa treatment at this elaborate facility. In Idaho, just 35 miles southeast of Pocatello, you must find Lava Hot Springs, (800) 423-8597. Enjoy the Olympic-size pool for lap swimming and several different temperatures of hot pools. The pools are open year-round.

I is for Ice Skating

Sharpen up your blades and skate your way through Yellowstone country. In Bozeman, Montana, there are three free ice skating rinks. At Southside Park on West College Street and South 7th Avenue, you can play a pick-up game of hockey or just skate. Beall Park at Villard and Black Streets offers broom ball on certain days of the week and recreational skating the rest of the time. Or if you are serious about hockey, head for Bogert Park at 325 South Church Avenue. If temperatures outside warm up too much for the ice to stay solid, there is always the Valley Ice Garden, 269 Jackrabbit Lane, (406) 585-1415, home to the Ice Dogs hockey team. This massive complex offers skating and hockey lessons, as well as regular family skating sessions. In Livingston, Montana, you can get a taste for the way ice skating used to be—the beautiful but ungroomed pond in Sacajawea Park is a lively gathering place for kids after school. West Yellowstone, Montana, makes a skating rink each winter on Electric Street, and there is also a neat skating rink at Mammoth

Hotel in Yellowstone National Park. You can rent skates for the whole family at Mammoth.

In Jackson, Wyoming, you can pay a few bucks to skate at the indoor Snow King Center Ice Rink at 100 East Snow King Avenue, (307) 733-5200. The rink is open from August to mid-April. And if you don't feel like skiing (or tennis), try out the skating area at Grand Targhee in Alta, Wyoming (the ski area floods the tennis courts and maintains the ice). Call Grand Targhee at (800) 827-4433 or drive up on Ski Hill Road out of Driggs, Idaho.

J is for Jigsaw Puzzles

When the sun goes down in Yellowstone country things get awfully quiet around here. Many hotels in and around Yellowstone Park have no phones or televisions in the rooms, that's all part of the charm. So in the quiet of the evening, why not revive a forgotten tradition. In Pray, Montana's Chico Hot Springs Lodge, 1 Old Chico Road, (406) 333-4933, you will find a large selection of puzzles in the lobby area. It's common to see families sitting together at one of the tables piecing the puzzles together. Get back to the basics on your trip and check out the puzzles at Old Faithful and Roosevelt Lodges, too, (307) 344-7311.

K is for Kites

You can fly a kite anywhere there is wind, of course, but in Livingston, Montana (supposedly the third windiest town in America), they even hold an annual Wind Festival, (406) 222-0580 to celebrate gale-force gusts in the area. Every October the community sponsors a contest for the best "wind catcher." The competition brings out school kids with handmade kites and many local artists, who create elaborate sculptures that blow with the direction of the wind like weather vanes. The community comes out for an afternoon of kite flying (wind and weather permitting) and contest.

L is for Licking Ice Cream

On a hot day there is nothing better than the cool, sweet flavor of homemade ice cream. In these parts you can find special flavors, like Huckleberry, Chocolate Moose, and Rocky Mountain Road. Look in any Hamilton Store throughout Yellowstone National Park for Wilcoxson's Ice Cream, made in Livingston, Montana, at 314 S. Main Street, (406) 222-3270. This old-fashioned creamy ice cream comes in 50 flavors and has been made here since 1912. Try the Peanut Butter Chip, Cookies and Cream, or Praline Pecan. Look for Wilcoxson's outside of the park, too, in West Yellowstone and other Montana towns.

Teton Valley may be the Huckleberry Shake capitol of the world, so make sure you stop at the Victor Emporium for an old-fashioned treat made with hand-picked huckleberries and lots of smooth, rich ice cream. Victor Emporium is at 45 N. Main St., Victor, Idaho, (208) 787-2221. Around Ashton, you can get a fine milkshake served by a for-real carhop. It'll be a blast from the past for mom and dad, so be sure you make them stop at the Frostop Drive-in, 26 N. U.S. Highway 20, Ashton, Idaho.

M is for Mining

Montana isn't known as the treasure state for nothing: The 1860s kicked off the gold rush near Virginia City. From there the state's mining industry grew to include copper, coal, and the famous Yogo sapphires. In West Yellowstone, Montana, you can mine for gold and gems like the old timers at Yellowstone Mining Company inside the Rare Earth Store, 111 Yellowstone Ave., (406) 646-9337. They will show you how a real working sluice operates and dazzle you with Montana's largest amethyst geode, as well as displays of rocks, fossils, and minerals.

You can also search for treasure during Bozeman's annual Gem and Mineral Show at the Gallatin County Fairgrounds, 901 N. Black Ave. Rockhounds from all over the state gather here to show off giant geodes and magnificent minerals. One vendor sells cups of rock and sand for $2 so you can sift through them to find gemstones like garnets, sapphires, and amethyst. You're guaranteed to find some pretty colored stones and learn a thing or two about where they come from.

N is for Nature Walks

You are surrounded by more than 2 million acres of wilderness and forest service land out here. To learn about wildflowers, wildlife, and environmental issues, try one of many different field courses that get kids outside seeing, smelling, touching, and hearing, including Bridger Outdoor Science School (BOSS), 111 South Grand Avenue, (406) 582-0526.

Just eight miles east of Mammoth Hot Springs you'll find the Northern Yellowstone Trail, where you can race your kid brother the half-mile distance along the boardwalk. But take it easy on the way back to the car and read some of the signs at trailside exhibits, which talk about wildlife habitat and fire ecology after the massive burn of 1988—you can get down on your hands and knees to investigate any new post-fire signs.

Lone Mountain Ranch, in Big Sky, Montana, (406) 995-4644, offers summer wildflower walks with a naturalist guide. Both Teton Science School and Snake River Institute offer classes for kids, too, mostly in summer. (Teton Science School also has great winter programs for area schools and school groups.) Teton Science School, within Grand Teton National Park, is all about nature—lucky students spend as much as six weeks learning hands-on about ecology and the natural world while they live in cabins within the park. Nonresidential programs are also available for kids and adults. Call (307) 733-4765 or see our Education Chapter.

> **Insiders' Tip**
>
> If you want to spend an adults-only evening out or try a particularly strenuous hike, ask about childcare at the front desk of your hotel. Many resorts and guest ranches keep a reliable list of baby sitters whom they call regularly to watch kids on the premises, or they may be able to suggest a local daycare center.

Finally, Yellowstone and Grand Teton Parks are home to ranger-naturalist programs that can teach you about elk, bears, bison, geysers, forest fires, and mountain formation. In Yellowstone National Park, check the *Yellowstone Today* newspaper that the ranger will give you at the entrance gate; Grand Teton's newspaper, available at all visitor centers and park entrances, is called *Teewinot*. Both publications provide descriptions of programs. You can also check the bulletin board at your campground for a schedule of evening campfire talks. Often the evening programs are geared for children and adults.

O is for Old West

This is where the legends of mountain men, cowboys, and even outlaws were born. Half a million settlers crossed through this region on their migration to the west coast. Signs of the Old West's booms and busts have been left throughout Montana, Wyoming, and Idaho—wagon ruts, abandoned mines, homestead cabins, and most of today's towns. You can talk to mountain men and Pony Express riders during Jackson, Wyoming's Old West Days, (307) 733-3316, a celebration of 1800s life and legends in the area. Held each May in the Town Square, locals re-enact the famous Mountain Man Rendezvous, made famous by characters such as John Colter, Jim Bridger, and Davey Jackson. Wander through a village of authentic wagons circled around campfires and teepees where you can taste traditional fry bread. You'll see gunslinger shoot-outs, rodeos, and maybe even learn to promenade with your mom and dad during a street dance.

Get a glimpse of life on the frontier at Old Trail Town, 1831 DeMaris Dr., Cody, Wyoming, (307) 587-5302. Walk along the boardwalks where outlaws Butch Cassidy and the Sundance Kid strolled, where Buffalo Bill strutted, where Jeremiah "Liver Eatin'" Johnston traded furs. Imagine when times were simpler in these parts, when there were good guys and bad guys, when people didn't have the modern conveniences of electricity, indoor plumbing, or cars. This cluster of 200 year old buildings stands as a monument to the frontier era and walking through the dusty main street you'll feel like you are there. (Our Annual Events and Attractions chapters can give you more details.)

P is for Parades

You could be the one spinning cartwheels down main street and tossing candy into the crowd, or if you need moral support dress your dog up as a clown, put him in a little red wagon and walk the walk. Yellowstone country is loaded with parades, some exclusively for kids. Each year for July 4, Cody, Wyoming, kicks off its famous Stampede Rodeo with a kids-only parade on July 2. Bozeman and Livingston, Montana, both have kids-only parades in early December, when the towns welcome in the holiday season with annual Christmas strolls. We suggest you contact the local chambers of commerce to learn about exact times and starting points for these parades. Cody Chamber of Commerce, (307) 587-2777, 836 Sheridan Avenue; Bozeman Chamber of Commerce, (800) 228-4224, 1205 E. Main Street; Livingston Chamber of Commerce, (406) 222-0850, 303 E. Park Street. (See our Annual Events chapter for more details.)

Q is for Quakes

Did you know that the greater Yellowstone ecosystem sits on one of the largest fault lines in North America? At Quake Lake Visitor Center, located just eight miles north of West Yellowstone, Montana, you will see the proof. On August 17, 1959, an earthquake that rated 7.1 on the Richter scale was felt all the way to the Pacific Ocean, and took the lives of 28 people. The visitor center sits above the location of a major landslide that put half of a mountain into the Madison River on that day. Quake Lake is the scar left from that day. You'll see trees growing from its depths and houses left in their watery grave. At the visitor center you can learn more about seismic activity in the area and the details of that great earthquake. It is located in the Hebgen Lake area on U.S. Highway 287, (406) 646-7369. (Check out our Attractions chapter for more details.)

R is for Rodeos

Nearly all area rodeos offer kids' events. Sometimes it's mutton busting, where contestants try to ride sheep. Sometime its calf riding. Sheep bolt and calves buck, so it's hard to say which is more fun to watch or more difficult to do. You usually have to sign up in advance to participate, but in Cody, Wyoming, the Cody Nite Rodeo announcer invites kids out of the stands to join in the rodeo fun. In the calf scramble, a calf with dollar bills stuck to it (sometimes it's someone's pet cow) is turned loose in the arena. A herd of kids chases the calf around the arena trying to grab the bills off the calf.

At Jackson Hole, Wyoming's twice-weekly J.H. Rodeo, two unlucky calves have ribbon tied to their tails, while 50 to 100 kids ages four to eleven chase the calves to capture the winning ribbon. J.H. Rodeo is held at the fairgrounds on Snow King Avenue, (307) 733-2805. Kids from five to 12 can get wild and woolly at the Livingston Roundup Rodeo when they compete in a mutton busting contest. Each contestant tries to ride a sheep for eight seconds before the buzzer goes off to signal the end of the ride. Most kids get a mouthful of rodeo arena dust, but the ones who stay on win prizes. Check our Attractions chapter for more rodeo locations and times.

S is for Skiing

Steep slopes and beautiful bunny hills at ski areas around Yellowstone await your arrival. All offer extensive kids' programs with snowboard and ski instruction for all ages and abilities. Equipment rentals are also available at these ski meccas: Big Sky Ski and Summer Resort, Big Sky, Montana, (800) 548-4486, (406) 995-5000; Bridger Bowl, 15795 Bridger Canyon Road, Bozeman, Montana, (406) 586-1518, (800) 223-9609; Red Lodge Mountain Resort, Red Lodge, Montana, (406) 446-2610, (800) 444-8977; Jackson Hole, just to name a few. (Check out our Winter Sports chapter for names of the area's smaller ski hills, too.)

T is for Treats

Walking into the Montana Candy Emporium, 7 S. Broadway, Red Lodge, Montana, (406) 446-1119, is better than walking onto the set of Willie Wonka and the Chocolate Factory. (Plus, there are no Oompa Loompas to get you into trouble here). This is Montana's oldest and biggest candy store, where, in addition to 22 kinds of fudge made while you watch, they carry 2,300 kinds of candy. Don't leave without a taste of fudge, but then there are also caramels, taffy, mints, chocolates, and every kind of hard candy imaginable.

JoNae's Candies, 229 East Main Street, Bozeman, Montana, (406) 585-9818, greets you with the mouth-watering aroma of chocolate when you walk in the door. JoNae's sends candy to loyal patrons all over the world. The shop is famous for huckleberry truffles and a double chocolate Montana mint. In Jackson Hole, Wyoming, don't miss the Yippy I-O Candy Co. at 84 East Broadway Avenue, (307) 739-3020. This sweet shop is lined with barrels, baskets, and jars full of candy—every color and flavor you can dream up—including hand-dipped chocolates. The cream and butter fudge is made fresh in the store.

U is for Underground Caves

You and your parents will marvel at the stalactites and stalagmites jutting out of Lewis and Clark Caverns State Park near Three Forks, Montana, (406) 287-3541. You'll learn about resident bats and the formation of this geological wonder on a 2-mile, guided tour available from Memorial Day through Labor Day.

Skiing can be great fun for kids. PHOTO: BIG SKY RESORT

V is for Virginia City, Montana

The gold rush days will seem real in this historic mining town with its old buildings and boardwalks. You can peek into storefronts and houses from the Wild West days and ride the narrow-gauge railroad three miles to Nevada City. Go to Boot Hill and check out the gravestones of the Plummer Gang. Play the nickelodeons in the Bale of Hay Saloon and don't miss the melodrama by the Virginia City Players—you don't get to throw tomatoes, but you do get to cheer, boo, and hiss with the rest of the audience.

W is for Whitewater Rafting

One way to stay cool and take in some of the area's most spectacular scenery is to hit the rivers. The Gallatin, Madison, and Yellowstone in Montana and the Shoshone and the Snake Rivers in Wyoming all have big whitewater rapids. Local guides make the promise that you will not leave the raft with dry clothes. In Gardiner, Montana, Yellowstone Raft Company, (800) 858-7781, will take you and your folks down the scenic Yellowstone River (the longest undammed river in the lower 48)—and if your timing is just right you may be able to attempt the six-foot standing wave in Yankee Jim Canyon. For a little tamer perspective, talk your parents into an easy float down 13 miles of the Snake River outside of Jackson, Wyoming, with Teton Expeditions, (800) 700-7238. With the Grand Teton Mountains towering over you, this trip is bound to be memorable. But if you want to get back to the wild part of the Snake, set up a river run with Jackson's Mad River Boat Trips, (800) 458-RAFT. Their experienced guides will teach you about how to "read" the water as you navigate The Big Kahuna rapid. If you vow to wear your life preserver, maybe your parents will let you go down the Gallatin River to meet the challenge of House Rock and its field of rapids with Geyser Whitewater Expeditions, (800) 922-RAFT, near Big Sky, Montana.

> **Insiders' Tip**
>
> Mountain Sky Guest Ranch, south of Livingston, Montana, is renowned as a family vacation haven. The extensive kids' program includes day hikes, nature crafts, clowns, swimming, and trail rides. Call (406) 587-1244 for more information or reservations.

X is for X-ing Off Pictures

Page eight of your Yellowstone National Park Junior Ranger Activity Paper has a check list of animals to help you keep track of all the creatures you see in the park. The paper is for kids eight to 12 years old, but the park also has papers for younger kids, too. At the end of your park visit, you can turn your activity paper in. If you've done everything required, you become a Junior Ranger and get a patch to prove it. In order to qualify, you must attend at least one ranger-naturalist program, view a visitor center or roadside exhibit and tell about it, take a walk on a park trail, read and understand the Junior Ranger pledge, and understand six basic park rules. You must also complete a certain number of pages of your activity paper. For $2 you can buy one of these at any one of the visitor centers in Yellowstone National Park.

Y is for Yellowstone Buddies

This children's environmental education program in Yellowstone National Park teaches kids about volcanoes, Yellowstone's bird population, geysers, and other environmental issues in the four regions of the park through story-telling, games, nature crafts, and hikes. The two-hour segments are offered at Old Faithful, the Grand Canyon of the Yellowstone, Mammoth Hot Springs, and Yellowstone Lake. Classes focus on a theme each session: earth, wind, fire, or water. The cost is $20 per child and includes a "buddy busy bag" with activity books, pins, patches, and postcards. The program began in 1999 and is designed for seven to twelve-year-olds. Programs are available twice a day at 9:30 A.M. and 2:30 P.M., June 15 to August 15. There are eight different courses offered throughout the park, each ending with kids taking the "Buddy Pledge" to protect the environment for future generations. For more details about the Yellowstone Buddies Children's Program, call Yellowstone Park Lodges at (307) 344-7311.

Z is for Catching some ZZZs

After all of this kidstuff, you're going to want to get some rest.

Kayaking is a popular sport among Yellowstone Country adventure seekers. PHOTO: DONNIE SEXTON/TRAVEL MONTANA

Fishing and Watersports

Yellowstone country's waters include vast mountain lakes, roiling rivers, and tiny, meandering trout streams. From blue ribbon fishing, to wind surfing, water-skiing, and whitewater rafting—you can choose just one thing or do them all. Either way, you'll find that our area has a bounty of recreation opportunities on the water.

In this chapter we've highlighted some of the most talked about spots and some of the local treasures. If an area is famous for its angling, we'll tell you a bit about regulations and the best equipment to use to catch those wily fish. If it's whitewater, we'll focus on typical water conditions for that area. If it's open to motorized crafts, we'll tell you about boat ramps and other essentials. At the end of each region's description, look for listings of fishing guides, floatboat outfitters, powerboat tours, and equipment rental. With this information we hope to give you a jumping-off point, but when you get out here, you will find your own resources, as well.

Change in Rocky Mountain weather is an ever-present factor for any outdoor pursuit, so remember to prepare for a wide range of conditions. Even if the forecaster predicts sunny skies and warm temperatures, come prepared for snow—you never can tell out here. Bring along extra supplies and dress in layers so that you can easily adjust to the daily temperature fluctuation. Use our write-ups and your own experience as general guidelines only. You should always obtain current information about an area before you set out.

For regular up-to-date info, call area sporting goods stores and outfitters. Park rangers, the Fish, Wildlife, and Parks Department, as well as the Forest Service can provide most of the information you'll need to plan your excursion. (Look for contact numbers in our Resources chapter.)

Throw in a Line

Talk with anyone who has fished in Yellowstone country and you won't hear stories about the one that got away, but how many they caught. The region's streams yield astounding catches. On the most popular stretch of the Yellowstone River, by Sulfur Caldron in the park, catches of 50 to 60 trout a day occur regularly. That's because these fisheries are comparatively free of pollution and serious habitat degradation. With underwater hot springs flowing into many area rivers originating in Yellowstone National Park, fish thrive on the added nutrients and food sources encouraged by the warmer water. It helps keep fish metabolic rates and temperatures higher in winter cold and supports aquatic vegetation for prime habitat. Also, the region's heavy snows act as reservoirs, feeding into streams from spring to fall to keep water levels up and temperatures cooler during summer months—key factors for fish to survive the heat.

Because the climate throughout Yellowstone country is similar, so is the fishing. The waterways are linked within the ecosystem, giving each stream, mountain lake, and fast-flowing river a unique role in the big picture. This means you will find many of the same fish in this region. Trout are the mainstay of Rocky Mountain waterways, and you will largely encounter the same species of fish throughout this region: cutthroat, brown, rainbow, and lake trout, as well as grayling and mountain whitefish. Cutthroat, the only native species, are so named for the red slash under their throats. The other species were introduced mostly by government agencies beginning in 1890. A few, such as chub, sucker, and shiner, were planted inadvertently by bait anglers dumping unused minnows into rivers and lakes.

As far as fishing lore, each state offers a distinct experience for both the expert and novice. In Yellowstone Park, you might go after some of the mightiest native cutthroat trout in legendary Yellowstone Lake, where they are said to grow up to 18 inches long. In Idaho's impossibly clear waters look for the red-bodied kokanee salmon. Within Grand Teton National Park, the lake trout are big enough to tip your canoe on Jenny Lake, where the fish can weigh as much as 30 pounds. Montana's famed fisheries are home to great numbers of big, tricky browns, while Wyoming's secret is its hefty brookies.

Each state has its own set of fishing regulations and licenses. Generally, everything you'll need to get your rod on the river can be found at local sporting goods stores, or in the parks at visitor centers and ranger stations. Check out our Resources chapter for regional fishing guidebooks.

Fishing Outfitters

Hiring an outfitter won't guarantee that you'll catch a fish, but it will make the logistics of your fishing easy. Local guides have the insider expertise, and can take you where the fishing is hot while cluing you in on what the fish are eating. They know the regulations, so you won't mistakenly end up on the wrong side of the law. Plus, most guide services supply transportation to and from the fishing area, a boat, meals and drinks, and sometimes even equipment. Expect one day of guided fishing in Greater Yellowstone to cost between $200 and $300 per person (plus tip). Package deals that combine lodging or group rates are common.

River Outfitters

A local guide's knowledge of the river is a great asset, but even better is how simple he or she will make your time on the water. The outfitter provides most of the gear—boat, life preservers, food, water, transportation, and expertise. You just bring the sunglasses and the sunscreen. Whether you opt for a scenic river trip or heart-plunging whitewater, you can count on local guides and their gear to be reliable. Many companies pride themselves on their guides' knowledge of local history, flora, and fauna. Rates vary depending on the length of your trip, shuttle distance, and other factors, but generally you can expect to spend between $50 to $100 per person for a one-day float trip (about three or five hours on the water, plus lunch). Some shorter trips can be as little as $35 per person.

Rating Rivers

In the descriptions that follow, we refer to the international rating scale for rivers. It provides a general idea of a river section's difficulty. Remember, these ratings change as water flows rise and fall throughout the year. The difficulty of a section also depends on the craft and your ability to maneuver it. Wading fly fishers can use this scale also, as it gives an idea of water turbulence and gradient. A class IV, V, and VI river will be mostly or entirely turbulent, and will likely be very steep. Most of the region's best fishing rivers are rated I to III.

River Rating Scale

- Class I (practiced beginner): Easy moving water with small or no waves.
- Class II (beginner to intermediate): Regular waves, fast current, unobstructed rapids; may require some maneuvering.
- Class III (intermediate to advanced): Large waves and obstacles; maneuvering required; clear route exists, but may not be obvious.
- Class IV (expert): Large, chaotic waves; maneuvering difficult but not required; route often not obvious; clear route may not exist; scouting recommended.
- Class V (expert with previous Class IV experience): No beginners on board; scouting strongly recommended; most people choose to portage.
- Class VI (expert with previous Class V experience): No beginners or intermediates on board; extremely dangerous; most people choose to portage.

Yellowstone National Park

Within Yellowstone National Park's 3,472 square miles are over 800 miles of broad rivers and smaller backcountry streams, plus 175 lakes. The sheer variety leaves enough water for any level of angler. Experienced anglers often seek the calm waters of the Firehole or the Gibbon Rivers, where advanced fishing skills are necessary. Less experienced anglers can fulfill their trout goal at Yellowstone Lake or the Buffalo Ford stretch of the Yellowstone River.

But to fish Yellowstone you should know the water and have the right gear. Grab a set of regulations and a permit, which you can find at any fly shop or sporting goods store in Yellowstone's gateway towns. Anglers 16 and older must buy a fishing permit. You can fish for 10 days for only $10 or spend $20 for a season permit. Permits are available at ranger stations, visitor centers, and Hamilton Stores. Unless you haul in a lake trout (also called Mackinaw), fishing in Yellowstone Park is catch and release. Humans are at the end of the food chain out here, and wildlife—the grizzly, otter, mink, pelican, osprey, eagles, and others—prey on fish as a mainstay in their diets.

Generally Yellowstone National Park's fishing season begins on the Saturday of Memorial Day weekend and continues through the first Sunday in November. For complete information on park fishing, we suggest you pick up a set of regulations. Write the Chief Ranger's Office, P.O. Box 168, Yellowstone National Park, WY 82190, or call (307) 344-2107.

Yellowstone is not exactly a boater's paradise, only because access is limited within the park. Be advised that with the exception of the Lewis River channel between Lewis and Shoshone Lakes, there's no boating on Yellowstone National Park rivers, and limited motorized boat access is permitted on park lakes. Motorized boats are allowed on Yellowstone and Lewis Lakes. Non-motorized vessels, including float tubes, are permitted on all lakes except Sylvan, Eleanor, and Twin Lakes, as well as Beach Springs Lagoon.

All vessels, including float tubes, require permits with a sticker displayed. You can purchase boat permits at several places. You can pick up motorized boat permits at the Park's south entrance, the Lewis Lake Campground, Grant Visitor Center, Bridge Bay Marina, and the Lake Ranger Station. For non-motorized boat permits, you'll have to go to the Bechler Ranger Station, the Park's west or northeast entrance, or the backcountry office at Canyon and Mammoth Visitor Centers. In 2001, an annual motorized permit cost $20, while a 10-day permit cost $10. For non-motorized boats an annual permit cost $10 and a 10-day permit cost $5. For information about boat and slip rentals, call the Bridge Bay Marina from the first week in June until the end of September, at (307) 242-3876. The rest of the year, call (307) 344-7901.

Yellowstone Lake

In the blink of an eye Yellowstone Lake can change from glassy calm to churning treachery. At 20 miles long and 14 miles wide, this inland ocean is rimmed with layers of mountain ranges. Though it is popular with boaters and anglers, the waters of this lake are so frigid that swimming is discouraged even on the hottest August day. With an average depth of 140 feet, the water of this 89,000-acre lake is so cold (41 degrees on average) that hypothermia can set in within 20 minutes should you capsize a boat. These are important facts to know, but don't let them scare you. Just be sure to check current water and weather conditions at the visitor center or ranger station before heading out onto the lake.

> **Insiders' Tip**
> Of Yellowstone Lake's 110 miles of shoreline, 75 miles cannot be reached by park roads, but are ideal for exploring in a canoe or kayak.

Fishing

Those seeking consistent action for cutthroat in the 15- to 17-inch range head to legendary Yellowstone Lake. About 50,000 anglers (nearly half of all those who fish in the park) come to cast their lines into its icy waters. Since cutthroat trout live and spawn in shallow waters, most people fish from shore between Sedge Bay and Grant Village. Check out the inlet streams, especially during spawning time in June. One of the secrets of the lake, however, is that you'll catch more fish when you're out in a boat. This could simply be because there is less competition combined with the fact that you can cover more miles. Regardless, because of unpredictable winds and storms, fishing from a boat on Yellowstone Lake shouldn't be taken lightly.

Yellowstone Lake is also home to the notorious lake trout, which dwell in deep water. Although these abundant fish are big and fun to play once you hook them, they are considered the scourge of Yellowstone. Illegally introduced to the park, lake trout prey on cutthroat and currently threaten to offset the balance of the park's ecosystem since cutthroat are food for key species like grizzlies, pelicans, and eagles. Catch and release is the norm within Yellowstone, but if you catch a lake trout, please keep it and turn it in to the ranger station. Thanks to efforts like gill netting of lake trout, the wild cutthroat population is still at a healthy level. Yellowstone Lake is the gauge of fishery health throughout the park, and though it is heavily fished, so far so good.

Insiders' Tip

Most of Yellowstone is off-limits for bait fishing, but Panther, Obsidian, and Indian Creeks are reserved for bait fishing by children.

Floatboating

Early park explorers compared Yellowstone Lake to the shape of a man's left hand, although there are only three "fingers," or arms, as they are known, to the lake. (West Thumb gets its name from this early description.) It is within these three arms that kayakers and canoeists can best explore Yellowstone's wilderness. Access the Southeast Arm by putting in at Sedge Bay; the Flat Mountain Arm and South Arm are accessible from the Grant Village boat ramp. Because of tempestuous winds and storms, canoeists and kayakers should travel along the shoreline at all times. Crossing Yellowstone Lake in small watercraft is not encouraged here.

Powerboating

All but 13 miles of the 110 miles of Yellowstone Lake's shoreline is accessible by powerboat. There are two boat launches: one at Grant Village near the campground and another that's operated by AmFac at Bridge Bay Marina, (307) 242-3876. Most people seem to opt for either riding with AmFac or renting one of its boats. Each summer AmFac hosts 5,000 anglers on guided lake trips and another 15,000 who tour the lake on one of the hour-long scenic cruises. These cruises run five to seven times a day from the first week in June to the last week in September. As of 2000, the cost for adults was $8.50 and $4.50 for children between the ages of two and eleven.

AmFac's guided fishing trips cost $50 or $65 per hour depending on the size of the boat. You can also rent rowboats for $5.75 per hour and outboards for $26 an hour. At Bridge Bay you'll find 110 dock slips for rent, starting at $9 per night for boats 16 feet or less. The marina sells fuel.

Shoshone Lake

At over 80,000 acres, Shoshone is the second largest lake in the park. All seven miles of this backcountry lake are protected wilderness. This deep, icy lake is accessible by trail, boat, or canoe from Lewis Lake (see below). Although getting here isn't easy, the payoff comes in the form of watching undisturbed wildlife, such as moose and sandhill cranes. According to Yellowstone Park historian Lee Whittlesey, Shoshone Lake had six different names before Park Superintendent P.H. Norris christened it in the 1870s after the Shoshone Indians who sometimes visited the lake during summer months.

Insiders' Tip

Wyoming's Fish, Wildlife, and Parks Department holds the Wyoming Cutt Slam in which fishers try to catch the state's four native cutthroat trout: Yellowstone, Colorado River, Snake River, and the Bonneville from their original drainages. As of 2000, only 65 people had completed the challenge successfully. The challenge was started in 1998 to help anglers learn more about Wyoming's cutthroat sub-species.

Fishing

Shoshone boasts large brown and lake trout along with some good-sized brook and cutthroat trout. But the best fishing opportunities here are in the fall when the huge old lake trout come to spawn in the shallows.

Floatboating

If you plan on canoeing or sea kayaking to Shoshone Lake you should begin on the south shore of Lewis Lake near the campground and then travel down the Lewis River Channel. Inside the heavily forested channel it is calm and protected from the regular winds of both lakes. You'll pass gorgeous rock formations. Depending on the time of year, water conditions could be high enough to warrant a wet suit and good shoes to cross the river on foot while you pull your boat. It's hard work, but worth it once you get to Shoshone Lake to explore its fragile Shoshone Geyser Basin (there are over 70 geysers here) and surrounding wilderness. There are several nice gravel beaches for camping along the eastern shore.

Lewis Lake

The third largest lake in the park, Lewis Lake is only 12 miles from the south entrance of Yellowstone. At the southeast end is a campground and boat launch. At the opposite end is the mouth of the Lewis Channel, which connects to Shoshone Lake.

Fishing

Lewis hosts mainly brown trout but is also sprinkled with lake and brook trout. There's roadside access, as well as a boat launching ramp—an important element since the best fishing often results from a boat on this lake. High winds and rough water can make it dangerous to canoe on this lake, so you might opt to fish from the safety of the shoreline. If you're canoeing, float tubing, or kayaking on this 2,000-plus-acre lake, hug the shoreline even if you're headed up the Lewis River Channel to Shoshone Lake.

Floatboating

Just off of Lewis Lake you can enjoy a rare privilege. The Lewis River Channel is the only stream in Yellowstone that allows canoes or kayaks. The 3.5-mile stretch of water drains from Shoshone Lake, so from Lewis Lake boaters must haul their crafts up the river using ropes in order to enjoy the trip downriver later. Water in the channel is high in June, but by August it is knee deep and peaceful.

Powerboating

Along with Yellowstone Lake, Lewis Lake is the only other lake in the park where power-boats are permitted. Morning is the best time to enjoy calm waters and sunrises reflecting off the lake.

Firehole River

With its source at Madison Lake, south of Old Faithful on the north side of the Continental Divide, this is one of America's most famous rivers. It moves and meanders gently through Yellowstone for 35 miles before tumbling through the canyon leading to Madison Junction. Wandering through the Midway and Upper geyser basins, the Firehole is fed by thermal springs that warm its waters throughout the year, thus making it popular with both anglers and swimmers, as well as lazy bison, which are often seen soaking their feet in its waters. Mountain man Jim Bridger told folks this river ran so fast downhill that it was hot at the bottom.

Fishing

It's fly fishing only on the Firehole, and though it's not written anywhere, it may as well be experts only, too. The fish are wily in this stream and aren't fooled easily. Veteran guides suggest the use of tiny flies to catch this river's crafty ones. You can't keep any rainbow, but you're allowed two browns smaller than 13 inches and up to five brookies. What's great about this river is that, unlike most of the other park streams, which aren't in peak fishing form until late June or July, the Firehole is in gear when the park opens in late May. No fishing is permitted from Old Faithful to Biscuit Basin.

Gibbon River

The Gibbon flows for 38 miles from Grebe Lake to its confluence with the Firehole at Madison Junction. Its cascading route passes through the Norris Geyser Basin and through Elk Park and the Gibbon Meadows until it plunges over Gibbon Falls. The Gibbon is accessible via the Madison-Norris Road, which parallels most of its length.

Fishing

A 5-mile stretch of water winding through Gibbon Meadows is home to some big browns and good-size rainbows. The water here can be deceptively deep. Be aware that from Gibbon Falls downstream to the Firehole, the river is restricted to fly fishing. The upper river, from Grebe to Elk Park at Norris Geyser Basin, has small brook trout and rarely caught grayling. Fishing is best at this river during early summer and early fall.

Slough Creek and the Lamar River

Stake your claim in the Slough Creek Campground the night before so that you can get on the river by dawn—this is the fly fisher's Mecca. Conditions on this stream are rarely crowded, since it covers so much terrain. From the campground, trails lead to a series of three meadows through which Slough Creek creeps along until it tumbles to its next sleepy slither and at last into the Lamar River in the northern portion of the park.

    The Lamar River, famous as the site where the re-introduced wolves were released in 1995, coasts along for 66 miles before rushing through the Canyon and dumping into the Yellowstone River near Tower Junction. The Lamar Valley is rimmed by the Absaroka

Mountains to the east and offers supreme opportunities for wildlife watching. It's also one of the last streams to clear from spring runoff, and it muddies easily after heavy rains. For best results, fish here in late summer. We recommend the Little Lamar River, Cache, South Cache, Soda Butte, Amphitheater, Flint, Cold, and Miller Creeks. If you feel discouraged at first, be aware that the Lamar can be moody, so move around until you find fish.

Fishing

Hidden in the pools, glides, riffles, and side channels of Slough Creek, you'll find the world-famous cutthroats (as big as 24 inches). Fishing for the cutts is strictly catch and release, but you can keep two rainbow and five brook trout. Both Slough and Lamar offer easily accessible meadow fishing. The season runs from Memorial Day through October 31.

Grand Teton National Park

The Tetons jut up from glacial lakes and divide Wyoming and Idaho with a sheer granite wall. If there is anything that makes being on the water more dramatically scenic or breathtaking than these mountains in Grand Teton National Park, we haven't found it. Unlike Yellowstone, Grand Teton National Park does not require its own fishing license. Generally, fishing rules are the rules of Wyoming, with a few special restrictions. Just be familiar with park fishing regulations, which you can pick up at Moose Village Store, Signal Mountain Lodge, Colter Bay Marina, Flagg Ranch Village, and many locations outside the boundaries. A one-day, nonresident Wyoming fishing license costs about $6. Nonresident children under 14 may fish without a license, as long as they're accompanied by an adult with a valid fishing license.

Permits are required to float your boat in the park's lakes and rivers. You can buy craft permits at Moose Visitor Center year-round; in summer you can get them at Colter Bay and Flagg Ranch visitor information centers and at Buffalo and Signal Mountain ranger stations. A one-week, non-motorized permit costs about $5. A season permit costs $10. Motorized permits cost about $10 for one week and $20 for the year. Motorized craft larger than five horsepower must display a state registration sticker. Grand Teton and Yellowstone National Parks honor the other's permits, although Yellowstone requires Grand Teton craft permits check in at a ranger station.

Scenic paddling is mostly what you'll experience in Grand Teton, since there really is no whitewater here. The bonus of that is that kayaks, canoes, and quiet crafts allow you to observe wildlife easier and possibly get closer than in a louder boat. The park's lakes and waterways also give you the opportunity to leave busy roads and experience a side of the Tetons you might otherwise miss.

Leigh and String Lakes

The square, black top of Mount Moran stands ominously over Leigh Lake. Its deep, glacial waters butt up against the mountain and are not accessible by road. To get here you must paddle the shallow, wandering length of String Lake (accessed along an offshoot of Teton Park Road), until you reach a portage on a short but hilly trail. You can also get here on foot to fish the shore via a short hiking trail. The trail into Leigh continues about halfway around its perimeter. Numerous attractive backcountry campsites sit along the trail near the lakeshore.

Fishing

Since Leigh Lake is generally more difficult to reach, it sees less fishing and boating traffic than any other lake in the park. Like Jenny and Jackson Lakes, the chilly, deep water is home to massive lake trout, a few brook and brown, as well as stocked cutthroat. The fishing here is better compared to shallow String Lake. The lake is open to anglers all year. The limit is six fish per day, although size limitations do apply.

Floatboating

Unlike the placid String Lake, Leigh's deep waters are known for sudden winds kicking up rough choppy waves. Because of this, most boaters hug the shoreline. One of the more popular canoe trips on Leigh takes you from the put-in after the portage from String to the base of Mount Moran. Most climbers looking to conquer Moran paddle this 2.5-mile one-way trip. There is also a trail leading to the foot of the mountain.

Jackson Lake

Grand Teton's largest lake is also its most popular. The average depth here is 400 feet and the lake offers miles of shoreline and numerous islands that are good for exploring. Spanning 31 square miles, Jackson is a natural lake formed by glacial run-off 5 million years ago, but it wasn't always this big. The dam at its southern end—built for farmer's irrigation purposes—increased its size. Be sure to make reservations for one of the several backcountry sites along the shore.

Fishing

Although fishing is great any time of year on Jackson Lake (except in October when it's closed to fishing), ice fishing has become increasingly popular here. It's easy to access the lake from several points along the shore and any one of the three marinas. The time to fish is in the spring and fall. During the summer months the fish go deep and are harder to catch. You may also hook cutthroat here. The limit is six fish per day. Other regulations, including size, may apply.

Floatboating

With high winds likely to whip up an unexpected storm, most paddlers hug the shores on Jackson Lake. Access to the lake is good, so you have many options for paddling trips. One popular route begins at Spalding Bay and takes you to Moran Bay, on the secluded, roadless side of the lake. Hikers like to paddle across the northern arm of the lake from Lizard Creek Campground to access hard-to-reach backcountry trails. Because of Jackson Lake's popularity, you might not get that wilderness experience you're looking for, particularly on weekends. Powerboats hauling water-skiers, sailboats, personal watercraft, and windsurfers compete with each other on sunny summer days.

Powerboating

Jackson Lake's three marinas offer everything you need to make your powerboat experience on the water memorable. You can rent boats, hire a guide, and buy gasoline and groceries at both Signal Mountain, (307) 543-2831, and Colter Bay, (307) 543-2811. Leek's Marina, (307) 543-2494, offers limited services. Of the other lakes in Grand Teton National Park, only Phelps allows motorized traffic. Only Jackson Lake allows sailboats, water-skiers, and personal watercraft.

Close-up

Paradise Valley Spring Creeks

When the rivers are running high and muddy, the crystalline spring creeks in Montana's Paradise Valley are ideal for anxious anglers who are ready to start the season off right.

"The spring creeks offer the best fishing there is this time of year, because they aren't affected by run-off," says George Anderson, owner of the Yellowstone Angler in Livingston.

Located a few miles south of Livingston, these spring-fed streams, known as the Armstrong, Depuy, and Nelson Creeks, are celebrated for their crystal clear water and abundant, but finicky, wild trout. Meandering at their own sweet pace almost parallel to the wide, raging waters of the Yellowstone River, the spring creeks only make up a few scant miles of pristine fishing before joining the river. But in that stretch of water there are countless challenges for both the expert and the novice fly fisher.

According to Anderson, the key is to "match the hatch." Since the spring creeks consistently maintain a moderately warm 50- to 60-degree temperature year round, the insect hatches are fat and frequent. But with this comes a savvy rainbow, brown, or cutthroat that will accept only the finest imitation cast with precision.

"What you have is an ideal habitat with a food source that fosters an increased fish population," Anderson explains, "The spring creeks have 10 times the number of fish per square mile compared to the Yellowstone."

Though the spring creeks are heralded by experts, even the best angler can get frustrated without the right equipment. Long leaders, fine tippets, and specific flies are essential for success on these tricky streams. Rods in the 3 to 5 weight range and reels spooled with a floating line are considered standard.

Spring hatches generally consist of midges, blue-winged olives, and pale mourning duns. Accurate representations of these insects in No. 16 to 20 sizes are effective. Wet fly selections for late summer should include small pheasant-tail nymphs, sowbugs, scuds, San Juan worms, brassies, and midge larva patterns. Fished with weight and an indicator in the deeper runs, these flies can be quite productive and offer beginners an excellent opportunity at landing a finicky spring creek trout. The average fish is between 14 to 16 inches long, with some up to 20 inches.

As the weather warms in June and July, the emergence of sulphur duns, midges, pale morning duns, and caddis flies offer a continued food source and terrific surface activity for the dry fly fisher. Ants are effective as well and are a good option if you can't seem to match the current hatch.

The months of August and September provide prime terrestrial fishing as hoppers become a staple in the trout's diet. Imitations work well when fished tight along the grassy banks. October and November continue to provide consistent fishing with midges and blue-winged olives. Wooly buggers may also fool a few fish when stripped through the deeper runs.

For the hardy angler, the months of winter still provide solid fishing when weather permits. Though some surface action does take place, most fish are caught below the surface with midge larva, sowbugs, and small nymph patterns.

Beyond their reputation as famous wild trout fisheries, the spring creeks are a prime spawning ground for the Yellowstone's trout. The record floods of 1996 washed the Yellowstone over the fragile banks of Depuy and Armstrong Creeks, ruining that essential habitat. Through careful planning and reconstruction, a dike was designed to divert the river away from the creeks. As a result, these special fisheries have made a strong comeback.

"It was important to the entire ecosystem to re-route the Yellowstone after the flooding," says Anderson.

The spring creeks are privately owned and require a fee in order to fish. Certain rules apply, such as fly-fishing only, as well as catch and release. A valid Montana fishing license is necessary. For information on current fishing conditions, be sure to contact a fly shop in the Bozeman or Livingston area. For reservations call the following numbers: Dupuy's: (406) 222-0221, Armstrong's: (406) 222-2979, and Nelson's: (406) 222-2159.

Jenny Lake

Necklaced by a rolling trail, Jenny Lake is considerably smaller and quieter than Jackson Lake. Its 2 square miles lie at the base of Mount Teewinot, where a ferry shuttles back-country hikers and climbers to trailheads. This lake is open to the public throughout the year.

Fishing

Big fish like deep water and Jenny Lake has that. The lake trout here are fabled to weigh as much as 40 pounds. To hook the biggies, you'll probably need to get into a boat. There are several acceptable boat launch areas on the lake and a marina on the southeast end. Motorcraft with more than eight horsepower are not allowed on this lake. For shore fishing, the trail encircling the lake makes it easily accessible. You may catch a few cutthroats, browns, and brookies. The limit is six fish per day, although other restrictions may apply. Ice fishing is also popular on Jenny Lake.

Floatboating

To get the best from boating on Jenny Lake, we recommend getting up early and paddling out to the middle to see the sun come up over the Tetons and their image reflecting off the dark, glacial waters. The best launching point is at the lake's East End boat dock at South Jenny Lake.

Powerboating

Jenny Lake allows small watercraft with motors less than eight horsepower. No personal watercraft, sailboats, or windsurfers are allowed. Jenny, Jackson, and Phelps (not listed here) Lakes are the only lakes in the park where motorized boats are allowed.

Fishing and Boating Outfitters

Whether it's gear, a boat, or local knowledge, hiring a guide will be worthwhile. Expect a day-long guided fishing trip to run between $250 to $300 per person.

Floating in Grand Teton National Park means the Snake River. The long, meandering river is pretty tame, with almost no whitewater except in Alpine Canyon. Most float trips will be calm, scenic ones, unless you opt for whitewater rafting down the canyon. Expect float trips to take between three and five hours and cost around $35 for an adult. Extras such as Dutch-oven dinners or private boats will cost more.

Adventure Sports
Dornan's at Moose, Grand Teton National Park, WY
(307) 733-3307

These folks rent stable canoes and kayaks for beginner boaters, anglers, and families. These boats are intended for lake floating, not for the Snake River or any other river. The full-day rate for a canoe is around $30. The shop is closed during winter months.

Barker-Ewing Scenic Tours
Moose, Grand Teton National Park, WY
(307) 733-1800, (800) 365-1800

Providing scenic raft tours in the park since 1963, this company is considered an old-timer. Trips run from Deadman's Bar to Moose, a 10-mile float on Class II water. Some trips include a gourmet cookout.

Flagg Ranch Float Trips
John D. Rockefeller Jr. Memorial Parkway, WY
(307) 543-2861

Flagg Ranch offers the only commercial trips on the upper Snake above Jackson Lake. The river is smaller and less traveled here. Both Class III whitewater and Class I and II scenic trips are available.

Grand Teton Lodge Company
Colter Bay Village and Jackson Lake Lodge,
U.S. Hwy. 89, Grand Teton National Park, WY
(307) 543-2811, (800) 628-9988

Regular fishing boats depart at flexible times from Colter Marina if you want to catch a ride. You can fish Jackson Lake for giant lake trout without planning the logistics. You can also rent a boat or aluminum canoe here for the day. Guided fishing trips require advance reservations.

Scenic floats leave every morning and afternoon from Colter Bay and Jackson Lake Lodge. Some Snake River float trips include picnic lunches or dinners at Deadman's Bar. Transportation is provided for the scenic 10.5-mile float. Colter Bay also runs four regularly scheduled scenic cruises of Jackson Lake daily. Its most popular cruise includes breakfast or dinner on Elk Island.

Signal Mountain Lodge
Teton Park Rd., Grand Teton National Park, WY
(307) 543-2831

Perched on the shore of Jackson Lake, Signal Mountain Lodge offers daily guided fishing trips. If you don't need a guide,

---

Insiders' Tip

The Big Springs National Water Trail is a 5-mile stretch of the Henry's Fork River that restricts fishing in order to protect the fishery downstream.

---

you can rent your own fishing boat here. Canoes and oar boats are available for $8 per hour; Signal Mountain also rents fishing skiffs with outboard motors. Signal Mountain Lodge also offers scenic trips on the Snake below Jackson Lake Dam. Reservations are suggested.

If you feel like a scenic cruise of the lake on your own, pontoon boats and deck cruisers can be held for groups of eight to ten people. Deck cruisers rent for $50 an hour or $225 for the day. Guest buoys and other services for boaters are available.

Teton Boating Company
S. Jenny Lake, Grand Teton National Park, WY
(307) 733-2703

This is the only company that rents motorized and non-motorized boats on Jenny Lake. Teton Boating also runs a regular ferry service across the clear waters of the lake to the western shore. Climbers and hikers appreciate the shorter trip to some of the area's more popular backcountry attractions such as Hidden Falls.

Triangle X—Osprey Float Trips
U.S. Hwy. 89, Grand Teton National Park, WY
(307) 733-5500, (307) 733-6455

It's hard to beat the choices offered by the Turner Brothers. You can opt for a sunrise, afternoon, or evening scenic float on the Snake in Grand Teton National Park. Some trips travel the 10 miles between Deadman's Bar and Moose, but trips as short as 5 miles are also an option, as are the extra-long, 20-mile floats. All trips are on Class I or II water. You can also arrange a dinner float and lodging at the Triangle X Ranch.

Jackson Hole

It is no secret that Jackson Hole has legendary skiing, but with so much attention focused on those darn Teton Mountains, sometimes the area's waterways are forgotten. By location alone, you should be able to guess that this region, just on the edge of Grand Teton National Park, is a fishing and boating paradise.

Wyoming fishing regulations apply throughout Jackson Hole. You can pick up regulations and other fishing information at the local office of the Wyoming Department of Game and Fish, 360 N. Cache Street, Jackson, Wyoming, (307) 733-2321.

Green River

About an hour's drive east of Jackson, the Green River meanders along the flats between the Windriver and Salt mountain ranges. Only a stone's throw from Jackson's summer crowds, the Green's wide oxbow turns and fast moving straights make this an off-the-beaten-path river. Most people put in at the Warren Bridge on U.S. Highway 191/189, 20 miles north of Pinedale.

Fishing

After the spring runoff, this river tends to clear about two weeks before other area fisheries. You can expect to catch Snake River cutthroat, brookies, browns, and rainbows. If you're a fly fisher, the Green is well known for its gray drake hatch in early July. You can float this river early in the season, but there is also plenty of shore access. On the north side of the highway, a Bureau of Land Management road runs along the river for about 10 miles and offers a dozen access points.

Floatboating

The wide stretches of the Green River are ideal for canoes and wooden fishing boats. You might want to leave that rodeo kayak strapped to the roof of your vehicle, however, since there is virtually no whitewater to be found on this river. But if you are in the mood for a scenic float, this is your river. With views of the Windrivers to the north and the smaller Salt Range to the south, you can't go wrong.

Hoback River

Hoback River runs rocky and shallow through 43 miles of sagebrush. It livens up a bit for boaters when its pace quickens in the canyon until it crashes into the Snake River at the bottom of Jackson Hole. U.S. Highway 191 runs parallel to this shallow stream and provides easy access. Otherwise, much of the river is bordered by private land. This fact keeps Hoback somewhat isolated compared to the bigger Jackson-area rivers.

Fishing

Although fishing is not as good here as on some of the more famous waters, the scenery more than makes up for it. If a little peace and quiet are what you yearn for, this is the river for you. This small, rocky stream is best fished from shore or by wading. You can fish all year on this water. Most people focus on the pockets of water in the lower section above the confluence with the Snake, where they find cutthroat and brookies.

Floatboating

This river is narrower and shallower than its cousin the Snake, but the boaters who frequent Hoback like the challenge. Akin to the Snake River's Alpine Canyon, the 12-mile stretch of water between the Granite Creek put in and the Hoback Junction take out is popular with kayakers and really brave whitewater canoeists. Although the rapids are a steady Class II and III (during spring runoff it's a solid Class III river), log jams add to the difficulty of this section of water. You can shorten or lengthen your trip by using lower put-in points or the lower take out at Astoria Hot Springs on the Snake.

Snake River in Alpine Canyon

This is no isolated river float. Alpine Canyon on the Snake River is the Jackson area's whitewater expressway. You'll see enough raftloads of tourists in this stretch of the Snake to fill several buses. Jackson, Wyoming, residents stop here after work to get a couple hours of hole riding and wave surfing in with their kayaks. It may be over used, but it is a fun spot with legendary rapids known as Lunch Counter and the Big Kahuna (in spring they can reach a Class IV rating).

Mostly you'll see rafts, whitewater canoes, and kayaks in this part of the river. It is an expert and intermediate waterway, so play it safe and study the water. The put in is called West Table, and the take out is Sheep Gulch.

Fishing and Boating Outfitters

Barker-Ewing Jackson Hole River Trips
45 W. Broadway, Jackson, WY
(307) 733-1000, (800) 448-4202

This company has a solid regional reputation as a fine outfitter. For scenic floats, Barker-Ewing guides will take you through the Snake River's South Park area. When it comes to whitewater, Alpine Canyon is a thrill a minute in a raft or whitewater canoe. The best is a combo scenic-whitewater trip combining these two stretches of the Snake.

High Country Flies
185 Center St., Jackson, WY
(307) 733-7210

Owner James Jones is a 20-year veteran fishing guide. His fly shop and guide service can take you floating down the Snake River near Jackson, the New Fork, and the Green River to the south. Or you can fish the famous waters in Yellowstone National Park. Jones can offer instruction and even arrange for casting, entomology, knot tying, and playing and releasing sessions with a fish on your line. Trips are catch and release only.

Jack Dennis Fishing Trips
50 E. Broadway Ave., Jackson, WY
(307) 733-3270

Jack Dennis Sports is home to one of the better-known fishing guide services in Jackson. The fishing celebrity opened his fly shop and guide service here in 1967. His guides can take you to the rivers and lakes of Yellowstone National Park, to the remote holes of the New Fork, the Green, and through the Upper Snake River. Through an Idaho outfitter, you can also book trips on eastern Idaho's South Fork of the Snake, famed for its native cutthroat fishing. Besides organizing the heralded one-fly trout derby, Dennis also offers seminars and fly-casting instruction.

Jackson Hole Whitewater
650 W. Broadway Ave., Jackson, WY
(307) 733-1007, (800) 548-2602

This raft company has been voted a local favorite again and again. The scenic/whitewater combination trip is popular. You'll meander along the upper Snake for a sleepy, but beautiful eight miles before reaching the legendary Alpine Canyon for a fast set of rapids. Along the float, guides will give you information on the area's geology, history, and wildlife, and they will make you lunch, too.

Lone Eagle Whitewater
U.S. Hwy. 89/191, near Hoback Junction, WY
(307) 733-1090, (800) 321-3800

Coupled with breakfast, lunch, or dinner, Lone Eagle tries to provide quality river trips by not overcrowding the boats. Running Alpine Canyon, they promise no more than eight to ten guests per raft. Scenic floats are also available. They put in at Wilson Bridge and float for about three hours. When you finish, the resort's hot tubs will be waiting for you.

Mad River Boat Trips
1255 S. U.S. Hwy. 89, Jackson, WY
(307) 733-6203, (800) 458-7238

If it makes you feel more comfortable, rental wetsuits are washed and dried after each use at Mad River Boat Trips—but

that's just one of the perks. They also offer a free tour of the Mad River's River Runners Museum, where you can learn about the roots of rafting. But the best thing after jamming down the rapids of Alpine Canyon is the lunch or barbecue dinner they'll serve you at the end of the line.

West Bank Anglers
3670 N. Moose-Wilson Rd., Teton Village, WY
(307) 733-6483

Outdoor clothing, reels, rods, flies, and waders won't necessarily make you a better angler, but you can still buy the stuff here. You can also arrange fishing adventures for nearby Flat Creek and the Upper Snake in Jackson Hole, the South Fork of the Snake, the Firehole, Gibbon, Madison, and Yellowstone Rivers, but not all in one day. Half-day, full-day, and overnight trips are available throughout the region.

Craft Rentals

Leisure Sports
1075 S. U.S. Hwy. 89, Jackson, WY
(307) 733-3040

If you feel like you can hit the lakes, rivers, and streams on your own but don't feel like lugging your gear, this is the all-purpose stop for you. During the summer, you can rent rafts between 12- and 18-feet long (around $90 per day). You can also rent Coleman canoes and inflatable kayaks.

Rent-A-Raft/Jackson Hole Outdoor Center
Lewis Landing, 10925 U.S. Hwy. 89, Hoback Junction, WY
(307) 733-2728

Rod Lewis has been in the river business for decades. Now from his riverside location he rents Achilles and Hyside rafts. Lewis's staff can also rent you a trailer or help you load your rented raft. They will

even shuttle you up to the Hoback or down to the Snake. Other services here include inner-tube, sit-on-top, and inflatable kayak rentals.

Teton Aquatic Supply/Snake River Kayak and Canoe School
155 W. Gill Ave., Jackson, WY
(307) 733-3127, (800) 529-2501

This is the kind of place where you can go crazy buying all the gear to start you kayaking or canoeing and take lessons at their paddling school. Even in winter you can practice your rolls and rowing technique in the indoor training pool. The 45,000-gallon pool is 12 feet deep, equipped to simulate a four–mile-an-hour current, and is a much more forgiving place to practice than the chilly rivers and lakes around Jackson.

Besides operating a paddling school and watersports shop, these folks rent canoes, inflatable kayaks, paddle and oar rafts, and sea kayaks. Rafts rent for about $50 a day. You can also rent a canoe for a half-day price of $20.

Southwestern Montana

Some of North America's most renowned fishing holes are here in Montana—the Yellowstone, Madison, and Gallatin Rivers and many secret spots in between. The list of blue ribbon fisheries is so long that we can't cover enough here to do it justice. One guarantee is that no matter what your ability or experience, there is good fishing to be found here.

Make no mistake, folks take their fishing seriously in these parts. The teeny town of Ennis is so identified with angling that as you enter you will see a larger-than-life bronze statue of a fisherman casting his line across the highway and a sign reading "Home of 640 people and 11 million trout." You might find enough fishers on the water to match the trout population one-to-one in the more popular areas like Ennis's Madison River and in Paradise Valley's stretch of the Yellowstone, but there are countless other stretches of water to explore. Any fly fishing shop can tell you about the hot spots and the more out-of-the-way spots as well, so use these places as resources.

But the fish aren't the only thing jumping out here. If you like to water ski, windsurf, and boat, read on to find out about Ennis, Dailey, and Hebgen Lakes and great paddling water, too. The good thing about southwestern Montana waters is that they are very accessible—you can be on any one of three different rivers within a 45-minute drive out of Bozeman. If you're visiting and need equipment, we've listed several sources for renting gear.

Ennis Lake

When locals say "Let's go to the beach!" they mean Ennis Lake. A short drive west of Bozeman, this lake covers about three square miles. It is a haven for water skiers and windsurfers from June through September. Formed in 1905 when Montana Power Company built a dam on the Madison River at the head of Bear Trap Canyon, the lake has slowly been getting shallower because of silt deposits from the river. The good thing about this is that it keeps the water warmer, a boon for recreationists. High winds sweep in from the Madison Valley and off the Spanish Peaks to create ideal windsurfing conditions on most afternoons. Spectators congregate at Sandy Beach, on the north side of the lake.

Most of the lake is surrounded by private property, but there is one primitive public campground on the west end and another one along the river's channels south of the lake. The area has enough room for about 10 sites and has a vault toilet with an informal boat launch at each site. The channel site, however, is used more as a take out since the shoreline downstream is entirely bordered by private homes. The private property aspect of Ennis Lake makes this more of a day-use area, but that doesn't mean you can't have fun.

Fishing

Fishers troll along the lake during summer months, but the high level of motorized traffic makes the fishing pretty slim. Your chances are better during winter months when ice fishing is popular. Look for rainbow and brown trout from the Madison River. Each spring after ice is out, thousands of trumpeter swans land on the lake and spend a few days here before flying on.

Powerboating

Near the mouth of the lake, on the north side, the Bureau of Land Management acquired Sandy beach, which has a vaulted toilet and informal camping. Also on this end you'll find the Lakeshore Lodge, (406) 682-4424, which offers a boat ramp and a marina for guests. They also rent small motorboats for fishing.

Hebgen Lake

Located just eight miles northwest of West Yellowstone, Hebgen offers some of the finest stillwater fishing in the state. That's what it's known for, but you'll also see water skiing, windsurfing, and sailing out here. Formed in 1915 by the construction of a Montana Power Company dam, Hebgen is 16 miles long, with 57 miles of shoreline, most of which is public land managed by the National Forest Service. This means there are very few private homes or services around the lake, and that makes it seem kind of remote.

You can reach the water via three Forest Service boat ramps at Lonesomehurst and Rainbow campgrounds and at an informal launch on the north shore. Four private resorts also have launch sites they'll let you use for a minimal fee.

Fishing

Big fish don't necessarily live in big name rivers. While the famous titles of the Madison, the Yellowstone, or the Bighorn Rivers draw the crowds, other top-notch Montana fisheries go practically unnoticed. Hebgen Lake is one of those.

"It's the best brown trout lake in Montana," says Dick Greene, outfitter and owner of Bud Lilly's Trout Shop in West Yellowstone.

Three "arms," the Madison, Grayling, and South Arm, supply the lake with water and offer excellent fishing areas. This is primarily a trout fishery supporting an abundant population of Eagle Lake rainbows and brown trout that average 16 to 17 inches. Greene says the biggest he's caught was a 23- to 24-inch brown.

Hebgen is open all year, but without a doubt the lake is renowned for its summer "gulpers." On any given day an angler might encounter pods of trout rising, eager to inhale mayflies and other prolific insects. Anglers tell stories of how the fish make an almost audible gulping sound as they grab the fly off the top of the water. But they also caution that gulper fishing is probably the most difficult because you have to figure out which direction the fish are swimming.

One of the most popular times of the year to fish Hebgen Lake is at ice out in late April or early May. The water temperature begins to rise after a long winter and the fish become more active. This is a fantastic time to strip streamers like the woolly buggers, kiwi muddlers and zonkers. Both browns and rainbows can be spotted cruising the shoreline for prey at this time.

Important hatches during the summer months include the tiny Trico, the larger Callibaetis mayfly, and the caddis. On a perfect day an angler could fish the Trico hatch early in the morning, catch the Callibaetis emergence at midday (the parachute Adams is an effective imitation) and finish off the day witnessing the explosive strikes of the caddis hatch. Though these hatches are fished best with a float-tube or a boat, shoreline anglers can still get in on the action.

When the weather begins to cool in the fall, Hebgen's resident browns grow restless and start congregating to make their annual spawning journey up the Madison River into Yellowstone National Park. It is then, from October to late November, that many die-hard streamer anglers try their hand at one of the lake's big browns. Fishing is tough at this time of year. Expect foul weather and long days while on the quest for a trophy. Fly selections at this time include egg-sucking leeches, large sculpin patterns, and other ostentatious streamers.

Floatboating

With so much public land encircling Hebgen Lake, there are ample opportunities to see undisturbed wildlife as you cruise along the shore in a sea kayak or canoe. The more sheltered areas of the Madison and Grayling arms are where the deer, elk, and moose hide, especially in the early morning or near dusk. At certain times of year you might spot black bear and all kinds of waterfowl, as well. In the afternoons, when hot winds usually kick up, sailboats and windsurfers speckle the lake from July through September.

Powerboating

On warm days powerboats, scenic cruisers, and houseboats zoom around the lake. There are three marinas on Hebgen's north shore: Kirkwood Ranch Motel at (406) 646-7200; Yellowstone Holiday Resort at (406) 646-4242, (800) 643-4227; and the Happy Hour Bar at (406) 646-7281. The Madison Arm Resort and Marina at (406) 646-9328 is on the south shore. Each rents slips, sells gas, and rents watercraft ranging from rowboats to speedboats and party pontoons.

Cliff and Wade Lakes

Take a hint from Mother Nature and follow her sharpest anglers—the bald eagle and osprey—up to the chill, glassy waters of Cliff and Wade Lakes in the Beaverhead/Deerlodge National Forest. Nestled in cool mountain slopes at 6,400 feet, these icy sister lakes are a well-guarded treasure. Located a mere 18 miles northwest of Hebgen Lake, Cliff and Wade are serene, spring-fed lakes with a no wake speed limit and secretive fish. But more than that, these jewel-colored pools offer amazing scenery and fun camping spots near the water.

Although the lakes are busy with campers over national holidays, the rest of the time they are almost untouched. Cliff and Wade Lakes are accessible from May 15 through November 1 for most of us. The die-hard angler, however, can make the five-mile trek on snow shoes or skinny skis to a cast a solitary line into a hole on pristine Wade Lake in deep winter months.

Fishing

Wade Lake is the best of the two and the kind of spot that the regulars don't tell just anyone about. The state record for the largest brown trout was caught here and still stands since it was set in 1966: a 29-pound Loch Laven brown. The wild rainbow and Eagle Lake trout found here grow fat off year-round hatches in good weed cover.

"The water clarity is the greatest challenge," says Dave Schmidt, owner of Wade Lake Lodge and fly shop. "The key to catching them during the day is to fish with really long, thin leaders."

With the spring filling Wade at a steady 51 degrees, the Callibaetis and blue dun hatch early and continue through September. Unrivaled hopper fishing starts up in July and August. Bring the pheasant tail nymphs, sheep creeks, and dragonfly nymph imitations along. With its constant clear water, Wade is almost always fishable.

Cliff Lake is larger at 750 acres, but also deeper and not quite as fishable. Here the rainbows, browns, and sparse cutthroat are smaller due to a harsher habitat.

Floatboating

The no-wake rule on these tiny mountain lakes make for peaceful boating. The lakes are deep and not very big, but the sheer pristine atmosphere makes it a relaxing place to paddle a canoe or kayak. Since most of the camping sites lie on the north and south shores of Wade and the north shore of Cliff, you can paddle to uninhabited sides for a quiet picnic lunch.

Madison River

From the border of Yellowstone National Park to the confluence with the Jefferson and Gallatin Rivers at Three Forks, the Madison River covers over 100 miles. The river flows through a wide valley coming out of the park, through ranchlands, and through a canyon with mountain ranges rising up on either side. It is a fly fishing paradise, usually packed with guided boat trips from mid-June through September. The stretch between Ennis and Three Forks is the most popular, and along these banks you might see moose or even some black bear during certain times of the year.

The best access points for this river are Quake Lake, Hebgen Lake, Slide Inn, Lyons Bridge, McAtee Bridge, and Varney Bridge, along with a host of other public accesses. U.S. Highway 287 parallels the river from Yellowstone to 40 miles past Ennis.

Fishing

There is arguably no western river more popular or more famous than the Madison, according to expert fishing guides around here. The big river supports an amazing number of trout and an even more amazing number of trout fishers. The Madison River has a variety of characteristics and water types, insect hatches, and moods. You could fish any one-mile section of the river for a year and still not know it fully.

Unlike many other productive trout fisheries, the Madison lacks many of the usual trout haunts, including the deep pool. There just aren't many deep pools or much still-water on the rushing Madison River. The banks aren't cluttered with roots, rocks, or moss. Still, the angler needs to look for any slower water available, any current seams, behind and in front of boulders, in the back eddies, against the banks, and in the braided channels, and in the riffles. Many local anglers believe the riffles are the only type of water on the river.

This sweet, shallow river has good, solid hatches of mayfly and caddis throughout the year, and excellent dry fly fishing after runoff. The most famous (read: most crowded) time of year to fish a hatch is in late June and early July as anglers chase the salmonfly hatch. If you catch the hatch—many locals have tried and failed for years—then it is indeed an experience to last a lifetime. The salmonfly are as long as your index finger and clumsy. They sputter along in the air, then splash into the stream, when one, maybe two, trout streak from their hidden lies to grab the insect with a heartstopping slash.

They do the same for size 2 Sofa Pillows, and they cause the same cardiac arrest. To imitate these large insects, any number of dressings will suffice, including the Sofa Pillow, Stimulator, Bird's Orange, McSalmonfly, and Madam X, but check in with the local fly shops for their creations to imitate the salmon fly. Some of the best fishing on the Madison is in the spring and fall when the crowds clear.

Nevertheless, the river has faced some tough times the last two years. Whirling disease has robbed the great river of several classes of rainbow trout. In one stretch, the Madison River lost about 95 percent of its rainbow trout population. Whether or not the Madison recovers from this problem is anybody's guess. Whether or not whirling disease affects the length of the Madison is unknown. There are no known cures for this malady. Most of the river has been affected and it might recover quickly.

The trout in this mighty stream are plentiful and often finicky, sometimes requiring match-the-hatch angling from an increasingly sophisticated fishing crowd. But part of the charm of the river is that it is many things to many people. For trout cover, the Madison has pocket water, riffles, eddies, undercut banks, boulders, underwater structure, side channels, braids, beaver ponds, and more. Typically, the river has movement and is rarely slow, meaning that these fish have lots of well-oxygenated water and resulting energy. Don't be surprised when these trout take enough line off the reel to go into the backing and cause your palms to sweat. The average size trout here is somewhere between 13 to 17 inches, probably closer to 13. Many go over 17 inches, and there are some large fish in the river. There are some biggies in this river, but if you nab a rainbow it is catch and release only. You can keep two brown trout less than 13 inches.

Waders should be prepared for the constant pressure exerted on their legs from the heavy current. It pays to be on your toes when wading the river, as some places can be either slippery or tricky. You can wade between high water marks of the stream, but cannot trespass on private land above the line, nor gain access to the river by crossing private land. From Reynolds Pass Bridge to Varney Bridge, there is a catch-and-release, artificial-flies-and-lures-only regulation. There are other regulations along the river on a smaller scale, so check the rulebook from the Montana Fish and Game Department.

Floatboating

Mostly what you'll see on the Madison are wooden fishing boats and recreational rafters. The river is floatable, except for the stretch below Slide Inn all the way to Lyon Bridge and from Ennis Bridge to Ennis Lake where no boats are allowed, only wading anglers. One of the most popular float areas is below the confluence of the West Fork of the Madison. The sight of drift boats and rafts queuing up in the morning at launches is mildly comical with so many people milling around, but this is a big river and can handle all its fans.

Beartrap Canyon below Ennis Lake is an undiscovered treat. This stretch of the Madison is filled with treacherous rapids, deep pools, and followed by slower water. On the slow parts you can enjoy the coolness of the steep canyon walls. The water isn't deep enough for sporty kayakers, but it is perfect for a fun and scenic river run in a whitewater canoe.

Gallatin River

Even if the Gallatin River wasn't ranked a blue ribbon fishing stream, it would be rewarding just to walk along its stony banks, wade waist-deep into a slow green eddy or float on its steady currents. The fact that this river parallels U.S. Highway 191 doesn't even take away from its beauty; in fact it makes the Gallatin very accessible for fishing, boating, and camping.

Fishing

Parts of Robert Redford's movie *A River Runs Through It* were filmed on this river and when you experience the way the sun filters through the trees onto the rippling, swirling, glistening water through Gallatin Canyon, you'll understand why.

But fishing the Gallatin is not all Hollywood glam and glimmer—it's the real thing. Generally this is a wader's stream, although you need to be wary of deep holes and fast currents. Some of the holes here are very tricky and can be reached best if you are casting from the shore.

Just barely over the boundary into Yellowstone you will find the Gallatin braids into a series of channels flowing through a wide, green meadow. (We've never been through this area without spotting a moose here). The fishing in these channels is for light-weight rods only, and if your touch is just right you might catch a pretty little cutthroat. Just outside the park is the confluence of Taylor Creek, which largely dictates downstream fishing conditions, based on whether it is running clear or muddy. You'll find rainbow, brown, and hatchery grayling from the Taylor Creek all the way through Gallatin Valley until the Gallatin joins with the Madison and Jefferson rivers outside of Three Forks.

In Montana the Gallatin is fishable year-round, but the park closes for the winter. You must release grayling, but you can keep up to five trout, with one longer than 18 inches allowed. In Yellowstone it's catch and release for cutthroat, with a two-fish limit on rainbows and browns.

Floatboating

Whether you are looking for wild rapids or a relaxing float, the Gallatin has it. The legendary stretch of whitewater frequented by a half-dozen local rafting guides and groups of kayakers is House Rock and the subsequent field of rocks following it. But from the put-in at Moose Flats you'll find plenty of medium-sized rapids to frolic in as well. This 13-mile stretch of water is scenic and fun. Although the rapids rank between Class II and IV, by mid-summer there are some slow sections where you can take quick plunges off the side of your boat to cool off. Most people take-out at Squaw Creek about two miles after House Rock. If you don't want to go through House Rock, then you will want to take-out just before the 35 mile an hour bridge (as Insiders call it because the speed limit is posted right on the bridge), or you'll get pulled right into fast water.

Yellowstone River

The venerable Yellowstone is a river that has always gotten good press. It became legendary as the thoroughfare of the Lewis and Clark Expedition. Both of Robert Redford's movies *A River Runs Through It* and *The Horse Whisperer* filmed scenes along this stream, but most of its fame comes from being the largest undammed river in the Lower 48 states. For the many ranchers and farmers who live along its banks, the Yellowstone is a lifesource for their businesses.

From its source in the high mountains of Wyoming through Yellowstone National Park, into Yellowstone Lake, over the Grand Canyon of the Yellowstone, into the serene Paradise Valley of Montana, and finally out onto the prairie past Billings, this river crosses some of our country's most rugged terrain. Its 678-mile course is wide, long, and swift up to where it finally merges with the Missouri River in North Dakota.

Fishing

The Yellowstone River is the most popular river in Yellowstone National Park for fishing. There is some exquisite angling within the park, particularly above Fishing Bridge. Those 16- to 24-inch cutthroats are only available from July until October, while the rest of the Yellowstone is open year round. The 30-mile stretch of water from Paradise Valley through Livingston and on to Sheep Mountain is famous for sport and scenery.

Because of the distance between access points, most anglers float this section and do the majority of their fishing from a boat, occasionally getting out to cover areas where islands divide the river and create more interesting water. Some high banks near Mallard's Rest access house deep pools that hold plenty of fish, particularly cutthroat. There are a few creeks that dump into the river, and their mouths provide attractive areas to find fish: Big Creek, Dry Creek, Six Mile Creek, Fridley Creek, and Mill Creek all flow into the river.

You should be careful in one area along this stretch of the river. About midway into the float, there is an area that has some underwater hazards, but they are clearly marked with a sign. Also, look for an irrigation ditch off the river on the left side: it resembles a channel, and some anglers have mistakenly floated down this ditch, only to be surprised by a small dam, which can put a damper on a day's floating. Otherwise, there is no water that can be considered difficult or dangerous in this section, and any type of craft, from canoes to drift boats, will have no trouble navigating it.

Floatboating

Outside the park the Yellowstone River becomes a very tame, snaking stream. But for rafters, canoeists, and kayakers the rapids in Yankee Jim Canyon will get your heart pounding. During spring run-off you could meet up with a six-foot standing wave in the canyon. Most boaters do their best to skirt around it. To get in on the whitewater, most people put in at Gardiner's Queen of the Waters access and float the 16-mile stretch to Carbella access. This Class III section is frequented by a lot of river outfitters.

From Carbella on through Livingston the river flattens out and is a popular scenic float. With the stately Absaroka Mountains sweeping into the flats of Paradise Valley, you'll see why. On a clear day you can see the far-off Crazy Mountains to the north. Keep your binoculars out along this float for bald eagles who like to nest in the high cottonwoods lining the Yellowstone, and it's almost a guarantee you'll see deer on the shore among the willows.

Quite a few working kayakers put in after work at the Ninth Street Bridge and skim down about a half mile to a sweet set of rapids to play before the take out downstream at Mayor's Landing. But if you are boating upriver, locals warn about the currents around Carter's Bridge just before Livingston. Because the river hits the bridge at an angle, kayakers and canoeists can be pulled into the bridge supports. Navigating this stretch of river is for experienced paddlers only.

Fishing Outfitters

The great thing about fishing is that it is something that can be a family affair or a solitary pursuit. With the number of fishing outfitters located in southwestern Montana, you should have no problem finding someone to set you up for your first angling experience or to fine-tune your life-long love. During peak fishing months (July through September) guides are booked up months in advance. Make the best of your time out here and contact an outfitter ahead of time to make a reservation for your trip. The rates quoted here for each listing are from 2001 and include guide service, transportation, lunch, and beverages for the day. Also, in case you didn't realize it, tipping your fishing guide is standard. According to area guides, they average between $40 to $100 a day per person.

West Yellowstone, Montana

Bud Lilly's Trout Shop
39 Madison Ave., West Yellowstone, MT
(406) 646-7801, (800) 854-9559

Bud Lilly no longer owns this little shop, but the new owners are pretty effective at maintaining his household name and reputation in the fishing and guiding arena. If you don't want to lug your own gear, your guide will be able to provide you with all the essentials plus the extras for your trip. You can choose from eight knowledgeable, full-time guides who can direct you through regional fisheries from waters inside Yellowstone to equally famous rivers outside the park. Float trips cost $310 per person, while a walk-and-wade daytrip costs $265 for one person and less for groups. Bud Lilly's is open all year long.

Livingston, Montana

George Anderson's Yellowstone Angler
U.S. Hwy. 89 S., Livingston, MT
(406) 222-7130

World-famous fly fisherman George Anderson could be your trusty guide if you plan to drop in at the Yellowstone Angler. Anderson grew up fishing and his passion for the sport grew into his profession. He has fished all over the globe and is best known as the personality for ESPN's "Fishing the World" program. He and his five full-time guides love to share their expertise with other fishers, but Anderson is a real showman with a fish story for every occasion. His shop is located just south of Livingston and is a full-service store. Yellowstone Angler guides have exceptional expertise in their home waters on Paradise Valley's Yellowstone River and spring creeks, but they also travel as far as the Big Horn River and offer equal knowledge in other area streams. A one-day wading trip for one person costs $285; two people $315; three people $445. A float trips for one person is $300; two people $330; three people

$465. There may also be additional rod fees on private lakes or creeks.

Gardiner, Montana

Parks' Fly Shop
U.S. Hwy. 89 S., Gardiner, MT
(406) 848-7314

This landmark local shop has been around since the 1950s. Owner/guide Richard Parks took over the business from his father. Parks is a Yellowstone National Park fishing expert—he knows every riffle, hole, and hatch on park waters. He'll take you to other areas, too, of course and guides on all the big rivers. He does much of the guiding himself, but also works with independent outfitters. A float trip or walk/wade trip starts at $295 for two people, $40 for a third person.

Bozeman, Montana

The Bozeman Angler
23 E. Main St., Bozeman, MT
(406) 587-9111, (800) 886-9111

New owners Rod and Pam King have a marriage bound by fish, water, and traveling all over the world in search of both. The couple recently purchased this downtown retail shop and run guided fishing trips primarily on the big local streams: the Gallatin, Madison, Yellowstone, and the Missouri. They offer fishing classes throughout the year, with topics ranging from a women-only fishing clinic to the entomology of Montana streams. Their standard day float, walk/wade, or float tube trips (includes tube and fins) for one or two anglers begins at $300 per day, depending on what river you choose. Add $75 for each additional person. Bozeman Angler also offers an overnight horsepack trip in Yellowstone.

Big Sky, Montana

Gallatin Riverguides
U.S. Hwy. 191, Big Sky, MT
(406) 995-2290

Owners Steve and Betsy French opened their fly shop here in 1981. They offer affordable casting clinics at their 2-acre pond behind the shop. The pond is set up with a casting platform and target rings, not to mention some hefty rainbows. They employ eight guides, almost all of whom have at least five years of experience fishing southwestern Montana's waters.

Fishing the Madison and Gallatin Rivers, as well as Yellowstone National Park, they also do overnight trips on the Beaverhead and Missouri Rivers. A day of guided walk-and-wade fishing costs $275 for two people. A float trip costs $300 for two people.

Floatboat Outfitters

Adventures Big Sky
U.S. Hwy. 191 at the Big Sky Resort
entrance, Big Sky, MT
(406) 995-2324

Barbara and Patrick Dillon offer full or half-day trips on flatwater and whitewater along the Gallatin River. You can take the river in a paddleboat, inflatable kayak, or with a group in a big rubber raft. Either way, you'll work up an appetite, and full-day trips include lunch, so you're in luck.

Geyser Whitewater Expeditions
47200 Gallatin Rd., Gallatin Gateway, MT
(406) 995-4989, (800) 914-9031

Located on U.S. Highway 191, just south of the Big Sky turnoff, Geyser Whitewater Expeditions may be the only river runner to offer horseback riding combination rafting trips. It's a great way to see Gallatin Canyon off the beaten path. They also run half and full-day river trips on the Gallatin River.

Montana Whitewater
U.S. Hwy. 191, Gallatin Gateway, MT
(406) 763-4465, (800) 799-4465

Bill Zell and his fun-loving group of guides may seem a little crazy at first glance, but they are solid whitewater experts. They run half- and full-day white-water and scenic floats on the upper and lower Gallatin River. They also offer trips on the Yellowstone River.

Wild West Rafting
Yellowstone Outpost Mini Mall
(Headwaters Angler), U.S. Hwy. 89, Gardiner, MT
(406) 848-7110, (800) 862-0557

Wild West Rafting caters to family river trips. Their experienced guides will lead you down the Yellowstone River through gentle or rough water and in some cases, a little of each. They also offer horseback riding packages.

Yellowstone Raft Company
406 Scott St., Gardiner, MT
(406) 848-7777, (800) 858-7781
10043 U.S. Hwy. 191, Big Sky, MT
(406) 995-4613, (800) 348-4376

In business since 1978, Yellowstone Raft Company has two locations in Big Sky and Gardiner. This makes it easy for them to offer full- and half-day trips down both the Gallatin and Yellowstone Rivers. They also have a wonderfully scenic trip down the Madison with a little whitewater thrill as you go through Beartrap Canyon. Ask about their guided fishing trips, too.

Floatboat Rentals

Northern Lights Trading Company
1716 W. Babcock, Bozeman, MT
(406) 586-2225

Not only is this the place to rent rafts, canoes, kayaks, and wind surfing boards, but this is Bozeman's all-around outdoor outlet. With the oldest outdoor store in town, owner Mike Garcia can tell you how he has watched the recreation scene in southwest Montana blossom. You'll pay $20 to $40 per day for a touring kayak and around $35 for a canoe. There are discounts for multi-day rentals. For rafts, rates range between $100 to $200 per day. You must leave your credit card for a deposit; in the event that the raft is lost or damaged you may be charged between $1,000 to $4,000. When you return to the shop with the raft intact, they return your card uncharged. Northern Lights also rents watersports accessories, such as paddles, wetsuits, dry bags, life preservers, and helmets. This is also a great place to find used equipment listed on their ad board in the entryway.

Paradise Mercantile
U.S. Hwy. 89, Emigrant, MT
(406) 333-4060

Located right next door to the Emigrant General Store, the Mercantile rents Avon six-man rafts for $50 a day or $250 per week. These rafts come with paddles, life jackets, and foot pumps. They are made for scenic float trips, not whitewater.

Rubber Ducky River Services
Mount Baldy and South Park St.
Livingston, MT
(406) 222-3746

This little rental shop is easy to miss, behind the railroad tracks across Livingston's main thoroughfare. They rent inflatable kayaks and sit-on-top kayaks for $20 per day. In August they offer free boating on the lagoon in Sacajawea Park during the annual Summer Fest celebration.

Eastern Idaho

With so much hype focused on the area of Sun Valley, this little corner of Idaho doesn't get the attention it deserves. But seasoned fishers and boaters daydream about the kind of water in the Targhee National Forest on the border of Montana and Yellowstone National Park.

Quiet, lazy rivers, raging rapids, serene lakes, or a fun-filled day of water skiing— that's the Targhee. Fishing is very popular here and requires a state license. The Island Park area is world renowned for its excellent stream and lake fly fishing opportunities. Other parts of the Forest can provide more solitude and similar successes. Game fish include rainbow, eastern brook, brown, and cutthroat trout, kokanee salmon, and whitefish. Rafting, kayaking, and canoeing are popular sports in the Island Park Ranger District on the North Fork of the Snake River.

For anglers, it's a good idea to hire a fishing guide to help you enjoy your time in the area. There are enough nuances to fishing here to make it challenging even for experts. If you don't opt for guided fishing trips, get the skinny on area conditions at the fly shop where you purchase your license. You can also call Idaho Fish and Game Department at (208) 525-7290, or check out the other contacts listed in the Resource chapter. Boaters and paddlers should be aware of unique conditions resulting from dams and irrigation systems on regional waterways.

Henry's Fork

The Henry's Fork of the Snake River is one of the most highly regarded streams in the nation for trout fishing and wildlife watching. Though silting, logging, cattle grazing, and the construction of dams has troubled this area in the past, Henry's Fork has shown an uncommon resilience. It winds across the Island Park Caldera at a slow, steady pace, casting a golden light across the otherwise plain landscape. Cornered by two reservoirs, it rages through Cadillac Canyon before coasting another 100 miles downstream to join the South Fork of the Snake River. Together they form the Snake River and meander through Teton Basin in shallow but swift Class I or II waters.

Fishing

You'll see the big, fighting rainbows of the Henry's Fork jumping out of the stream before you even have a chance to wet your line. That's what this river is known for, along with lots of brown trout, a few brookies, cutthroat, and cutt-bows (the combination hybrid rainbow-cutthroat), as well as several species of salmon. The fish are abundant but hard to catch because the Henry's Fork is both shallow and narrow.

Winding and riffling its way through the Island Park Caldera, access to this famous river is good for the sections outside of canyons where wading, bank, and drift-boat fishing are popular. There are many fishing accesses along the water, since Big Springs Road/Idaho Highway 47 and U.S. Highway 20 run along much of its length.

Fishing regulations are complex and strict on the Henry's Fork, since it sees such high use by recreationists and agriculture. For instance, Box Canyon to Riverside Campground is catch and release only, Big Springs National Waterway allows no fishing, and Harriman State Park is fly fishing only. Check the regulations at a ranger station (the numbers are listed in our Resource chapter) before you set out on the water.

Floatboating

The clear water and mild temperatures along this narrow waterway aren't just for fish. Rafting, kayaking, and canoeing are popular sports in the Island Park Ranger District on the North Fork of the Snake River. This river offers challenges for paddlers with intermediate skills. Put in at Island Park dam; take out at Last Chance. Dams, large falls, and irrigation canals present hazards along stretches of the river, so paddle with care.

Put in is at Last Chance for paddlers with advanced skills, take out at Hatchery Ford. Another put in is at Grandview Campground, with a take out at Warm River. This section demands "advanced plus" skills, a large raft, and the launch is described as "poor." Find out about other access areas from the Ashton, St. Anthony, or Island Park Ranger Stations. (The numbers are listed in our Resources chapter.)

Henry's Fork, Big Springs Water Trail

This National Scenic Water Trail was the first one established by the Forest Service. From the cool, clean source of Big Spring, this water tumbles over smooth-washed pebbles for a five-mile stretch of unhampered aquatic wilderness. It's a fine scenic float for beginners and offers a great opportunity to view wildlife. You're likely to see bald eagles, osprey, and kingfishers all diving and vying for fish as long as your arm.

To protect the health of this mini-ecosystem, fishing is not allowed on the Big Springs Water Trail, so the only way to catch a fish is by taking a picture (don't worry, you'll get so close to some fish that you won't even need a zoom lens.) Expect to spend about four hours on this stretch of water if you just plan to float with the current. The route is easy to navigate. Put in at the sign on Big Springs Road/Idaho Highway 84 and the take out at Mack's Inn.

Henry's Lake

In the shadow of the Targhee, Centennial, and Gravelly ranges, Henry's Lake stays relatively cold all year, but that doesn't take away from its beauty or its popularity with anglers and wildlife. You can watch bald eagles soar above this tempestuous mountain lake. At its narrowest, the lake is two miles wide, but it expands to four miles wide and stretches five miles in length. Although it is a natural lake, it was expanded by a dam and is known for sudden winds that cause high waves.

Fishing

Henry's Lake is an angler's paradise and a haven for trophy-sized trout. Mostly it's the cutthroat (both wild and stocked) that break the records, but you can also look for rainbow, cutt-bow (the rainbow-cutthroat hybrid), and brook trout. You'll find the cutthroat near the shoreline in the shallows, which most people cast for from a boat or float tube. Since most of the lake is surrounded by private land, there isn't much access to shore fishing. In August the lake's tributaries open to fishing, except for Hatchery Creek.

The limit is two fish and you must stop fishing once you catch your limit. You can fish Henry's Lake from Memorial Day to October 31.

Floatboating and Powerboating

Unpredictable winds and cold temperatures keep most paddlers off Henry's Lake. For the same reason, most powerboats, sailboats, and personalized watercraft avoid this lake as well. In fact, Henry's Lake is pretty much for anglers in motorized boats. Everyone else gravitates to nearby Island Park Reservoir (listed below).

Island Park Reservoir

Of the two large lakes in this area, 8,400-acre Island Park Reservoir is the powerboater's hang out. Its twin, Henry's Lake, draws more anglers because of its cold, often choppy waters. Neither lake attracts many rafts, canoes, or kayaks since maneuvering across and around these large bodies of water is a lot of work. But camping, picnicking, and hiking are all accessible around Island Park Reservoir's heavily forested shores. Anglers catch brook, cutthroat, and rainbow trout, as well as coho and kokanee salmon. There are only two boat ramps on the lake.

Fishing Outfitters

Henry's Fork Anglers
Last Chance in Island Park, ID
(208) 558-7525

Mike Lawson was born in this area and has fished here his whole life. If that's not enough to make him an expert, then maybe you'll be encouraged knowing he writes for fly fishing magazines and presents lectures on the sport during the off season. But when rainbows are biting on the Henry's Fork, he'll be fishing. Mike and his guides also offer trips on the Madison, Firehole, Gibbon, Yellowstone, and Gallatin Rivers in Yellowstone National Park, as well as on Island Park

Reservoir. A full-service fly shop is on the premises.

Hyde Outfitters Inc.
3408 N. U.S. Hwy. 20, Last Chance in Island Park, ID
(208) 558-7068

Local guides and outfitters will take you out in a locally built Hyde drift boat.

Hyde Outfitters offer day trips from the South Fork of the Snake, the Henry's Fork, Teton River, Henry's Lake, Palisades, and Island Park Reservoir all the way into Yellowstone National Park. Your base price includes the guide, lunch, a Hyde drift boat, and transportation. Hyde's has a complete fly shop.

Watercraft Rentals

Mack's Inn Resort
U.S. Hwy. 20, at Mack's Inn in Island Park, ID
(208) 558-7672, (208) 558-7272 (Henry's Fork Landing)

This is the place to come to rent rafts and canoes to float the tranquil Big Springs Water Trail. For $25 to $50 you'll get a boat, life jackets, and a ride to the put in. Reservations are a good idea. Mack's Inn is at the junction of the Henry's Fork and U.S. Highway 20 (you can't miss it). It also rents watercraft by the hour for paddling around the immediate vicinity.

Northwestern Wyoming

The rivers and lakes near Cody in northwestern Wyoming may not get the same press as other regions, but that doesn't mean there isn't an abundance of water to explore here. The fishing here is good, the water is clean, the rivers are swift and scenic, but what else would you expect so close to Yellowstone National Park? Although we've listed only one lake here, there are many in the area. Ask at a local fly fishing shop for more details.

North Fork of the Shoshone

President Teddy Roosevelt called this slice of Wyoming the most scenic 50 miles in the U.S., but he wasn't the first to discover it. Buffalo Bill Cody himself used the area for his early Yellowstone National Park tours and before him, explorer John Colter traveled down this river. With its red rock spires standing sentinel over a steadfast stretch of wild river, it's no wonder the North Fork of the Shoshone has carved its way into western history. U.S. Highway 20 parallels the river for 40 miles between Pahaska Teepee and Buffalo Bill Reservoir.

Fishing

When hungry bears roust from hibernation in the spring, they know where to go for fine fishing—the North Fork of the Shoshone. If that isn't proof that there are fish in this stream, then nothing is. The North Fork is easily accessed and holds good-size Yellowstone cutthroat, rainbow, browns, and brookies. Because so many small tributaries run into the North Fork, you have the chance to fish several different streams. The Grinell, Clearwater, Sweetwater, Elk Fork, and Eagle Creeks all offer good fishing.

The North Fork is not a big river, but it is deep. One of the deepest areas on the river is below the reservoir, although it's hard to access. The limit here is three fish with only one bigger than 20 inches.

Floatboating

This narrow river is wrought with log jams, frequent downfalls, and surprise drops. It's an experts-only kind of river and even they only run the upper stretches. Spring runoff raises water levels to Class V on some rapids and then quickly down to Class III and IV later in the year. The North Fork is frequented by local commercial raft companies, which guide clients down the 12-mile stretch from Rimrock Ranch to just below the Buffalo Bill Reservoir. Early in the season is the time to take this trip; otherwise the water mellows out late in the summer.

Shoshone River

You can count nine rapids on the Shoshone River from Demaris Hot Springs to Corbetts Crossing. That's what makes this route a commercial rafting mainstay from early spring until late summer. But the truth is, this stream is used more for irrigating Bighorn Basin than for recreation. Sure, some daring kayakers put in just below Buffalo Bill Dam and traverse the hairy rapids for the next four miles, but for the most part everyone else stays on the tamer stretch of river downstream. It's those 11 miles of water that bring visitors and local boaters out to enjoy Class III waters for the season.

There is no real fishing of note on this river, although there are cutthroats, rainbows, and browns in there somewhere. The river's many small diversion dams (used for irrigation) don't bode well for fish.

Clarks Fork of the Yellowstone River

From high in the Beartooth Mountains, the Clarks Fork carves its way down through Sunlight Basin along a route used by Chief Joseph when his Nez Perce band fled from U.S. troops in 1878. That's just the recent history of this river. Along its scenic 140-mile route, it traverses through some of the world's oldest mountains down into Wyoming and back up into Montana. You can see the Clarks Fork from the Chief Joseph Scenic Highway between Colter Pass to Crandall Creek.

Fishing

The Clarks Fork of the Yellowstone isn't that easy to get to and perhaps that's just what makes fishing here so satisfying. You won't see droves of other anglers lining up at access areas. You may not see another person fishing here for the whole day you're on the water. From the Montana-Wyoming state line to Crandall Creek you'll find a 16-mile stretch of water winding through a high mountain forested valley. Most of the fish here are cutthroat, but you'll also see brown, rainbow, and good-sized brookies. The upper Clarks Fork has mostly rainbow, with a few brook trout and browns; the lower area has about the same, but with a few grayling as well. Fishing regulations vary greatly depending on what part of the river you plan to fish. Check with the Wyoming Game and Fish Department or local fishing shops for details.

Floatboating

There is one five-mile stretch of challenging water on the Clarks Fork through one of Wyoming's most beautiful canyons. But the going is hard and for expert paddlers only because of a treacherous Class V rapid at the end of the canyon. A few local rafters and kayakers brave this stretch of water. The rest of us head for the breathtaking views on the next 12 miles of water where the Red Rock River joins the Clarks Fork. From here you can cruise at an easy pace with views of the Beartooth Mountains and imagine yourself as an early explorer to this spectacular land.

Buffalo Bill Dam Reservoir

Feeding water onto the once-dry lands of Bighorn Basin, the Buffalo Bill Reservoir plays an important role in northwestern Wyoming. Unfortunately the frigid waters and high winds on this lake keep most everyone away except anglers and windsurfers. In fact, in the 1980s Buffalo Bill Reservoir made it on *Outside Magazine's* top 10 list of national windsurfing lakes. A hearty core of windsurfers put the place on the map and decided to share it with the world by organizing a three-day national windsurfing event. And for the first time in anyone's memory the wind did not blow on this lake tucked into the pretty North Fork Canyon. And so the story goes that Buffalo Bill Reservoir remains the best kept windsurfing secret in Wyoming.

Fishing

This is a lake that can be all things to all different kinds of anglers, from trolling with bait to matching the hatch for fly fishers. Either way, you'll be fishing for some seriously big lake trout, rainbows, browns, and cutthroat. The legendary lake trout have been found up to 30 pounds, the rainbows as high as 12 pounds, while the browns and cut-throats average around 6 pounds. Chinook winds make for poor ice fishing conditions here in winter, causing unevenly frozen or "rotten ice."

Fishing Outfitters

North Fork Anglers
1107 Sheridan Ave., Cody, WY
(307) 587-7274

Operating out of its store on Cody's main thoroughfare, North Fork Anglers not only has a full-service fly shop with hand-tied flies customized for the area, but also offers a range of guided fishing trips in and out of Yellowstone National Park. In tune with fishing conditions, Tim Wade and his guides weigh your needs and capabilities with area conditions to personalize your experience on area fisheries.

In addition to a week-long horsepack trips combined with fishing in summer and fall, Wade also offers trips in Yellowstone National Park, the Shoshone National Forest, the North Fork of the Shoshone, and the Clarks Fork.

Floatboat Outfitters

Red Canyon River Trips
1374 Sheridan Ave., Cody, WY
(307) 587-6988, (800) 293-0148

Red Canyon River Trips is the only local rafting company to offer guided trips down the Clarks Fork of the Yellowstone River and that's something you won't want to miss. The views and history down this 12-mile stretch of water are unbeatable. But RCRT also runs three other river trips, one in a "Duckie" (a.k.a. inflatable kayak) down the Shoshone River. They bill this as a trip for the more adventurous traveler, in which you float the river solo accompanied by an experienced guide in his own Duckie. All trips depart daily and cost between $20 to $50 for adults, while children 12 and under pay $18.

Wyoming River Trips
233 Yellowstone Hwy., Cody, WY
(307) 587-6661, (800) 586-6661

For 22 years Rick and Ron Blanchard have been guiding family rafting trips on the rivers around Cody. They offer five different raft and kayak trips during the season. Four of them, including an inflatable kayak trip, are on the Shoshone River. The fifth is on the North Fork of the Shoshone. Clients return year after year to float with Wyoming River Trips. They pride themselves on experienced guides who enjoy sharing the freedom of wild rivers with visitors. You can find them in two locations: The Holiday Inn complex on Sheridan Avenue and on the Yellowstone Highway west of Cody. Most trips cost between $20 and $50 per person, between $18 to $24 for children under 13.

The tram at Big Sky Resort whisks skiers to the summit of 11,166-foot Lone Mountain. PHOTO: BIG SKY RESORT

Winter Sports

After the hustle and bustle of the summer season is over, a chill starts to set in around the Yellowstone region, which can mean only one thing: Winter is in the air, and snow is on the way. And from November to April, that's all people seem to talk about. You'll hear it in the coffee shops, on the radio, and read about it in the local newspapers. Though it both elates folks and irritates them, the subject of snow won't go away. After all, it's winter in Yellowstone Country, and winter here revolves around snow.

For adventure seekers, this means downhill and cross-country skiing, snowmobiling and snowboarding, and dogsled and sleigh rides. For others it means relaxing in a thermal hot pool in the middle of the woods or simply soaking in the hot tub while the kids are busy skiing. Either way, there is plenty to do when the cold sets in and the flakes are falling.

Winter is perhaps the most beautiful time of the year around here. Snow-capped mountains stand perched against bright blue skies. The cold air turns rivers into frozen landscapes. Elk and moose come down from the high country and frolic in the valleys. Snowbank-lined streets give towns a certain magical charm not felt any other time of the year. It can be quiet and peaceful.

Insiders' Tip

Driving around Yellowstone Country in the winter takes special care. Generally there are three main rules to follow: Visibility, common sense, and patience. First, see and be seen. Keep headlights, taillights, and windshields clean. Leave plenty of room between your vehicle and those around you, and drive defensively. Test the road for traction. Give yourself extra time to travel. Being in a hurry on icy roads can get you and others into trouble. Only drive as fast enough as road conditions allow and leave the cruise control off. Finally, be prepared with road and weather information before you set out on your trip, and it's always a good idea to carry emergency gear. Call (800) 226-ROAD for Montana road conditions, (307) 772-0824 for Wyoming and (888) IDA-ROAD for Idaho.

It can also buzz with the excitement of winter visitors. Snowmobiles invade West Yellowstone, legally cruising on snow-covered streets headed for the hundreds of miles of trails that surround the town. Ski slopes in Montana and Wyoming are dotted with jubilant locals and eager visitors, hoping to catch one of the region's renowned powder days. Still others come by ski, snowcoach, or snowmobile to see two of our finest National Parks under the white shroud of winter. It sounds clichéd, but this time of year Yellowstone Country is a veritable winter wonderland.

Bring your warmest clothes when you visit during the winter. It's not uncommon for below-zero temperatures even during the day, and nighttime can be brutally cold, especially in the higher elevations. The flip side of this is that temperatures can warm up into the 40s and even 50s—which seems like summer to us—drawing people outside of their homes in a pre-spring frenzy. Generally, daytime temperatures will be in the 20s to 30s with nighttime lows between 0 and 15. The important thing to remember is that in Yellowstone Country, if you don't like the weather, just wait about 15 minutes. It's bound to change.

If you plan on visiting Yellowstone or Grand Teton National Parks during the winter, be sure to read the respective chapters in this book about what shuts down and when roads open and close. Otherwise, enjoy the frosted scenery of what are sure to be some of the prettiest sights you'll ever see.

Winter Safety Tips

Winter in Yellowstone Country is serious stuff. Simply driving your car can be hazardous, as road and weather conditions can change instantly. Always call the road reports and remember to carry emergency gear with you at all times. Remember, help can be far away and cell phones don't always work. Carrying extra clothes, blankets, flashlights, food, and water is a good and safe idea.

If you're venturing out into the backcountry, exercise extreme caution. The best advice is to be prepared for anything. You should always travel with a partner and let someone know where you are going and when you expect to be back. Check with rangers if you'll be in one of the parks or in a national forest. They will always be happy to tell you what conditions are like where you are planning to go. Carry emergency gear and don't get in over your head. Hire a guide if you don't know what you are doing.

Hypothermia is extremely dangerous but can be prevented with the right knowledge. Carrying a backpack with extra layers of clothing, food, water, and waterproof matches or a lighter is a must, as it could literally be days before someone may rescue you if you or your partner is hurt. Learn to recognize the symptoms of hypothermia: drowsiness, numbness, confusion, and frostbite. This means your body's core temperature is dropping and must be warmed immediately. Drink plenty of liquids, stay dry, snack frequently, and wear warm layers.

Wind in cold weather can cause frostbite in a hurry, usually signaled by numbing in the extremities and whitening tissue. Your face will be especially susceptible, so cover it immediately when the wind picks up.

Avalanches are another concern to backcountry travelers in Yellowstone Country. Backcountry use is up, and snow conditions are a popular winter subject around these parts. Even if you are not an expert on avalanches, there are several basic things you can do to prevent yourself from being put in a situation where an avalanche could occur. Snowmobilers and backcountry skiers should be especially alert, but anyone who travels in terrain steeper than 25 degrees should pay attention.

Again, prevention is the key, and understanding snow conditions is the primary method of prevention. Luckily, there are certain avalanche centers in the Yellowstone region that list daily snow conditions and forecasts. Calling one of these numbers listed below is the first step, but no substitute for getting educated about avalanches. Here are a few other basic rules to help you out:

- Avoid steep terrain after heavy snowfall or prolonged high winds. Most avalanches occur on slopes between 30 and 45 degrees, and wind deposits significantly increase the load on buried snowpack.

- Try not to cross steep slopes. If you must, do so one at a time and dig a snow pit before crossing to examine layers and slide conditions. Travel on ridges away from cornices.

- Notice the terrain and any previous slide activity. You can usually spot where avalanches typically occur.

- Carry and know how to use an avalanche transceiver, shovel, and probe, as they could save your life.

- Examine the snowpack during your activity. Check for a "whoomp" sound while walking, indicating collapsing snow, and take notice of the snowfall rate, buried layers, and type of snow on the ground.

- Dig a snow pit to examine snow layers, especially those near the bottom. Grainy, sugary snow anywhere in the snowpack is bad, since heavy snow deposits can cause this underlying snow to slide under pressure.

If you are caught in an avalanche, try to keep calm and remember what to do:

- If you are on a snowmobile, get away from your machine.

- Fight to stay on the surface and try to "swim" toward the safety zone on the side of the slide.

- As you come to a stop, try to make an airspace around your face with your hands. This will give you more time if you are buried.

- If you are a survivor, watch the victim carefully and try to spot where he or she was last seen. Probe downhill from there. Keep searching and do not leave the victim. Most buried victims don't survive past 30 minutes.

In the Bozeman area, the Gallatin National Forest Avalanche Center covers a large area and gives daily advisories before 7 A.M. during the winter season. For the mountains near Bozeman, Big Sky, and West Yellowstone, you can call (406) 587-6894. Around Cooke City call (406) 838-2341. You can also get advisories on the center's website, www.mtavalanche.com.

Near Jackson Hole, you can call the Avalanche Hazard Forecast Hotline at (307) 733-2664 for updated information, or you can visit www.untracked.com/forecast.

Jackson Hole Mountain Resort is known for feather-light powder and amazing scenery. PHOTO: JACKSON HOLE CHAMBER OF COMMERCE

Downhill Skiing

Montana

Big Sky Resort
1 Lone Mountain Tr., Big Sky, MT 59716
(406) 995-5000, (800) 548-4486
www.bigskyresort.com

Big Sky is Montana's largest ski area, with 3,600 acres of skiing on three mountains and more than 120 trails served by 18 lifts. Big Sky is built around Lone Mountain, an 11,166-foot, pyramid-shaped peak that you can actually go up to and come down. A 15-passenger tram was installed in 1995, whisking skiers to the steep, rocky summit, and giving Big Sky a whopping 4,350-foot vertical drop. The ride alone is worth it, as you can watch expert skiers descend the wild Big Couloir from the window. You can opt to return down on the tram if you're not feeling up to testing your skills. Technically there is no easy way down from the top, although

the black diamond Liberty Bowl can be tackled by most advanced intermediate skiers.

The skiing at Big Sky, which lasts from mid November until April (although it opened on October 16th for the 2000–01 season, a resort record), is nothing short of fantastic. Whether you're a seasoned veteran or a willing first-timer, there is enough terrain to keep you riding different trails each day of your visit. Advanced skiers will find rocky chutes and steep bowls off the Challenger double chair, the Lone Peak triple chair, and the Tram, as well as excellent glades off the Ramcharger and Thunderwolf quad chairs. The Explorer is an excellent beginners-only lift, while the trails off the Swiftcurrent quad will test advanced beginners through expert skiers. The snow falls often here, to the tune of 400 inches a year, so conditions are usually soft and fun for all levels.

You can find food in the Mountain Village base area and at the base of the Iron Horse chairlift on the north side of the mountain, as well as at the top of the Ramcharger quad. Nightlife isn't something Big Sky is known for, but there are plenty of après ski activities going on after the lifts close. You'll also find live music in many of the bars in the Mountain Village. For more information, see the Big Sky chapter in this book.

Big Sky has a very Euro-Western flavor and a relaxed atmosphere. Most people come here to get away from some of the busier ski areas in the West, and find Big Sky a quiet, out-of-the-way gem that they return to often. Much of it is upscale, with world-class restaurants, boutiques, and accommodations, but Big Sky can also be done on a budget. Either way, it is a great way to experience all that Montana has to offer.

In the 2000–01 season, full day lift tickets were $54 for adults and $42 for youths 11 through 17, while kids under 10 ski free. Rental and instruction are available, and the ski area is located 43 miles south of Bozeman on U.S. Highway 191.

Bridger Bowl
15795 Bridger Canyon Rd., Bozeman, MT, 59715
(406) 586-1518, (800) 223-9609
www.bridgerbowl.com

Bridger Bowl is Bozeman's local ski area and is located 16 miles north of town on Montana Highway 86. Bridger offers an excellent combination of terrain, atmosphere, and value, and is a great spot for families, hardcore skiers, and snowboarders alike. The resort sits on the east side of the Bridger Mountains, below a long ridge, and offers more than 60 runs on 2,000 acres and 2,000 vertical feet. There are seven lifts that serve a variety of terrain, including open bowls, glades, chutes, and groomed trails. Bridger is well known for the 350 inches of light, fluffy powder, what the locals call "Cold Smoke," that falls each year.

Beginners will want to stick to the lower mountain, serviced by the Virginia City double chair and the quad chair at the base, while experts can find great runs from every chair. The Bridger double chair travels furthest up the mountain but not all the way to the top of the ridge. Advanced skiers with an avalanche beacon, shovel, and partner are allowed to hike the remaining distance to access some of the best terrain in the West. Check with the ski patrol shack at the top of the Bridger lift if you are a first-timer up the Ridge.

You can grab a bite at the Deer Park Chalet half way up the mountain or at the base lodge cafeteria. In the base area, Jimmy B's is the après ski hotspot, offering great burgers and sandwiches, and the newly constructed FaceShots features occasional live music. The often sun-drenched patio at the base lodge is also a great spot to relax after a day on the slopes.

Lift tickets for the 2000–01 season were $33 for adults, $13 for children (age

5 and under free), and complete rental packages started at $20 a day. Lodging packages are also available.

Red Lodge Mountain
P.O. Box 750, Red Lodge, MT 59068
(406) 446-2610, (800) 444-8977
www.redlogemountain.com

Red Lodge is a medium-sized mountain perched at the foot of the Beartooth Mountains, a vast alpine plateau with more peaks over 10,000 feet than any other place in the country. Although Red Lodge is only about an hour from Cooke City and the northeast entrance to Yellowstone, the section of U.S. Highway 212 that connects the two is closed during the winter. You can only access Red Lodge from the north.

Once you get there, you won't be disappointed. The mountain offers 2,400 vertical feet of skiing spread out over 1,600 acres in the Custer National Forest. There are more than 70 trails, with 15 percent for novices, 55 percent for intermediates, and 30 percent for experts. Snowmaking covers 40 percent of the trails and the area receives an average of 250 inches of snow per year.

Advanced skiers should head for the top of Nichols Peak (9,390 feet) via the Cole Creek quad chair to access some recently developed terrain, which includes the Headwaters glades area and a few double black diamond runs. The Grizzly Peak double chair also hits some great expert terrain, like the West and East Park glades and the Buckin' Chute.

The middle of the mountain is reserved for novice skiers and there are some great green runs off of the Triple Chair in the base area. Some fun intermediate cruisers can be found near the Palisades quad chair.

The best time to ski Red Lodge is toward the end of the season when the Beartooths see most of their snow. It is a great mountain for all abilities and the quaint, Western town of Red Lodge is a unique and fun place to stay. The shop-lined Main Street is a nice example of small town Montana. For the 2000–01 season, lift tickets were $34 for adults and $28 for kids ages 12 through 18. Children 12 and under pay $13. Rates are discounted on Mondays and Tuesdays, except holidays. These low prices and fun terrain make Red Lodge a great value.

> ## Insiders' Tip
> If you are skiing at Jackson Hole and want to take a break from the slopes, a naturalist-led snowshoe hike is complimentary with your alpine or Nordic lift ticket, snowshoes included. Call (307) 739-2753.

Wyoming

Grand Targhee Ski and Summer Resort
Ski Hill Rd., Alta, WY 83442
(307) 353-2300, (800) 827-4433
www.grandtarghee.com

Only one word can accurately describe the Grand Targhee skiing experience: powder. With an annual snowfall total of more than 500 inches, this somewhat undiscovered resort proudly proclaims that it gets its "Snow From Heaven, Not Hoses." It's light, fluffy, and plentiful.

Targhee is located 42 miles west of Jackson Hole, over the steep and winding Teton Pass. The pass may close during inclement weather, so call ahead. The mountain is located in Wyoming, but you will go through Idaho and the rustic town of Driggs before getting there. If you arrive early on a powder day, head directly to the summit on the Dreamcatcher quad chair and pick a trail and go. You won't believe how effortlessly you float in the feathery powder. Advanced skiers will want to stick to Dreamcatcher and the Blackfoot chair, which access all of the intermediate and expert terrain on the mountain. The only beginner runs are serviced by the Shoshone quad chair at the base area.

Targhee's long season often gets the jump on Jackson Hole, and is one reason why even Jackson locals make the one-hour drive over the pass to ride powder all day. It isn't as steep as Jackson Hole, but who cares when there is a foot of fresh powder? Typically the season runs from mid-November until mid-April.

There are 1,500 acres of terrain at Targhee and 2,200 vertical feet of skiing. Only 300 acres are groomed, however, leaving the trail busting to you. If you have some extra cash, you can pay about $225 (includes lunch) for a day of incredible snowcat powder skiing on more than 1,500 additional acres.

The quaint base area has a variety of great lodging, restaurants, shops, and services. There is also a full-service rental and repair shop. Lift tickets for the 2000–01 season were $44 full day, $32 half day (12:30 P.M.), which is a bargain for the fresh tracks you're likely to get.

Jackson Hole Mountain Resort
3395 W. McCollister Dr., Teton Village, WY 83025
(307) 733-2292, (888)-333-7766
www.jacksonhole.com

Jackson Hole is one of the premier ski destinations in the world, where skiers and snowboarders come for a real Western experience—spectacular snow and friendly folks amid the cowboy charm of a small, vibrant town.

The ski area is located in Teton Village, about 10 miles from the town of Jackson, at the base of 10,450-foot Rendezvous Mountain. A 50-passenger aerial tram takes you to the top, where views of the majestic Grand Teton can be had on a clear day. Skiing all the way down will give you a leg-burning 4,139 feet, the tallest continuous vertical rise of any ski resort in North America. There are 2,500 acres of it to choose from.

Jackson Hole is truly an expert's mountain, as 50 percent of the in-bounds terrain is marked advanced or expert. The resort's open gate policy, initiated at the start of the 1999–2000 season, adds another 2,500 skiable acres and access to numerous bowls, glades, and peaks. This terrain is for skiers and snowboarders with knowledge and possession of avalanche safety and rescue equipment. Much of Jackson's in-bounds expert terrain is accessed by the Tram and the Sublette quad chair, as well as the Thunder quad. The Hobacks offer powder turns, and the gnarly Corbett's Couloir is one of best-known expert-only runs in the world.

If you're just beginning or are an intermediate, don't be discouraged by Jackson's steeps, because there is plenty for you, too. The Bridger Gondola, the Casper Bowl triple chair, and the Après Vous quad chair offer confidence-building intermediate terrain and fun, long runs. Beginners and first timers will want to stick to the Teewinot quad, which serves the only green runs on the mountain.

It literally can take days to explore all of Jackson Hole's terrain, but the time spent is well worth it. Mountain hosts lead complimentary orientation tours for intermediate-level skiers daily at 9:30 A.M. from the Mountain Host Building. Advanced riders can also hire a guide from the Jackson Hole Ski and Snowboard Guide Service by calling (307) 739-2663.

The Jackson Hole Nordic Center, (307) 739-2629, also offers 17 kilometers of groomed trails at the base of Teton Village.

Jackson Hole gets an average of 400 inches of snow every winter, making the skiing and snowboarding here unforgettable. Lift tickets for the 2000–01 season were $56 full day, $47 for a half day (12:30 P.M.). Call the snow report at (888) 333-7766.

Close-up

Altitude without the Attitude

The big ski resorts of Yellowstone country are among the best in the world. But if you want to get away from their big crowds and big prices, there are many smaller ski areas that make great day trips from wherever you are staying in our region. Taking a trip to one of these has many advantages. First, you'll be away from the hustle and bustle of resort towns. These small ski areas are often located in out-of-the-way smaller towns that don't depend on dollars from the ski area. Second, you'll be able to see some more of the beautiful country that surrounds the Yellowstone region without having to go too far. These small ski areas are bargains. They are great for families, offer plenty of bang for the buck, and are an unforgettable off-the-beaten-path adventure.

If you are staying in the Bozeman area during the winter, you have a few options. The first is Discovery Ski Basin (406) 563-2184, www.skidiscovery.com, located about two hours west of Bozeman near the old mining town of Anaconda. Discovery has a vertical drop of 1,300 feet and more than 40 runs, evenly divided between beginners, intermediates, and experts. The lift on the backside serves some of the steepest terrain in the state. All-day tickets were $24 in 2000–01, half that for kids. Rentals and instruction are available. Nearby Fairmont Hot Springs, (800) 332-3272 or www.fairmontmontana.com, offers two-day ski and soak specials for as little as $110 per person.

Showdown, (800) 433-0022 or www.showdownmontana.com, about two hours north of Bozeman on U.S. Highway 89, is a neat little area that offers 34 trails and a 1,400-foot vertical drop. There's also a half pipe and terrain park for snowboarders and more than 240 inches of snow falls here each year. Full-day tickets were $27 in 2000–01, but a great midweek package gives you three days of skiing and three nights lodging for only $110 per person, based on quad occupancy.

About 90 miles south from Jackson on U.S. Highway 191, you'll find White Pine Ski Area, a bargain at only $22 (307) 367-7222 or www.whitepineski.com. The 1999–00 season marked the first time the resort was open for full operations in 15 years. The 9,500-foot summit produces outstanding views of the rugged Wind River Mountains, the Continental Divide, and 11-mile long Fremont Lake. The drive from Jackson is a designated scenic route and passes through the Gros Ventre range and the small community of Pinedale. White Pine is open seven days a week until Easter.

Outside Cody is one of America's oldest ski areas, Sleeping Giant, (307) 587-4044, located on U.S. Highway 20 just outside the east entrance to Yellowstone National Park. It is small—the vertical drop is only 600 feet—but it's not about the skiing here. It's more about being out in the middle of the wilderness, as Sleeping Giant looms beneath numerous 11,000-foot peaks and the forested slopes of the Shoshone National Forest. The resort does get about 300 inches of snow each year, so if you happen to be there on a powder day chances are you'll have the mountain to yourself. There are also 35 kilometers of groomed Nordic trails that connect to Yellowstone, and the on-site Shoshone Lodge can accommodate up to 65 guests.

About 90 miles east of Cody on U.S. Highway 14 in the beautiful Big Horn Mountains is Antelope Butte, (307) 655-9530 or www.skiantelopebutte.com, with 18 runs on 250 acres and a vertical drop of 1,000 feet. Don't let the small stature fool you, as there are numerous double black diamond runs off of the Big Horn summit chair. Average snowfall is 200 inches, and lift tickets during the 2000–01 season were a modest $25 for adults. Antelope Butte is typically open from Wednesday through Sunday and holidays and also offers 5 kilometers of groomed cross-country trails.

Snow King Resort
400 E. Snow King Ave., Jackson, WY
83001
(307) 733-5200, (800) 522-5464
www.snowking.com

Snow King—founded in 1939—was Wyoming's first ski area, and is affectionately called the Town Hill by Jackson locals. While the Jackson Hole Ski Resort may get all the attention from the skiing world, a ski trip to Jackson wouldn't be complete without spending a day at Snow King.

Literally minutes from Jackson's town square, Snow King offers 1,571 vertical feet of skiing—and most of it is vertical. The ski area has some of the steepest lift-served terrain in the country, with numerous double black diamond runs off of

the Summit chairlift, including Bearcat, Upper Exhibition, and Belly Roll. The Rafferty chair and surface tow are perfect for beginner skiers, and the Cougar chair serves the middle of the mountain and most of the ski area's intermediate terrain.

Snow King is a popular and convenient spot for locals who just want to get a few runs in, and therefore offers hourly tickets ($8 in 2000–01) for those wanting to spend their lunch hour on the lifts. There is also a terrain park and half pipe, and night skiing from 4 to 8 P.M. Tuesday through Saturday. Full day lift tickets for the 2000–01 season were $30, half day were $20, and night tickets were $14. If you want to stay on the mountain, you can choose from more than 200 hotel rooms and condos.

Insiders' Tip

By purchasing a Jackson Hole Ski Club membership you can get great deals on area activities and help the youth skiing community. Both locals and visitors can pay $30 and receive discounts on lift tickets, passes, tunings, snowmobile tours, meals, drinks, and more. Money collected helps finance local youth skiing and racing programs. Memberships are available at most local ski shops, or call (307) 733-6433 for more information.

Cross-country Skiing and Snowshoeing

Montana

B Bar Guest Ranch
818 Tom Miner Creek Rd., Emigrant, MT
59027
(406) 848-7523
www.bbar.com

This full service guest ranch lies in a beautiful basin bordering the northwest corner

of Yellowstone National Park and provides 40 kilometers of groomed trails for all skill levels. The B Bar is only open in the winter from mid-December until the end of February, and trails are open to the public on weekends from 9 A.M. until 4 P.M.

The Rendezvous Complex in West Yellowstone, Montana, is one of the premier cross-country skiing trail systems in the region. PHOTO: DONNIE SEXTON/TRAVEL MONTANA

Bohart Ranch
16621 Bridger Canyon Rd., Bozeman, MT 59715
(406) 586-9070
www.bohartranchxcski.com

Bohart Ranch is an outstanding facility offering 25 kilometers of groomed and tracked trails with spectacular views of the Bridger Mountains. Trails are groomed for diagonal and skating techniques, and there is a biathlon range, rentals, lessons, snacks, and a warming hut. Bohart Ranch is located just north of the Bridger Bowl ski area, 16 miles northeast of Bozeman on Montana Highway 86. Daily rates for the 2000–01 season were $8 for adults, $5 for kids seven to twelve, and kids six and under and adults over 70 are admitted free.

Lindley Park
E. Main St., Bozeman, MT

This beautiful Bozeman park has a 1.5-kilometer loop trail that winds its way through huge trees, rolling hills, and flat meadows. It's a popular local spot when there is snow, usually from November until April. Lindley Park is located on the south side of East Main Street as you are heading out of town toward Interstate 90.

Lone Mountain Ranch
P.O. Box 160069, Big Sky, MT 59716
(406) 995-4644, (800) 514-4644
www.lmranch.com

Lone Mountain Ranch is a full service winter vacation resort with 75 kilometers of groomed, tilled, and tracked trails for all skill levels. Trails are groomed for traditional skiing and skating. Portions of the trails meander through the Gallatin National Forest, and the views of Lone Mountain and the surrounding peaks are nothing short of incredible. Lone Mountain Ranch was named by Mountain Living magazine as the top cross-country ski resort in the western U.S. Don't worry, you don't have to be a guest at the ranch to ski. Full day ($15) and half day ($12) rates are available. See the Big Sky chapter in this book for details on the resort, including lodging, dining, and other activities.

Mountain Meadows Guest Ranch
P.O. Box 160334, Big Sky, MT 59716
(406) 995-4997, (888) 644-6647
www.mountainmeadowsranch.com

You can enjoy 30 kilometers of groomed trails at Mountain Meadows, which offers full resort packages, including lodging, dining, and other winter activities, such as snowshoeing, sleigh rides, ice skating, sledding, and downhill skiing. The trails are also open to the public for $10 a day, and rentals are available, too. The ranch consists of the main lodge and two cabins on 640 acres of beautiful land. The main lodge has seven guest rooms with private verandas, a lounge area with a gigantic fireplace, an outdoor Jacuzzi, a sauna, and the Thirsty Moose Bar. Since Mountain Meadows only accommodates up to 20 guests, your vacation here should be a relatively peaceful experience.

Red Lodge Nordic Center
P.O. Box 1668, Red Lodge, MT 59068
(406) 425-1070, (406) 446-9191

The Red Lodge Nordic Center is located two miles west of the town of Red Lodge on Montana Highway 78. It offers 15 kilometers of groomed trails, rentals, instruction, snacks, and snowshoe rentals. Trails range from open meadows to rolling loops through Aspen trees. Full day rates are $7 and a half day is $5.

Wade Lake Resort
963 U.S. Hwy. 287 N. #1, Cameron, MT 59720
(406) 682-7560
www.wadelake.com

This small resort—elevation 6,300 feet—is located 30 miles west of West Yellowstone on Wade Lake, part of a designated Montana Wildlife Viewing site. There is little development around this area, except for the five small cabins and main lodge, which must be accessed by skis from the parking area during the winter. The 35 kilometers of groomed trails as well as miles of backcountry areas cover

Insiders' Tip

If you're going to be in the area for a while, take a course at the Yellowstone Association Institute, a nonprofit field school operated in conjunction with the National Park Service. Winter courses are held at park hotels and the Lamar Buffalo Ranch—a campus like setting with heated guest cabins and a common building with bathrooms, classrooms, and showers.

Courses run a minimum of two days, and include Wilderness First Aid, Exploring Yellowstone on Snowshoes, Wolf Watching in Yellowstone, Snow Tracking, and Exploring Yellowstone's Winter World on Skis. The institute also offers Lodging and Learning packages with rooms at Mammoth or Old Faithful. Complete program information can be found on www.Yellowstone-Association.org, or by calling (307) 344-2294.

lakeshores, riversides, aspen groves, rolling hills, and old growth fir forests. Winter cabin rates range from $85 to $150, depending on number of people and duration of stay.

Yellowstone Expeditions
P.O. Box 865, West Yellowstone, MT 59758
(406) 646-9333, (800) 728-9333
www.yellowstoneexpeditions.com

Yellowstone Expeditions offers backcountry, cross-country skiing tours from the Yellowstone Yurt Camp near the Grand Canyon of the Yellowstone in Yellowstone National Park. The main camp consists of two, large heated yurts where guests eat and socialize before heading to bed in private, heated tent cabins—large, sturdy canvas structures. Four, five, and eight-day tours are offered, with trips to the Rim of the Canyon, Mount Washburn, Cascade Creek, and everywhere in between. Snowcoaches transport guests to and from West Yellowstone and to the trailheads for the daily tours. The yurt camp also includes a sauna and shower. Package excursions include ski guides, all meals, lodging, and transportation. The camp only accommodates 10 guests, so this is a great way to see parts of the park that few get to see in the winter. Prices range from $660 to $1,080 per person.

Close-up

Snowshoe Heaven

Not comfortable on a pair of skinny skis? Looking for something to do after you drop the kids off at the ski hill? Snowshoeing is an easy and inexpensive way to take care of both problems.

With the advances in snowshoe design and construction over the past 10 years, the sport of snowshoeing has exploded in popularity. Gone are the heavy, wooden frames of the past (although you'll see them hanging in many lodges and homes throughout the area). They have been replaced with lighter, more durable materials such as aluminum and plastic.

The great thing about the sport is that it is perfect for all ages and abilities. If you can walk, you can snowshoe. The shoes may feel slightly clunky at first, but you'll get the hang of it in a few steps. The free heel design of today's snowshoes make for easy walking, or even running.

Not surprisingly, Yellowstone Country is the perfect place to strap on a pair and head out for an adventure. Basically, any trail that you can hike on during the summer becomes a snowshoe trail in the winter. You don't have to worry about grooming, your snowshoes will plod through the deepest snow. Check national forest trail maps for snowshoeing opportunities. Both Yellowstone and Grand Teton National Parks abound with trails for both skis and snowshoers. Most Nordic centers described in this chapter offer snowshoe rentals and instruction. In addition, many outdoor shops in towns like Bozeman and Jackson offer rentals for $5 to $10 a day. Some folks like to rent poles, which give your upper body a workout and allow you better balance going up and down hills.

Snowshoeing is just another way for you to see our beautiful area in the winter. Go ahead, give it a shot. The opportunities are only limited by your imagination.

Gallatin National Forest Trails

This immense forest has hundreds of miles of groomed and backcountry trails. Some trails are described below, but for more information contact the forest headquarters at 3710 Fallon St., Bozeman, MT 59718. Phone is (406) 522-2520, or check out the informative website: www.fs.fed.us/r1/gallatin.

Bear Creek Road

More than 6 kilometers of easy, groomed trail skiing takes you up through the tall timber above Gardiner. For information, contact the District Ranger in Gardiner at (406) 848-7375.

Bozeman Creek to Mystic Lake

To get to the trailhead of this 10-mile (one way), moderate, uphill route, follow South Third Avenue from Bozeman to Nash Road. Head west on Nash and make a left on Bozeman Creek Road. The trailhead is one mile south from there. Climbing from 5,220 to 6,550 feet and ending at the Mystic Lake Ranger Station, the trail provides expansive views of the Hyalite Range. You can combine this with the New World Gulch trail to make a nice loop, although this makes the route steeper and much more difficult.

Rendezvous Ski Trails

Over 30 kilometers of trails groomed daily begin at the intersection of Geyser Street and Obsidian Avenue in West Yellowstone. Trails, which range from easy to most difficult, are open from December 1 through March 30 and provide great snow and scenic beauty. Day passes are $3, season passes are $20, and family passes are $40. All are available at the West Yellowstone Chamber of Commerce, (406) 646-7701), the Hebgen Lake Ranger District Office, (406) 646-7369), and several ski shops in town. It's no accident that these trails are among the finest in the country, as many of the top national teams in the world use them as training grounds. Groomer Doug Edgerton has been selected Chief of Grooming for the cross-country and biathlon trials of the 2002 Winter Olympics in Salt Lake City.

Yellowstone National Park

Yellowstone's 2.2 million acres provide hundred of miles of trails for you to explore. From groomed track skiing to backcountry touring, Yellowstone is a cross-country paradise with breathtaking winter scenery, abundant wildlife, and plenty of snow. There are trails in all areas of the park, including Old Faithful, Tower, Mammoth, Northeast, and Northwest. Remember that only the road from Mammoth to Cooke City is open during the winter and all other areas must be accessed by snowcoach, snowmobile, or skis. Conditions can change rapidly, so be prepared by carrying extra clothes and emergency gear, even if you are sticking to groomed trails. All unplowed roads are open to cross-country skiing and snowshoeing, and a permit is required if you want to camp in the backcountry. There are many more trails than listed here, so check at the visitor centers for detailed maps and information.

Northeast Region

There are many trailheads along the open road between Mammoth and Cooke City. The Tower Fall Trail begins at Tower Junction and follows an unplowed road for 2.5 miles to Tower Fall. There are great views of the Yellowstone River Canyon and you may run into bald eagles, bison, or bighorn sheep. From the fall, you can continue along the 5.5-mile Chittenden Loop Trail or return the way you came.

Advanced skiers should try the 6-mile Bunsen Peak Trail, reached by taking a snowcoach from Mammoth to the trailhead. The trail is steep in spots and has some sharp turns, but gives you splendid views of the Gallatin Mountains and the Gardiner River Canyon.

The Blacktail Plateau Trail begins 7.5 miles east of Mammoth and is 8 miles long. It is a great trail to spot wildlife, including bison, elk, deer, and coyotes. The scenery isn't bad either, as broad meadows give way to high, snow-covered peaks.

The Upper Terrace Trail gives you great views of the steaming lower terraces. If you've seen these in the summer, imagine them surrounded by a white blanket of snow with steam rising all around. The trail is 1.5-miles and follows Upper Terrace Drive, and starts right in Mammoth. Remember to stay on the trail, as the ground around thermal features is very unstable.

Northwest Region

There are several excellent trails leading from U.S. Highway 191 south of Big Sky into the Park. There is no gate or entry fee here, and trailheads are located in pull-outs on the side of the road. At milepost 20 you'll find the trail to Big Horn Pass, which follows the Gallatin River for a while and can be a great spot to watch for elk, eagles, moose, and coyotes. The Fawn Pass Trail leaves at milepost 22 and goes through timber and meadows after crossing the Gallatin River. It hooks up with the Big Horn Pass Trail after about 6 miles. Specimen Creek is another favorite and is found at milepost 27. This enjoyable trek follows the creek as it gradually rises through forest and meadows. Look for elk, moose, and petrified trees on the exposed ridges above you.

A nice trail with great views of high peaks and open meadows is the Bacon Rind, which begins a few miles south of Specimen Creek on U.S. 191. The trail begins in the park and then goes back into National Forest land, following a drainage ditch for 5 miles of gentle open terrain. Look for numerous 9,000-foot peaks as the trail climbs.

A well-kept secret is Telemark Meadows, found on the west side of U.S. 191 at mile post 18. As the trail gains elevation you can test your telemark powder turns on a variety of gentle to steep slopes, while enjoying great views of the Madison and Gallatin Mountains.

Old Faithful Area

Part of the beauty of skiing in Yellowstone Park is the numerous thermal features you will encounter. Gone are the crowds of summer and you will feel like you have the park to yourself. The contrast between the cold snow surrounding the geysers and hot pots and the rising steam is breathtaking. The Lone Star Geyser Trail is no exception. This moderate, 9-mile trail begins at Old Faithful Lodge, takes you past Kepler Cascades, and alongside the Firehole River to the geyser. The geyser erupts about every three hours from a 12-foot high cinder cone. Advanced skiers can return via the Howard Eaton Trail, but it is steep and should be skied with caution.

The 8-mile Fairy Falls Trail is another favorite. Hop on a snowcoach from Old Faithful Lodge to the trailhead and follow the signs. The trail winds past spectacular ice encrusted waterfalls and through burned trees. You can head back to the lodge by following the snowcoach road until the Biscuit Basin Trail, which will take you past the scenic Upper Geyser Basin, Morning Glory Pool, and Geyser Hill.

Grand Teton National Park

Grand Teton has about 40 miles of ungroomed skiing and snowshoe trails that are among the most popular in the region. It's hard to blame skiers for flocking here, as the views alone are worth it even if the skiing is crowded. Snow isn't usually a problem, as an average of four feet falls even in the lowest elevations. Trails range in difficulty to suit novice and advanced skiers.

Skiing and snowshoeing are not limited to marked trails, and to get away from some of the crowds it may be necessary to explore the park on your own. If you choose this route, make sure the area you are planning to ski in isn't closed. Check with the Moose Visitor Center upon entering the park, and while you're there pick up any one of several good maps.

Only marked trails will be described here. Generally tall flags stick out of the snow, allowing you to follow the markers after a fresh snowfall if previous tracks are covered.

Jenny Lake Trail

This trail—great for any level of skier—provides some of the best views in the park. The 9-mile rail starts at the Taggart Lake parking area and heads north along Cottonwood Creek, climbing slowly through wide meadows with panoramic views of the Tetons. You'll skirt the base of the range until the Jenny Lake Overlook, where you'll hope you still have film in your camera. The return trip is mostly level, taking you back to the parking area.

Signal Mountain

If you're feeling confident after the Jenny Lake loop, try this 10-mile round trip that takes you to the top of this popular peak. Start at the end of the road near the Signal Mountain Lodge, then ski south along a snowmobile trail until you see the Signal Mountain Road heading up to the east. The climb to the summit is a gradual 4 miles, and you'll be rewarded with outstanding views across the valley of the entire Teton Range, as well as the icy Snake River on the valley floor. The return trip is a blast—downhill all the way to your car.

Jackson Area

Grand Targhee Ski and Summer Resort
Alta, WY 83422
(307) 353-2300, (800) TARGHEE
www.grandtarghee.com

Grand Targhee is about an hour west of Jackson and offers 15 kilometers of groomed tracks and fresh powder that accommodate skating and classic skiing styles. Adult passes were $8 in 2000–01, seniors and children paid $5. Group and private lessons are available.

Jackson Hole Nordic Center
Teton Village, WY 83025
(307) 739-2629

This full-service Nordic center lies at the base of Jackson Hole Mountain Resort and offers 17 kilometers of professionally groomed trails as well as rentals, instruction, dog sledding trips, snowshoe tours and rentals, guided backcountry nature tours, and more. A full day is $8 for adults and $4 for juniors and seniors. You can also transfer your downhill lift ticket for a Nordic pass, so you can ride the lifts in the morning and skate in the afternoon. And 10 kilometers of trails are open to your four-legged friend. The center is open daily from 8:30 A.M. to 4:30 P.M.

Pahaska Tepee Area
183 Yellowstone Hwy., Cody, WY 82404
(307) 527-7701, (800) 628-7791
www.pahaska.com

Three miles from the east entrance to Yellowstone National Park lies the Pahaska, a cross-country skiing paradise in the Wapiti Valley. Buffalo Bill Cody built the Pahaska Tepee near the base of Sylvan Pass, where the original lodge still greets visitors before they head into Yellowstone National Park. The Park County Nordic Ski Association has linked existing and new trails to a 35-kilometer trail system, thanks to an agreement with the Sleeping Giant ski area. Two backcountry trails, the Cow Creek Trail and the Sunlight Wilderness Trail, head off from the groomed trail. For a map and more information, contact Pahaska Tepee at (307) 527-7701 or (800) 628-7791. Skiing is free and usually lasts from early December to mid-March, and rentals are available.

Spring Creek Ranch and Nordic Center
1800 Spirit Dance Rd., Jackson, WY 83001
(307) 733-1004, (800) 443-6139
www.springcreekranch.com

The Spring Creek Ranch sits 1,000 feet above the town of Jackson and is a full service guest resort, offering lodging, dining, and numerous activities. The Nordic Center offers 15 kilometers of groomed trails for skating and classic skating. Snowshoe and ski rentals and lessons are available, as well as guided backcountry cross-country skiing and snowshoeing in Grand Teton National Park. The center is open from 9:30 A.M. to 4:30 P.M. daily.

Teton Pines
3450 N. Clubhouse Dr., Jackson, WY 83002
(307) 733-1005
www.tetonpines.com

Everyone loves cross-country skiing on golf courses, and the Arnold Palmer-designed course at Teton Pines makes for an excellent day of snow-filled adventure. There are 13 kilometers of machine groomed trails here, all with the scenic backdrop of the Tetons rising up from the valley. There are skating and diagonal tracks, and rentals and instruction are available.

Idaho

Harriman State Park
U.S. Hwy. 20, Island Park, ID
(208) 558-7368

Although Island Park is a snowmobiling hotspot, skinny skiers can visit Harriman and avoid the sled traffic. No snowmobiles are allowed here, and 15 kilometers of groomed trails await you.

The easy Ranch loop takes skiers past the historic Railroad Ranch, along the north side of Silver Lake and back to the main trail. You can stop in at the Jones House warming hut to thaw out by the fire. Look for trumpeter swans in the park's open water. There are several other trails to choose from after this good warm-up. Thurman and Silver Lake loops are moderate and the more difficult Ridge loop has a few steep hills.

It's $3 to get into the park, and you can rent a pair of skis at the Last Chance Texaco, (208) 558-7399), just north of the park. Call the Island Park Ranger District, (208) 558-7301) or the Ashton Ranger District at (208) 652-7442 for more information and ski conditions.

Cross-Country Skiing Rentals

Yellowstone National Park

AmFac Resorts and Services
Mammoth, Yellowstone National Park
(307) 344-7901

You can rent skis and snowshoes from the park's main concessionaire, AmFac, at Mammoth and Old Faithful. In 2000–01, full-day ski touring packages were $14.25, $9.25 for a half day. Full-day snowshoe rentals run $11, and $8 for a half-day. Instruction is available and children under 12 get a 20 percent discount on any package, rental, or lesson. AmFac also offers guided ski tours from Mammoth and Old Faithful.

Montana

Bangtail Bike and Ski
508 W. Main St., Bozeman, MT
(406) 587-4905

Bangtail—named after a mountain range northeast of town—has the largest selection of Nordic equipment in Bozeman, and the shop rents cross-country skis for $9 a day. Skis with metal edges (telemark) run $16 a day and snowshoes are $9. The shop also rents bikes in the summer.

Bud Lilly's
39 Madison Ave., West Yellowstone, MT
(406) 646-7801

You can rent a pair of cross-country skis at Bud Lilly's Ski Shop for $15 per day, and showshoes are available for $12 per day.

Cooke City Bike Shack
U.S. Hwy. 212, Cooke City, MT
(406) 838-2412

Visit Bill Blackford for cross-country and telemark skis, as well as snowshoes and backcountry accessories. Nordic skis are $10 a day, telemark skis are $18, and snowshoes are $10. Every third day is half price. If telemarking is your thing, Blackford will take you by snowmobile to Daisy Pass, where you can choose a variety of

ascents or ski right back down to town. The 2,500-foot run is epic—powder conditions and glade skiing through the burned trees of the 1988 Yellowstone fires. The Bike Shack also has a nice selection of topographic and other maps.

Free Heel and Wheel
40 Yellowstone Ave.
West Yellowstone, MT
(406) 646-7744

You can rent all kinds of skis at Free Heel and Wheel, including touring, skate, and classic styles. Standard cross-country packages run $15 a day, or $4 per hour if you're running short on time. The shop also rents snowshoes for the same rates.

Winter visitors can take snow coaches into the Old Faithful Snow Lodge of Yellowstone National Park.
PHOTO: JACKSON HOLE CHAMBER OF COMMERCE

Grizzly Outfitters
Meadow Center, Big Sky, MT
(406) 995-2939
www.grizzlyoutfitters.com

Grizzly Outfitters moved into a more convenient location in 2000, and rents cross-country skis and snowshoes for $10 a day with reduced rates for multiple day rentals. Grizzly Outfitters also rents bikes in the summer.

Northern Lights Trading Company
1716 W. Babcock St., Bozeman, MT
(406) 586-2225

The friendliest staff in town will rent you a pair of Nordic skis for $20 a day for skating skis, $15 for classic style. Snowhoes are also available for $8. The staff is also full of tips on where the best skiing is and how to get there.

The Round House Ski and Sports Center
1422 W. Main St., Bozeman, MT
(406) 587-1258

The Round House offers a large selection of alpine and Nordic ski rentals in town and at their location at the base of the Bridger Bowl ski area (587) 2838. Nordic ski packages are $10 a day, as are snowshoes. Snowboards are also available and both shops offer waxing and tuning.

Jackson Area

Flagg Ranch Resort
U.S. Hwy. 89 (John D. Rockefeller Jr. Memorial Pkwy.)
(307) 543-2861

There's not much activity on the highway from the north end of Grand Teton National Park to the south entrance to Yellowstone, but the Flagg Ranch is an oasis of winter adventure. You can rent cross-country skis for $15 a day and snowshoes for $12, and enjoy the 10 miles of ungroomed trails around the resort and even more in the parks. Most trails are for beginners and intermediate skiers.

Skinny Skis
65 W. Deloney Ave., Jackson, WY
(307) 733-6094
www.skinnyskis.com

As its name implies, this is Jackson's skinny ski headquarters. The shop rents touring, telemark, and skate skis as well as snowshoes. Prices are $15, $25, $18, and $12, respectively. The Skinny Skis staff is very knowledgeable about trails in the area, so ask around for some helpful hints. Also pick up a copy of *Trailhead*, published twice a year, an area magazine that will lead you in the right direction.

Teton Mountaineering
170 N. Cache St., Jackson, WY
(307) 733-3595, (800) 850-3595
www.tetonmountaineering.com

This full-service skiing, climbing, and mountaineering shop rents cross-country skis for $15 a day, and snowshoes for $10 per day.

Cody

Sunlight Sports
1251 Sheridan Ave., Cody, WY
(307) 587-9517

Cody's oldest sporting goods store rents cross-country gear for $8 for adults, $5 for kids ages 8 to 13, and $3 for kids seven and under. You can also rent snowshoes for $9 a day.

Teton Valley

Grand Targhee Ski and Summer Resort
Ski Hill Rd., Alta, WY
(307) 353-2300, (800) 827-4433
www.grandtarghee.com

The ski resort rents full cross-country packages for around $18 for a full day. Lessons are also available, and there are 15 kilometers of groomed tracks around the resort.

Yöstmark Mountain Equipment
12 E. Little Ave., Driggs, ID
(208) 354-2828

This one of the Teton Valley's finest shops, specializing in telemark and back-country ski gear. You can rent Nordic equipment for $14 per day and snow-shoes for $10 per day. Call for prices and availability of telemark and snowboard rentals.

Dog Sled Tours

Absaroka Dogsled Treks
Chico Hot Springs, Pray, MT 59065
(406) 333-4933, (800) 468-9232
www.extrememontana.com

Veteran musher Mark Nardin runs these tours from the historic Chico Hot Springs, located 30 miles south of Livingston in the beautiful Paradise Valley. The difference here is that you get to drive. You'll get a "Mushing 101" lesson, then you'll hit the trail up the Mill Creek drainage of the Absaroka Mountains. Half-day treks with a picnic lunch run $130, and two-hour treks are $65. A full day of mushing, complete with a steak and trout lunch, is $175. The season usu-

ally runs from Thanksgiving to Easter, and reservations are required. If you can't get enough, sign up for a three-day "rookie" training session, usually held in December.

Continental Divide Dogsled Adventures
P.O. Box 84, Dubois, WY 82513
(307) 739-0165, (800) 531-6874
www.dogsledadv.com

Besides the usual full- and half-day trips, Continental Divide offers the mother of all dogsled adventures: three days of guided dogsledding in the rugged and snowy Wind River Mountains. Experienced musher Scott Smith will assign you a team of dogs and give you a basic course in sled control, commands, handling, harnessing, feeding, and care of your dogs—yours for three days. Nights are spent in the warm, cozy yurt or backcountry lodge, where you'll feast on a hearty meal and get a good night's rest. Optional cross-country skis and snowshoes are available at the rest stops for those who want more diversions. This multi-day tour ($1,570 per person) includes transportation to and from Jackson, instruction, meals, and expedition sleeping bags. If that sounds like too much, full day trips ($215) take you back to Brooks Lake Loge, and half day trips ($145) as well as two-night ($1,070) and overnight ($455) are available.

Dog Sled Tours by Washakie Outfitting
P.O. Box 1054, Dubois, WY
(307) 733-3602, (800) 249-0662
www.dogsledwashakie.com

Jacki and Billy Snodgrass have operated a commercial mushing operation for more than 10 years at their mountain home outside of Dubois, about 90 miles east of Jackson. The fourth generation Wyomingites use and breed Alaskan Huskies for their strength, longevity, and heritage of sled pulling. Half day, full day, and overnight trips are available. The Brooks Lake Lodge tour takes you back into the spectacular Absaroka Mountains, where you'll enjoy lunch beneath the splendor of the Pinnacle Buttes and next to a beautiful, alpine lake. After lunch your guide will mush you around the lake and back to the trailhead.

Jackson Hole Iditarod Sled Dog Tours
P.O. Box 1940, Jackson, WY 83001
(307) 733-7388, (800) 554-7388
www.jhsleddog.com

Jackson Hole Iditarod veteran Frank Teasley hosts your adventure here, where you'll mush through Grand Teton National Park or the Bridger-Teton National Forest. Meals, transportation, and extra clothing are provided and you can learn how to mush your own team. Full day trips leave at 9 A.M. and return at

approximately 4:30 P.M. A full day trip will take you back to Granite Hot Springs, where you can warm up by taking a dip in the natural spring. After you dry off, you'll be served a lunch of trout or steak. Frank has been the recipient of the Iditarod's Leonard Seppala Humanitarian Award for the best cared-for team, so you know you're in good hands. He also finished sixth in the race in 1991.

Klondike Dreams Sled Dog Tours
P.O. Box 268, West Yellowstone, MT 59758
(406) 646-4988
www.klondikedreams.com

Learn how to give commands and handle a powerful team of Alaskan huskies on half- or full-day tours of Gallatin National Forest trails. Half days are $100 per adult, $85 per child under 10, and are approximately three hours and include a snack. A full day tour ($165 per adult, $150 per child under 10) is about six hours and includes a lunch.

Moon Mountain Ranch
Grand Targhee Ski and Summer Resort
Alta, WY
(307) 353-2300, (800) TARGHEE
www.sharplink.com/dogsled

On the "other" side of the Tetons you'll find the Moon Mountain Ranch at Grand Targhee, where professional mushers will take you as high as 9,000 feet—3,000 feet above the valley that you came from. Sweeping views of three states, two national parks, and countless mountain ranges await, as does a snack lunch inside a warm and cozy teepee. Half-day backcountry tours (with or without lunch), BBQ cookout tours, and moonlit tours are available.

Spirit of the North Sled Dog Adventures
P.O. Box 1321, Ennis, MT 59729
(406) 995-3424, (406) 682-7994
www.huskypower.com

Spirit of the North offers half-day trips beginning at 9:30 A.M. and 1 P.M. seven days a week; make reservations at least one day in advance. Adults (13 and over) pay $99, children 7 to 12 are $75 and children under six travel free. Groups of four or more get a 10 percent discount. You'll get hands-on instruction before you and your huskies set out from the Moonlight Basin Ranch near Big Sky. The trail affords great views of Lone Mountain and the Spanish Peaks.

Snowmobiling

For many winter visitors, Yellowstone Country is best enjoyed by snowmobile. And why not? Our region offers endless miles of groomed and backcountry trails, big powder-filled basins and high alpine ridges. There are places that you can only get to by snowmobile, and when you get there and see the view you'll realize why this powder playground is so popular.

Snowmobiling in the west is unlike other places. Because of the powdery, often steep terrain, sleds are bigger and more powerful and use longer tracks and wider skis. These "powder sleds," as they're called, are what you need if you intend to go off-trail and head for the hills. And if you decide to do that, be prepared with avalanche knowledge and equipment. Every year snowmobilers die in Yellowstone Region avalanches and in most cases their deaths could have been prevented. This chapter has some basic information, but it's best to take a class and read up on proper procedures.

If you just intend to stick to the trails, a "trail sled" is what you need. These are often more comfortable on bumpy trails and usually have more room for two. These sleds are big and powerful, too, but aren't made for deep powder or climbing hills.

The town of West Yellowstone is recognized as the snowmobile capital of the world. Streets that are paved in the summer become snow-covered byways in the winter. It's one of the few places you can actually drive snowmachines on the roads. You can literally find hundreds of miles of trails—perfect for novice and advanced riders—beginning right from your hotel parking lot. If you want to head into the national parks, plan now. The National Park Service will phase out the use of snowmobiles in the parks by the winter

Insiders' Tip

The Three Bear Lodge, (800) 646-7353, and the Holiday Inn SunSpree Resort, (406) 646-7365, became the first rental operators to offer snowmobiles with quieter, more efficient four-stroke engines during the 2000-01 season. Called the "Yellowstone Special" by the manufacturer, Arctic Cat, these 660cc fuel-injected sleds run at only 70 decibels and get about 25 miles to the gallon while burning no oil. Traditional snowmobiles use whiny, two-stroke engines (like motorcycles) and often leave a trail of blue haze behind them. These new sleds are restricted to use in Yellowstone National Park and demonstrate of what the future of snowmobiling holds.

of 2003–04. This is a very controversial subject, and businesses and towns surrounding the park say their economies will crumble if snowmobilers aren't allowed park access. Proponents of the ban argue that the parks are for people and animals, not loud, polluting machines, and that towns and businesses will survive because park trails make up only a fraction of the terrain found in Yellowstone Country. Snowmobile manufacturers have come out with quieter, more efficient machines, but they are not yet mass marketed. However, several places in town offer them for rental.

Pay attention to the signs and rules while riding. Both Yellowstone National Park and the Gallatin National Forest have a 45-mph speed limit, and you must stay on the trails while in the parks. Never approach wildlife on a snowmachine and always give animals the right of way.

You must also have a valid driver's license to drive in the national parks. You'll see why, as the trails can be crowded and often seem like highway driving. It is now common to have as many as 800 snowmachines operating on the park road system each day, so hand signals and other rules apply. Read the literature handed out at the entrances for further rules and regulations.

Whether you stick to the trails or head for the hills, snowmobiling is a great way to experience the winter splendor around our region. The list below is only partial. Check forest ranger stations and visitor centers for complete maps and information.

Two things to keep in mind: If you're bringing your own sled registered in another state, you don't need to display a Montana registration. If your sled is unregistered, a non-resident, temporary use permit is required. You can get one by contacting the Montana Fish, Wildlife, and Parks Dept. at (406) 444-2535. You can also get statewide snowmobiling information by contacting the Montana Snowmobile Association, Box 4714, Missoula, MT 59806, or Travel Montana at (800) 847-4868 or www.visitmt.com.

Montana

Big Sky Area

The area south of Big Sky on U.S. Highway 191 is a mecca for thrill-seeking snowmobilers. Buck Creek Ridge is one of the most popular spots, and the trailhead is found just across from the Rainbow Ranch. The trail winds back 19 miles up the Buck Creek Ridge Road to excellent snow play areas on the ridge. The trail passes alongside the Lee Metcalf Wilderness boundary and offers great views of two of our favorite mountains, the Helmet and the Sphinx—easy to pick out on the horizon because of their namesakes. The trail is marked but ungroomed, and watch out for cornices on the main ridge.

Another great trail can be found by taking the Taylor Fork Road, which is about 18 miles long, west from U.S. 191. The road leads to a trailhead with ample parking, and the trail goes back past the Wapiti Forest Service cabin into the Carrot and Sage Creek Basins. There are plenty of powder play areas and this fun trail can occupy an entire day. Check the conditions of the Taylor Fork Road, as it is not plowed and heavy snow could make it impassable. If so, you can park at the junction of the road and the highway.

There's one other trail to mention— The Big Sky Trail, an iffy, ungroomed trail from Bozeman to Big Sky, is for experienced riders only. Many riders say that there's not really a trail at all, just parts that aren't well connected, and it's not worth searching for it.

Bozeman Area

You have to drive a little bit to get to the trails here, but they are worth it. About 22 miles north of town on Montana Highway 86 just past the Bridger Bowl ski resort,

The old mining town of Cooke City is a favorite winter spot for powder-hungry snowmobilers. PHOTO: DONNIE SEXTON/TRAVEL MONTANA

you'll find the Brackett Creek Parking Area. Taking the Brackett Creek Trail west into the North Bridger Mountains will lead you to numerous play areas with jaw-dropping views of this small, rugged range. Stay alert on the trail, since skiers and hikers also use the sledding hill about ¾ miles in. Highmarking is popular in the big bowls here, but be aware of avalanche danger. This trails system links up with the popular Fairy Lake Trail, which can also be accessed by driving another six miles past Brackett Creek on Montana Highway 86. This scenic trail looms beneath Sacajawea Peak, the highest in the range at 9,466 feet.

The Olsen Creek area is another popular spot. This is found a few miles south of the Bridger Bowl ski area on Montana Highway 86. The parking lot is on the west side of the road, and you'll have to cross the highway to get to the trail. The trail, which is a Forest Service road during the summer, climbs steadily for about four miles to a wide-open area on top of a ridge. From here you can continue north or south on the ridge, toward Skunk Creek Road or Jackson Creek Road, respectively. You'll see numerous powder-filled meadows along the way.

Contact the Gallatin Valley Snowmobile Association at (406) 763-4387 for more information about Bozeman and Big Sky area trails.

Cooke City

Cooke City calls itself a community of about "80 people, dogs, moose, and an occasional bison," and in winter the old mining town is an isolated place. Except, of course, for the hundreds of snowmobiles that pass through daily on their way to some of the best riding in the state. So good, in fact, that both Yamaha and Arctic Cat use the area as a test site.

The best thing about Cooke City is the

easily accessible, high-elevation trails. Heading east out of town toward the Beartooth Highway (closed in winter) opens up numerous possibilities, including the popular Daisy Pass Road. The trail heads north through the burned trees of the 1988 Yellowstone fires, switchbacking up to 9,345-foot Daisy Pass. From there, choose your powder play area or continue on the trail down into the basin below the pass.

Other trails include Lulu Pass Road, Round Lake, and Henderson Mountain, and the trail system connects with 50 miles of groomed trails in Wyoming.

Cooke City and the surrounding area get huge amounts of snow so avalanches are a frequent concern. Be well versed in avalanche knowledge or don't go, and pay attention on and off the trails. Call the avalanche advisory, (406) 838-2341, for detailed information on conditions.

For more information, call the Upper Yellowstone Snowmobile Club at (406) 838-2212 or (406) 838-2414, or contact the Gardiner Ranger District of the Gallatin National Forest, (406) 848-7375.

Virginia City/Ennis

If you're staying in the West Yellowstone area, a drive to the old mining town of Virginia City is a worthy diversion. From West, head north on U.S. Highway 287 until you reach the small town of Ennis, then head west on Montana Highway 287 over the pass and into Virginia City. The town, established in 1863 when gold lured early settlers into Alder Gulch, is primarily a summer destination but its close proximity to the trails of the Gravelly Range are making it more and more popular with snowmobilers. Trails begin right from town and you can ride on the streets. The main trail from town follows Alder Gulch through the ghost town of Summit City. Two options exist at the Lyons Bridge trailhead off U.S. 287. A 50-mile loop trail takes experienced riders to the spine of the Gravellys, while an easier route through Antelope Basin gives riders access to resorts at Elk and Cliff Lakes. A

total of 130 miles of trails are nearby.

Contact the Vigilante Snowmobilers at (406) 843-5484 or (406) 682-7755, or the Madison Ranger District of the Beaverhead-Deerlodge National Forest, (406) 682-4253, for more information on these and other trails in the area.

West Yellowstone Area

If you're basing your snowmobile trip in and around West Yellowstone, you'll have 580 miles of trails at your disposal, 180 of them in Yellowstone National Park. If you decide to ride in the park, there is a $15 entrance fee per machine, which is good for seven days in both Yellowstone and Grand Teton. Trails open in mid-December and close in early March. Fuel stops are located in Mammoth, Old Faithful, Fishing Bridge, and Canyon. Warming huts are located in Mammoth, Indian Creek, Madison Junction, Old Faithful, West Thumb, Fishing Bridge, and Canyon.

Taking the Grand Loop Road will lead you past several the park's main attractions. If you start from West Yellowstone, head 14 miles straight to Madison Junction, where you'll make a right and continue for 16 miles to Old Faithful. Along the way are the Fountain Paint Pot, Midway Geyser Basin, Biscuit Basin, and Black Sand Basin. A short loop along Firehole Canyon Drive is a nice diversion. Full services, including fuel, lodging, medical, and dining, are available at Old Faithful. Watching the famed geyser erupt in the winter is a marvelous sight.

From Old Faithful, continue 17 miles over the mountains to the West Thumb, where you can thaw out in the warming hut. From there, you can head south toward Grand Teton (22 miles), or continue along Yellowstone Lake up to Fishing Bridge. This 21-miles jaunt is one of the prettiest in the park. You'll find fuel and a warming hut at Fishing Bridge. From here, heading east 27 miles will take you toward Cody and out the east entrance of the park. If you choose this route, be careful of the avalanche danger about 18 miles in. Heading north from

The Two Top Loop is near West Yellowstone, Montana, is a popular snowmobiling trail. PHOTO: DONNIE SEXTON/TRAVEL MONTANA

Fishing Bridge leads you along the Grand Canyon of the Yellowstone, where huge frozen waterfalls plunge hundreds of feet down to the Yellowstone River. Follow the signs for the best viewing points. When you reach the canyon area, head back 12 miles west to Norris, then 14 miles southwest to Madison Junction. From Norris, you can also head 21 miles north to Mammoth, where you'll find the most services in the park.

If you are snowmobiling outside of the park, you're in for some incredible scenery. The nation's first designated snowmobile trail, Two Top, begins just west of town and curls its way up to the Continental Divide, passing numerous powder playgrounds along the way. When you reach the top you'll see the Tetons on a clear day.

Experienced riders should check out the wild Lionhead Loop, a steep 10-mile trail full of tricky, windblown snow. You'll get great views of the rugged Lionhead and Lower Madison Ranges, but do not take this trail unless you possess and know how to use avalanche equipment.

Other nice trails include the Madison Arm Loop, the South Plateau, and the Horse Butte Trail, all of which offer inspiring vistas around every corner. For more information and trail maps, contact the Hebgen Lake Ranger District, (406) 823-6961), the West Yellowstone Chamber of Commerce, (406) 646-7701) or Yellowstone National Park, (307) 344-7381, ext. 2206). It's best to contact these agencies anyway to get detailed and up-to-the-minute information on trail conditions and closures.

Idaho

Island Park

Island Park is snowmobiler's paradise, with more than 400 miles of groomed trails that spurt off in every direction. From Island Park, you can access the trails in Yellowstone National Park and around West Yellowstone, as well as the trails in the Gallatin and Targhee National Forests and all the way down to Flagg Ranch on the northern end of Grand Teton National Park.

Snowmobiling is popular here because of the long season and abundance of snow. The town sits at an elevation of about 6,000 feet, high enough to let the snow stick around all winter. Another reason for the popularity is that the town caters to snowmobilers. Just about every business in town can be reached by snowmobile, creating a great atmosphere for riders and making it a great place to take your snowmobiling vacation.

One of the most popular trails leads up to 8,710-foot Two Top Mountain, about nine miles from town. This ride offers plenty for the beginner and expert. Beginners will want to stick to the trail, then soak in the view from the top as the more advanced riders play in the powder of the many off-trail bowls. This trail can be a little crowded, with more than 80,000 sledders using it each year.

Thirty miles from Island Park is Upper Mesa Falls, a flat and easy trail that ends at a 110-foot frozen waterfall, a prime example of the region's winter beauty.

Since enough snowmobilers descend on Island Park each year, there's really no need for a guide. Trails are extremely well marked and maps are available in just about every business. For more information and trail maps, contact the Island Park Ranger District at (208) 558-7301.

Insiders' Tip

First time on a snowmobile? Several companies around the region offer guided tours. Grand Teton National Park Snowmobile Rental, (800) 563-6469, offers half- and full-day trips to Togwotee, Jenny Lake, Old Faithful, and more. Rates start at $79 per person. Togwotee Snowmobile Adventures offers Yellowstone, Gros Ventre, Granite Hot Springs, and Greys River day tours out of Moran, Wyoming. Call (800) 543-2847. Best Adventures (800) 851-0827, offers snowmobile tours of Yellowstone for $165, and Back-country Adventure, (800) 924-7669, has tours in the Gallatin National Forest and Yellowstone National Park from West Yellowstone.

Wyoming

Cody

The best bet for snowmobiling around Cody is to head to the Pahaska Tepee area (described earlier) just outside the east entrance to Yellowstone National Park. A groomed trail connects riders to the rest of the trails in the park, where you can ride down to Flagg Ranch, over to West Yellowstone or up to Mammoth. Other options include taking the incredibly scenic Chief Joseph Highway (U.S. 287) northwest to nearly 60 miles of groomed trails and numerous playgrounds in the Beartooth Mountains. From here you can actually hook up with the trails around the Cooke City area. East of Cody you'll find the Bighorn Mountains, where more groomed trails exist.

Jackson Area

Jackson isn't exactly known as a snowmobiling mecca because you need to drive out of town to access the trails. But many feel the extra work is well worth it. You can drive to Flagg Ranch at the northern end of the park and start snowmobiling from there, but most people head south to the Togwotee Pass area to access the Continental Divide Snowmobile Trail, which runs from the Lander area up to Grand Teton and Yellowstone National Parks and on to West Yellowstone. It would take several days to ride the whole trail, so most riders head to Togwotee or the Gros Ventre River Road to access parts of the trail. You can also hop on the trail at the Grand Teton National Park RV Resort in the Buffalo Fork Valley, the Signal Mountain Lodge in Grand Teton National Park, or at Flagg Ranch just south of Yellowstone.

One popular trip with a warm ending is the 10-mile ride to Granite Hot Springs, a commercial resort with a 104-degree, natural-fed pool that beckons bathers for a relaxing dip after an invigorating ride.

Guide services are popular in these parts, mostly because you have to drive to ride. A large number of outfitters and a few offer a variety of guided snowmobile trips, and there are a few rental companies as well. Whatever way you choose, snowmobiling here produces some of the most beautiful scenery in the country.

Snowmobile Rentals

Yellowstone National Park

AmFac Mammoth Hotel Snowmobile Shop
Mammoth Hot Springs
(307) 344-7311
www.travelyellowstone.com

AmFac Old Faithful Snow Lodge
Old Faithful
(307) 344-7311
www.travelyellowstone.com

You can rent sleds at Mammoth and Old Faithful for $130 for one rider or $145 for two. Children under 12 ride free with a licensed adult. Clothing rentals are available for $20. Both locations offer Winter Getaway packages, including one-day snowmobile rental, two nights lodging, breakfast, hot tub rental, and ice skating. Prices start at $149 at Mammoth and $249 at Old Faithful per person based on double occupancy.

Montana

Canyon Adventures
U.S. Hwy. 191, Big Sky, MT
(406) 995-4450, (800) 520-SLED
www.canyonadventures.com

This Big Sky business rents sleds from its location one mile south of the Big Sky entrance. Full-day rates range from $89 to

$145; a half-day is $65 to $95. Complete clothing rentals are available for $15. Canyon specializes in guiding you to some of the best spots in the Gallatin Canyon, including Buck Creek Ridge. Guide service runs $150 per day or $75 for a half day. Trailer trips are available for larger groups.

Cooke City Exxon and Polaris/Ski Doo
U.S. Hwy. 212, Cooke City, MT
(406) 838-2244

If you didn't bring your sled to this little mountain town, Cooke City Exxon has about 16 rentals from $125 to $150 per day, plus gas. You can also rent clothing and gear for $30 a day.

Rendezvous Snowmobile Rentals
415 Yellowstone Ave., West Yellowstone, MT
(406) 646-9564, (800) 426-7669
www.snowmobileyellowstone.net

Owner Randy Roberson has three generations of Yellowstone hospitality behind Rendezvous, where you'll find eight different models of Polaris sleds for rent. Prices range from $109 to $175 depending on what kind of machine you want. All of them have hand warmers and Rendezvous gives discounts to Big Sky skiers. They also offer a $25 per-person transportation package from Big Sky to West Yellowstone, so you can spend more time on the trail. Clothing is also available for rental.

Two Top Snowmobile Rental
645 Gibbon Ave., West Yellowstone, MT
(406) 646-7802, (800) 522-7802
www.twotopsnowmobile.com

Serving Yellowstone snowmobilers since 1966, Two Top offers four single rider and four double rider Polaris sleds. Prices range from $89 for the Lite GT 340 to $119 for the RMK 500 Liquid. If you're staying in Big Sky, Two Top has some great specials. Just tell owners Dave and Jamie McCray, "I saw you at Big Sky," and you'll get $10 off. Clothing is available for $15 per day.

Yellowstone Tour and Travel
P.O. Box 410, West Yellowstone, MT
(646) 9310, (800) 221-1151
www.yellowstone-travel.com

This full-service travel service is affiliated with three hotels in town (Holiday Inn, Three Bear Lodge, and the Big Western Pine) and specializes in multi-day bed and sled packages. Price depends on how many people you have, what kind of sled you want, and where you want to stay. They start at around $665 for two days and three nights. You'll get complimentary tickets to the Grizzly Discovery Center (see Attractions) and a prime rib dinner as well. Yellowstone Tour and Travel also started renting environmentally sensitive, four-stroke sleds in 2000–01.

Wyoming

Flagg Ranch Resort
P.O. Box 187, Moran, WY 83013
(307) 543-2484, (800) 443-2311
www.flaggranch.com

Flagg Ranch is the center of winter activities at the south entrance of Yellowstone National Park. Daily snowmobile rentals on new Polaris sleds are available for around $150. Additional adult riders are $60, and children are $30. Rentals include helmet, suit, boots, gloves, and the first tank of gas. If you're staying in the Jackson area, the folks at Flagg Ranch will pick you up and take you back for an additional $15.

Other Activities

High Mountain Heli-Skiing
Jackson, WY
(307) 733-3274
www.heliskijackson.com

A day of heli-skiing with High Mountain consists of six runs and up to 15,000 feet of skiing. Two Bell 407 helicopters transport you to terrain south of the Jackson Hole ski resort, including all of the Snake River and Palisades Mountain Ranges and portions of the Hoback, Teton, and Gros Ventre ranges. Groups are made of five clients and one guide. Terrain runs from intermediate to expert and skiers and snowboarders are grouped accordingly. You should be at the advanced level and be able to link parallel turns if you want to give it a try. Fat powder ski rentals are also available. Packages with five nights at Teton Pines and three days of skiing start at $1,878 per person. High Mountain's offices are located in Teton Village at the Renaissance Resort and Spa, and hours are 2 P.M. to 7 P.M. daily during the winter.

Snow King Tubing Park
Snow King Resort, Jackson, WY
(307) 734-TUBE

Some people can't ski, but everyone can tube. A rope tow lift takes you to the top of Snow King's tubing park, then you glide down the lanes on provided inner-tubes for an exhilarating and slippery ride. Hours are Monday through Friday 4 P.M. to 8 P.M. and on weekends from noon until 8 P.M. Adults pay $8 per hour, $12 for two hours. Kids pay $6 and $9, respectively.

Ice Climbing

This is a popular sport in Yellowstone Country, as the winter temperatures allow for excellent ice conditions from around Thanksgiving (sometimes much earlier) through April. Good waterfall ice can be found in several spots, and challenging mixed routes exist for those who have the skills. If you just want to give it a try, several opportunities exist for guided excursions.

If you're staying in the Jackson area, try Exum Mountain Guides, (307) 733-2297, in Grand Teton National Park, which offers everything from introductory lessons to winter ascents of a major peak. Ice climbing areas include Death Canyon, Lake Louise, Torrey Canyon, and the Dubois area 90 miles east of Jackson. Rates are $275 for one person, $165 each for two climbers.

Jackson Hole Mountain Guides, (307) 733-4979, www.jhmg.com, has been leading Teton adventures since 1968. The company's acclaimed school offers an introductory ice climbing class for $125, and a basic snow school class for $100.

The center of the ice climbing universe in Cody is Bison Willy's Ice Climbing Bunkhouse, (307) 587-0629, www.bisonwillys.com, a climber's hostel where diehards gather each winter to explore the area's excellent routes. You'll find information about the latest conditions here and tips on where to find the best ice. You can also register for the annual Waterfall Ice Roundup, held during February, where there's plenty of beer, food, and entertainment to go around. Also try Sunlight Sports at (888) 889-2463 for information on where to go.

The Bozeman area offers several ice climbing opportunities, including waterfall-filled Hyalite Canyon. When you get to town, stop by Northern Lights Trading Company, (406) 586-2225, or Barrel Mountaineering, (406) 582-1335, for information. The staff at both of these establishments will answer questions about ice climbing in the area. Both locations also rent harnesses, ice tools, and crampons.

Ice Skating

Beall Park
N. Black and Villard Sts., Bozeman, MT

A popular north-side city park, the ice rink here is large and accommodates plenty of recreational skaters and a few games of pick-up hockey or broomball. It's open from noon to 10 P.M. on weekdays and 10 A.M. to 10 P.M. on weekends.

Bogert Park
325 S. Church Ave., Bozeman, MT

This covered rink is reserved for hockey after 4 P.M., so check the schedule posted at the rink for recreational ice skating times.

Haynes Pavillion
Gallatin County Fairgrounds, Bozeman, MT

Bozeman's newest covered rink, built with the help of the Bozeman Amateur Hockey Association, allows recreational skating and hockey. The fairgrounds are located on Tamarack Street, between North Rouse and North Seventh Avenues.

Mammoth Hotel
Mammoth Hot Springs, Yellowstone National Park, WY
(307) 344-7311

If you're staying in Mammoth, you can skate on this flooded rink outside the hotel. Skate rentals are available by the hour or day.

Snow King Center Ice Rink
100 E. Snow King Ave., Jackson, WY
(307) 733-5200
www.snowking.com

This big indoor rink at the Snow King ski area is open from August through April and has skate rentals, snacks, and beverages on-site. Public skating sessions, which cost around $7, are regularly scheduled during the week. A less expensive session is available on Saturdays, but call ahead as the rink hosts many other activities.

Southside Park
W. College and S. 5th Ave., Bozeman, MT

This rink is on the south side of town near the university and is open from noon until 10 P.M. on weekdays and 10 A.M. to 10 P.M. on weekends. Recreational skating and hockey are allowed.

Valley Ice Garden
269 Jackrabbit Ln., Bozeman, MT
(406) 585-1415
www.valleyicegarden.com

This regulation-sized hockey rink is home to Bozeman's Junior Pro hockey team, the Icedogs. The Garden also has open public and figure skating during the week and on the weekends. Call for times, as they change weekly.

Relocation

Education
Real Estate
Healthcare
Retirement
Worship

Yellowstone Country has an intangible allure. The simple greatness of so much space free from development and crowds is impressive. But the sky, the mountains, and the rivers have nothing on the hospitality and friendliness of the people out here. We have been wrapped up in the magic that this area casts upon us and it's a pleasure to share it with you. If you can't get enough of our area and are considering relocation or a vacation home, the listings that follow will help you get started.

Although the landscape dominates our culture, this is also a place where people are interested in the arts, education, and community. In this chapter we cover adult education opportunities, real estate markets, medical facilities, and retirement information. The Resources chapter has information about area chambers of commerce. Request a relocation packet (for a fee) from the town of your choice.

Education

BYU-Idaho (Ricks College)
Rexburg, ID, 83460
(208) 356-2200
www.ricks.edu

Ricks College was founded in 1888 as Bannock Stake Academy, developed by the Church of Jesus Christ of Latter-day Saints. Ricks became the official name in 1917, and then the school became known as Brigham Young University–Idaho in June 2000. It changed from a two-year junior college into a four-year institution with the affiliation of BYU.

With an enrollment cap of 8,600 students, the small college offers 40 majors within 9 academic departments.

Montana State University
Bozeman, MT
(994) 2452, (888) 678-2287
www.montana.edu

More than 11,000 students from 50 states and 47 countries attend MSU, which offers baccalaureate degrees in 50 fields, master's degrees in 39 disciplines, and doctorates in 13. The 1,170-acre campus is filled with trees and surrounded by mountains, and is a nice place to stroll

around. A brochure detailing a leisurely walking tour of campus landmarks and school history is available at the Strand Union Building, the main student gathering place, located on the south end of campus.

The land-grant university was founded in 1893 as the Agricultural College of the State of Montana, then changed its name to the State College of Agriculture and Mechanical Arts, then to Montana State College, and finally to MSU in 1965. In 1994, the college merged with Northern Montana College, Eastern Montana College, and two colleges of technology, so it is occasionally referred to as MSU–Bozeman.

The university contributes much to Bozeman's atmosphere, offering art, theater, music, and sports events all year long. The Exit Gallery in the Strand Union Building and the Helen E. Copeland Gallery in Haynes Hall display student, faculty, and juried art exhibits, while Reynolds Recital Hall offers a variety of recitals and concerts. Several theater companies perform in the Strand Union Theater, and the school is also the home of Montana Shakespeare in the Parks. The Brick Breeden Fieldhouse—where many of the sports are played—hosts big-name concerts a few times a year.

The sports teams, known as the Bobcats, compete at the Division I level in the Big Sky Conference, while rodeo competition for men and women is conducted through the Big Sky Region of the National Intercollegiate Rodeo Association. Games are always competitive and fun to watch.

Northwest College
231 W. 6th St., Powell, WY
(307) 754-6111

The neighboring community of Powell, some 50 miles to the west, is closely linked to Cody. Northwest College offers two-year programs in classic arts and sciences. Founded in 1949 as a satellite branch for the University of Wyoming, enrollment at the residential college has grown to 2,000 students.

Northwest College operates Mickelson Field Station in the Absaroka Mountain Range off the Chief Joseph Highway (Wyoming Highway 296). This year-round research facility is used for retreats or outdoor education classes, and it includes 12 cabins and a three-building complex. Call for availability and reservations.

Teton Science School
P.O. Box 68T, Kelly, WY 83011
(307) 733-4765

Located within Grand Teton National Park, Teton Science School has provided natural science education for kids and adults since 1967. Summer programs include two-to-five-week residential field ecology and field natural history courses for junior high and high school students, as well as week-long, non-residential programs for students in third through eighth grades. A one-year, master's level graduate program in Environmental Education and Natural Science is also offered.

For those visiting the park and wanting to educate themselves a little more, the scince school offers up to 40 one- to four-day field seminars taught by expert instructors.

The Yellowstone Institute
Mammoth Hot Springs, Yellowstone National Park, WY
(307) 344-2294

Learn to track wolves in Yellowstone's Lamar Valley. Identify native songbirds as they migrate into Yellowstone each year. Spend a day perfecting your plein air painting technique from Artist's Point overlooking the Grand Canyon of the Yellowstone. Or practice your wildlife photography skills along Specimen Ridge.

This is only a sampling of the Yellowstone Institute's courses offered throughout the year within the park. Established in 1948, the Yellowstone Institute provides visitors with hands-on educational experiences using Yellowstone as their classroom. The Yellowstone Institute is the education arm of the park's non-profit Yellowstone Association. Each year more than 850 students enroll in 80 different classes, with subjects ranging from geology, ecology, and history to mysteries of Yellowstone. Sounds serious, but these courses are laid back and enjoyable. They are a far cry from sitting at a desk taking notes from a dry lecture series; most of them are conducted while you are out hiking, backpacking, llama packing, canoeing, or cross country skiing.

Based at the historic Buffalo Ranch in the Lamar Valley, courses range in length from single session to multi-day. College credit is available for many classes. The wilds of Yellowstone are the classroom, but students stay at the ranch in sleeping cabins, and a historic bunkhouse, and use a communal kitchen. Most classes take place between June 1 and September 1, but some winter courses are offered as well. A complete catalog of classes comes out twice a year. Write to the institute at P.O. Box 117, Yellowstone National Park, WY 82190 for a catalog. Classes fill quickly, so don't hesitate if you would like to participate in one.

Real Estate

Not since the gold rush and homesteading days has there been such a clamoring for land in Yellowstone Country. This time the treasure is mountain views, riverfront getaways, and estates on rambling acreage. Greater Yellowstone is one of the fastest growing regions of the West. Part of that is good marketing, part of it is just luck, most of it is location. Tagged by *Outside* magazine as the "Last Best Place," southwestern Montana communities have been booming since the early 1990s. World class skiing, shopping, and celebrities like Harrison Ford and Mel Gibson buying real estate have showcased Jackson Hole, Wyoming, and subsequently its neighboring communities. Blue ribbon fishing in the Idaho's Island Park region has made it the hotbed for second homes. Regardless of the source of the region's growth, it's happening. Many of the markets are inflated by high-end second homes, but there are still great deals to be found out there. Whether you are buying to invest, to relocate, or to retreat, you can find your dream property.

What you will see in Yellowstone Country are wide open spaces, jagged mountains, cascading streams, and quaint western towns, but the magnitude of this beauty shrinks as more people move in. As a result, Greater Yellowstone communities grapple with drawing lines to preserve the scenic beauty and wildlife habitat of our land without setting limitations on newcomers. City and county planning meetings are brimming with zoning issues, development proposals, and new plans to incorporate growth as well as open space. It's not easy to find a balance, but bit by bit, towns are finding their own way. Many communities such as Jackson Hole, Wyoming, and Bozeman, Montana, have formed land trusts to save wildlife migration corridors, viewsheds, and farm land within their area. Basically private land owners agree to set aside property under a conservation easement, forever forfeiting their rights to develop or subdivide the designated land. Currently over 300,000 acres of land are managed under conservation easements. There are real estate companies and brokers who work with this specific goal in mind, but you can also ask the realtor of your choice for more information on conservation easements.

> ## Insiders' Tip
> Montana is one of the nation's major producers of log homes. Two types of house logs are made here—hand-hewn, and machine-lathed. Twenty percent of the log houses produced here stay in Montana.

In this chapter we've briefly described property markets in communities and listed some real estate agencies to help you get started.

Southwestern Montana

Bozeman, Montana

Bozeman is one of Montana's fastest growing cities, and houses are springing up all over the city and the surrounding Gallatin Valley. Because of this, downtown housing costs have soared to the point that most working class families have to look elsewhere. On Bozeman's more desirable south side—historic homes close to downtown and the university—it's not uncommon to find small, two-bedroom homes for more than $120,000.

Larger homes are harder to find, and many go for upwards of $300,000. The north side of town is where you'll find bargains, if you like to fix up and add your own charm. This section of town is actually older, more industrial, and eccentric. Many folks can find a house that needs lots of work and put their own imaginative touches into it. Still, it's nearly impossible to find a house under $80,000.

Most new construction is taking place on the west side of town, where subdivision after subdivision sprawls over former farmland, and is made up of a combination of single family homes and townhouses. Generally prices in these neighborhoods start at around $120,000 for a modest, three-bedroom home. Upscale housing can be found all over, especially in the Bridger Canyon, Springhill, and Sourdough areas—anywhere on the outskirts of town.

Naturally, people look to the surrounding area. Belgrade, eight miles west of Bozeman along the interstate, has benefited the most from Bozeman's skyrocketing housing costs. Houses here are significantly cheaper, while residents still enjoy all the amenities of the surrounding area. The prices drop even more the further west you go, toward Amsterdam, Churchill, Gallatin Gateway, Three Forks, and Manhattan. You'll also find chunks of land out this way that aren't outrageously expensive.

Bridger Realty
85 W. Kagy Blvd., Bozeman, MT
(406) 586-7676, (888) 586-7676
www.bridgerrealtyy.com

Most of broker/owner Mike Basile's 20 agents have more than 20 years experience in the field. Bridger can research your housing needs in advance through their Multiple Listing Service, and can show you any property that meets your guidelines even it's listed with another real estate office.

Bridger Realty offers a full line of residential, commercial, and acreage listings.

ERA Landmark Real Estate
1805 Dickerson #1, Bozeman, MT
(406) 586-1321, (800) 788-2372
www.eralandmark.com

ERA Landmark has been one of Bozeman's leading real estate agencies since 1976, and the top all-around ERA broker in the nation since 1998. ERA specializes in residential, new construction, commercial, acreages, and vacation properties. With offices in Big Sky and Bozeman, ERA's nearly 30 real estate professionals can find something to suit your needs. The agency also provides international relocation, in-house mortgage programs, and a free 16-page real estate guide.

Gardiner and Cooke City, Montana

As the original entrance to Yellowstone, growth in Gardiner is limited by the surrounding national forest and park boundaries. However, this fact is principally what keeps the town from losing its real western character.

Most people who move to Gardiner come for the proximity to Yellowstone (only five miles from Mammoth Hot Springs) because they work there or soon will be. There is a small pocket of people who also choose Gardiner for recreational retreats or second homes, but these residents are generally north of town through Yankee Jim Canyon. Within Gardiner, homes are not available often and land is scarce. You'll find riverfront property with a modest two acres jumping as high as $500,000, while acreage in Yankee Jim Canyon ranges between $2,000 to $6,000. In 1998 a three-bedroom, two-bathroom house on a small lot cost $100,000.

Through Yellowstone National Park and up to 7,500 feet, real estate in Cooke City is even less common. The tiny town is isolated by winter snows from October to June, but hosts a strong skiing and snowmobiling business during that time. But it is during summer months when the town's population balloons from 90 to 300 and floods with tourists. It's not an easy place to live, nor is it an easy place to find property to buy. The steep mountains, designated wilderness, and other federal lands make Cooke a limited land market. When something does come up for sale, the prices tend to be inflated. A one-acre lot within the city limits was listed at $37,900, while we saw a large restaurant and bar priced at $350,000.

Century 21 Payne Realty
124 W. Lewis St., Livingston, MT
(406) 222-6377, (800) 637-7911
Gardiner Office, (406) 848-7904

After 25 years in the Livingston real estate business, brokers Bob and Dee Payne provide an inside edge to buying farm and ranch properties, as well as recreation properties in and around Livingston. They team up with Karen Hayes in Gardiner to offer specialized service to clients. In Gardiner, associate broker Karen Hayes is the person you need to contact. She has her finger on the pulse of the community and can tip you off to the rare residential property within the area.

Livingston, Montana

Though it is only 25 miles east of Bozeman, this tiny old pioneer town bursts with growing pains but has managed to maintain its easy small-town feel. With a population of around 7,500, easy access to mountains and rivers, and close access to Bozeman, Livingston is charming and ideally located.

The real estate market in Livingston is divided into two different worlds: town and the valleys. In Livingston proper you can still find reasonably priced historic homes within the $80,000 to $100,000 range. Town offers the sweet conveniences of provincial life—with the post office, restaurants, shops, and schools all within walking distance. The community has a rich arts culture and is home to many painters, writers, and actors.

Land prices get crazy outside of town. The region includes the ever-popular Paradise Valley to the south, the Shields River Valley to the east, and the Boulder Valley to the southeast. Newsman Tom Brokaw and actors Michael Keaton, Dennis Quaid, and Meg Ryan have planted roots here and put the area on the high profile map. Add Hollywood exposure to breathtaking scenery and boundless recreation opportunities and you've got a pretty nice package. Expect to pay anywhere between $5,000 to $20,000 per acre and don't expect to find your ideal property easily. The influx of second home residents has scooped up the larger parcels over the last 15 years, so now prime pieces of land with more than 20 acres rarely come up for sale.

Coldwell Banker/Maverick Realty
125 E. Callendar St., Livingston, MT
(406) 222-0304, (800) 676-8189

Broker-owner Michelle Goodwine was born and raised in Livingston and has been with Maverick Realty since 1986. While she sells all kinds of properties, including ranches and businesses, she sells more small acreages and homes than anything else. In fact, Coldwell Banker/Maverick Realty has been the leader in residential sales in the Livingston area for six years. The agency has nine sales associates, a licensed assistant, and a full-time property manager.

Red Lodge, Montana

Red Lodge sits at the base of the massive Beartooth Mountains as they tumble to the valley floor and stretch out into the expanse of Montana prairie. Two golf courses, a ski mountain, access to wilderness, Yellowstone National Park, and a major airport within

60 miles are just a few of the things that make this Montana town so appealing. With a population of 2,300, the small town western flavor of Red Lodge is pervasive and real. It is a place that feels undiscovered, a little sheltered, a little too quaint. Yet the real estate market here does not reflect the naiveté that the town first projects.

You won't find bargains here, where few residential homes come on the market and outlying acreage goes for top dollar. In 2000, we saw a 2.75-acre lot on the edge of town with outstanding mountain views listed for $59,900. A small, three-bedroom, finely renovated 1920s bed and breakfast was priced at $390,000, while a new condo between town and Red Lodge Mountain Ski Area was $142, 000. Attribute these kinds of prices to the initial Montana boom sparked by the movie *A River Runs Through It*, filmed in 1990. By 1996 interested buyers leveled out, but Red Lodge's prices did not. There is hope, however. If you don't mind being about 30 miles from Red Lodge proper, it's possible to find raw land for roughly $1,300 an acre.

C Mor Real Estate
110 S. Broadway, Red Lodge, MT
(406) 446-2123, (800) 752-2499

Red Lodge's oldest and largest real estate agency, C Mor has eight agents who know the area well, including how far you'll have to drill for a well, how deep the snow is in winter, and how far you'll have to drive or walk to school. C Mor's agents pride themselves on their community involvement and have sold all types of real estate for more than 20 years. They also offer a relocation service.

> **Insiders' Tip**
> If you're older than 62 and heading for Grand Teton or Yellowstone national parks, make sure you buy a Golden Age Passport. It costs $10 and buys you lifetime entrance to all national parks.

Northwestern Wyoming

Cody, Wyoming

Views of mountains and prairie instead of traffic jams are what Cody promises. Look a little deeper and you'll see a town deeply rooted in its heritage and quietly standing at the forefront of Western culture. These undercurrents shine when locals talk about town founder Buffalo Bill Cody and the famous Buffalo Bill Cody Historic Center. You'll also find quality medical and educational facilities combined with boundless recreational opportunities.

. While other Greater Yellowstone communities sport property prices in the multi-millions, Cody's real estate pace has slowed since 1998. There are exceptions, of course, but in 1999 the average home in town sold for around $109,700

and $171,500 out of town. Homes within the historic downtown district sold for higher prices, around $200,000, but throughout the community prices are relatively reasonable.

ReMax Real Estate Group
15 07 Beck Ave., Cody, WY
(307) 587-3883

Owners Mike and Theresa Donley are a husband and wife broker team who specialize in residential properties and working with families to find that perfect home. Since they opened in 1997, the Donleys have used their roots in the community to match people and places. With 15 years of real estate experience between them, they share an affection for Cody country and offer this to their clients.

Western Real Estate
1143 Sheridan Ave., Cody, WY
(307) 587-4926, (800) 538-5122

As Cody's oldest real estate firm, Western Real Estate sells every kind of property. Six full-time agents work together as one big team specializing in farm, ranch, and recreational properties as well as commercial pieces. The agency is staffed mostly by long-time residents of Cody and is owned by Shirley Lehman, a fourth-generation Wyoming native, and Ed Higbie, a second-generation Cody native. Western Real Estate leads the market in selling recreational property.

Jackson, Wyoming

Jackson is one of the premier places to live in the West, especially if you can afford to live here. The price of the average home has skyrocketed to more than a million dollars, and you'll be hard-pressed to find a place near town for under $300,000. Even townhomes and condos are pricey, but if you are only considering living here for part of the year, that may be the best option. That way, perhaps you could make some money back on daily or weekly rentals during the busy tourist seasons.

For these reasons, many people are finding out about Jackson's equally impressive surrounding small towns. On the east side of Teton Pass, these include Alpine, Pinedale, Bondurant, Thayne, and Afton. The west side of the pass—Idaho—is also booming. Towns like Driggs, Tetonia, and Victor are capturing many of those who can't quite afford to live in Jackson proper, but still want to be in the shadow of the Tetons.

American Realty West, Inc.
189 N. Main St., Driggs, ID
(208) 354-2348
www.arwest.com

Many people are finding out that the Teton Valley area—on the Idaho side of Teton Pass—is less crowded, less expensive, and equally beautiful. American Realty West has a variety of ranch and home sites available in the valley. Towns include Driggs, Victor, Tetonia, and Rexburg.

Jackson Hole Realty
185 W. Broadway Ave., Jackson, WY
(307) 733-9009, (888) 733-9009
www.JHRealty.com

Jackson Hole Realty has been serving the region since 1964, offering everything from in-town locations and large ranches to ski area condominiums and pristine Jackson acreage. In fact, the company sold more than half of the entire dollar volume in Jackson Hole during 1999. There are eight locations around the valley to serve your real estate needs.

Mountain View Real Estate
251 Vista Ave., Thayne, WY
(307) 883-3792
www.silverstar.com/mvr

Broker Susan Anderson specializes in real estate in the area south of Jackson along U.S. Highway 89. As Jackson's real estate prices soar, many folks are looking at outlying areas to build or buy their dream home. From Alpine to Afton, Mountain View can find something for you.

Real Estate of Jackson Hole
P.O. Box 1027, Jackson, WY
(307) 733-6060, (888) 733-6060
www.rejh.com

This exclusive real estate agency has four locations around the area: 110 E. Broadway in Jackson; the Broadway Shops; the Resort Hotel; and the Village Center in Teton Village. The agency has recently teamed up with Christie's Great Esates, the largest network of independent brokers specializing in the sale of important properties, and has access to properties all over the world. Contact the company for a free brochure highlighting all of its listings.

Healthcare

When pioneers first settled in Yellowstone country doctors made house calls. It was easier then for that one caregiver to travel to patients few and far between in this desolate country. As populations grew, country doctors had to travel further and further to care for their patients. Eventually towns were platted and became hubs for commerce and services. The bigger, centrally located towns built medical facilities and drew patients from far and wide to their doors.

Even today, great distances separate some rural towns from complete and reliable medical care. Many towns only have clinics for day-to-day health needs, while full service hospitals are 50 to 100 miles away. Still, rural clinics are well connected with major hospitals and you will be able to receive respectable medical assistance throughout our region.

Emergency 911 service is available in all areas of Greater Yellowstone, including the parks. The people who answer your call are highly trained individuals, many of whom are emergency medical technicians (EMT). Except for larger towns like Bozeman, Billings, and Idaho Falls, most emergency crews consist of volunteers. These men and women are the people who fight our fires, answer the calls for help or tragedy, and willingly put their lives on the line to ensure the safety of our area.

> ## Insiders' Tip
> The cool clear water of mountain streams and lakes looks clean enough to drink, but don't do it. Although waterways are relatively free of pollutants, natural bacteria in the water can cause severe illness in people. Stick to treated water from a faucet or a bottle.

What we tell you in this section is where to find the hospitals and clinics and what services they provide. If you have special medical needs, it's a good idea to figure out where you'll be able to access a hospital or clinic during your trip.

In the Parks

It's not too far off base to say that Yellowstone and Grand Teton National Park's clinics administer care for some of the oddest ailments, including embedded fishing hooks, poison ivy rashes, altitude-related cardiac problems, and burns caused by scalding geothermal features. Primarily, the three park clinics treat injuries from automobile accidents. With three million people traveling on unfamiliar, narrow, winding highways gawking at roadside attractions, the parks can be dangerous.

Yellowstone's two clinics and one hospital and Grand Teton's one clinic serve park visitors each summer. Of the millions who pass through here, less than one percent need medical care, but park facilities and emergency medical services are equipped to provide assistance for minor and major injuries. Yellowstone and Grand Teton rangers all have EMT status and many are certified Wilderness First Responders, while a few of them are trained medics. We hope you won't need medical attention when you come here, but if you do, trust that you are in good, qualified hands.

Yellowstone National Park

Lake Hospital
Lake Village, 713 Lake, Yellowstone
National Park
(307) 242-7241

This tiny medical facility has the honor of being the country's only seasonal hospital. Managed by West Park Hospital in Cody (see subsequent entry), the 10-bed facility opens with a new batch of healthcare professionals each May. From mid-May until mid-September the small staff provides 24-hour service to tourists, with one doctor at the hospital and one on call. Three and sometimes four share the workload throughout the season.

Mammoth Clinic
Mammoth Village, Yellowstone National
Park
(307) 344-7965

In the dead of winter Yellowstone's Mammoth Clinic is the only medical facility within 100 miles. Built in the 1960s, it is Yellowstone National Park's only year-round clinic. The staff provides care not just for year-round park employees, but for the residents of Gardiner and Cooke City, Montana.

Mammoth Clinic is open seven days a week between Memorial Day and Labor Day weekends, and Monday through Friday the rest of the year. Check with either the clinic or the Park Service for hours of operation, which vary seasonally.

Old Faithful Clinic
Old Faithful, Yellowstone National Park
(307) 545-7325

Even though you might be too sick to stand outside and watch Old Faithful Geyser blow, you can still see it from the waiting room of Old Faithful Clinic. That's not the only good thing about this medical facility (built in 1996); it also offers excellent aid for basic illnesses or injuries. With a staff of nurses and two doctors, the clinic stays busy, but walk-ins are welcome.

Grand Teton National Park

Grand Teton Medical Clinic
Jackson Lake Lodge, Grand Teton
National Park
(307) 543-2514

This clinic is located next to the Chevron gas station at the Jackson Lake Lodge, and is open daily from 10 A.M. to 6 P.M. mid-May to mid-October.

Southwestern Montana

Beartooth Hospital and Health Center
600 W. 21st St., Red Lodge, MT
(406) 446-2345

The numerous rural towns between Red Lodge and Billings rely on the Beartooth Hospital and Health Center for the finest medical care. Owned by the community since 1993, this 22-bed hospital has an attached nursing home and offers 24-hour emergency care. In addition, it offers a range of outpatient surgeries, including knee surgeries, plastic surgery, mastectomies, and appendectomies. The facility includes a daycare center and a pharmacy. Obstetrics, cardiac rehabilitation, and community health education are also

among the hospital's services. Mountain View Medical Center, a private clinic across the street from the hospital, also encourages appointments, but will accommodate walk-ins.

Big Sky Medical Clinic
P.O. Box 160609, Big Sky, MT
(406) 995-2797

Dr. Jeff Daniels and his staff are the main source of care in and around Big Sky, with a slopeside location especially handy for injured skiers and snowboarders. It's a fully equipped facility capable of handling just about any injury or illness. Hours are 10 A.M. to 5 P.M. daily.

Bozeman Deaconess Health Services
915 Highland Blvd., Bozeman, MT
(406) 585-1007
www.bozemandeaconess.com

BDHS is a community owned, nonprofit organization made up of Bozeman Deaconess Hospital, Highland Park Medical Campus, and Hillcrest Retirement Community. BDHS has more than 600 employees and has annual payroll and benefits exceeding $16.5 million.

The hospital is the only one in Gallatin County, with its service area including Gallatin, Park, and Madison Counties. The center of the hospital is an 86-bed acute care facility that provides inpatient and outpatient services and a 24-hour emergency room. Other services include day surgery, hospice care, nutrition counseling, physical therapy, radiology, and X-rays.

The Highland Park Medical Campus consists of three buildings that house medical practices for 74 physicians and multiple outpatient services. Hillcrest has been providing independent living for the elderly since 1963, and is currently constructing a brand-new facility on its top-of-the-hill location on Bozeman's east side.

Bozeman Urgent Care Center
1006 W. Main St., Bozeman, MT
(406) 586-8711

Urgent Care offers emergency room services seven days a week, with no appointment necessary. From allergies and colds to fractures and sports injuries, treatment is available Monday to Friday, 9 A.M. to 8 P.M., and on weekends from 9 A.M. to 5 P.M. There's an X-ray lab on site, and Urgent Care is staffed with several doctors and nurses.

Deaconess Billings Clinic
2800 10th Ave. N., Billings, MT
(406) 657-4000

Since it opened in 1927, this hospital has evolved from a family-oriented, 58-bed facility to a regional medical center employing more than 1,000 people. Today the 275-bed non-profit regional clinic, hospital, and trauma center is recognized for its patient-focused care. Services here include emergency, trauma and walk-in care, family practice, internal medicine, obstetrics and gynecology, cardiology, renal dialysis, psychiatric and behavioral health services, orthopedics and sports medicine, neurology, and women's health services. Deaconess operates DEACARE/ALS, a fixed-wing air-ambulance service that uses two prop jets.

Livingston Memorial Hospital
504 S. 13th, Livingston, MT
(406) 222-3541

Livingston Memorial Hospital is a nonprofit, community-owned facility servicing an area spanning roughly 150 miles within Sweetwater and Park Counties. Built in 1995, this 45-bed facility offers 24-hour emergency care and a four-bed intensive/critical care unit. A full-service facility, patients have access to a full lab, birth center, mammography, ultrasound, and surgery. The hospital is also known for its post-op care, with echocardiography, respiratory therapy, physical therapy, cardiac, and pulmonary rehabilitation available.

Saint Vincent Hospital and Health Center
1233 N. 30th St., Billings, MT
(406) 657-7000, (800) 762-8778

With 15 clinics in and around Billings as part of the Saint Vincent Primary Care Network, Saint Vincent's offers progressive healthcare. Billings' oldest hospital has been providing care for the people of the region for over a century. With 302 beds, Saint Vincent offers a range of services, including a notable neonatal intensive care unit, an emergency helicopter air service, cancer care, The Women's Center, and the Sports Medicine Institute. Additionally, they also provide a 24-hour service called Ask-A-Nurse, which gives free healthcare information and can assist in finding a physician.

West Yellowstone Health Associates
125 Madison Ave., West Yellowstone, MT
(406) 646-4137

This is West Yellowstone's primary care facility, offering urgent care for all simple illnesses and ailments. Prescription refills and immunizations are also available.

Jackson, Wyoming

St. John's Hospital and Living Center
625 E. Broadway Ave., Jackson, WY
(307) 733-3636
www.tetonhospital.org

St. John's has provided a continuum of health care services for the Jackson Hole area for more than 80 years. The hospital is a nonprofit community healthcare facility and a member of the Voluntary Hospital Association, the Wyoming Hospital Association, and the Quality Health-care Foundation of Wyoming. Comprehensive care includes 24-hour emergency services, general surgery, professional home care, sports medicine, wellness programs, and an outpatient surgical center. There is also physical therapy, a pain clinic, and the Hospice of Tetons. The hospital also includes the St. John's Living Center, a long-term care facility.

Northwestern Wyoming

Cody Family Practice
225 W. Yellowstone Ave., Cody, WY
(307) 527-7561

With three physicians on staff, this clinic welcomes walk-ins during regular daytime office hours. After hours you'll have to head for the emergency room at West Park Hospital.

West Park Hospital
707 Sheridan Ave., Cody, WY
(307) 527-7501, (800) 654-9447

As the regional medical center for the entire Bighorn Basin, West Park Hospital provides general medical care as well as specialty care. The hospital is also responsible for medical services within Yellowstone National Park, and patients who need more extensive care than park facilities can provide are frequently sent here. West Park Hospital has 24-hour emergency/ambulance services and the latest technology, including MRI and renal dialysis equipment. Physicians at West Park also specialize in family practice, pediatrics, general surgery, obstetrics, gynecology, internal medicine, orthopedic surgery, and urology. Attached to the hospital is the Coe Medical Center, which accommodates 30 physicians. The 12-bed inpatient Chemical Dependency Center is one of only four resident facilities in Wyoming. West Park Hospital is the largest employer in Cody.

West Park Urgent Care Clinic
702 Yellowstone Ave., Cody, WY
(307) 587-7207

Opened in 1998, this clinic encourages walk-ins seven days a week from 9 A.M. until 7 P.M., except Sundays when they close at 5 P.M. Operated by the West Park Hospital, the clinic is staffed by a doctor, physician's assistants, and a registered nurse.

Retirement

Yellowstone country is an oasis of good clean living with its close-knit communities, majestic mountains, open space, and clean water. Low crime, access to education, recreation, and healthcare make our region an appealing place to retire.

Larger towns such as Bozeman, Cody, and Jackson have strong programs for older citizens at area senior centers. They also offer ready access to medical care, which may be important for seniors with failing health. Smaller communities such as Gardiner and Ennis, Montana or Driggs, Idaho, are quaint, but may be isolating (especially in winter) because they are without organized senior programs, public transportation, or ready medical facilities.

Do your homework before you select a town for your retirement. Before you make your decision, come visit the area at different times of year. Too many people fall in love with Yellowstone country in the summer only to be jolted into the reality of long, cold, harsh winters. To get you started, here are some contact numbers throughout the region: Gallatin County Council on Aging in Bozeman, (406) 586-2421; Cody Council on Aging, (307) 587-6221; and Idaho's Region VII Council on Aging, (800) 632-4813.

Southwestern Montana

Bozeman Senior Center
807 N. Tracy Ave., Bozeman, MT
(406) 586-2421

Like much of Bozeman's population, the town's seniors are an active bunch and the Bozeman Senior Center is the place to be for many of them. Noon meals are served Monday through Friday and a Sunday dinner is served once a month. Reservations should be made for any meal. The center also offers organized trips and has a busy social events calendar, which includes music, dances, arts and crafts. Galavan—a free senior shuttle—may be the center's most valuable asset. The wheelchair-accessible bus takes passengers from around the area to Bozeman, dropping them off at the supermarket, drug store, or just about anyplace else. Call (406) 587-2434 for schedules and more information.

Darlinton Manor
606 N. Fifth St., Bozeman, MT
(406) 587-2981

Located on Bozeman's north side, the 100-unit Darlinton Manor offers apartment-style senior citizen housing with on-site management. Its convenient spot is a block away from a supermarket and is adjacent to a partially developed city park. Utilities are included with monthly rent, and rental assistance is available.

Red Lodge Senior Citizens' Center
207 S. Villard Ave., Red Lodge, MT
(406) 446-1826

The Mother's Day brunch, card parties, and bingo aren't solely what bring Red Lodge's older citizens to the senior center. It's also a place to share experiences and stories about the past and present. The 150 members pay $5 for organized activities, as well as a little camaraderie. This volunteer-run center serves three meals a week: soup and sandwiches at noon on Wednesday, a full meal on Thursday at 11:30 A.M., and lunch on Friday at noon.

Senior Citizens' Center of Park County
206 S. Main St., Livingston, MT
(406) 222-7195

Located at the center of town, Livingston's senior center is a gathering place and a source for information on area physicians, fitness programs, local clubs, and fun get-togethers. Started with a grant in the 1960s, the center has grown dramatically and now boasts 400 members. The board offers low-income housing for seniors by maintaining 26 apartments in the building. A staff of several part-time employees manage events and an in-house thrift store. Members pay annual dues of $7. Besides serving lunch Monday through Friday, the center offers card parties, dances, bingo, a pool table, exercise, and a wellness center, and publishes a monthly newsletter. Members also participate in many volunteer activities throughout the community. The facility prohibits the practice of politics or religion on the premises. It's open Monday through Saturday.

Wyoming

Cody Senior Citizens' Center
613 16th St., Cody, WY
(307) 587-6221

This hub for older citizens boasts a growing membership and some say it's because the meals here are so tasty. Big on home cooked meals shared with lots of friends and lively conversation, the Cody Senior Center serves up the vittles in the 200-seat dining room. A crew of volunteers operates a thriving thrift shop Monday through Saturday from 10 A.M. to 3 P.M. The store netted $25,000 in 2000. The center offers a senior bus service, as well as medical and personal services. A membership at the Cody Senior Citizens' Center is free.

Senior Center of Jackson Hole
830 E. Hansen Ave., Jackson, WY
(307) 733-7300

Stop in the Senior Center of Jackson Hole for a daily lunch if you're 60 and older. The center asks for a $2 donation and reservations are required. The center also delivers meals and provides home care, and its monthly newsletter includes a lunch menu and an activities calendar.

Worship

At the core of Yellowstone country's traditions of worship is the westward expansion movement sparked in the 1840s. Overland routes such as the Oregon, California, and the Mormon trails brought more than 500,000 emigrants through Yellowstone country on their way to better lives in the West. Some of them stayed here and left their mark of faith by establishing churches that still stand in our communities today.

Most of them were Christian and their churches were not just places of formal worship, but community centers and gathering places for early settlers who depended on one another to survive. These roots have spread throughout our region, in different denominations. In many small towns out here churches are still the bedrock of communal bonds. The Church of Jesus Christ of Latter-day Saints and the Catholic Church are also well represented.

At the turn of the century, industrious Mormon families traversed Wyoming on their way to settle in Salt Lake City, Utah, and some were dispatched later to colonize in surrounding areas. They worked as farmers mostly and often were responsible for laying foundations of faith and prosperity. Both Wyoming (particularly in Cody) and also in Idaho, the Mormon church's roots are strongly planted and still thriving today.

In turn, Jesuit priest Father Pierre Jean de Smet celebrated the first Catholic mass in Wyoming territory in 1840. Additionally, according to Aubrey Haine's account in The Yellowstone National Chapel, Fr. Francis Xavier Kuppens, a Belgian Jesuit, accompanied a band of Blackfoot Indians within Yellowstone's boundaries in 1865. Their influence spread and remains powerful in Wyoming and Montana communities. The churches of early Catholic congregations are some of the oldest buildings in towns throughout the region.

Predominantly conservative and traditionally Christian, the religious foundations of greater Yellowstone communities share a vaster commonality: the land. With cathedral-like mountains standing guard over our homes, it's hard to deny the presence of something greater than ourselves. Some people even feel that being outside is akin to attending church.

You'll find regular worship services scheduled from Memorial Day to Labor Day throughout the amphitheaters, lodges, and chapels of Yellowstone and Grand Teton National Parks. The national organization of Christian Ministry in the National Parks has provided this service for almost 50 years. It took root in Yellowstone in 1953 and has since spread to 65 national parks, where volunteers conduct nondenominational services each Sunday.

Look for worship schedules posted at hotel front desks, visitor centers, campground offices, and amphitheater bulletin boards throughout both parks.

Media

Newspapers

Radio Stations

Television Stations and
Network Affiliates

Newspapers

In the Parks

Teewinot
Grand Teton National Park, Moose, WY
(307) 739-3600

When you enter the park, you'll be handed the current issue of *Teewinot*, which contains information on the park and the John D. Rockefeller Memorial Parkway. Published each summer and winter, this paper includes campground listings, and information on roads, trails, attractions, wildlife, and much more. A comprehensive map details trailheads and visitor centers, and you'll also find interesting facts about the park's history, geology, and plants. There is also a schedule of ranger-led activities, hikes, evening talks and other programs.

Yellowstone Today
Mammoth Hot Springs, Yellowstone National Park
(307) 344-2258

As a visitor to Yellowstone National Park, this is the first thing you should pick up. In this quarterly paper produced by the National Park Service, you will find basic listings and directions to all the park attractions, from Old Faithful Geyser to Uncle Tom's Trail. Campgrounds, visitor centers, and ranger-led activities are listed here as well. This little paper gives you everything you'll need to get started on your tour of Yellowstone, but it's not just a directory. It's also packed with informative articles on topics such as on-going research on geothermal formations at the bottom of Yellowstone Lake, wolf activity, or history.

Each year, close to 1 million copies of *Yellowstone Today* are handed out by the Park Service at park entrance gates. Originally, the paper began publication in 1974 as *Yellowstone Explorer*. It has been going strong ever since.

Dailies

Billings Gazette
401 N. Broadway Ave., Billings, MT
(406) 657-1200

If Yellowstone country could claim just one newspaper, the *Billings Gazette* would be it. With a circulation of 200,000 people, Montana's largest paper covers over 90,000 square miles, from the Canadian border to central Wyoming and from the western Dakotas to Helena, Montana. The bulk of the paper covers state and national stories with well-done features mixed in. Most residents read the *Gazette* and their own small-town paper for a well-rounded perspective. Owned by Lee Enterprises, this daily also supports bureaus in Cody, Wyoming, and Bozeman and Helena, Montana. In addition to "Enjoy!" the regular weekly arts and entertainment supplement, the *Gazette* also publishes 60 special sections each year, including a tab on Yellowstone National Park. Available by 6 A.M. daily, a weekday paper costs 75 cents. The Sunday paper is $1.25.

Bozeman Daily Chronicle
2820 W. College St., Bozeman, MT
(406) 587-4491, (800) 275-0401
www.gomontana.com

For a small paper, the *Chronicle* supplies ample amounts of regional and national news seven days a week. The morning paper—which has been voted the state's best in the past—has a circulation of about 16,000 and covers Bozeman and its suburbs—Big Sky, Belgrade, Three Forks, Livingston, West Yellowstone, and everywhere in between. Environmental coverage and issues concerning Yellowstone National Park are particularly strong. "This Week," the *Chronicle's* weekly enter-tainment section, comes with the Friday issue and covers arts, music, movies, theater, and more. The paper costs 50 cents. The price increases to $1.25 on Sunday.

Livingston Enterprise
401 S. Main St., Livingston, MT
(406) 222-2000

The *Livingston Enterprise* prides itself on covering the provincial happenings within Park County, Montana. Because of proximity to Yellowstone (only 50 miles from the northern entrance), the *Enterprise* often gets the scoop on what's happening in the park. Publishing city and county news every weekday afternoon, you'll find local features mixed in with a generous dose of Associated Press stories.

With a current circulation of 3,300, the *Enterprise* is one of Livingston's oldest continuously operating businesses. It first began as the *Livingston Post* in 1889 and was published from a small stone building on Callender Street, where the Blue Slipper Theatre currently operates. Today, publisher John Sullivan is president of the *Enterprise's* parent company, Yellowstone Newspapers. The paper costs 50 cents.

Semiweeklies

Cody Enterprise
1549 Sheridan Ave., Cody, WY
(307) 587-2231

Founded by none other than the legendary Buffalo Bill Cody, the *Cody Enterprise* is the town's oldest business. With a circulation of 6,025, this paper is published every Monday and Wednesday afternoon. In addition to local feature articles and coverage of Yellowstone National Park issues, the *Enterprise* is heavy on local sports stories. This award-winning paper combines excellent photography with solid reporting. Locally owned by Sage Publishing, it costs 50 cents.

Weeklies

Carbon County News
202 S. Hauser St., Red Lodge, MT
(406) 226-2222

The photos and copy of the lively *Carbon County News* mirror this town's dedication to community issues. Stories on tourism, recreation, and Yellowstone Park issues make the headlines in this weekly. First published in 1907, the *Carbon County*

News has a staff of seven and a circulation of 3,000. Owned by News Montana, Inc., the paper comes out on Wednesdays and costs 75 cents.

Gardiner Community Newsletter
233 Main St., Suite A, Gardiner, MT
(406) 848-7971

Gardiner may have only 200 year-round residents, but it's not too small to have a collective voice. That voice can be heard in the *Gardiner Community Newsletter*, which hits the streets most Wednesday mornings throughout the year. The Gardiner Chamber of Commerce produces the two-sided legal-sized paper featuring listings of upcoming events and meetings, local advertisements, and a classifieds section. It is distributed at most local businesses for free.

Jackson Hole Guide
P.O. Box 648, Jackson, WY
(307) 733-7841

The *Guide* has been Jackson's weekly news source for 50 years. The paper comes out every Wednesday, and has lots of columns, editorials, features, sports, and more. "Tempo," the entertainment guide, is a great place to find out what's going on around town. For a weekly, the *Guide* is as informative as any paper around and gives a good representation of the town. It costs 50 cents.

Jackson Hole News
P.O. Box 7445, Jackson, WY
(307) 733-2047

For a town as small as Jackson, you wouldn't think that two competing weeklies could survive, but the *News*—not quite as edgy as its competitor, the *Guide*—has been going strong for more than 30 years. The 50-cent paper also comes out on Wednesdays, and features strong and informative stories and editorials about local issues.

Lone Peak Lookout
P.O. Box 160123, Big Sky, MT
(406) 995-7133
www.lonepeaklookout.com

The *Lookout* is owned by the *Bozeman Daily Chronicle* and is Big Sky's free source for news, sports, and features. It comes out every Thursday, and also includes the *Chronicle's* "This Week" arts and entertainment section. As the Big Sky community grows, the *Lookout* has become the loudest voice on issues concerning the resort town. It also features a calendar of events around the area, and has a staff of four.

Park County Weekly
306 S. Main St., Livingston, MT
(406) 222-9500

Packed with local columns, quirky editorials, and interesting, homespun feature articles, the *Park County Weekly* reflects the values of its community. This free weekly comes out every Tuesday and is delivered to the doorsteps of residents throughout Livingston, as well as local businesses. Geared toward citizens in Livingston, Wilsall, and Clyde Park, it offers in-depth coverage of school board meetings, county planning issues, and events. Published by Sharon Walker since 1996, the *Park County Weekly* calls itself "the paper that's read from cover to cover."

West Yellowstone News
309 Canyon St., West Yellowstone, MT
(406) 646-9719
www.westyellowstonenews.com

This 50-cent weekly paper has become West Yellowstone's voice, especially as the town deals with impending legislation that will ban snowmobiles in Yellowstone National Park by the 2003–04 season, and is part of a three-paper system operated by the *Bozeman Daily Chronicle*. You'll find news, editorials, columns, sports, and classifieds in the tabloid-sized paper, which comes out every Thursday. Look for it in racks around town or stop by the office in downtown West Yellowstone.

Radio Stations

Adult and Soft Contemporary

KBMJ 95.5 FM, Billings, MT
KOHZ 103.7 FM, Billings, MT
KYYA 93.3 FM, Billings, MT
KTAG 97.9 FM, Cody, WY
KMXE 99.3 FM, Red Lodge, MT
KEZQ 92.9 FM, West Yellowstone, MT

Christian

KULR 730 AM, Billings, MT

Contemporary

KCTR 102.9 FM, Billings, MT
KSCY 96.7 FM, Bozeman, MT
KZ 95 FM, Jackson, WY
KMTN 96.9 FM, Jackson, WY

Country

KDWG 970 AM, Billings, MT
KGHL 790 AM, Billings, MT
KIDX 98.5 FM, Billings, MT
KXLB 100.7 FM, Bozeman, MT
KPRK 1340 AM, Livingston, MT
KZLO 99.99 FM, Bozeman/Livingston, MT
KSGT 93.3 FM, Jackson, WY
KGST 1340 AM, Jackson, WY
KPOW 1260 AM, Powell, WY

News/Talk/Sports

KBLG 910 AM, Billings, MT
KWYS 920 AM, West Yellowstone, MT

Oldies

KKBR 97.1 FM, Billings, MT
KODI 1400 AM, Cody, WY
KWYS 920 AM, West Yellowstone, MT

Public Radio

KEMC 95.9 FM, Big Sky, MT
KEMC 91.7 FM, Billings, MT
KEMC 102.1 FM, Bozeman, MT

Rock—Alternative/Classic

KRKX 94.1 FM, Billings, MT
KPRK 97.5 FM, Bozeman, MT
KMMS 95.1 FM, 1450 AM Bozeman, MT
KTMN 96.9 FM, Jackson, WY
KLZY 92.5 FM, Powell, WY

Television Stations and Network Affiliates

Here is a listing of major television stations along with their network affiliate:

KHMT Channel 4 (FX) Billings, MT
KSVI Channel 6 (ABC) Billings, MT
KTVQ Channel 2 (CBS) Billings, MT
KULR Channel 8 (NBC) Billings, MT
KBZK Channel 4 (CBS) Bozeman, MT
KTVM Channel 6 and 42 (NBC) Bozeman, MT
KUSM Channel 9 (PBS) Bozeman, MT
KJWY Channel 2 (NBC) Jackson, WY

Hiking and Other Recreation

Hiking

Horseback Riding

Hunting

Mountain Biking

Golf

On the surface, Greater Yellowstone's regions appear similar: mountains, forests, valleys, and rivers. But the people who populate its regions have many differences, in politics, upbringing, occupation, and lifestyle. It's safe to say, however, that the outdoors is our great unifier. Whether it's hiking or hunting, horseback riding or mountain biking, rock climbing or golfing, there's plenty of room for everyone to pursue their own version of getting outside.

In this chapter we'll share some of the popular pursuits that showcase a whole different side of Yellowstone country. What you'll find here is only a glimpse of what is out there; the rest is for you to discover in your own way. Learn more about your choice of outdoor recreation in guide books for the region and detailed information on specific areas. Falcon, an imprint of The Globe Pequot Press, publishes a series of hiking guides for the Greater Yellowstone regions.

Hiking

Each year millions of visitors flock to Yellowstone National Park. Tangled in crowds at popular attractions and hung up in traffic jams along park roads, few realize what they are missing just beyond the pavement. With only 3 percent of this huge park accessible by roads, they are missing a lot, perhaps even the essence of Yellowstone itself. You can access the rest of the park along more than 1,000 miles of designated, marked trails. Grand Teton National Park offers an additional 200 miles of trails. The seven national forests in the region add to this bounty, with hundreds of miles of footpaths into their wilderness. The Gallatin, Bridger-Teton, and Shoshone National Forests alone combine some 6,300 miles of designated trails.

Both hiking and backpacking are popular in the area, but here we have primarily included day-hikes throughout the region. Most are well traveled and easily accessed. This is a good place to begin your forays into the Yellowstone country wilderness. For more rigorous hikes and extended backpacking trips, check out Falcon Publishing's series of hiking guides. Going into the backcountry should not be undertaken lightly. It requires knowledge of area geography, first aid, map and compass reading, and survival skills in case of an emergency. It's best to go with a seasoned hiker, take an outdoor class, and read about the area you plan to explore.

From this chapter we hope you will discover the beauty of Yellowstone country away from roads, traffic, and crowds. There is a lot to see and experience, and the possibilities are endless.

Mount Washburn

Picking out just one superlative hike from among Yellowstone's 1,000 miles of trail is no mean feat, but the Mount Washburn Spur Trail is a pretty safe choice. Starting from the Glacial Boulder Trailhead in the Canyon area, this trail follows the north side of the awe-inspiring Grand Canyon of the Yellowstone on the Seven-Mile Hole Trail before climbing steeply up the east face of Mount Washburn for a 12-mile, one-way trek. Less ambitious hikers can reach Washburn via the more heavily trafficked trails that begin at Dunraven Pass and the Old Chittenden Road, both off the Tower-Lake Road, for shorter roundtrip hikes of 6 miles and 10 miles respectively. Whichever route you choose, this hike offers an amazing breadth of high-country wildlife, midsummer wildflowers, and views. A large herd of bighorn sheep summer near the summit; yellow-bellied marmots and red foxes are also common. On a clear day, the 10,243-foot peak offers views all the way to the Gallatins, Absarokas, and Tetons, along with panoramas of the Grand Canyon, Hayden Valley, and Yellowstone Lake.

Riddle Lake Trail
South Entrance Rd.

Rolling hills and meadows splashed with wildflowers are the main attractions along the 3.5-mile hike up to Riddle Lake. You can cruise along this well-maintained trail without seeing another hiker. Be on the lookout for wildlife, because this trail is prime habitat for moose and grizzly. In fact, you'll find this area is often closed through the month of June due to grizzly sightings.

Once you reach the lake, walk around to the north shore for a majestic view of Mount Sheridan's 10,308-foot peak and the colorful Red Mountain Range. Peaceful little Solution Creek flows from the lake. Riddle Lake was named during the 1870s, by the way, when it was believed that a lake existed in this area containing major drainages to both oceans. Once the actual location of the Continental Divide was determined, however, the "riddle" was solved, and the creek flowing from the lake was the "solution." Although you'd never know it from the easy terrain on this hike, the Continental Divide is only another mile to the southeast.

Start from the South Entrance Road, about 4.3 miles from Grant Village. The trailhead is plainly marked and is a moderate seven-mile, round-trip hike.

Shoshone Lake
Old Faithful–West Thumb Rd.

Yellowstone's largest backcountry lake offers an unspoiled destination for wildlife watching, fishing, camping, or as a remote picnic spot. Head out on the

Insiders' Tip

Increasing numbers of outdoor recreationists have significantly impacted America's wildlands. The national Leave No Trace program promotes responsible outdoor ethics. Please help minimize impact on our wilderness by practicing these principles: Plan ahead and prepare; travel and camp on durable surfaces away from water sources; properly dispose of waste; leave what you find; minimize campfire impacts; and be considerate of other visitors.

Close-up

Walking Yellowstone National Park

You can be your own expert guide to Yellowstone along the park's system of boardwalks and paths that meander through steep canyons and scenic thermal areas. Trail guides and signs lead you along to most of the locations, accompanied by informative explanations of the sights. A free visitors' guide is available at all entrance stations to Yellowstone National Park, listing complete details of these interpretive trails.

Mammoth Hot Springs Terraces

You won't find travertine terraces like these anywhere else in the park. As an early visitor described them, "The hot springs fall over a lofty hill of snowy whiteness, resembling cascades."

A walking trail through the Lower Terraces and a one-way drive through the Upper Terraces offer views of these fascinating formations.

Norris Geyser Basin

Explore the hottest, most active thermal basin in the park. Trails start at the Geyser Basin Museum. Porcelain Basin is open terrain with hundreds of densely packed geothermal features. The features in the Back Basin are more scattered and isolated. The world's tallest geyser, Steamboat, is here, but its last eruption was in the fall of 1991.

Fort Yellowstone Historic Trail

Most of the buildings constructed in Mammoth during the time that the U.S. Army managed the park (1886 to 1918) are still standing and are now used by the National Park Service as its headquarters. There is an established walking tour through the major areas of the fort.

West Thumb Geyser Basin

Situated on the shore of Yellowstone Lake, the boiling springs in this basin, including the famous Fishing Cone, discharge their waters into the icy lake. With the Absaroka Mountains as a backdrop to the east, this is truly one of the prettiest boardwalk trails found anywhere in the park.

Upper Geyser Basin

The world's largest concentration of geysers is located here, with Old Faithful among its most famous. But there is much more to explore in this area. Several miles of trail begin at the visitor center, winding past geysers and hot springs too numerous to count. Names such as Beehive Grotto, Castle, Spasmodic, Grand, Giant, Riverside, and Morning Glory only hint at the wonders you will see. Stop at the visitor center for orientation and geyser information.

Grand Canyon Of The Yellowstone

The Canyon as well as the Upper and Lower Falls can be seen from overlooks along the rim drives. The North Rim Drive takes you to Inspiration, Grandview, and Lookout Points. A spur road leads to an overlook at the brink of the Upper Falls. The South Rim Drive leads to Uncle Tom's Trail and Artist Point. From there you can take a harrowing two-mile walk down to the base of Lower Falls, but be prepared for the steep hike back up. Walking trails also wind along both rims of the canyon.

Mud Volcano

Discover turbulent and explosive mud pots, including Mud Volcano and Dragon's Mouth. View—and smell—Sulfur Caldron from the overlook just north of the Mud Volcano area. It is located on the road between Lake and Canyon, six miles north of Fishing Bridge Junction.

Active, ever-changing mud pots; constant geysers; hissing fumaroles; and colorful boiling hot springs make this area a worthwhile stop. Park in the large parking area eight miles north of Old Faithful on the road to Madison Junction and take a leisurely walk through this unforgettable spot.

DeLacy Creek Trail, which begins from Old Faithful–West Thumb Road about eight miles east of Old Faithful. Look for moose along the trail, especially as you cross the wide meadow where the creek flows for about three miles down to the lake. Once you get to Shoshone Lake, you'll see fine gravel beaches and great views of the surrounding mountains.

Eleven campsites circle this lake and you'll find a ranger cabin near the Lewis Channel. If you plan to stay overnight, you might want to add a little side trip to your stay with the seven-mile trek from the lake up to Shoshone Geyser Basin. This is one of the park's most impressive geothermal areas and from the lake you can find a loop trail to access it.

Grand Teton National Park

Surprise Lake and Amphitheater Lake

Hidden Falls and Lake Solitude
Near Jenny Lake Visitor Center

There are two ways to get to the refreshing mists of Hidden Falls. You can either hike the 2.5-mile trail around Jenny Lake or ride the ferry straight to the trailhead. If you take the boat you'll shave this quintessential Grand Teton day hike down to two miles round-trip. From the East Shore boat dock the climb to the falls is pretty steep, although you gain very little elevation. Since most Grand Teton hikes begin at 6,800 feet, unless you head out on a longer hike, you're not likely to get much higher than a few hundred extra feet.

This trail brings you quickly to Hidden Falls, where you will no doubt encounter a flock of other hikers (with the ferry departing every 20 minutes from 8 A.M. to 6 P.M. every day from June through late September, this can't be avoided). However, don't let the crowds dissuade you, because the falls are impressive and the view from Inspiration Point (another half-mile up the trail) is fantastic. From there you will get a bird's eye view of Jenny Lake, Jackson Hole, and the Gros Ventre range. To make this a more strenuous day hike, assuming you're in good physical

condition, you can also travel on to Lake Solitude. This deeply carved glacial lake lies another six miles up a very steep route through Cascade Canyon. The canyon is a classic U-shaped glacial cut, and well named. An enormous volume of water rushes down the canyon, dropping violently in chute after chute. Lake Solitude, at 9,035 feet, is a spectacular setting for viewing Teewinot, Mt. Owen, and the Grand Teton. This is a popular area for both people and bears—you're likely to catch a glimpse of a black bear from afar.

You can pick up maps at the Jenny Lake Ranger Station or at the trailhead. Remember that the last ferry across Jenny Lake leaves the trailhead at 6 P.M., so time your hike accordingly or you will add another 2.5 miles onto your return trip.

Surprise Lake and Amphitheater Lake
South Jenny Lake Junction on Teton Park Rd.

For a strenuous day hike, the trip up to Surprise Lake and Amphitheater Lake is outstanding. Starting from Lupine Meadows, the trail begins with an abrupt hill. The whole route is a steep but well-switchbacked climb gaining almost 3,000 feet in elevation over just 4.8 miles (one-way). The cool air floating off the creek paralleling the trail and, of course, the reward of these two jeweled mountain lakes at the end make it worthwhile. Along the way you'll get a panoramic view of Jenny, Taggart, and Bradley Lakes.

The trailhead for Amphitheater is at Lupine Meadows. Find the trailhead by turning onto an unpaved road a mile south of the South Jenny Lake Junction. About 1.5 miles in, you'll see a parking lot and a restroom marking the trailhead.

Phelps Lake Overlook
Moose-Wilson Rd.

You'll find that there is no such thing as a middle-ground hike in Grand Teton National Park. Most trails are either extensive overnight treks or easy day hikes. Phelps Lake Overlook is the latter and a perfect jaunt for the whole family. The two-mile, round-trip hike gently gains 400 feet as it climbs to a scenic overlook of the fourth largest lake in the park

> ## Insiders' Tip
> In Grand Teton National Park most of the trails begin at 6,800 feet and gain elevation. If you're unaccustomed to high altitudes take it slow and give yourself extra time.

and the portals of Death Canyon. This well-used path travels quickly through forests and lush wildflowers fed by snowmelt and springs.

The walking path begins at the Death Canyon Trailhead, accessed off Moose–Wilson Road.

Jackson Hole, Wyoming

String Lake Trail
North Jenny Lake Junction

If you're the kind of hiker who needs a treat at the end of line, String Lake Trail is for you. The lake is perfect for swimming and a favorite with families because of the easy 3.5-mile round-trip walk. On top of that, you'll see nice views of the Tetons, from pleasant little picnic areas lining the shallow mountain lake.

From the trailhead, walk around the lake clockwise along a gentle rolling path through a dense lodgepole pine and Douglas-fir forest. The trail soon forks; the left route takes you around Jenny Lake to Hidden Falls. Take the right fork and continue around String Lake. On the west side of the lake, the trail begins to climb and distance itself from the lake, giving hikers a nice view of the lake and valley. About a quarter-mile past the rocky area the trail passes an avalanche zone. Evidence of past snowslides down the slopes

of 11,144-foot Rockchuck Peak will be obvious. Here, all the trees have been swept clean off the mountainside almost to the valley floor. The tremendous power of avalanches can be seen in the effects on the trees and rocks.

Fortunately for hikers, the danger of avalanche is long gone by late spring. Snow often covers this stretch of the trail into early summer. If snow is present, be careful with your footing as you cross. The trail continues to climb until it comes to another fork. The left fork goes up Paintbrush Canyon, a very strenuous hike into the heart of the Tetons. Take the right fork. From here, the trail goes downhill to cross a footbridge over the Leigh Lake outlet. Head left to pick up the Leigh Lake trail or right to return back to your vehicle and the picnic area.

Hiking here is good from May through October. To get to the trailhead, drive 14 miles north of Jackson on U.S.

Highway 89 to Moose Junction. Turn left (west) and drive 11 miles to the North Jenny Lake Junction and turn left (west). Drive 2.5 miles to the String Lake picnic area and park at the first parking lot near the footbridge.

Ski Lake Trail
Off WY Hwy. 22, west of Wilson, WY

A short, moderate 2.3-mile walk along a path sprigged with wildflowers will lead you to the crystal-clear waters of Ski Lake. You'll get all the rewards of high-mountain hiking without much work. Along the way you can relish great views of Jackson Hole and the Gros Ventre range. At the one-mile mark, the trail forks at the expanse of two sprawling meadows. The right fork heads up to Phillips Pass, which is another three miles up. Even though this trail climbs to the crest of the Tetons, most of the hiking is moderate. Much of this is due to the fact that the trailhead starts out at such a high elevation. This is a popular starting point for hikers connecting with the Teton Crest Trail—a trail that traverses the length of the mountain range.

The left fork trail continues to the lake, following the outlet stream of Ski Lake.

Ski Lake is a beautiful lake jewel about a dozen acres in area and tucked right up against the peaks. As you walk around it you will notice that its bottom quickly drops out of sight. The deepest part is up by the mountain. Another view of the lake can be obtained with a bit more effort by taking the side trail that climbs up the north side of the lake.

Find the trailhead from Wilson by driving 4.5 miles west on Highway 22 toward Teton Pass. Watch for the sign for Phillips Canyon. Pull off the road there and into a parking area on the left (south) side. From the parking area, walk across the highway and up the jeep road for about 0.3 mile. The sign for the trailhead is on the left.

Southwestern Montana

Bozeman, Montana

Sacajawea Peak and Hardscrabble Peak Trail
Off Bridger Canyon Rd.
31 miles west of Bozeman

The long, bumpy drive up to Fairy Lake Campground, where the trailhead for this hike begins, will be worthwhile once you see the view from the top of Sacajawea Peak. This two mile, one-way trail sounds short, but you'll be huffing and puffing with the altitude gain of 2,065 feet to the summit. Most of the trail switchbacks through part of a snow field and then a long stretch of boulders up the steep slope to Hardscrabble saddle. At this point the trail divides: to the left is the summit of Sacajawea Peak, just a few hundred yards up the trail, and to the right is the 9,561-foot Hardscrabble Peak about two more miles up. If you feel up to it, you can stand atop two mountains on one hike. Hardscrabble is at the very edge of the Bridger Mountains and offers a closer view of the Shields Valley.

The trail on the back side is hard to follow at times, as it gets lost in the rocks. But there is only one way to go, and that is up. Along the way, you'll enjoy an excellent view of the Crazy Mountains, the Shields River valley, and the Bridger Range from most points along the trail. The 9,665-foot Sacajawea Peak affords a good view of the Gallatin Valley, with refreshing, cool winds drifting up from the valley. Have a seat in one of the grassy areas and recover from the climb while you take in the view.

This trail is accessible summer through fall. From the Bozeman city limits, take Montana Highway 86 (Bridger Drive) for approximately 24 miles to Forest Road #74. Turn west and continue for 7 miles to Fairy Lake Campground. The trail begins at the campground. The road to Fairy Lake is rough and is not recommended for trailers or large campers.

There are other trails in the area as well. In fact, this is the starting point for the annual Bridger Ridge Run, a 21-mile race along the jagged spine of the Bridgers that ends at the M trailhead off of Bridger Canyon Road. Fairy Lake Campground is located at the trailhead with adequate parking available.

History Rock Trail
Hyalite Canyon

This easy day hike is ideal for getting acclimated to the Rocky Mountains. The 1.2-mile trail up to History Rock rises from 550 feet to 7,000 feet. History Rock is a limestone outcropping with dates, initials, and inscriptions carved by early settlers and many more recent visitors. From the trailhead, it follows History Rock Creek through stands of Englemann spruce and lodgepole pine. It is a nice walk for the entire family.

From Bozeman, take 19th Street due south for 7.5 miles to Hyalite Canyon Road #62. Proceed south for 9.7 miles to the History Rock turnoff. The turnoff is on the west side of the road just 1 mile north of Hyalite Reservoir.

Livingston, Montana

Pine Creek Falls and Lake
Off East River Rd. south of Livingston

From Pine Creek Campground, this popular trailhead begins in the cool forest of the western Absaroka Mountains and traverses pleasantly for a mile to lovely little Pine Creek Falls. This portion of the trail is popular with families, because it is relatively easy, despite a rocky ascent just before the falls. From the trailhead to the falls you'll see quite a few other hikers, but beyond that the numbers thin. So does the air, as the trail grows steeper on its way to a 3,406-foot elevation gain up to Pine Creek Lake at 9,062 feet. But you will be rewarded for your travels with an astounding view of Mount McCowan and a dip in the chilly glacier water of the lake. This five-mile hike up to the lake is a popular overnight trip for backpackers, but is also a satisfying ten-mile day hike if you begin in the early morning. About three miles up the trail you will need to fjord Pine Creek, which can be spooky if the water is high during spring run-off. But later in summer the creek is tame and poses little danger. There are several rocky areas on the trail, but plenty of shade for when the summer temperatures begin to soar.

From Livingston, take U.S. Highway 89 South to Pine Creek turn-off to East River Road (about five miles) and continue to the tiny hamlet of Pine Creek, where you will turn right (south)and drive about one mile until you see the brown Forest Service sign for Pine Creek Campground. The drive up to the trailhead alone is invigorating with its views of the broad, sweeping Paradise Valley and the Absaroka Range.

Red Lodge, Montana

Island Lake Trail to Becker Lake
Off U.S. Hwy. 212

For day hikers, the Beartooths are ringed with trailheads and a greater concentration of alpine lakes than anywhere else in the world. On the south side of the range, Becker Lake is a fairly easy yet worthy destination about four miles in from the Island Lake Trailhead.

Starting at 9,518 feet, Island Lake Trailhead is an enduring favorite to begin this top-of-the-world hike with an elevation gain of only 200 feet. The trail winds through wildflower meadows studded with boulders, hugging the west shore of spectacular Island Lake en route to Night Lake at only one mile into your trek. From there you will reach Flake Lake at the 2.5 mile mark and then Mutt and Jeff Lakes less than a mile further up the trail. Once you arrive at Becker Lake you'll be dazzled by the sheer cliffs rising from its west shore and 11,409-foot Lonesome

Mountain to the north. Becker is not on official maps, but the lake is easy to find. Cross the small stream between Mutt and Jeff, traverse the rock field, then climb the small hill in front of you for your first views of Becker. The terrain, vistas, and distance make this a popular camping destination for families.

Island Lake Trailhead is at the end of the marked Island Lake Campground Road, located off U.S. Highway 212, approximately 25 miles east of Cooke City, and 38 miles west of Red Lodge.

Big Sky, Montana

Garnet Mountain Lookout Trail
Off U.S. Hwy. 191, north of Big Sky

The Garnet Mountain Lookout Trail begins at the Forest Service horse pasture at the mouth of Squaw Creek. From there it gains 2,000-plus feet of elevation, but the trail is moderate and well maintained. Along this four-mile climb you'll see a sec-

tion of the trail that parallels the path of a recent avalanche, giving you an opportunity to view the results of this natural phenomena. Most of your jaunt keeps you low in Gallatin Canyon until you get to the lookout cabin at 8,245 feet. From there you will have terrific views of the surrounding area, including the Gallatin Range, Hyalite Peaks, and the Spanish Peaks, with 25 summits topping 10,000 feet. The lookout is no longer manned; all fire detection on the Bozeman-Gallatin District is now done with aircraft. The Garnet Mountain Lookout is one of many Forest Service cabin rentals available to the public through the Gallatin National Forest Ranger District.

To get here, follow U.S. Highway 191 south of Bozeman for 25 miles to Squaw Creek Ranger Station. Follow Squaw Creek Road #132 south for approximately 1.5 miles to the trailhead.

Eastern Idaho

Teton Valley

Table Mountain
Off Ski Hill Rd. from Driggs, ID

This popular trail allows you to be engulfed by the dramatic Teton Range. When you finally crest the 11,106-foot

summit of Table Mountain, you can lie on top of its warm flat granite and bask in your accomplishment. But to get there you will traverse a well-worn but rocky trail, with an elevation gain of 4,000 feet over 12.5 miles (round-trip) and a hearty scramble the last hundred yards to the top. But once you're up there it's just you, the thin mountain air, and the spine of the Tetons spanning across the border between Wyoming and Idaho.

You'll need lots of water on this hike and it won't be enjoyable unless you are in good physical condition.

Northwestern Wyoming

Cody, Wyoming

Clarks Fork Trail
U.S. Hwy. 296, 55 miles northeast of Cody

With nearly 2.5 million acres of some of the most raw and rugged country in the Lower 48, the Shoshone National Forest offers endless opportunities for hiking. One of its most breathtaking areas is the Clarks Fork of the Yellowstone River, which starts high above Cooke City and runs into Wyoming before slipping back into Montana to converge with the Yellowstone River near Billings. Early on its way just south of Cooke City, Montana, the river runs through narrow granite gorges, its waters plummeting over frequent waterfalls that make the river itself virtually impassable. Eventually it opens into a broader valley with long stretches of smooth water, but here the river is only teasing. Again the gradient steepens and the stream carves the Box, the sheer-walled canyon that earned it wild and scenic status. You can see solid granite walls towering 1,200 feet above the river in a spectacular gorge from the Chief Joseph Scenic Highway. Hikers can get a better view from the north side trail. The trail along the north side of the Clarks Fork is great for anything from a long day hike to several days of camping. Along the way, you will encounter spectacular canyon vistas and varied ecologies.

The trailhead starts about five miles from where the Chief Joseph Highway turns off to Highway 212. The Hunter Peak Campground of the Shoshone National Forest is on the left and the trailhead is on the left just before the campground. Hikers out for the day can explore the land along the Clarks Fork Canyon rim. For eight miles the trail gently wanders through the benchland above the river.

To get here, turn right from Ski Hill Road, which leads to Grand Targhee Ski and Summer Resort, onto a dirt road marked with a sign for Teton Campground. Drive five miles to the trailhead parking area at one end of a Forest Service campground.

If you're an experienced backpacker out for a few days, you can descend to the canyon bottom. The trail drops down just beyond Table Creek and follows the canyon bottom for a couple of miles to Thief Creek. Beyond this stream, the path climbs and heads further east along the high benches above the river. From here you can retrace your route to Hunter Peak Campground, or if you have arranged transportation, keep going. The one way hike ends at the Morrison Jeep Road, about eight miles beyond the ascent from Thief Creek. The Jeep Road is on the north side of the river. Hikers can also be picked up on Highway 296, but beware of the river crossing to the south side. It can be harrowing and local Forest Service officials should be consulted before planning it.

The Clarks Fork trail offers a great wilderness experience that relatively few hikers have discovered.

Insiders' Tip

Nathaniel Langford led the first climbing party to the Grand Teton's 13,770-foot summit in 1843.

As of 2000, a grizzly bear special order is in effect for the Shoshone National Forest. Please check trailhead bulletin boards for possible closures and current information.

Horseback Riding

There is no image of the West with longer staying power or greater reach than the cowboy. Modern day rodeos preserve the cowboy's ways and traditional garb, while our imaginations preserve their heroism. And what would a cowboy be without a horse? If you long to experience Yellowstone country on horseback, there are literally hundreds of outfitters in the region who will be happy to oblige.

Outiftters offer varying lengths of trail rides as well as multi-day pack trips, and none of it will be like anything you've seen before. Because, cowboy-wanna-be or not, there is just something energizing about sitting in the saddle, hearing the leather squeak in rhythm to your horse's gait, the scent of sage, and mountain air in your nostrils. Your eyes will soak up the electric colors of wildflowers along the trail and the view of skyscraping mountains will seem somehow closer than when you are just walking on your own.

We're not saying the view is better sitting on the back of a horse. But one thing is certain: By horseback you will see this country from a new perspective. Rates for horseback rides range between $15 and $20 per hour. Most stables prefer that you make a reservation. Outfitters and dude ranches have a wide range of rates depending on the length, location, and activities of your horsepack trip.

What follows is a sampling of area outfitters. There are so many more operations out here, it's impossible to list them all. We suggest you contact the Outfitters and Guides Association in the appropriate state to obtain more details.

Yellowstone National Park

AmFac Parks and Resorts
Mammoth Hot Springs, Yellowstone
National Park
(307) 344-7411

From Mammoth, Roosevelt, and Canyon Village, AmFac offers daily one- or two-hour trail rides throughout the summer. These are slow and easy rides along gentle, scenic trails. The horses know the routine well enough that all you need to do is enjoy the view. Wranglers lead you and sometimes as many as 24 riders along a loop nearby, talking about area history and wildlife. Roosevelt Lodge also offers stagecoach rides five times a day. Children must be 8 years old and 48-inches tall to ride; children 11 and younger must be accompanied by someone aged 16 or older.

For a more extensive trip through the park, look into packages offered by area outfitters and dude ranches. There are several dozen area outfitters who offer pack trips through Yellowstone. A popular ride for operations near Jackson, Wyoming is the Thorofare—the route from Yellowstone's southeastern corner north to the tip of Yellowstone Lake's Southeast Arm. It was used for centuries by Indians to get from Jackson Hole to points north, and by mountain men and trappers during frontier days. The scenery is spectacular: Thousands of elk summer here, and in the distance the crags of the Absarokas rise to the east and the Wind River Range is to the south. These days, the Thorofare is one of the largest, most remote expanses of wilderness in the Lower 48.

Bear Safety

Yellowstone Country is also bear country and whether you are a mile from a heavily traveled trailhead or a day's walk into the backcountry, you should be prepared for an encounter with bears.

Each year area newspapers report unnerving entanglements between bears and humans, including horrific maulings, unfortunate bear killings because of aggressive behavior, and many near-misses where recreationists escape unhurt. This makes it sound like the country is crawling with bears, but in fact the vast majority of visitors will never see a bear at all. There is always the possibility of a chance encounter, however.

Experts say the best weapon against bear attack is knowledge. So read up on grizzly and black bear behavior and learn to respect them and their territory. Be alert—look for bear sign such as tracks, droppings, or diggings. Be noisy—talk, sing, clap your hands, or attach "bear bells" to your gear. Be social—a bigger group makes more noise and looks more formidable than a single person. Travel between 11 A.M. and 3:30 P.M. when wildlife are likely to be bedded down. Stay on trails, as bears tend to avoid them during the day because they know humans travel there. If you smell something dead or see a carcass, steer clear. It could be a grizzly food cache—even black bears will aggressively defend a kill. If you see a bear cub, know that its mama is somewhere nearby and back off. Avoid bringing pungent foods or smelly deodorants.

More and more people are also carrying pepper spray when they are in bear country. It works as a bear repellent when sprayed in the face and eye area. The high-powered pepper spray comes in a canister that works from 10 to 15 feet away (but who wants to get close enough to try it?) and has proven to be an effective tool in the event of an attack. It is, however, no substitute for caution and knowledge.

If you do encounter a bear, Yellowstone National Park officials recommend backing away slowly, talking quietly to the bear, refraining from sudden movements, and avoiding eye contact with it. A bear can outrun you so don't run for a tree. Black bears, young grizzlies, and even some adults can also climb trees. If you are actually attacked by a bear, most authorities recommend playing dead by dropping to the ground, putting your knees to your chest and your hands behind your head. Usually a bear will swat and bite a couple of times before running off. Don't move from that position until you are positive the bear is gone.

Before you venture into the backcountry, it's a good idea to check with the appropriate ranger district or forest service office (check our Resources chapter) for information on trail conditions and information on bear activity. When you are in the backcountry, be sure to set-up camp at least 100 yards away from your cooking and food storage site. Store your food by hanging it from trees and don't store any food in your tent.

Grand Teton National Park

**Colter Bay Village and Jackson Lake
Lodge Corrals
Grand Teton National Park
(307) 543-2811**

Operating from two locations, the Grand Teton Lodge Company offers a variety of trail rides within the park. You can choose from breakfast rides, evening campfire rides, and wagon rides. All last one to two hours and are led by a wrangler. Reservations are recommended.

**Scott's Jackson Hole Trail Rides
Teton Village, WY
(307) 733-6992, (307) 739-2753**

Located near the Moose–Wilson Road entrance to the park, the Scott family offers one- and two-hour trail rides into Grand Teton National Park. The entrance sees less traffic than other park roads and is convenient for quick trips offering wonderful views of the Tetons. The Scott family has been guiding horseback rides throughout Jackson Hole since the 1960s.

Southwestern Wyoming

Jackson Hole, Wyoming

**Yellowstone Outfitters
P.O. Box 1156, Afton, WY
(307) 733-2418, (800) 447-4711**

Ride for two hours or take all day in the Teton wilderness. Yellowstone Outfitters will provide the guides and the food to keep you going on your trip. They run short trail rides and week-long excursions throughout the Bridger-Teton National Forest and Teton Wilderness Area. For a taste of the Old West, you can step back in time on a covered wagon trek through Teton country. The wagons look and feel authentic (all but the rubber tires, which are thankfully shock absorbent) as they bump and roll along the remote dirt roads.

**Snow King Stables
400 E. Snow King Ave., Jackson, WY
(307) 733-5781**

If you already have experience riding horses, Snow King Stables is one of the few places where you can arrange an unguided ride. The owners use their own discretion and provide clients with very detailed directions for their ride. From these stables at the edge of town you can choose to have a guide as well. The one-hour ride will take you onto the flanks of Snow King Mountain, with a view of Jackson Hole, the Tetons, and Flat Creek winding through the National Elk Refuge. Two or three hours will take you to the top of the mountain and back. These folks have been in business since the mid-1980s.

Southwestern Montana

Big Sky, Montana

**Jake's Horses
U.S. Hwy. 191, Big Sky, MT
(406) 995-4630**

Jake has been running guided pack trips and trail rides in Big Sky since the early 1980s. He offers multi-day packages in Yellowstone and throughout the Gallatin National Forest. From the corrals in Gallatin Canyon you can saddle up for an all-day fishing and riding trip to a nearby lake or hit the trail for just a couple hours. The shorter, one- or two-hour rides will take you along the foothills of the Spanish Peaks and eventually give you a vantage point to take in the gorgeous view of 11,000-foot Lone Peak.

Diamond K Outfitters
Rainbow Ranch Lodge, U.S. Hwy. 191
Big Sky, MT
(406) 995-4132

One of the Diamond K's most popular trips is their four-day expedition over the Hyalite Mountains. Traveling from west to east, you start out near Big Sky and end up near Pray in Paradise Valley. The trip's steep ascents offer rewarding vistas from Hyalite Peak and a true wilderness experience. Shorter rides ranging from one to two hours, and half- and full-day jaunts from the Rainbow Ranch along a nearby trail in the Gallatin National Forest, can also be arranged.

Livingston, Montana

Chico Hot Springs Lodge
1 Chico Rd., Pray, MT
(406) 333-4933, (800) HOT WADA

Even if you are not a guest at the resort, you can start here with a trail ride (and soak in the hot springs, too). Outfitter Buzz Feeley has been running horses at Chico for 25 years and you could say he knows the area pretty well. You can arrange for rides as short as 30 minutes or as long as a day. The shortest ride, which is great for kids under 12, takes you up a well-trod path to a small trout pond above the resort. Just before the trail heads into the trees you will have an outstanding view of Paradise Valley all the way to the Crazy Mountains. Longer rides take you through Emigrant Gulch and to cool, cascading Emigrant Falls. Chico also offers wagon rides that include lunch or dinner.

Eastern Idaho

Teton Valley

Beard Outfitters
Leigh Canyon, WY
(307) 576-2694

Born and raised in the Teton Valley, Joe Beard guides trail rides by the hour or by the day from his family ranch at the base of the Tetons. Beard is licensed to take trips into the Bridger-Teton National Forest and Yellowstone National Park. His family also offers commercial elk hunting trips from the ranch in fall and winter.

Insiders' Tip

If you are experienced in the backcountry, to truly experience the Tetons, nothing is better than backpacking the Teton Crest. The full route is 39 miles, from Teton Pass on Highway 22 south of the park to String Lake, just north of Jenny Lake. A good option is to take the gondola from Teton Village and hike to Marion Lake for the first night, then pick up the Crest Trail. Marion Lake has limited campsites, which require a permit.

Cody, Wyoming

K Bar Z Guest Ranch and Outfitters
Off U.S. Hwy. 296, Cody, WY
(307) 587-4410

Located off the Chief Joseph Scenic Highway, the K Bar Z is a little out of the way, but its location in the Shoshone National Forest adjacent to Yellowstone will make the extra effort worthwhile. Offering rides ranging from one-hour to all day, as well as week-long pack trips, the K Bar Z wranglers will guide you through some of the most breathtaking views in the area. No matter how long you ride, you won't believe how gorgeous the expanse of Sunlight Basin is or how desolate the Beartooth Plateau can be.

Gateway Ranch
Yellowstone Hwy., Cody, WY
(307) 587-6507, (307) 527-5981

Old timer Speed Spielberg has been taking folks horseback riding since 1955. Located halfway between Cody and the Stampede Rodeo Grounds west of town, Gateway Ranch is home to Spielberg's wrangler, who will guide you along the banks of the Shoshone River. He'll tell you about explorer John Colter who discovered the area in the 1800s and likely rode along the same path. An hour-long trip will take you down to the river; longer rides take you into the mountains.

For Further information

Wyoming Outfitters and Guides
Association
P.O. Box 2284, Cody, WY
(307) 527-7453

Montana Fish, Wildlife and Parks
Department
P.O. Box 200701, Helena, MT
(406) 444-2535

Montana Outfitters and Guides
Association
P.O. Box 1248, Helena, MT
(406) 449-3578

Hunting

Hunting is the very thread that connects humans to this tapestry we know of as Yellowstone Country. Even the prehistory of this land, unearthed by archeologists and paleontologists, tells us of the Clovis people who tracked big game animals across the land bridge from Asia to Yellowstone. Those people, like the Plains Indians after them, were subsistence hunters who utilized every scrap and bone and tooth of elk, bison, or bear for food, shelter, and clothing. The very act of pursuing an animal and killing it was embedded in their cultural and spiritual practices as their sacred connection in the circle of life.

Later the plentiful prospects for fur trade and for hunting the bounteous bison attracted trappers, businessmen, and eventually settlers. Though without the same reverence for the hunt, those who came here before us relied on the abundant wildlife.

The ritual is still a popular practice throughout the Rocky Mountain area, although not permitted within national park boundaries. In Yellowstone country we hunt for sport, for trophy, for food, and even as a rite of passage. Hunters travel from all over the world to hunt the region's big game animals: mule deer, white-tailed deer, elk, antelope, bighorn sheep, mountain goat, Shiras moose, black bear, and mountain lion. They also come for unparalleled upland bird hunting, in search of wild turkeys, geese, ducks, pheasant, and grouse.

For some, hunting is even a means to taste and smell and feel the wilderness that we have become so separate from in these modern times. Although today's supermarket society isn't dependent on the meat, fur, or feathers gained from a kill taken in the thick forests, the snow covered foothills, or the boggy wetlands, hunting is special for some people. Perhaps it is a way to reconnect with history, nature, and wildness of this land.

The practice of hunting and what is hunted can spark the fire of discord within communities. It has often been the source of conflict, as many people believe that the practice of hunting trophy animals such as bighorn sheep, mountain lion, and bears is a barbaric way to appreciate nature. Advocates argue that it is man's "natural right." For the state agencies who regulate hunting, it is a management tool used to keep herds and flocks and land in a healthy balance.

Throughout our region the hunting regulations and seasons vary drastically, often changing from month to month within a calendar year. For this reason, we have listed Fish, Wildlife and Parks departments for Montana, Idaho, and Wyoming, as well as the Guides and Outfitters associations to assist you with details on hunting. By far the most popular animals hunted are elk and deer, because they are prolific in this region. Check out our Resources chapter for books on hunting.

Idaho Fish, Wildlife and Parks Department
Upper Snake Region, 1515 Lincoln Rd.,
Idaho Falls, ID
(208) 525-7290

Idaho Outfitters and Guides Association
P.O. Box 95, Boise, ID
(208) 342-1438, (208) 342-1919

Wyoming Department of Game and Fish
Information Section, 5400 Bishop Blvd.,
Cheyenne, WY
(307) 777-4600

Wyoming Outfitters and Guides Association
P.O. Box 2284, Cody, WY
(307) 527-7453

Montana Fish, Wildlife and Parks Department
P.O. Box 200701, Helena, MT
(406) 444-2535

Montana Outfitters and Guides Association
P.O. Box 1248, Helena, MT
(406) 449-3578

Mountain Biking

Mountain biking is just another way to access what Yellowstone country has in abundance: trails. From harrowing summer routes that scream down area ski runs to lazy, rolling trails along rivers or through residential areas, there is plenty to do. In places such as Jackson, Wyoming, Big Sky and Bozeman, Montana, or Driggs, Idaho, you'll find a counterculture of bikers who test themselves regularly on their area's most challenging trails.

Outside of Yellowstone and Grand Teton National Rarks is where you'll find most of the mountain biking action. Just like hiking or horseback riding, your bike can take you to the far reaches of wilderness that you might otherwise miss from the paved roads. What follows is general information on surrounding areas, as well as listings of bike shops that sell or rent gear. The local bike shop is probably your best resource for getting the scoop on mountain biking hot spots. Generally you'll find bike rentals by the hour, half-day, and full-day ranging from $15 to $30.

Yellowstone National Park

Although snowmobilers can access thousands of miles of trails in Yellowstone, off-road biking is very limited here. Largely what you'll find are short jaunts of only a few miles on old spur roads or utility roads. For specific bicycle trails in Yellowstone National Park, check out the close up, "Pedaling Yellowstone National Park" in our chapter.

However, touring park roads via bicycle is very popular in spring or fall when there is less traffic. Many cyclists even choose to brave the crowds along Yellowstone's frighteningly narrow roads in the summer. If you are determined to see Yellowstone on two wheels during summer months, try to travel early in the morning or in the evening when traffic is lighter. It's a good idea to install side mirrors on your helmet and to pack extra provisions, since full-service rest areas are far apart. Bicycle entrance fees cost $10 in Yellowstone.

Grand Teton National Park

Grand Teton, like Yellowstone, is not the best location for technical biking. Other than a seven-mile loop on Shadow Mountain's gravel road, no off-trail biking is permitted in the park. If you're tired of seeing the national parks framed by your windshield, you can cruise on your bike around Jenny Lake and Antelope flats. Both are paved 15 and 12-mile rides, respectively, and offer outstanding Teton views. Bike passes cost $10.

Adventure Sports
Dornan's at Moose, Grand Teton
National Park, WY
(307) 733-3307

Ride in style on the newest models of Diamondback, Cannondale, Giant, and Marin, for rent or sale. Dornan's staff can provide area maps and ideas for rides to suit your skill and fitness levels. They'll also supply a shuttle if you are renting gear.

Jackson Hole

An abundance of old logging roads and hiking trails throughout Jackson Hole provide fun two-lane routes or challenging single tracks.

One popular, but strenuous technical loop is the 18-mile-long Cache Creek ride, which goes up Cache Creek Road, turns single track, and includes a steep ascent and matching technical descent. You return to Jackson on Game Creek Road.

For a more leisurely ride, try the Elk Refuge's dirt road, accessed from Broadway in Jackson. You can travel the road for as long as you like across rolling hills and head back to town whenever you feel like it. The route is popular with runners and bikers during summer months, although you'll see an occasional vehicle here, too.

For information on bike/pedestrian paths within city limits contact: Friends of Pathways in Jackson, (307) 733-4534.

Hoback Sports
40 S. Millward St., Jackson, WY
(307) 733-5335

Fat Tire Tours operates right out of this outdoor store. They can treat you to guided mountain biking adventures to the Elk Refuge or the more formidable descent on the backside of Snow King Mountain (you take the tram up the ski hill) on a single track trail.

You can also pick up local trail maps and rent Specialized, Trek, and Voodoo performance mountain bikes, including full-suspension bikes.

Wilson Backcountry Sports
Fish Creek Center, Wilson, WY
(307) 733-5228

The advice here is free, but you'll have to pay for the bikes. You can rent or buy a bike and ride out the front door to the base of Teton Pass, where you'll find a bunch of loop trails that climb and crest to mountain vistas. Rental bikes are this year's Gary Fishers. Bike repair is also available.

The Edge Sports
490 W. Broadway, Jackson, WY
(307) 734-3916

With more than 2,000 bike rentals to choose from, you should be able to find something to suit your needs. This shop's experienced staff offer advice on the best local trails and tips on technique. You'll find area trail maps and bike accessories here, too.

Southwestern Montana

West Yellowstone, Montana

The trails you'll find around West Yellowstone are mostly flatland routes through forests or around lakes. This is a boon for beginning riders or families. One of the more popular courses is the system of ski trails bordering town. This 40-kilometer trail system loops around rolling hills and through timber for a pleasant, not too challenging ride.

Additionally, the local Chamber of Commerce organizes two races each year: One in early October is in the park; the other, in April, goes past Hebgen, Wade, and Henry's Lakes, over Targhee Pass, and back into West Yellowstone.

Free Heel and Wheel
40 Yellowstone, West Yellowstone, MT
(406) 646-7744

If you need an energy boost before pedaling around West Yellowstone, get a jolt of caffeine from the espresso bar in this store. You can also rent Trek and Special-ized mountain bikes with the gear to accompany it. Owners Kelli Criner and Melissa Buller can suggest the best biking routes for you—easy or hard. They occasionally organize a women-only ride from the shop during summer months.

Big Sky, Montana

It's safe to say that Big Sky would not exist if it weren't for Big Sky Ski and Summer Resort. This means that most of the residents live here to ski and in the summer (when they are not daydreaming about winter) they hit the trails on two wheels. Mountain biking in the Spanish Peaks and Gallatin Canyon is not beginner terrain. What you'll find up the popular Beehive Basin or Squaw Creek trails are steep ascents and fast, rocky downhills for the technical biker. But for the great amount of energy you exert on these types of rides, you will be rewarded with the freedom of the sun on your face, wind in your hair, and 360-degree mountain views. Ask about specifics in local bike shops.

Grizzly Outfitters
Meadow Center, Big Sky, MT
(406) 995-2939

Big Sky's only full-service bike shop, Grizzly Outfitters offers a bike rental package to suit your skill and fitness lev-els. Owner Ken Lancey is a seasoned mountain biker with a wealth of knowledge about area trails. Grizzly also offers reduced rates for kids.

Bozeman, Montana

The Bozeman area offers such an abundance of mountain biking trails that you could take a different one every day of the summer for five years. From the Hyalites, to the Bridgers, you'll find easy access to trails suitable for all levels and abilities. Traversing the switchback road of Bridger Bowl Ski Area is a local favorite for its prolific wildflowers and views of the neighboring Crazy and Absaroka Mountains. For strenuous, all-day rides head to Hyalite Reservoir. But if you just want to get in a quick after-work cruise, join the rest of this outdoorsy population on the miles of trails that secretly meander through town.

For more information on Bozeman's Mainstreet to Mountains trail system, contact Gallatin Valley Land Trust at (406) 587-8404.

Bangtail Bicycle and Ski
508 W. Main St., Bozeman, MT
(406) 587-4905

Owner Chris Saboda won't tell you how to ride, but he can tell you where to go and the right kind of bike to get you there. This veteran cyclist has logged enough miles to travel every trail in the county and then some. Bangtail specializes more in road biking, but also offers mountain bike rentals, trail maps, and local expertise.

Summit Bike and Ski
26 S. Grand Ave., Bozeman, MT
(406) 587-1064

This is the place to come for the inside scoop on area mountain biking. Through the spokes of bicycle wheels hanging from the ceiling of this shop you might get a glimpse of a staff person who can tip you off to where the single tracks are plentiful, but the crowds are not. This tiny shop does a lot of bike repairs and offers this year's Diamondback, Trek, and Cannondale bikes for rentals. You can also buy clothing, repair kits, and other accessories.

Chalet Sports
108 W. Main St., Bozeman, MT
(406) 587-4595

Open since the early 1980s, Chalet Sports has seen the population of mountain bikers explode over the years. The crew of veteran recreationists can outfit you with top of the line bikes from Cannondale, Giant, and Rockhopper. They offer experience to go with the gear, so be sure to ask about area trails and buy the trail map to go with the advice you get.

Livingston, Montana

Because the surrounding Absaroka, Crazy, and Gallatin ranges are so steep, there are not a lot of biking trails to choose from around Livingston. Many local cyclists drive the distance over to Bozeman's Gallatin Valley to access loads of trails there. But the great thing about the few challenging rides around Livingston is that you will more than likely have them all to yourself.

A popular trail from town can be accessed off Swingley Road about one mile north of Livingston. Pedal along this wide dirt road until you see the Forest Service sign marking the Livingston Peak trailhead. From there the road narrows and begins to climb up the trail, traversing private land and finally turns to single track. Most of this 20-mile ride is forested single-track along the rocky rim of a small drainage that dips and dives in through the Absarokas. It is an intermediate to advanced ride with a lot of technical maneuvering once you get to the trailhead.

For a pleasant beginner to intermediate ride, try Emigrant Falls. This short, six-mile out-and-back trail begins about five miles past Chico Hot Springs Resort and takes you to a gentle, cascading waterfall. You'll ride up the old logging road beside Emigrant Peak for most of the way and take the left fork in the road along a tree-covered single-track for the last half-mile.

Timber Trails
309 W. Park St., Livingston, MT
(406) 222-9550

It's hard to miss this hip outdoor shop at the edge of the historic district—there is a bicycle mounted on the rooftop. Owner Dale Sexton is a do-everything kind of outdoorsman and his store reflects that. But as the only shop in town renting mountain bikes, this is the place to go for local knowledge and expertise on what equipment you will need out on local trails. Wednesdays during the summer a bike club meets here for a weekly ride.

Red Lodge, Montana

The slickrock formations west of Red Lodge are only one of the features that has turned this into a mountain biking haven. The town hosts its annual Fat Tire Frenzy in July, attracting mountain bikers from around the country. This event offers a criterion and cross-country race. Even if you are not ready to start competing, there are enough trails around Red Lodge to accommodate any level, from beginner to expert. Willow Creek and Upper and Lower Red Lodge Creek Roads—both west of town off Route 78—are ideal for family rides, while a more challenging ride can be found along the Silver Run trails, where a series of interconnected loops allows you to choose from rides of different lengths along the West Fork of Rock Creek. For technical, single-track riding try the Greenough Lake Trail along the Main Fork of Rock Creek. Ask for details and trail maps at local outdoor shops.

Beartooth Mountain Shop
U.S. Hwy. 212, Red Lodge, MT
(406) 446-1952

The crew at Beartooth Mountain Shop will point you in the right direction for mountain biking adventures around Red Lodge and give you information on the annual Fat Tire Frenzy races held here each July. They'll also rent you the latest Trek, Cannondale, and Diamondback bikes for any of your rides. This shop is the hub for area trails.

Eastern Idaho

Teton Valley

On your mountain bike you can criss-cross Teton Valley's wildflower-washed meadows, endure excruciating climbs for close-enough-to-touch views of the Grand Teton, or test your technical skills on a lift-assisted downhill along the ski runs at Grand Targhee Ski and Summer Resort. The possibilities are limitless here in this vast outstretch of land on the "backside" of the Tetons.

For starters, try the Horseshoe Canyon area west and northwest of Driggs, where you'll find three good beginner or intermediate rides. The Big Challenge trail is single-track with few obstacles, so it's suitable for intermediates. The trail begins as a gravel road, becomes two-track, then narrows to single-track. The first part of this 12.5-mile ride is uphill; the downhill is fairly steep, but not technical. Enjoy good Teton views and heavily forested sections. The Grand View Point ride is a bit longer. It takes off from the end of Packsaddle Road. Since it's mostly two-track, some beginners may enjoy this ride as well, but they may find themselves walking parts of the climb. You'll ride through forest and wheat field and stop for panoramic views of the Snake River Plain and the Teton range. The Horseshoe Canyon loop itself is a good beginner ride. It starts where Packsaddle Road ends. Cross the cattleguard and simply pedal up the Forest Service road. More difficult trails branch off for more experienced riders.

Peaked Sports
70 E. Little Ave., Driggs, ID
(208) 354-2354, (800) 705-2354

Peaked is the valley's Schwinn headquarters in summer. The shop rents mountain bikes (the price includes helmet, extra tube, seat pack, pump patch kit, and advice about where to go). Two-hour, four-hour, per-day, and multi-day rates are available You can rent standard performance Schwinn models and even a bike trailer to haul the kids in. And since many rides are a drive out of town, they rent bike racks to mount on your vehicle.

Teton Teepee Lodge
Ski Hill Rd., Alta, WY
(307) 353-8176, (800) 353-8176

Teton Teepee Lodge rents Research Dynamics mountain bikes by the hour, half-day, and day. The shop also provides a guide service that includes transportation, bike rental, and snacks. They can personalize tours to your skill level and interests for a fee of about $30 per hour. Teton Teepee Lodge is just inside the Wyoming border near Driggs, Idaho.

Northwestern Wyoming

Cody, Wyoming

With a thick network of trails around Cody, mountain bikers can coast or climb. Favorite fat tire haunts include numerous trailheads from the North Fork of the Shoshone River and Carter Mountain south of town. For the latter ride, locals have a friend shuttle them to the top so that they can coast down through the trees, across streams, and over meadows. You can also try the trail by the remnants of the Heart Mountain Relocation Center, west of town off of U.S. Highway 120.

Old Faithful Bicycles
1362 Sheridan Ave., Cody, WY
(307) 527-5110

Owners Doug and Leslie Shinaver not only rent mountain bikes, they know every good trail or road in the area. Because of this, their shop has become

the hub for cyclists in the area and the Shinavers like it this way. They publish their humorous, handy newsletter, "Chainletter," offering everything from maintenance tips to a calendar of regional biking events. Behind the store is the Cody BMX Track.

Golf

Winter in Yellowstone country makes for a short golf season. But when there's no snow on the ground you'll be pleasantly surprised with the options you'll find out here. Municipal courses, some pleasantly mature, others relaxed and funky, allow play for prices that may surprise you—some are as reasonable as $10. The region's resort towns are home to award-winning courses (with the higher greens fees you might expect). Greater Yellowstone courses often make use of the lovely mountain scenery to enhance the beauty of their courses.

Jackson Hole, Wyoming

Jackson Hole Golf and Tennis Club
5000 N. Spring Gulch Rd., Jackson, WY
(307) 733-3111

The Teton Mountains aren't the only thing that gets national press in Jackson. *Golf Digest* ranked this set of 18-holes among the top 10 resort courses in the country. Course designer Robert Trent Jones knew this course had to be world-class. Among other challenges, he built water hazards on 11 of 18 holes. Each hole provides excellent views of the Teton and Gros Ventre mountain ranges.

The par 72 course is rated 72.5 with a slope of 126 from the championship tees. It measures 6,756 from the white tees. Reserving tee times is essential. No metal spike shoes are allowed. Green fees range between $50 and $100, depending on the season and time of day.

Teton Pines Resort and Country Club
3450 N. Clubhouse Dr., Jackson, WY
(307) 733-1733 for tee times

If playing a round of golf in the shadow of the Tetons isn't impressive enough, then you should know that Arnold Palmer designed this course, which was built in 1987 and is located just 6 miles west of Jackson, off Teton Village Road. Teton Pines is open to the golfing public in summer and then in winter it is transformed into a snaking course of cross country ski trails. The 18-hole par 72 course is rated 74.8 with a slope of 137 from the gold championship tees. It measures 6,330 from the white tees.

Please wear spikeless shoes; a few complimentary pair are available for use. Greens fees range between $50 and $140, depending on the season and day. Lodge guests receive a discount. Lessons area available for $75 to $85 per hour. Reservations are necessary.

Southwestern Montana

Bozeman, Montana

Big Sky Ski and Summer Resort
Mountain Village, Big Sky, MT
(406) 995-5000, (800) 548-4486

When you hit the ball across the fairway on this course you are apt to startle the resident moose, deer, or elk. While this is not a destination golf course, it's hard to beat it for setting. Nestled within the Spanish Peaks, the original 9-hole course designed by Arnold Palmer has been recently expanded to 18 holes. Located in the Meadow Village, it is owned by Big Sky Resort. The pro shop has a complete line of golf rentals.

Bridger Creek Golf Course
2710 McIlhattan Rd., Bozeman, MT
(406) 586-2333

Voted one of Montana's top 10 golf courses by *Golf Digest*, Bridger Creek sits on the edge of town along the foothills of the Bridger Mountains. At the clubhouse you'll find a pro shop with space for catered gatherings and cart rentals. Greens fees for nine holes are $15 weekends and $13 weekdays. For 18 holes, the fees are $25 and $22. Bridger Creek is open from April 1 to November 1.

Red Lodge, Montana

Red Lodge Mountain Resort Golf Course
828 Upper Continental Dr., Red Lodge, MT
(406) 446-3344

Besides the sheer beauty of the Red Lodge Mountain Golf Course's location, you'll also find a challenging set of 18 holes. Three tree-lined streams flow through this golf course at the base of the Beartooth Mountains. The first half of the course offers a formidable par-three on the sixth and eight holes. The back nine holes weave through trees and over hazards. Built in the mid-1980s, Red Lodge Mountain Resort bought the site in 1995. After your game you can enjoy the views from the clubhouse. This course is open from April to early October.

Northwestern Wyoming

Olive Glenn Golf and Country Club
802 Meadow Ln., Cody, WY
(307) 587-5551

Golf Digest ranks Olive Glenn as the fifth-best golf course in Wyoming. On top of that, this 18-hole course offers a beautiful view in every direction. This 72-par course also has a fully staffed pro shop and clubhouse, and offers club and cart rental. Many Wyoming Golf Association events are held at Olive Glenn each year. A buy-in membership here costs $2,800, and monthly dues are $105 (per family). Visitors can play for $28.

Eastern Idaho

Aspen Acres
4179 E. 1100 N., Ashton, ID
(208) 652-3524

Arthur and Velma Anderson were ahead of their time when they built Aspen Acres golf course 30 years ago. Like the traditional courses in Scotland, the Andersons let their original three-hole course grow organically along the contours of the existing aspen groves. It was a creative solution to their post-retirement addiction to golf. Replacing their potato fields with greens, the couple has created a funky, laid-back family golf course where you are just as likely to cross paths with a moose as you are with another golfer.

A small pro shop and snack bar are on the premises. Golf carts are available to rent. No tee-time reservations are necessary. The cost to play 18 holes is $10.

Resources

Real Estate/Relocation

Idaho Land Magazine
Rocky Mountain Publishing
P.O. Box 6062, Pocatello, ID 83205-6062

The Montana Land Magazine
P.O. Box 30516, Billings, MT 59107

Homes and Land of Southwest Montana
(406) 522-7800
www.montanahomesandland.com

Homeseekers
Bozeman and Livingston, MT
(406) 587-0440

www.move.com
You can find average house sales, current listings, and compare neighborhoods and schools by typing in the town you want to live in. The site gives you a list of local real estate companies and agents, as well as information on rentals, the job market, and recreation by town.

Regional Information

Montana

Bozeman Chamber of Commerce
2000 Commerce Wy., Bozeman, MT 59715
(406) 586-5421, (800) 228-4224
www.bozemanchamber.com

Gardiner Chamber of Commerce
P.O. Box 81, Gardiner, MT 59030
(406) 848-7971

Livingston Chamber of Commerce
305 E. Park St., Livingston, MT 59047
(307) 222-0850

Red Lodge Chamber of Commerce
601 N. Broadway, Red Lodge, MT 59065
(406) 446-1718

West Yellowstone Chamber of Commerce
P.O. Box 458, West Yellowstone, MT 59758
(406) 646-7701
www.westyellowstonechamber.com

Wyoming

Cody Country Chamber of Commerce
836 Sheridan Ave., Cody, WY 82414
(307) 587-2777

Jackson Hole Chamber of Commerce
532 N. Cache St., Jackson, WY 83001
(307) 733-3316
www.jhchamber.com

Idaho

Greater Idaho Falls Chamber of Commerce
(208) 523-1010, (800) 634-3246
www.idahofallschamber.com

Island Park Area Chamber of Commerce
(208) 558-7755
www.islandpark.org

Teton Valley Chamber of Commerce
(208) 354-2000
www.tetonvalleychamber.com

National Parks

Grand Teton National Park
Moose, WY 83012-0170
(307) 739-3600

Yellowstone National Park
P.O. Box 168, Yellowstone, WY 82190
(307) 344-7381

Outdoor Recreation

Southwestern Montana

Fish, Wildlife, and Parks Department
Region 3 Headquarters, 1400 S. 19th Ave.,
Bozeman, MT 59715
(406) 994-4042

Gallatin National Forest
Bozeman Ranger District, 3710 Fallon St.,
Bozeman, MT
(406) 522-2520

Gallatin National Forest
Hebgen Lake Ranger District, P.O. Box
520, West Yellowstone, MT
(406) 646-7369

Gallatin National Forest
Livingston Ranger District, 5242 U.S. Hwy.
89 South, Livingston, MT
(406) 222-1892

Wyoming

Bridger-Teton National Forest
P.O. Box 1888, Jackson, WY 83001
(307) 739-5500

Shoshone National Forest
808 Meadow Lane, Cody, WY 82414
(307) 527-6241

Wapiti Ranger District
Clarks Fork Ranger District
Greybull Ranger District
203A Yellowstone Ave., Cody, WY 82414
(307) 527-6921

Wyoming Game and Fish
360 N. Cache St., Jackson, WY
(307) 733-2321

Eastern Idaho

Island Park Ranger District
P.O. Box 220 Island Park, ID 83429
(208) 558-7301

Targhee National Forest
420 North Bridge St.
P.O. Box 208, St. Anthony, ID 83445
(208) 624-3151

Teton Basin Ranger District
P.O. Box 127 Driggs, ID 83422
(208) 354-2312

Books

A Guide to Exploring Grand Teton National Park, by Linda L. Olson and Tim Bywater. RNM Press, 1995.

The Complete Climber's Guide to the Teton Range, by Leigh N. Ortenburger and R.G. Jackson. The Mountaineers Press, 1996.

Creation of the Teton Landscape, by J.D. Love and John C. Reed, Jr. Grand Teton Natural History Association, 1989.

From Trapper to Tourist in Jackson Hole, by Elizabeth Wied Hayden. Grand Teton Natural History Association, 1992.

Greater Yellowstone National Forests, by Todd Wilkinson. Falcon Publishing/Globe Pequot, 1991.

Hiking Grand Teton National Park, by Bill Schneider. Falcon Publishing/Globe Pequot, 1999.

Knee Deep in Montana's Trout Streams, by John Holt, Pruett Publishing, 1991.

Mark of the Grizzly, by Scott McMillion, Falcon Publishing, 1998.

Rocky Mountain Wildlife of Yellowstone and Grand Teton National Parks, by Bill Perry. Homestead Publishing, 1995.

Scenic Driving Yellowstone and Grand Teton National Parks, by Susan
Springer Butler. Falcon Publishing/Globe Pequot, 1999.

Short Hikes and Easy Walks in Grand Teton National Park, by Bill Hayden and Jerry Freilich.
Grand Teton Natural History Association, 1968.

The Wildlife Watcher's Guide to Yellowstone and Grand Teton National Parks, by Todd Wilkinson. NorthWord Press, 1999.

The Yellowstone Fly-Fishing Guide, by Craig Matthews and Clayton Molinero. Lyons and
Burford, New York, New York, 1997.

The Yellowstone Story: Volumes One and Two, by Aubrey L. Haines. University Press of Colorado, Niwot, Colorado, 1996.

Websites

www.gorp.com

This website—an acronym for Great Outdoor Recreation Pages—specializes in information on national parks and adventure travel packages. With complete listings of trails, lodging, scenic drives, and attractions, this website has everything you can imagine to get you outside. It's a must for virtual traveling.

www.nps.gov

The official National Park Service website has links to all national parks, with information on history, roads, trails, campgrounds, and more.

www.defenders.org

A website for those who want to learn more about how we can protect our earth's amazing animals. The official site for the Defenders of the Wildlife.

www.weather.com

Find out what your stay in our area will be like ahead of time.

Index

About the Authors

Brian Hurlbut

Brian Hurlbut is a journalist and freelance writer living in Big Sky. He began hiking around the Adirondack Mountains of upstate New York as a young boy, but the lure of the high peaks was eventually too much. In 1993, a year after graduating from the State University of New York at Buffalo, he packed his belongings into a microscopic Nissan Sentra and headed west. He landed in Missoula, where he continued his studies in journalism at the University of Montana and began to explore the state's vast physical and cultural geography. Since then, he has hiked in most of Montana's mountain ranges and visited many of the region's small towns, immersing himself in everything the Treasure State has to offer. Hurlbut spends most of his free time in the outdoors and is particularly interested in backpacking, backcountry snowboarding, and music. His work can be seen regularly in publications around the state, and he is often on stage as a drummer in a local rock and roll band.

Brian Hurlbut. PHOTO: DIANE HURLBUT

Seabring Davis

Award-winning journalist Seabring Davis, has worked as a reporter, backcountry hiking guide, waitress, kayak instructor, wedding planner, English teacher, camp cook, and public relations director—not necessarily in that order. She has wrirren about rodeos and history, among other topics. What these have in common are a sense of place rooted in the West, which is what Davis loves to write about most. Her work has taken her to the cobblestone streets of Mexico, the pagodas of Japan, the gothic terraces of Spain, and the beaches of Tahiti. But Montana is the place she will always consider home.

Originally from Hawaii, Montana's dramatic seasons seduced Davis ten years ago. She attended Montana State University in Bozeman and traded the ocean for canoeing big rivers, mountain biking, skiing, and hiking. Her day is not complete without at least a short foray onto local trails, summer or winter. She lives in Livingston, Montana, with her husband, Colin, their daughter, Isabel, and two errant dogs, Stella and Bay.

Seabring Davis. PHOTO: COLIN DAVIS

Help Us Keep This Guide Up to Date

Every effort has been made by the authors and editors to make this guide as accurate and useful as possible. However, many things can change after a guide is published—establishments close, phone numbers change, hiking trails are rerouted, facilities come under new management, etc.

We would love to hear from you concerning your experiences with this guide and how you feel it could be made better and be kept up to date. While we may not be able to respond to all comments and suggestions, we'll take them to heart and we'll also make certain to share them with the author. Please send your comments and suggestions to the following address:

The Globe Pequot Press
Reader Response/Editorial Department
P.O. Box 480
Guilford, CT 06437

Or you may e-mail us at: editorial@globe-pequot.com

Thanks for your input, and happy travels!